THE ROUGH GUIDE TO

Comedy
Movies

**ROUGH
GUIDES**

www.roughguides.com

Credits

The Rough Guide to Comedy Movies

Additional writing: Sam Cook
Additional contributions: Andrew Lockett, Peter Perkins, Kaushik Bhaumik
Senior contributing editor: Sam Cook
Editors: Andrew Dickson, Andrew Lockett, Katie Stephens
Layout: Michelle Bhatia and Link Hall
Picture research: Michele Faram
Proofreading: Ken Bell
Production: Julia Bovis and Katherine Owers

Rough Guides Reference

Series editor: Mark Ellingham
Editors: Peter Buckley, Duncan Clark, Daniel Crewe, Matthew Milton, Joe Staines
Director: Andrew Lockett

Publishing Information

This first edition published September 2005 by
Rough Guides Ltd, 80 Strand, London WC2R 0RL
345 Hudson St, 4th Floor, New York 10014, USA
Email: mail@roughguides.com

Distributed by the Penguin Group:
Penguin Books Ltd, 80 Strand, London WC2R 0RL
Penguin Putnam, Inc., 375 Hudson Street, NY 10014, USA
Penguin Group (Australia), 250 Camberwell Road, Camberwell, Victoria 3124, Australia
Penguin Books Canada Ltd, 10 Alcorn Avenue, Toronto, Ontario, Canada M4V 1E4
Penguin Group (New Zealand), Cnr Rosedale and Airborne Roads, Albany, Auckland, New Zealand

Printed in Italy by LegoPrint S.p.A

Typeset in Bembo and Helvetica Neue to an original design by Henry Iles

A catalogue record for this book is available from the British Library

ISBN 10: 1-84353-464-9
ISBN 13: 978-1-84353-464-8

1 3 5 7 9 8 6 4 2

THE ROUGH GUIDE TO

Comedy Movies

by
Bob McCabe

Contents

The Icons:

Funny World:

The Information:

Introduction

The task of providing a *Rough Guide to Comedy Movies*, perhaps the most constant and durable of cinema genres, provides an ample supply of banana skins to pratfall over, but nonetheless, here are a few additional words on what to look out for on the slippery terrace of this movie guide.

The book, whilst offering a few clear personal favourites, hasn't tried to pin down "academic-style" what comedy movies are according to theory. Comedy is what comedy does. It makes some people laugh, while some others might sit there with a face more etched in stone than Buster Keaton's himself. Not everyone finds the Farrelly Brothers a riot; likewise others have never really seen the mirth in the movies of Pedro Álmodóvar.

For some Chaplin is still cinema's greatest comedian; for others he is simply to be ignored as too sentimental and irrelevant to twenty-first century tastes. In all the above cases though, these filmmakers have been influential; they have made some people laugh and the world of humour in the movies has been irrevocably altered by what they've done – for better or worse according to your tastes. Therefore I've taken a wide view of which funny movies should be looked at, acknowledging that for some people there will be movies discussed that leaves the ribs untickled, the funny bone untouched. The brush is correspondingly broad and the comedy canvas dauntingly wide, with space given to everything from "gross out"

comedies to European arthouse comedy drama, and, following the Rough Guides travel principle, we have pushed the critical boat out a little to encourage exploration further afield.

The Canon section provides a detailed look at 50 major comedy movie classics. These are largely personal favourites with a couple of nods to advice from my editorial team and I hope you enjoy reflecting on these films and rewatching these movies as much as I did. Likewise the section on Comedy Icons discusses comedy personalities that have made a mark in different ways. It is a large section and could have been a heck of a lot larger, given that film comedy to a large extent is about performers and we weren't able to include everybody.

Back-tracking, the Early Years chapter briskly takes a look at the first great heyday of comedy movies and the Comedy Story tries to put the genre in some kind of general historical perspective, from the advent of sound to the present day. Scattered throughout the book are numerous capsule reviews of movies that don't make the comedy canon but you may want to use as a recommendation to rent, if you've not already seen the film. Funny World: International Comedy steps outside the Anglo-American mainstream for a quick tour of what's out there in a few major film-producing countries of the world that aren't covered elsewhere. The Information rounds out the picture with pointers on comedy festivals, the best of the books on comedy movies, and interesting websites and further information on favourites and funny men and funny women. There are also quick pauses in the form of boxes – looking forward and back – at perennial elements of the comedy mix, including drag, slapstick, military mirth, sport and musical comedy. The book can be read from the beginning to end but it's also designed to dip into, so we have added pointers to further coverage and there's always the index to check films and names for additional reference. For all the regrettable omissions – inevitable with so large a subject – apologies are proffered in advance. Some were deliberate – some of the so-called classics just are *not* funny films – for others I'll promise to think about them again if you feel strongly enough about anything to write in c/o Rough Guides. I'll adjust accordingly if I feel the case is strong – second edition permitting! I hope therefore, this *Rough Guide* throws a little extra light on familiar funny territory and points out new comedy directions to explore, for every reader. After all, as far as the film business is concerned there is never such a thing as the last laugh – only the next one to look forward to…

Bob McCabe, 2005

Acknowledgements

Despite the fact that writing such a book as this involves many solitary hours either locked away in a library or, preferably, in a darkened room in front of a DVD player, there are still several people to whom I am indebted. First and foremost Andrew Lockett and the team at Rough Guides, whose editorial process is stringent but always fair and welcome. They have done a superb job of keeping everything moving. I owe a dear debt to Alan Jones for mutually angst-ridden conversations. Special thanks also to Rob Churchill for his fondness for a certain French fellah, also to Michael Samuels, Paul Gillion, and Mark Kermode. As always the BFI Library – and their staff – were both a font of knowledge and a haven of solitude. Love as ever to Mary McCabe. And as always, all my love to Lucy, Jessie and Jack.

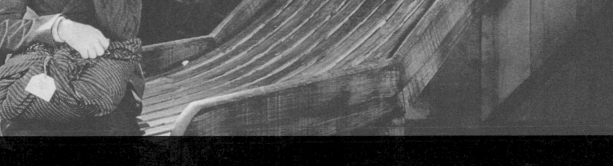

Film Comedy: early years

The art of slapstick: Harry Langdon's *The Strong Man* (1926)

Film comedy:
early years

It started with a sneeze...

When audiences first saw the **Lumière brothers'** film of a train arriving at a station (1895), legend has it they dived for cover, fearing that this huge locomotive was about to leap off the screen and mow them down. When a similar audience saw a man sneeze, however, they simply laughed. And thus was born screen comedy.

The notion that an image or idea could be captured on celluloid, simply for the audience's amusement, was one of the earliest indicators of the power of film as a medium of pure entertainment. There are many souls who can lay claim to the development of cinema: American Eadweard Muybridge, whose sequential photos of horses in action (1873–78) sowed the seeds for the idea of continuous motion pictures; John Rudge, of Bath in England, whose work with animation, shown via magic lantern (1884), defined the nature of projection; German Ottomar Anschütz, who developed the Tachyscope (1887), forerunner of the *What the Butler Saw*-esque peep show;

Fred Ott's Sneeze – the first movie gag

3

American George Eastman, founding father of Eastman Kodak (1885), a company that made rolls of photographic film available to all; and then, of course, **Thomas Edison**, who patented the Kinetoscope (1891), a cabinet designed to show moving film to one person at a time. Edison was also first off the mark with the earliest movie gag – in 1894 he filmed one of his workers, a man named Fred Ott (arguably the first movie star, if only by default), sneezing. Edison's assistant, William Dickson, was quick to follow, making brief films (often just twenty seconds in length) of vaudeville acts and performers, such as Buffalo Bill Cody who was then touring England.

In such primitive work was born the notion that film could be used as a medium to tell stories as well as depict photorealism. *Fred Ott's Sneeze* got us laughing – and as the likes of *American Pie* (1999) demonstrate, our tastes haven't come on much since then! The Lumières themselves were quick to catch on to the fact that audiences wanted to laugh, as one of their first pieces, *L'arroseur arrosé* (*The Sprinkler Sprinkled*, 1895), testifies. The film's central gag – someone stands on a hosepipe thus stopping its flow, a man examines it, then the other person moves only to have the water hit the man full force in the face – has remained a comedy staple ever since.

Early film comedy was made and maintained by a handful of pioneers who very quickly saw

Vaudeville: from comedy to comedy movies

Vaudeville was a form of variety entertainment consisting of short acts or turns. In its heyday this included acrobatics, song-and-dance routines, animal acts and, of course, comedy and clowning. The height of its popularity stretched from the late 1890s to the advent of the talkies, and it is closely related to the British music hall tradition. Early cinema itself, and screen comedy in particular, was closely tied not only to vaudeville, but also to fairground entertainments, circuses, dime museums and sideshows, and early filmmakers fought to get the best "exclusives" with leading entertainers. In cinema's first decade, travelling showmen with their own projectors put on shows at fairgrounds or at vaudeville houses, and comedy was an integral part of the mix.

Huge numbers of screen comedians received their training in vaudeville, where brisk "acts" provided ideal material for early films, which were often very short in length. Because movies were silent, and could not include music or verbal humour, filmmakers had to alter performances to feature the most visual elements on film – the so-called "dumb acts", for example, were tradition-

ally used at the beginning or end of the show as audiences noisily came and went. Clowning of various types in the slapstick vein was particularly popular, and the high-level skill of many early performers was largely due to their extensive live entertainment training. Vaudeville, in that respect, could be said to have been the *Saturday Night Live* of its day. Performers who made it big with the talkies, such as the Marx Brothers and Abbott and Costello (for both see Icons), served their apprenticeship there, as well as hosts of silent comedians, including Buster Keaton and Harry Langdon. Vaudeville and its risqué cousin burlesque (which was for adults only) prospered alongside the movies for decades.

But, as the Twenties moved on, audience demands became more sophisticated, and, as the novelty value of moving pictures wore off, fewer stage performers were filmed performing their "turns". The vaudeville stage itself remained an outlet for cinema screenings, but it became less appealing to see these acts on screen when a live version was still on offer on the stage. When the talkies arrived, vaudeville's days were numbered.

Slapstick

Slapstick, which dominated silent screen comedy, is an essentially physical form – the province of the pratfall, relying heavily on the sadistically comedic value of physical pain. (Indeed, its name derives from the Italian theatrical tradition of *commedia dell'arte*: the central performer would beat others with an object made of two sticks, which made a slapping sound on impact.) Charlie Chaplin revelled in it; Harold Lloyd excelled at it; Buster Keaton was a genius at redefining it; and Mack Sennett made his entire career out of it, his Keystone Kops (see p.8) providing the perfect answer to the question: "What's funnier than watching someone fall over?" – "Watching a dozen people fall over". Later, in the sound age Abbott and Costello and The Three Stooges (for both see Icons) struggled to keep the form alive, often by poking at least one member of their team in the eye (even Mel Gibson likes to reference it in his *Lethal Weapon* series, although, admittedly, somewhat more lethally). Without slapstick, we would never have experienced the trepidation of spotting a casually dropped banana skin, or witnessed the anarchic joy of the custard pie fight. Even Stanley Kubrick went for one of those in his dark comedy *Dr Strangelove* (1963, see Canon), but he cut it out of the finished film, proving perhaps that the basic gut reaction to slapstick doesn't sit too well with the more cerebral demands of satire. Slapstick remains very much about falling over. Artfully, of course.

and understood the power of the image, and the inherent punch this new art form could deliver. In France, **Georges Méliès** had already begun experimenting with the more technically challenging aspects of film, culminating in his groundbreaking *Le voyage dans la lune* (*A Trip To The Moon*, 1902), in which a comedic moon is somewhat shocked to experience a rocket landing right in the centre of "his" expressive face. Overall, however, the first two decades of cinematic comedy are defined by the limitations of the art form itself. Silent comedy depended on the visual nature of the medium – a heavy reliance on slapstick and physical humour, and on performance over technical tricks.

🎬 Slapstick Encyclopedia (DVD Collection)
dir Various, 1913–1929

Vols 1 & 2 *Film Comedy Pioneers; Keystone Tonight!*, 215m, b/w

Vols 3 & 4 *Sennett In The Twenties; Genders And Their Benders*, 221m, b/w

Vols 5 & 6 *Keaton, Arbuckle and St. John; Hal Roach's All-Star Comedians*, 229m, b/w & colour tinted

Vols 7 & 8 *Hal Roach; Chaplin And The Music Hall Tradition*, 217m, b/w & colour-tinted

Vols 9 & 10 *The Race Is On; The Anarchic Fringe* 207m, b/w & colour-tinted

This vast selection of silent comedy highlights goes well beyond the "Film Comedy Pioneers" of Vol 1 and indeed takes you forward nearly to the beginning of sound. Early highlights include fat funny man John Bunny in *A Cure for Pokeritis* (1912) and black vaudevillian Bert (Egbert Austin) Williams in *A Natural Born Gambler* (1916) with separate later volumes on Hal Roach, 1920s Sennett material and silent comediennes. There's also a selection on Chaplin and contemporaries including Billy West (*He's In Again*, 1918) – a brazen Chaplin copyist – and a chance to sample the *Our Gang* team (see p. 12) in 1923's *Dogs of War*. A bargain (given the extensive running time) at $70, albeit one that's a serious time commitment.

Comedy stars and star producers

Along with the notion of film as global entertainment (after all, celluloid could be shipped anywhere in the world to be screened, and, in the absence of dialogue, language wasn't an issue) came the idea of the movie star, and, rapidly following it, the long tradition of comedian comedy.

The success of André Deed's **Cretinetti** character (see p.6) ushered in a period of prolific production on comedian-led one-reel movies throughout the world, with stars like France's Charles Prince (who made nearly six hundred films); fat funny man **John Bunny** in America; many Italian competitors to Deed, including the innocent Ferdinand Guillaume; Antonin Fertner in Russia; and, in England, **Pimple** (Fred Evans). This international free-for-all in movie comedy ended, however, with World War I, when many European performers died in action. Subsequently, Hollywood comedy became internationally dominant, as it has of course remained ever since.

André Deed (Cretinetti)

French actor **André Deed** (1884–1938), whose Italian character Cretinetti (the name speaks volumes) shone in countless one-reel comedies, was one of the first international stars, not only of the comedy genre, but also of cinema itself. Experienced in music-hall singing and acrobatics, he developed a clowning style that harked back to the ancient tradition of the Pierrot, a stock clown-figure from Italian comedy and improvised theatre.

He was known by a variety of names in a variety of countries – Boireau in France, Torribio in Spain, Foolshead in England and the US, and Glupishkin in Russia – at a time when nobody really knew exactly what a "movie star" was. After a spell working with Méliès, and then Pathé, Deed grew famous for his work, from 1909, for the Turin-based Itala film company and became the first director-comedian, continuing to direct after his performing days. His performances lived up to his Italian name, displaying a surreal foolishness that descended into mayhem. Only a very few fragmentary images survive of his work, making his influence on future generations of comedy stars impossible to gauge.

Quickly following Deed in the comedy star stakes was **Max Linder**, probably the earliest movie star comedian still to be hailed as a genius today. His influence was profound, not only on the likes of Charlie Chaplin (see Icons) but also on a host of lesser performers, and, unlike most of his contemporaries, Linder had a successful career well beyond the end of World War I.

Max Linder: the first King of Comedy

It wasn't until the 1960s that the pioneering work of French comedian **Max Linder** was rediscovered and re-evaluated. Until then, Linder's work had lived in oblivion, his role in

Max Linder – silent comedy stylist

the history of screen comedy a brief footnote at best, and one that tended to focus more on his tragic demise – a double suicide pact with his wife – than on the impact of his work.

Born on December 16, 1883, Linder began working on the Paris stage under his real name Gabriel-Maximilien Leuvielle, later adopting the name Linder for his burgeoning film career – a career that soon came to dominate. His on-screen success was curtailed by a gas-poisoning incident in 1914 whilst he was on active duty in World War I, an event that was to have lasting personal and professional implications for him. Prior to this, Linder was very probably the most famous

screen comedian in the world. From 1905 he started work at Pathé films, mostly as an extra, and eventually made over four hundred films for the company, many very short, with his big break coming after André Deed (Cretinetti) left for Italy.

His comic persona was the most highly developed yet seen on the screen: a dapper would-be gent, impeccably turned out, with an eye for the ladies and the good life, and yet whose surface elegance was the foil to a series of slapstick mishaps. His relentless style – often creating variations on a gag or a situation (like having a bath) – is thought to have been a huge influence on both Mack Sennett and Charlie Chaplin (the latter is said to have referred admiringly to Linder as "the Professor").

After his time in active service, Linder forsook France for Hollywood. His career, however, never really managed to take off, plagued as he was by ill health, both mental and physical. One noticeable exception was his parody of Douglas Fairbanks' *The Three Musketeers* (1921), which Linder reworked in 1922 as *The Three Must-Get-Theres*. Despite this comic triumph (still only coolly received in America), Linder's career seemed to be already on the verge of fizzling out before his death on October 31, 1925.

Laugh With Max Linder! (DVD Collection)
1 DVD, US/France, 117m b/w

Seven Year's Bad Luck (1921) dominates this selection of Linder's work and illustrates one of the highlights of his American career. The mirror sequence (where a servant pretends to be Max's reflection) is justly famous. Rather more genteel than much of the rough-and-ready material of say Sennett's film factory, this is a collection which helps connect Linder with Chaplin. Fresh, amusing and well presented.

The Keystone Kops

Mack Sennett's **Keystone Kops**, whose heyday was between 1913 and 1916, were a riotous assembly of uniformed comics who tore around the streets of LA without permits, safety apparatus or sense, causing chaos and comic destruction wherever they went. Generally short on plot and long on (often physical) comic set pieces, the movies were shot in a fly-by-the-seat-of-your-pants manner, with a loose improvisational attitude. Editing was crucial, and Sennett himself fine-tuned the Kops footage, turning them into comic gems in his editing suite. Today the movies remain something of an artistic and logistical triumph of early cinema and offer a revealing glimpse into a lost world of turn-of-the-century America – all dusty streets, primitive automobiles and affronted respectability. Many comedy stars, such as Roscoe "Fatty" Arbuckle and Chester Conklin, gained valuable experience on "duty" with the Kops.

For once not in hectic pursuit – Mack Sennett's Keystone Kops

Mack Sennett: Comedy Colossus

For all the stars on offer, the real motivators in the early days of screen comedy were content to remain behind the camera, and none more so than **Mack Sennett** (see Icons). A truly prolific mover and shaker, Michael Sinnott was born to working-class Irish immigrants in Quebec, Canada, in 1880, and relocated to Connecticut seventeen years later. Having met the comedienne **Marie Dressler** by chance at the age of 22, he set off to New York to try his luck on the stage. Thus began a career in the Broadway chorus, as well as some work in the popular burlesque shows of the day. The name change to Mack Sennett was soon followed by a change in ambition as he began acting in films at Biograph Studios in Manhattan. He made a number of shorts under the direction of **D.W. Griffith**, and even landed a few lead roles, co-starring with the likes of **Mary Pickford** and **Mabel Normand**. For Griffith, he started writing scripts, including 1909's *The Lonely Villa* (famous for the first use of the technique of cross-cutting), and by 1910 was specializing in

comedy, directing shorts as well as appearing in them. Having honed his craft under Griffith, Sennett turned independent filmmaker and founded Keystone Pictures (with two former bookies for partners) in 1912.

When Sennett left Biograph he didn't leave empty-handed, cherry-picking from their talent roster and taking with him the likes of Fred Mace, Ford Sterling and Mabel Normand (he developed a strong, intimate relationship with Normand, and she also proved to be a fine comedienne and talented director). Alongside these stalwarts at Keystone Pictures, he built a

Harry Langdon

Harry Langdon is perhaps the least known of the "big four" silent comedians, after Charlie Chaplin, Buster Keaton and Harold Lloyd. Originally from Council Bluffs, Iowa, Langdon was a vaudeville veteran, starting work in 1903 before being signed to Sennett in 1923. Sennett worked productively with Langdon, but the latter's career really only took off in 1926 at the age of 40, with two of the three features for which he is still remembered: *Tramp, Tramp, Tramp* (with Joan Crawford as leading lady) and circus-themed comedy romance *The Strong Man*, for which his distinctive screen persona won serious acclaim. Langdon's baby-faced innocent usually survives the customary disasters of the silent comedy hero as if by the hand of God. **Frank Capra** had a hand in developing this persona, as did director Harry Edwards, but Langdon parted from both after his last triumph, the gangster-themed *Long Pants* (1927), in which Harry falls in love with a villainous moll.

Langdon subsequently struggled in the film industry, firstly by attempting to direct himself in 1927's *Three's A Crowd* (critical and box office reactions were muted), and then with the arrival of the talkies, when,, like Keaton, he was unable to build on his earlier suc-

cess. His thin voice and his slow, even weird, screen presence – frequently described as "eerie" by critics – failed to transfer to a medium that was picking up the pace with the arrival of the Marx brothers (see Icons) and music.

Harry Langdon (lower left) unawares in *The Strong Man* (1926)

Chaplin: First Among Indies

In 1914, when Chaplin went into a costume/props room at Mack Sennett's studios and picked out a cane, a bowler hat and an oversize suit – the trousers having previously belonged to Sennett regular **Fatty Arbuckle** – and added a stick-on moustache, he created a character known as "the Little Tramp". Whereas before producer Sennett had depended upon ensembles (could anyone tell one Keystone Kop from another?) and Chaplin had previously been a stock player, by creating a noticeable character for himself he became a comedy icon – as recognizable in silhouette as he was on screen. Knowing the value of this, he soon left Sennett behind for total autonomy, writing, producing and directing his own shorts, before expanding into features in 1921 with *The Kid*. (When sound came along he even started doing the music as well.) In 1919, alongside fellow stars **Douglas Fairbanks** and Mary Pickford, and director D. W. Griffith, Chaplin formed **United Artists**, a movie company that dictated its own terms and hired its talent out to the highest bidder or the right project – essentially creating independent cinema in a studio-run town.

veritable repertory company of comedy stars, including such names as Chester Conklin, Mack Swain and Roscoe "Fatty" Arbuckle (see Icons). Charlie Chaplin served his apprenticeship there in 1914, before being lured to Chicago-based company Essanay. Sennett proved himself an extremely competent filmmaker and a fine editor, and guided the early careers of Harry Langdon (see box), Harold Lloyd and Buster Keaton (for both see Icons). Success continued throughout the 1920s, with Sennett making the occasional feature; but, as with so many of his era, the coming of sound in the movies signalled the end of the career of a comedy giant.

To be fair, the runaway success of screen comedy in this period depended largely on two factors: firstly, it was recognizable and, secondly, it was cheap. Anyone with a spouse on their arm could relate to the fictional marital trials and tribulations of Vitagraph stars John Bunny and Flora Finch, who featured in a range of films made between 1910 and 1915. Depicting their domestic set-up certainly didn't break the bank. Other duos arrived in the movies with their acts already honed from vaudeville and the burlesque shows, including the physical comedian **Larry Semon** – a man who holds the distinction of having used both **Stan Laurel** and **Oliver Hardy** as the proverbial second banana in his popular shorts. (Wisely, Sennett realized Laurel was funnier than him and promptly had him fired.)

Hal Roach, the other giant amongst the comedy producers of the period, took a tip from Sennett and was soon fostering a comedy roster of his own, initially specializing in a similar brand of slapstick humour before moving towards a more sophisticated form of comedy when he teamed Stan Laurel with Oliver Hardy. When Charlie Chaplin took his tramp persona, along with his business, to his own studio in 1918, the power of the comedy performer reached a new peak. Comedy was truly big business.

Keystone Komedies (DVD Collection)
2 DVDs, US, Vol 1 118m, Vol 2 83m, b/w

A wonderfully exuberant Region 2-only selection of Sennett material mostly from the "teens" with lots of Fatty Arbuckle and Mack Swain (he of the Walrus moustache) – though regrettably little of the famous Keystone Kops. The elaborate outdoor staging of *Wandering Willies* (1929) offers a welcome contrast to earlier studio-bound fare in the colllection.

Harry Langdon...The Forgotten Clown (DVD Collection)

1 DVD, US, 193m, b/w

All the Langdon you are ever likely to need, including all three major films; two directed by Frank Capra, the second being *Long Pants* (1927). *The Strong Man* (1926) is humane and poignant – the best Langdon (& Capra) outing. Joan Crawford in *Tramp, Tramp, Tramp* (1926) also stands out.

Hal Roach: Comedy Mogul

Shaping the careers of such big names as **Harold Lloyd** and the **Little Rascals**, through Laurel and Hardy to Frank Capra (see Icons), **Hal Roach** was a hugely influential figure in twentieth-century screen comedy. Roach left New York for Hollywood in 1912 – stopping along the way to spend some time as a gold prospector – and was picking up small roles in silent comedy shorts

Silent comedy teams

Comedy teams in the silent era were everywhere abundant. That's not to say, however, that they always had a long shelf-life – witness the *Plump and Runt* shorts, circa 1916, which featured comedian Billy Ruge paired up with the "plump" Oliver Hardy.

Many of the first movie comedy teams grew out of the vaudeville and burlesque circuit, with already-established theatrical partnerships being plundered for the movies. One of the earliest duos, however, had never worked together prior to their movie debut. In 1910 Victor Potel and Augustus Carney (Hank and Lank) were taken from Essanay's pool of performers and assigned each other as comedy partners. This teaming quickly became a great success, with Hank and Lank cranking out a new short on an almost weekly basis. The popularity of this early team was soon matched by Mutt and Jeff, animated characters developed from Bud Fisher's popular comic strip. Male-female couples also became extremely popular, the earliest example being Bunny and Finch (John and Flora respectively), who made their debut as a duo in 1912. Bunny, who played henpecked husband to Finch's shrewish wife, died in 1915. They were rivalled by light-comedy duo Mr. and Mrs. Sidney Drew (he too a henpecked husband), who by 1915 were producing a one-reel short per week, but whose on-screen career came to an end following Sidney Drew's death in 1919.

Mack Sennett, of course, was keen to get in on the act, and in 1915 took the vaudeville team of Weber and Fields, and their ethnic knockabout humour, to the big screen. The producer/director also saw the potential of teaming the giant Mack Swain – who had been one of the largest and bulkiest Keystone Kops – with other smaller-framed performers, including character comedian Chester Conklin (like Swain he often made much mirth out of a big moustache), who was already an established comedy star. Thus was born a series of *Ambrose and Walrus* shorts – Swain as gentle giant, Conklin as cunning comrade – that had audiences begging for more. Swain would later continue to work the big man/small man gag by playing opposite Chaplin on many occasions, most notably as the prospector Big Jim McKay in *The Gold Rush* (1925, see Canon).

The Twenties also saw a temporary vogue for military comedies, most notably Paramount's series of movies with Wallace Beery and Raymond Hatton, which began with 1926's *Behind the Front*. However, Hollywood's ability to find humour in the Great War was short-lived and, for the most part, the 1920s and the dying days of silent cinema provided little in the way of durable comedy teams – save, of course, for Laurel and Hardy, the best comedy duo of them all.

when he happened upon Harold Lloyd at a small production company. Suspecting his own strengths lay behind the camera, he was soon promoting Lloyd as a comedy star in the making, forming his own production company with a $3000 inheritance, turning writer/producer/director and setting Lloyd on the road to fame (not an instant or easy path, as the early *Willie Work* shorts can attest). Roach's mixture of extreme tenacity and good taste, and his sharp eye for talent, all conspired to help him build his comic empire, which took off in the early 1920s. He was soon beating Mack Sennett at his own game.

Roach's greatest strength was in recognizing the talent around him, and helping them to fulfil their potential. It was he who had the inspired idea of teaming one-time vaudevillian turned writer Stan Laurel with one-time screen villain Oliver Hardy, creating in the process cinema's most enduring and best loved comic duo – often aped, never bettered. His strength also lay in understanding the power of the comedy short. When audience tastes turned to feature films, Roach's abilities failed him to a degree (despite some success with the 1930s ghost comedy *Topper* series), and he saw some of his biggest stars – Laurel and Hardy included – move on (often unwisely) to other producers. Attempts to diversify led Roach to continue with the enduring *Our Gang* kids series (later renamed for TV dissemination *The Little Rascals*), on which Frank Capra was to gain valuable training. But by the late 1930s his heyday

had passed. He eventually found himself producing for television, something he continued to do – in particular in association with the Walt Disney Company – until his death in 1992.

The move towards talkies

Always eager to corner any market going, both Sennett and Roach quickly discovered the need to diversify, ensuring that the producer remained a dominant power in Hollywood, rather than being overshadowed by the stars he produced. Sennett made a series of movies from 1916 specifically aimed at a male audience, and starring the famously alluring Bathing Beauties (a series that launched the careers of Hollywood goddesses **Carole Lombard** and **Gloria Swanson**); and for the kids he came up with the *Kid Komedies*, a rather less anarchic version of the Kops. He also went for the female market with the pairing of talented comediennes **ZaSu Pitts** and **Thelma Todd**. Roach, meanwhile, followed the success of Sennett's *Kid Komedies* with the incredibly popular *Our Gang* (1922–1938) series. But change was just around the corner. The heyday of physical comedy was soon to be laid to rest as the medium of cinema took on board another crucial element. Some – like Chaplin – would try to avoid it, but others welcomed it, and, in turn, cinema welcomed a whole new breed of comedy performer. One that could now be heard.

Film Comedy: the comedy story

Screwball catalyst *It Happened One Night* (1963)

Film Comedy:
the comedy story

Comedy is heard: the 1930s

The arrival of sound changed the movies forever. In terms of comedy, it meant that where once the visual had ruled, now the verbal was on at least an equal footing. Buster Keaton's deadpan visage and the slow surreality of Harry Langdon were supplanted by Bob Hope's rapid-fire cowardliness act and the mercurial banter of the Marx Brothers. Verbiage did, indeed, out.

As early as 1899, sound was available to film-makers. Frenchman Auguste Baron completed his system of sound-synchronized cinema and offered it up to a then uninterested world. It wasn't until 1927 that the commercial potential was seized upon, when Al Jolson told us we "… ain't heard nothing yet" in *The Jazz Singer*. For many performers, it was a blessing. Take, for example, **the Marx Brothers** (see Canon), a huge hit on stage who played venues coast to coast in such riotous shows as *The Cocoanuts,* an anarchic *tour de force* set in a Florida hotel. Up until this point, film had been of no use to them. True, Harpo's pantomime could easily have given silent clown Larry Semon a run for his money, but the wit of Groucho would have been as nothing without sound. The Marxes took to the talkies instantly, first adapting *The Cocoanuts* for the big screen in 1929. Its stage origins prevailed, however – the cast visibly leaves plenty of pauses for the audience to laugh, their

Comedy is child's play

Ever since **Charlie Chaplin** turned 6-year-old Jackie Coogan into the world's most famous infant in *The Kid* (1921), children have been a staple of the comedy film. Some, like **Shirley Temple** or Macaulay Culkin, helped define their cinematic era, but many faded into obscurity with the onset of adolescence. Studios liked child actors: for one thing, they were cheap; for another, they were interchangeable. Silent movie mogul Hal Roach caught on to this when he attempted to expand his comedy kingdom courtesy of the *Our Gang* series of shorts. The series began in 1922 and continued on for many years – and none of the cast proved to be indispensable. By the 1930s the idea had really caught on, and cutesy **Shirley Temple** replaced sad-eyed Coogan as the world's most famous child in a series of hugely popular comedy musicals such as *Baby Take a Bow* (1934) and *Dimples* (1936). Within a few years, all-American boy **Mickey Rooney** was giving her a run for her money when he began the extremely successful *Andy Hardy* series for MGM (see box, p.10). Both Rooney and his contemporary, song and dance prodigy Donald O'Connor, managed the difficult transition into adult stardom, going on to appear in such movies as *National Velvet* (1944) and *Singin' in the Rain* (1952); Temple did not, and opted for a political career later in life, becoming ambassador to Ghana under President Ford, and White House chief of protocol.

Historically, however, few child stars have received the recognition awarded their adult counterparts. One notable exception was **Tatum O'Neal**, whose precocious turn as a conman's 9-year-old daughter in 1973's *Paper Moon*, set in Depression-era USA, earned her a Best Supporting Actress Oscar. In her wake followed **Jodie Foster**, who began her career in such Disney comedies as 1976's *Freaky Friday*, and, shortly after, Alan Parker's splurge-tastic *Bugsy Malone* (1976), later developing into a highly acclaimed dramatic adult actress. By the 1970s, child stars had largely become the province of sappy primetime family-based television sitcoms. **Gary Coleman**, for example, was scouted early in his career for a TV revival of *The Little Rascals* (that never got

made), and later achieved huge success as cheeky 8-year-old Arnold Jackson in the TV show *Diff'rent Strokes*. Coleman became a prime example of someone whose fame never really allowed him to grow up – an increasingly familiar pattern. It was **John Hughes** who, having already cornered the teen market with hits such as *The Breakfast Club* (1984) and *Ferris Bueller's Day Off* (1986, see Canon), brought the big screen its last great child comedy star of the twentieth century. Hughes discovered 8-year-old **Macaulay Culkin** in 1989 for his John Candy vehicle *Uncle Buck*, and in 1990 made him the central focus of what became (in its day) the highest grossing comedy of all time, *Home Alone*. Culkin spent several years in the spotlight – firstly for his career and then for his troubled personal life – but then later struggled to emerge from the shadow of his childhood success.

Perhaps **"Baby LeRoy"** (LeRoy Winebrenner) had the right idea. Starring in a number of movies alongside famed curmudgeon W.C. Fields (who famously advised us never to work with children or animals – see Canon), Baby had the good sense to get out when the going was good – he started his career at the age of 1, and retired at the grand old age of 4.

LeRoy Winebrenner and W.C. Fields
(*It's a Gift*, 1934)

timing having been honed by continually playing the show on the road.

Laurel and Hardy (see Icons), already silent screen stalwarts, made the transition to sound easily, their fragile comic dignity ably abetted by the chance to speak their case. The likes of Harold Lloyd and Buster Keaton (see Canon), however, became casualties of invention; evocative faces who didn't seem to belong in a world in which you could hear what your screen heroes were saying. Other comedy acts that came to prominence in the age of sound cinema − Bob Hope's knowing asides and calculated smart-alec patter, the irascible W.C. Fields with his sly drawling pearls of cynical wisdom, and Mae West, queen of innuendo − are now unimaginable without their own dialogue and sound.

Music dance and comedy: Fred Astaire, Ginger Rogers and Erik Rhodes in *The Gay Divorcee* (1934)

Musical comedy

With the arrival of sound came the option to take **musical comedy** off the stage and onto the big screen. Early on, the genre had trouble outgrowing its theatrical origins – witness *Gold Diggers of Broadway* (1929) with its array of theatre turns presented in a loosely-strung-together backstage-set plot, and followed by more *Gold Diggers* films in 1933, 1935 and 1937. While many comedies, both on stage and on screen, featured musical numbers – most of the Marx Brothers' pictures, for example, in which the likes of Zeppo, or his later replacement Allan Jones, stop the proceedings for a song – a new form was emerging, and creating its own musical stars as it grew. **Maurice Chevalier** was among the first to croon his way to cinematic success in 1929's *Innocents of Paris*, while singers Jeanette MacDonald and Nelson Eddy teamed up for a series of comic operetta features, the first of which included *Naughty Marietta* (1935) and *Rose-Marie* (1936). The penchant for revue-style productions took a while to diminish, however, with hits such as 1932's *The Big Broadcast* turning radio entertainers Bing Crosby, George Burns and Gracie Allen into stars on the big screen. Crosby was soon crooning his way through such gentle comedy romances as *College Humor* and *Too Much Harmony* (both 1933).

The genre really began to find its feet when it bypassed Broadway and moved uptown: **Fred Astaire** and **Ginger Rogers** became worldwide stars in a series of movies, including *The Gay Divorcee* (1934) and *Swing Time* (1936), that brought sophistication to the form. Rejoicing in the joy of putting on a top hat, doing up a bow tie and brushing up some tails, this exuberant twosome was something of an antidote to the Depression. Fred and Ginger's romantic pairing wasn't unique, however, in the world of musical comedy. Young stars Judy Garland and Mickey Rooney enjoyed innocent romance in such movies as 1939's *Babes in Arms*, directed by choreographer Busby Berkeley, while MacDonald and Eddy, "America's singing sweethearts", had a string of hits in the 1930s with light musical romances such

as the lush Broadway-goes-to-Hollywood vehicle *Sweethearts* (1938). As the 1940s progressed, new musical stars emerged. Consummate dance stylist **Gene Kelly** stepped in for the maturing Fred Astaire just as the impact of World War II was being felt, adding his grace and masculine good looks to such movies as 1945's *Anchors Aweigh* (in which he dances with Jerry, of Tom and Jerry) and *On the Town* (1949), with Frank Sinatra. Bob Hope and Bing Crosby's *Road to...* movies (1940-1962) helped keep the genre alive, and versatile stars such as Danny Kaye were emerging.

As the 1950s moved on, however, musical comedy began to slow down– notwithstanding peaks like *Singin' in the Rain* (1952) and the Western musical comedies. *Calamity Jane* (1953) and *Seven Brides for Seven Brothers* (1954) may have made stars of the likes of Doris Day and Howard Keel, but, as the decade ended, so did the golden era of musical comedy. Musicals simply grew out of fashion as commercial and creative power moved over to the pop and rock music industries, and they were deemed too expensive by the studios. Rare exceptions, like Disney's *Mary Poppins* (1964) and the Gene Kelly-directed *Hello, Dolly!* (1969), starring a young **Barbra Streisand**, struggled to keep musical comedy alive; flops, like *Thoroughly Modern Millie* (1967), helped shoot it down. Since then, there have been few attempts to revive the genre, bar such notable efforts as 1975's *The Rocky Horror Picture Show* and 1986's *Little Shop of Horrors,* both based on stage musicals. More recent musicals, such as period revivals *Moulin Rouge!* (2001) and *Chicago* (2002), were certainly tuneful and glamorous, but the comedy was in fairly short supply. Not so, however, in the tacky animation of Trey Parker and Matt Stone's *South Park: Bigger, Longer & Uncut* (1999), and also in their satirical post-9/11 puppet action flick *Team America: World Police* (2004), where musical comedy found an unlikely new home. The fact that the theme song to the latter was entitled "America – Fuck Yeah!" shows in many ways just how much the genre has moved on.

Glamour, music and dance

During the American Depression, cinema – more than ever before – became the favoured escapist medium, and the comedies of the late 1920s and the 1930s reflected this. Laurel and Hardy were among the very few working (or non-working) average Joes shown on US screens during this period; audiences increasingly flocked to see a more glamorous life – often set in ritzy uptown New York – unfold in front of them. *The Purple Rose of Cairo* (1985), Woody Allen's (see Canon) homage to the cinema of that day, and to the power of cinema in general, evokes the era perfectly. Depression-era audiences were also hungry for stories set in the milieu of the Broadway musicals, with optimistic tales of penniless showgirls made good. Movies such as *Broadway Melody of 1936* (1935), *42nd Street* (1933) and *Gold Diggers of 1935* (1934), with their combination of heart-warming stories, great songs and fabulous sets (and, often, the surreal, erotic synchronized choreography of **Busby Berkeley**), offered the ultimate in escapist extravagance. In addition, a brief run of radio-inspired movies entitled *The Big Broadcast* (1932, 1936, 1937, 1938) offered up a melange of new talent – Bing Crosby and Jack Benny, for example, who were also making their names in radio and on the stage.

Dancers **Fred Astaire** and **Ginger Rogers** brought style and grace to the comedy musical, beginning their sixteen-year, fourteen-film partnership with the exuberant *Flying Down to Rio* (1933). At the other end of the spectrum, the Marx Brothers, having produced the two surreal masterpieces *Monkey Business* (1931) and *Horse Feathers* (1932), managed to go even further with their hysterical attack on tin-pot dictatorships in *Duck Soup* (1933, see Canon).

42nd Street
dir Lloyd Bacon, 1933, US, 89 m, b/w

One of the first really successful Hollywood musicals, that set the template for those that followed – witty banter and great songs in this case linked to a backstage story of a show in which the leading actress sprains her ankle and a chorus girl must go on in her place and, naturally, becomes a star. Ruby Keeler plays the girl, and Ginger Rogers also gets a look in, in an early role. Fresh from Broadway, Busby Berkeley provides the incredibly inventive choreography.

Flying Down To Rio
dir Thornton Freeland, 1933, US, 89 m, b/w

Fred Astaire and Ginger Rogers first teamed up on film as supporting players in this delight complete with aerial ballets and a sense of decadence that belied the Great Depression era. Nonetheless their chemistry was instant, as they went on to prove with several other films, all of which pitted high class sophisticated comedy with some of the finest tunes ever.

Gold Diggers of 1935
dir Busby Berkeley, 1934, US, 95 m, b/w

Choreographer Berkeley turned full-time director for this, one of a series of *Gold Diggers* movies, designed in many ways as a public salve to the American Depression. Here he cast Dick Powell as a medical student working in a hotel where – inevitably – people are trying to stage a show. Cue more backstage shenanigans and Berkeley's trademark risqué for their dance numbers.

The Gay Divorcee
dir Mark Sandrich, 1934, US, 107 m, b/w

Astaire and Rogers are the leading performers in a film that focuses largely on the music, with the bare bones of a plot from Cole Porter's original musical, then titled *The Gay Divorce*. She's a woman looking to get unhitched, he's a man mistaken for her new partner. Features Porter's "Night and Day", although it won an Oscar (the first awarded to a song) for the much more forgettable "The Continental."

Sweethearts
dir W.S. Van Dyke, 1938, US, 114 m

Nelson Eddy and Jeanette MacDonald proved to be one of American cinema's most popular musical comedy teams, here starring as a Broadway double act who get a shot at Hollywood movie fame (ironic given how Hollywood was milking Broadway at the time). A happy ending is never far away and the stars are eminently personable in this, MGM's first full-colour film. (*The Wizard of Oz*'s Scarecrow (Ray Bolger) and the wizard himself (Frank Morgan) also feature prominently.)

It's not so grim up north: British comedy in the Thirties

British audiences, meanwhile, were as eager to see homegrown talent as they were to see American stars. Between the wars, with British cinema in many ways still in its infancy, a new breed of movie star emerged, hailing from the variety club circuit of the north of England. Acts already established on their own turf were introduced to the rest of the country as their films found success at the box office, and many went on to become the biggest national movie stars of their day.

London's Ealing Studios (see p.27) led the way (as it would in its heyday two decades later), with founder Basil Dean and filmmaker Michael Balcon importing music hall entertainers **Gracie Fields** and George Formby down south for the amusement of the nation. Fields ("Our Gracie") was a popular singer, a Lancashire lass who suffered no fools, but took the time to sing a few rousing numbers in the likes of *Sally in Our Alley* (1931) and *Sing As We Go* (1934). Invariably playing working-class roles, she was the highest paid film star in Britain by 1937, and, with her grin-and-bear-it pluck, very much a favourite during the early years of World War II (until she

decamped to America with her Italian husband and lost a certain amount of supportive feeling back home). A contemporary of Fields was **Will Hay**, a former teacher from northeast England who had found success in music hall by playing a bumbling schoolmaster. He later transferred his act to radio, but eventually found success in the movies replaying his befuddled teacher role in films such as *Boys Will Be Boys* (1935) and *Good Morning, Boys!* (1937).

George Formby was an altogether stranger proposition. A buck-toothed former jockey, with a broad Lancashire accent and a penchant for playing the banjo ukulele (or banjulele, as he called it), Formby gets caught up in pure-slapstick scrapes in such movies as *No Limit* (1936), *It's in the Air* (1938) and *Let George Do It* (1940). He was extremely popular in his own country during World War II and, like Gracie, was invited by Field Marshal Montgomery to entertain the troops with ENSA in Europe and North Africa.

Sing As We Go!
dir Basil Dean, 1934, UK, 80m, b/w

Northern playwright J.B. Priestley had a hand in scripting this, one of Gracie Fields' most popular comedies in which she – inevitably – plays "Gracie", a strong-voiced young northern lass, this time having lost her job at the local mill, but repairing to the myriad delights of Blackpool in an attempt to keep up her spirits. In many ways it's a local version of the Hollywood comic musicals of the day.

Good Morning, Boys!
dir Marcel Varnel, 1937 UK, 79m, b/w

Will Hay is the typically flustered head teacher of a boys' school facing stiff competition from a stiff upper-lipped Colonel intent on seeing him off. Add in a plot involving a plan for one of the pupils' dads to steal the Mona Lisa and a small role for later *Carry On* regular Charles Hawtrey and you have one of his most endearing comedies.

Let George Do It
dir Marcel Varnel, 1940, UK, 84m, b/w

Having worked with Will Hay, director Varnel took on another popular northern comic in the shape of ukulele-playing George Formby, here cast as a man who ends up on the wrong boat, finds himself in Norway (with the ever present ukulele to hand) taking on the Nazis. Very much intended to keep everyone's spirits up in the UK as World War II escalated, this finds Formby on top form, even if he is one of the strangest movie stars the British film industry ever created.

Screwball and other developments

Perhaps the most enduring legacy of 1930s comedy movies, **screwball** contrasts with both the visual spectacle of musical comedy and the directness of the British comedy of the period. It was all about words, and about complications of all kinds, particularly romantic. In 1934, **Frank Capra**'s *It Happened One Night* (see Canon) captured the top five Oscars (Best Picture, Director, Actor, Actress and Screenplay) – a feat that wouldn't be matched until over forty years later with the black and anti-establishment *One Flew Over the Cuckoo's Nest* (1975). *It Happened* kick-started screwball. The word itself was borrowed from the baseball term for an unconventional pitch that moves in the opposite way to a conventional curve ball – screwball was not a little screwy.

Many explanations have been offered for the sudden emergence of screwball comedies: that their zany slapstick with sophisticated fast-paced dialogue formed a bridge between the physical clowning of silent comedies and the wordier appeal of the talkies; that the spirited clash of the

sexes was a displaced response to the harsh self-censorship strictures of the new Production Code (which discouraged not merely the sexual but the sexy); that the emphasis on the minor misdeeds of the rich and elegant offered escapism from the Depression in a more realistic and satirical mode than musicals; and that, simply, the time for sophisticated, romantic (but cynical) comedies, with rapid-fire overlapping dialogue, had arrived. Certainly, Capra was not the only new big movie name to succeed in screwball films. Directors William Wyler (*The Good Fairy*, 1935), Gregory La Cava (*My Man Godfrey*, 1936), Leo McCarey (*The Awful Truth*, 1937; *Love Affair*, 1939) and, above all, Howard Hawks with *Bringing Up Baby* (1938) and *His Girl Friday* (1939) had critical or

Clark Gable and Claudette Colbert; first stars of screwball

Andy Hardy: the pre-teen teenager

For a brief period, in the late 1930s, the toast of Hollywood was a nice small-town boy named Andy Hardy, played by **Mickey Rooney**. His father was a judge, his mother was a housewife, and Andy got into all the scrapes that any ordinary boy might in this idealized version of all-American family life. The fifteen films in the series, beginning with 1937's *A Family Affair*, made a star of Rooney and caught the imagination of pre-war audiences, who longed for nothing more than a big old barn and the determination to "put on a show right here". With titles such as *Love Finds Andy Hardy* (1938), *Judge Hardy And Son* (1939) and *Life Begins For Andy Hardy* (1941), the films kept family values very much to the fore – and there was a wholesome lesson or two to be learned every time. It was, in many ways, a light-hearted look at the life of one ordinary young man as he came of age, but by the time of the final instalment, 1958's *Andy Hardy Comes Home*, the audience, and also Rooney, had grown up. And grown tired. It was to be the last of the series. Although made on a low budget, the Andy Hardy series had, over the course of its 21 years, brought in enough money to enable MGM, the studio behind it, to expand considerably, and to groom a new generation of stars including **Judy Garland** and **Lana Turner**.

commercial successes with the genre. And the talent roster was impressive too. Cary Grant, Audrey Hepburn, Clark Gable, Claudette Colbert (the epitome of the screwball heroine) and Carole Lombard (who married Grant before her tragic early death in a plane crash) all had their talents showcased during the screwball golden age that ran from 1934 to the early 1940s.

Screwball plots varied from the road-movie scenario of *It Happened One Night*, to the Cinderella theme of *My Man Godfrey* and the court and press-room settings of *His Girl Friday,* but at the heart of it all was a witty and passionate battle of the sexes. By the 1940s, however, the mood was darker –with **Katharine Hepburn** a more subdued heroine in *The Philadelphia Story* (1940) – coupled with a greater self-consciousness about the genre, evident in **Preston Sturges'** *Sullivan's Travels* (1941, see Canon), a film which has even been credited with "ending" screwball.

Genres in the 1930s were beginning to cross-fertilize. A number of filmmakers, for example, used the Depression as a means to extol patriotic virtues – Frank Capra took *Mr Smith* (Jimmy Stewart) *to Washington* (1939), and *Mr Deeds* (Gary Cooper) *to Town* (1936); he also took time to remind audiences of the power of eccentricity, individualism and the ephemeral nature of life in *You Can't Take It With You*, 1938's big Oscar winner. These films weren't without humour, but they did develop their themes well beyond a screwball, or even comic, template. The Western met the comedy (arguably the two most popular genres of their day) in 1939's *Destry Rides Again*; in the same year Greta Garbo brought her dramatic intensity to Ernst Lubitsch's *Ninotchka*; and meanwhile *The Wizard of Oz* (also 1939) brought colour, fantasy and **Judy Garland** to the musical. Garland was frequently paired up with **Mickey Rooney**, one of the greatest comedy stars of the period, whose success (mostly playing all-American boy Andy Hardy, see box) also peaked in 1939 when he was the biggest box office star in the US.

The Good Fairy
dir William Wyler, 1935, US, 98m, b/w

Preston Sturges scripted this charming *Amélie*-like story – of an orphan usherette Luisa (Margaret Sullavan) who wants to do good for others – from a Ferenc Molnar stage

Drama and comedy in Old Europe, courtesy of Greta Garbo, in *Ninotchka* (1939)

play. Of course her plans don't go smoothly. Neither did the on-set romance between Sullavan and director Wyler, who married swiftly only to divorce in 1936.

My Man Godfrey
dir Gregory La Cava, 1936, US, 93m, b/w

Carole Lombard is at her delightful finest in this screwball fest, playing a ditzy socialite who, as a result of a party game, comes across William Powell's homeless, erudite, Depression-era bum whom she then hires as the family butler. He, needless to say, turns out to be the only sensible one amongst them.

Europe: comedy and tragedy

Throughout the 1930s, European cinemas continued to produce comedies, but, with the barrier of language in the export market, these were increasingly aimed at domestic audiences. **Luis Buñuel** followed his surrealist parade of images in *Un chien andalou* (*An Andalusian Dog,* 1928 codirected with Salvador Dalí) with the more satirical art-cinema comic fantasy *L'âge d'or* (*Age*

23

Of Gold, 1930). The French added sophistication to film comedy with **René Clair**'s *À nous la liberté (Freedom For Us,* 1931), a satire on the machine age and an inspiration for Charlie Chaplin's (see Canon) equally satirical *Modern Times* (1936).

Actor **Maurice Chevalier**, who was signed by Paramount at the end of the 1920s, offered a different form of elegance. Chevalier oozed a certain innuendo-laden *je ne sais quoi* in 1929's *The Love Parade*, and became hugely successful portraying very French characters in Hollywood films, before returning to France in the mid-1930s. *The Love Parade* was directed by **Ernst Lubitsch** (who often worked with Chevalier), a German émigré famous for his lightness of touch in many films of the 1930s, such as the Noël Coward-scripted *Design for Living* (1933) and *Angel* (1937), where Marlene

Dietrich stars (rather surprisingly in retrospect) as a neglected wife. **Alfred Hitchcock** was soon to join the exodus to the US with his big-screen adaptation of John Buchan's thriller *The 39 Steps* (1935), adding a fair number of comedy elements into the mix in one of his last British films. European émigrés were also very much to the fore in *Ninotchka* (1939) – "Garbo laughs!" – a satire in which Greta Garbo, Ernst Lubitsch (directing) and Billy Wilder (writing credits, see Canon) combined to superb effect in poking fun at Communism and "Old Europe". By then, of course, the biggest and most tragic show on earth was commencing in Europe in earnest just as Hollywood had hit a famous peak in 1939 that it found difficult to recapture once World War II had started.

A serious business: comedy in the 1940s

Comedy at war

Comedy dominated the Oscars at the start of the decade when 1940's *The Philadelphia Story* (which came to the movies courtesy of its star, **Katharine Hepburn**, who had snapped up the rights of the original Broadway show) won that year's statuette for Best Picture, as well as Best Actor for James Stewart. Mere months later, that movie's other male star, **Cary Grant**, teamed with Rosalind Russell – and delivered what apparently still remains the fastest

dialogue in movie history – in *His Girl Friday* (1940, see Canon), a reworking of the 1931 newspaper comedy *The Front Page,* which was scripted from an original stage play by **Ben Hecht** and **Charles Lederer**.

World War II became a global concern, with America entering the battle, and cinema increasingly reflected the changes in world politics. Britain produced a series of patriotic dramas, deeming the war too close to home to laugh at, while American cinema chimed in with Charlie Chaplin's ambitious *The Great Dictator* (1940), in

Comedy teams after Stan and Ollie

Notwithstanding the success of The Three Stooges and the Marx Brothers, the studios continued to look for a team that would match the popularity of Laurel and Hardy. They hit upon the idea of teaming established comic stars together and thus **Buster Keaton** was paired with **Jimmy Durante** for a trio of Edward Sedgwick pictures (*The Passionate Plumber*, and *Speak Easily*, both 1932, and *What! No Beer?* in 1933). If anything, however, this particular pairing only highlighted the great division that had occurred in movie comedy over the last few years – Keaton was firmly rooted in visual virtuosity, while Durante was a powerhouse of one-liners. The torch had truly been passed.

The comedy team who came closest to aping the success of Stan and Ollie were former vaudevillians **Bud Abbot** and **Lou Costello** (see Icons). Abbott, the taller, more cynical, opportunistic straight man, and Costello, the smaller, fatter buffoon, took to the big screen in 1941's *Buck Privates*, and proved to be an instant smash hit. They ably reflected something of a social shift in comedy cinema. Where Laurel and Hardy were generally innocents, awash and trying to scrape by in Depression-era America, Abbott was a guy who was always on the make, out to get ahead by any means available – including using his portly friend to do so. As World War II raged on, Abbott and Costello were a far more contemporary proposition. They proved such a hit with audiences that, for the next decade and a half, they were turning out roughly two features a year (and, like Laurel and Hardy before them, they too became the subject of a series of cartoons in the 1960s). Even more prolific were the **Three Stooges**. The varying line-up made over 200 shorts (1934-58) and inspired a cartoon series. Their direct physical style (loved by children) did not translate well into features but many eyes were poked during their prolific career in the name of humour.

Also vieing for Laurel and Hardy's crown were two already established cinema veterans – the fast-talking comedy coward **Bob Hope** (see Icons), and the more laid-back crooner **Bing Crosby**. Beginning with *Road To Singapore* in 1940, Bing and Bob made six *Road To...* movies, generally in the company of the delectable **Dorothy Lamour**. With their combined talents for comedy and song, and playing on their already well-established screen personas, the duo proved in many ways to be the template for the dominant screen comedy team of the 1950s – **Dean Martin** and **Jerry Lewis**.

The 'classic' Stooge line-up – Moe Howard, Larry Fine and Curly Howard

which Chaplin himself plays both a buffoonish Hitleresque dictator and a lookalike victim of the tyrant's politics. Even bolder was Ernst Lubitsch's sublime *To Be Or Not To Be* (1942, see Canon), an anti-Nazi farce set in Poland which failed to ignite the box office, but which has been lauded ever since.

The start of the new decade also saw Laurel and Hardy's popularity supplanted by comedy team **Bud Abbott** and **Lou Costello** (see Icons), who would drop a few hints to American audiences about the impending war in the musical comedy *Buck Privates* (1941). Director Preston Sturges reminded us of comedy's inherent responsibilities and its potential to affect social change in *Sullivan's Travels* (1941, see Canon), while Ole Olsen and Chic Johnson's *Hellzapoppin'* (1941) had nothing to do with the war, but everything to do with on-screen anarchy. As the war drew to a close, British cinema looked to **Noël Coward** to brighten things up – and David Lean's adaptation of Coward's supernatural farce, *Blithe Spirit* (1945), more than did the trick.

Road to Singapore
dir Victor Schertzinger, 1940, US, 85m, b/w

Bob Hope and Bing Crosby did some travelling – down numerous *Roads* – but this was their first time out, and, inevitably, it led to them delivering a few songs, making the best of a bad thing and desiring the attentions of Dorothy Lamour (not a bad thing either). Here they were on the road to Singapore – but it could have been anywhere – as Bing's trademark croon and Bob's trademark comic cowardice came into play. A great team, this immaculately balanced film set the template for the numerous sequels that followed.

Hellzapoppin'
dir H.C. Potter, 1941, US, 84m, b/w

Ole Olsen and Chick Johnson take vaudeville to the big screen but in a film that was in many other ways way ahead of its time. Their original Broadway show became a movie in which all hell breaks loose and rides rough saddle, courtesy of this team's wall-to-wall patter. Co-written by Bilko creator Nat Perrin, this insane collection of gags moves with a pace that would come to define wild screen comedy. It gives the Marx Brothers a run for their money, whilst also throwing more wiseass one-liners at the screen than most.

Blithe Spirit
dir David Lean, 1945, UK, 96m

Director Lean takes on playwright Noël Coward to perfect effect, adding Rex Harrison into the mix as a recently remarried widower who finds the "presence" of his late wife (Hammond) something of an inconvenience. As ever with Coward, it's all about social incompatibility – the very nature of farce – all delivered with the airs and graces of a high tea. The wonderful Margaret Rutherford steals the show as the medium who inadvertently brings Hammond back onto the scene. Inimitable.

Reconstructing comedy

After the war it was, for comedy movies, a case of something old, something new. **Bing Crosby** ruled the American box office (often playing a priest, as in *Going My Way* (1944) and 1945's *The Bells of St Mary's*) in a series of earnest, sentimental comedies. They vied for the public's attention with the emergence of *film noir*, the imported neo-realism school of Italy, and a handful of movies that brought a fantasy element into their look at the life of the ordinary man (Capra's *It's a Wonderful Life* and Powell and Pressburger's *A Matter of Life and Death*, aka *Stairway to Heaven* – both from 1946). Life after war in Britain became the subject of 1949's *Whisky Galore!* (aka *Tight Little Island*), which heralded the arrival of the Ealing comedies, and **Robert Hamer**'s deliciously black *Kind Hearts and Coronets* (1949, see Canon) soon followed.

In musical comedy, **Gene Kelly** emerged as the natural heir apparent to Fred Astaire, and even

Ealing Comedies

When founded in 1931 by Basil Dean, who was then head of Associated Talking Pictures, **Ealing Film Studios** in West London was the first dedicated sound studio in Europe. It cost a modest £140,000 to build, and was soon playing host to a raft of popular musical comedies like 1932 s *Looking On The Bright Side*, starring music-hall entertainers George Formby and Gracie Fields. Noted British producer Michael Balcon took over in 1938, and during World War II the studio took on a more realist tone, producing a number of British propaganda-flavoured war movies including *Went The Day Well* (1942) and *Undercover* (1943).

After the War the studio – in what would turn out to be its last burst of life – took its now trademark realist style and combined it with wild, fantastical plots to create a series of smart, often satirical movies that became known simply as the **Ealing comedies**. These quintessentially British films were firmly rooted in the sometimes bizarre world of postwar Britain, dealing with pressing issues such as rationing (Alexander Mackendrick's *Whisky Galore!,* 1949) or the advances and mistrust of big business and technology (Mackendrick's *The Man in the White Suit*, 1951). In

Henry Cornelius' *Passport To Pimlico*, which set the cycle in motion in 1949, the residents of a London suburb discover that it is actually an independent royal territory of France, and threaten to secede in order to avoid rationing and taxation. The comedy in the Ealing movies was also often matched with a deliciously dark and subversive side, particularly exemplified in Robert Hamer's *Kind Hearts And Coronets* (1949), and Mackendrick's *The Ladykillers (*1955), both of them murderous, dark comic fantasies.

Ealing comedies were generally populated by an ensemble of great British character actors, including **Alec Guinness**, Alastair Sim, Margaret Rutherford, Sidney James and Stanley Holloway, and were as much defined by their regular directors as by their stars. Along with Cornelius and Mackendrick, **Charles Crichton** was a major player in the Ealing team, helming such movies as *The Lavender Hill Mob* in 1951 and *The Titfield Thunderbolt* a year later. (In 1988, hoping to evoke the spirit of Ealing for his own pet project, John Cleese would later drag Crichton out of retirement to direct *A Fish Called Wanda*.) The Ealing comedy cycle drew to a close when the studios were sold to BBC Television in 1956.

---

took time to dance with Jerry Mouse in 1945's *Anchors Aweigh* – Jerry and cat pal Tom, meanwhile, became cinema's most popular (and most violent) cartoon stars. In France, **Jacques Tati** (see Canon) was also rapidly becoming a major comic force with his *Jour de fête* (*Holiday*, 1948).

Screwball received a shot in the arm as war themes persisted. Cary Grant saw out the decade in drag – a lead that many would follow in the coming years – in 1949's *I Was A Male War Bride* (aka *You Can't Sleep Here*). But, as one conflict receded, the threat of another arose, with serious consequences for comedy. Having seen off

Nazism, America started to look within itself to flush out the Communist "menace", most notably through the activities of the House Un-American Activities Committee, which led to the ousting of several supposed sympathizers in the film industry, and Charlie Chaplin leaving the country in 1952. (The events were well-documented in Martin Ritt's 1976 movie *The Front*, featuring **Woody Allen** and **Zero Mostel**, which was written by Walter Bernstein, who had himself been blacklisted in the 1950s.) Other signs of the times were the films *I Married A Communist* (aka *The Woman On Pier 13*, 1950), which, despite its title, was not a comedy, and *My Son John* (1952) by 1930s screwball director Leo McCarey, in which a mother turns in her communist spy son. With *film noir* still very much in the ascendant, and postwar prosperity beginning to take hold, it was time for a new generation of comedy icons to appear.

Passport to Pimlico
dir Henry Cornelius, 1949, UK, 85m, b/w

The movie that set the template for Ealing comedies – a specific location, a variety of strong characters and a strong element of absurdism. Here the residents of Pimlico, London, discover that cutting themselves off from the world around them isn't altogether a good thing in post-war, ration-heavy London. A delight.

Whisky Galore!
dir Alexander Mackendrick, 1949, UK, 82m, b/w

Quintessential Ealing comedy in which the residents of a small Scottish island are determined to keep a large cargo of whisky that floats ashore. As ever with Ealing, bureaucracy gets subverted – in this case in the form of the English laird (Basil Radford) who governs the island.

Funnies in the 50s

At the start of the decade, just as the box-office allure of Abbott and Costello was on the wane, another comic duo arrived to take their place. The radio team of goofy **Jerry Lewis** (see Icons) and debonair crooner **Dean Martin** became huge global stars in a series of knockabout comedies like *Sailor Beware* (1951) and *The Caddy* (1953) that for all their lowbrow humour showed that the double act had now become a more sophisticated, urbane beast. **Bette Davis** dug her teeth into one of her finest roles as a bitchy actress (typecasting anyone?) in Joseph L. Mankiewicz's

sharply witty *All About Eve* (1950; see Canon); it promptly picked up a handful of Oscars, including Best Picture. Hollywood also looked in on itself with *Singin' In The Rain* (1951), a knowing comedy musical that took a wry look at the coming of sound in the movies. Having made the role her own on stage, **Judy Holliday** brought a ditzy quality to her turn in George Cukor's *Born Yesterday* (1950), creating a dumb blonde, *idiote savante* persona that was to rear its head again and again in Hollywood over the course of the decade. It was another actress, however, Marilyn Monroe (see Icons), who above anyone came to personify the dumb blonde, her comic gifts shining bright in classic comedies *Gentlemen Prefer Blondes* (1953) and *The Seven Year Itch* (1955).

The early 1950s was also the era of **Francis The Talking Mule**, who starred with Donald O'Connor in six movies, among them *Francis Goes to the Races* (1951) and *Francis Joins the WACS* (1954), and with **Mickey Rooney** in one. He was eventually superseded by TV's talking horse *Mr. Ed*, but for many, Francis, with his backchat and wisecracks ruled supreme. (That was, at least until that lovable mutt Benji showed up in 1974.)

Over in Britain, along came Norman Wisdom – a diminutive, sentimental comic, much in the vein of **George Formby**, or, in the USA, Jerry Lewis – whose mixture of physical comedy, eternal optimism and flat cap made him Britain's biggest star of the early 1950s in such knockabout romps as *Trouble In Store* (1953). Britain was also busy making a star of Dirk Bogarde in *Doctor in The House* (1954), the first in a long-running series of broad comedy *Doctor* movies (later developed as a television series). New French sex symbol **Brigitte Bardot** joined him for the first sequel, *Doctor at Sea* (1955).

Flying the flag for a more genteel vision of Britain were Alastair Sim, Joyce Grenfell and

A decade of blondes-Judy Holliday in *Born Yesterday* (1950)

Margaret Rutherford in the farcical *The Happiest Days Of Your Life* (1950), set in that peculiarly British comic milieu, the schoolroom. Sim was to cast a long but benign shadow over British cinema comedy in the 1950s, returning to school and dragging up to play the headmistress in a series of movies set in a rowdy girls' boarding school, St. Trinian's, beginning with 1954's *The Belles Of St. Trinian's*.

In the USA, too, the late forties and fifties were a great era for drag comedies. Setting off in 1949 with the screwball-influenced *I Was A Male War Bride,* which sees Cary Grant suffer endless humiliation while dressed as a woman, the decade closed with one of the best drag acts ever – **Jack Lemmon** and **Tony Curtis** prettied up to play in an all-girl jazz band, in Billy Wilder's *Some Like It Hot* (1959; see Canon).

Back in England, the 1950s saw one of the country's major comic talents, Charlie Chaplin, make the flawed but interesting *Limelight* (1952), a dark reflection on getting older that had him playing opposite an ailing Buster Keaton. Ealing comedies, meanwhile, were getting allegorical with *The Man In The White Suit* (1951) and dark with *The Lavender Hill Mob* (1951); *The*

Never work with animals…

Animals have long been a staple of the comedy movie – **Laurel and Hardy** shared the screen with a dog named *Laughing Gravy* (1931), even if they did have to keep him hidden from their landlord, while another dog – Petey – was a staple of Hal Roach's *Our Gang* series. (Roach also had a fondness for chimpanzees, as witnessed in his *Dippy Doo-Dad* shorts of the 1920s.) Roach's contemporary Mack Sennett was also busy making use of a cat (Pepper), a dog (Teddy) and a horse (Butterfly) to elicit laughs when his human Keystone casts weren't delivering the goods. Despite being a nightmare to work with, much like kids, animals were cheap and dispensable – and audiences just loved them.

The screwball genre, with its reliance on spiralling anarchy and chaos, was the perfect arena for animal stars. Witness classics such as *Bringing Up Baby* (1938) in which a leopard – along with **Katharine Hepburn** – makes mincemeat of straightlaced palaeontologist **Cary Grant**, and *Monkey Business* (1952), in which a chimp creates a formula that leads **Ginger Rogers** and Cary Grant (again!) to regress to infancy.

Less successfully, future president Ronald Reagan came off looking like the lesser actor against another chimp, in 1951's *Bedtime For Bonzo*, while Clint Eastwood also later took a shine to a primate, teaming up with Clyde the slightly drunken orang-utan for the two movies *Every Which Way But Loose* (1978) *and Any Which Way You Can* (1980). Gorillas get a look in, too, most notably the one who sexually attacks Paul Gleason in *Trading Places* (1983) (a fate that also befell Homer Simpson on television, courtesy of an amorous panda bear).

Gophers and groundhogs – virtually unheard of, outside North America – are the latest members of cinema's comedy menagerie. Courtesy of **Bill Murray** and director Harold Ramis they are now known the world over. The former (admittedly in the form of a not-very-good puppet that would have the late Jim Henson spinning in his grave) tore up Murray's golf course in *Caddyshack* (1980; see Canon), while the latter poked his nose out of his tree in Gobbler's Gulch over and over again during the wonderful *Groundhog Day* (1993; see Canon).

Ladykillers (1955), another twisted Ealing tale, also helped to usher in one of Britain's biggest comedy stars, **Peter Sellers** (see Icons). Already a star of radio courtesy of his multi-character performances on *The Goon Show*, Sellers attacked cinema with a vengeance, forming short-lived alliances with the Boulting Brothers (*I'm All Right, Jack,* 1959) and going on to star in Stanley Kubrick's *Dr. Strangelove* (1963; see Canon) before becoming linked to director Blake Edwards courtesy of the *Pink Panther* franchise (see Canon).

In continental Europe, meanwhile, where Italy was roaring with laughter at the legendary comedian Toto, the 1950s saw another Italian,

Federico Fellini, announce the arrival of his prodigious talent to the world with the satirical *Lo sceicco bianco/The White Sheik* (1951). In France, **Jacques Tati** hit international comedy gold with his award-winning classic *Les vacances de Monsieur Hulot/Monsieur Hulot's Holiday* (1953). By the mid-1950s, Swedish filmmaker **Ingmar Bergman** had also sealed his global reputation with his first film, the delightful comedy of manners *Sommarnattens Leende/ Smiles of a Summer Night* (1955), which went on to inspire **Woody Allen**'s *A Midsummer Night's Sex Comedy* (1982).

Born Yesterday
dir George Cukor, 1950, US, 103m, b/w

Judy Holliday plays the girlfriend of dubious scrap metal tycoon Broderick Crawford who hires teacher William Holden to coach her to become more dignified. The trouble is, teacher and pupil fall for each other. A simple tale, it's wonderfully quick-witted thanks to Cukor's direction and Garson Kanin's smart script, adapted from his hit play.

Francis (aka Francis the Talking Mule)
dir Arthur Lubin, 1950, US, 91m, b/w

It had to be a winner. Take Donald O'Connor as a somewhat green soldier in need of a friend while romancing Patricia Medina's nurse, and suddenly a talking mule makes sense. Enough so that they made four sequels. Also features a young Tony Curtis, and an ageing Zasu Pitts.

The Happiest Days of Your Life
dir Frank Launder, 1950, UK, 81m, b/w

Typical post-WWII British comedy with Alastair Sim and Margaret Rutherford on ever-fine form as the heads – respectively – of a boys' school and a girls' school, who find their charges thrown together due to a bureaucratic mix-up as a result of the war. British comedy stalwarts Joyce Grenfell and Richard Wattis also make an appearance.

The Man in the White Suit
dir Alexander Mackendrick, 1951, UK, 85m, b/w

One of Ealing's finest comedies; a post-War morality tale in which Alec Guinness invents a cloth that never wears out or needs cleaning, thus threatening an entire fabric industry – workers and management. Guinness is on top form as the innocent boffin, and the movie takes on a Frankenstein-like quality as his suit is eventually ripped to shreds.

Lo sceicco bianco/The White Sheik
dir Federico Fellini, 1951, Italy, 88m, b/w

An early Fellini, and one that shows his more playful side. A honeymooning couple (Brunella Bovo and Leopoldo Trieste) face temptation in various forms; he from the local prostitutes, she from her photo comic-strip (*fumetti*) hero, the Sheik of the title (Alberto Sordi) – who turns out to be not quite the man of her dreams.

Sailor Beware
dir Hal Walker, 1952, US, 108m, b/w

The movie that established Dean Martin and Jerry Lewis as box office gold. The guys play chalk and cheese Navy buddies causing havoc on a sub; debonair ladies' man Martin makes the perfect foil for klutzy Lewis, whose allergy to women's make-up hinders him somewhat in the romance stakes.

Trouble in Store
dir John Paddy Carstairs, 1953, UK, 85m, b/w

Norman Wisdom is a typically British hero in that he – not a tall man – excelled at playing the little man. As ever with Wisdom, who here plays a department store window dresser, his penchant for sentimentality is married to a deft and always entertaining ability for physical comedy.

The Seven Year Itch
dir Billy Wilder, 1955, US, 105m

The premise – Marilyn Monroe's dress blows up in the street, men get distracted – holds true in a plot, based on George Axelrod's play, that's as old as the hills. Tom Ewell plays the man who becomes smitten by his gorgeous neighbour (Monroe, naturally). Monroe's astonishing screen presence and exemplary comic skills are to the fore.

Towards the 60s

A key feature of the second half of the 1950s was rapid technological change, and in particular the advent of television. Hollywood had a number of responses to this threat to its livelihood. One was to aspire to "high art", cherrypicking from a new group of actors and writers schooled in what became known as the Method approach to acting. Brooding stars such as **Marlon Brando**, Montgomery Clift and, later, James Dean brought a psychological angst to their work, while writers like Paddy Chayefsky – who originally started writing TV

What a drag

The notion of men playing women, which dates back to medieval times, reached its apogee on the Elizabethan stage, when all roles were played by men and teenage boys in costume and corsets (a tradition touched on in both John Madden's 1998 Oscar-winner *Shakespeare in Love* and Richard Eyre's *Stage Beauty* from 2005). Although no one appears to be sure where the term "drag" comes from – or, indeed, why it came from anywhere – it is generally assumed to be a corruption of Shakespeare's stage notation "dressed as girl". Others, however, date the earliest use of the word in this context to around 1870. Shakespeare, of course, gets quite a lot of comedy out of the man-dressed-as-woman-dressed-as-man thing, as did popular early forms of clowning, music hall, pantomime and even Punch and Judy puppet shows.

Drag was a must for the movies, the greatest popular entertainment of them all, and since the beginnings of screen comedy there has been one absolute – it's just plain funny when men dress up as women. As so often, Laurel and Hardy perfected the form early on, notably in 1933's *Twice Two*, in which they play each other's wives. The other great classic of American drag cinema is, of course, **Billy Wilder**'s incomparable *Some Like It Hot* (1959; see Canon), in which Jack Lemmon makes a remarkably convincing woman; equally, **Dustin Hoffman** should have picked up an Oscar for his *tour de force* as actor Dorothy Michaels, also known by his/her director as *Tootsie* (1982). It's no surprise maybe that Tom Hanks found his first success – on the small screen – as one half of TV's *Bosom Buddies* (opposite Peter Scolari), a *Some Like It Hot*-esque pair of guys dragging it up in order to be allowed to stay in an all-female hostel.

Drag's broad, music-hall influenced appeal has coursed through British comedy like a stream – from **Alastair Sim**, for example, who made a fine Lady Agatha in Ealing Studios' *Kind Hearts and Coronets* (1949) and was by far St. Trinian's finest headmistress, through the *Carry On* movies, to the *Monty Python* team, of whom there isn't a living member who hasn't thrown on a frock in the name of comedy. Even after the *Pythons*' demise many of them were still at it, **Eric Idle** taking ecclesiastical orders and joining Robbie Coltrane as *Nuns on the Run* in 1990.

In the 1990s the Australian hit *Priscilla, Queen of the Desert* (1994) provided fresh humour while taking drag seriously; its American counterpart, the clumsily named *To Wong Foo, Thanks For Everything! Julie Newmar* (1995), followed up by casting Patrick Swayze, Wesley Snipes and John Leguizamo as unlikely drag queens on a road trip. **Robin Williams** donned a frock for the runaway hit *Mrs. Doubtfire* (1993), a divorce-tinged family comedy with a politically correct agenda, and also starred in *The Birdcage* (1996), the American remake of the French arthouse hit *La cage aux folles* (1978). Perhaps returning to drag's broadest beginnings, in 2004 the Wayans brothers went one step further and swapped not only gender but also race in the outrageous *White Chicks*, a movie that saw Marlon and Shawn Wayans transform themselves into Paris Hilton clones. Billy Wilder may well have been spinning in his grave.

scripts – portrayed gritty reality in their movies. Hollywood also looked to pull in big audiences by reviving the epic. Cue a number of religious pieces, from *The Robe* (1953), the first movie filmed in CinemaScope (another response to the coming of TV) to **Cecil B. De Mille**'s *The Ten Commandments* (1956). Not a lot of laughs there. The comedy equivalent was offered by a new breed of all-star, globe-trotting comedy, including *Around the World in Eighty Days* (1956) with **David Niven** heading up a stellar cast that also included Shirley MacLaine, Buster Keaton,

Ava Gardner, John Gielgud, Frank Sinatra, Peter Lorre and Noël Coward.

Some directors, meanwhile, were breaking with tradition and pushing their own limits. Having made a name for himself with some of the best Ealing's comedies, **Alexander Mackendrick** headed to America and delivered the caustic drama *Sweet Smell Of Success* (1957), a scathing look at the job of the press agent and a timely reflection on the state of celebrity in America. Billy Wilder meanwhile moved on from such award-winning dramas as *Sunset Blvd.* (1950) and lent his prodigious talent to comedy on a more regular basis, delivering such gems as *Some Like It Hot* and *The Apartment* (1960; see Canon).

By 1958, **Rock Hudson** had become a star – the fact that he was one of Hollywood's leading homosexuals was a closely guarded secret, and he was presented to the world as very much a ladies' man, often teamed with the virtuous Doris Day in a series of frothy bedroom comedies that started with *Pillow Talk* in 1959. In the absence of Lewis and Martin, who split acrimoniously in 1956, Rock and Doris became Hollywood's leading comedy team.

Pillow Talk (1959) – Rock Hudson and Doris Day's first outing

Britain may have lacked a comedy duo, but they soon developed a whole raft of regular players with the arrival of *Carry on Sergeant* in 1958, a movie that began the long run of *Carry On* movies (see Icons). The series made stars of **Sid James**, Kenneth Williams, Barbara Windsor and numerous others over the next twenty years.

Around the World In Eighty Days
dir Michael Anderson, 1956, US, 167m

One of the first of a new breed of all-star comedies featuring scores of cameos, this rip-roaring take on Jules Verne's race against time pits David Niven as Phileas Fogg, ballooning, training and steamboating round the world on the back of a bet.

Pillow Talk
dir Michael Gordon, 1959, US, 105m

Rock Hudson and Doris Day first displayed their sparky chemistry in this romantic romp. Rock is a rakish songwriter (ably backed by the brilliant Tony Randall) who shares a party-phone line with Day's virtuous beauty. Through their phone conversations they fall in love – ensuring that all "pillow talk" stays far away from the pillow.

Comedy in the Sixties

In the early 1960s, while vast movies like the war epic *The Longest Day* (1962) and historical extravaganza *Cleopatra* (1963) were vying for attention with a slew of gritty British "kitchen sink" dramas like *The Loneliness Of The Long Distance Runner* and *A Kind Of Loving*, (both 1962), comedy was growing stale. There was a new level of cynicism seen in such movies as Billy Wilder's *The Apartment* and Stanley Kubrick's perfectly poised satire, *Dr. Strangelove, Or How I Learned to Stop Worrying And Love The Bomb* (1963; see Canon) – made in the shadow of the Cuban missile crisis – but very little being offered as a refreshing change or development.

Rock Hudson and Doris Day remained strong at the US box office, as did Elvis – though it's hard to call the sight of one of rock'n'roll's pre-eminent talents being deflated by a series of ever diminishing movies comedic – while Britain relied on more and more *Carry On* films. The Carry On team proved extraordinarily quick off the mark when they came out with *Carry On Cleo* (1964) making light of Liz Taylor and her own po-faced epic (a lesson in response-time that Mel Brooks could have learned for later life). **Audrey Hepburn** briefly dazzled in *Breakfast At Tiffany's (*1961) with her glamour masking the absence of some of the satirical bite of Truman Capote's novella lost in the transition from page to screen. One particularly sixties creature was the very Californian "Beach Party" movie. This series of films, generally starring crooner **Frankie Avalon** and former Mouseketeer Annette Funicello, and with titles such as *Beach Party* (1963), *Bikini Beach* (1964) and *Beach Blanket*

Glamour before the storm – Audrey Hepburn dazzles in *Breakfast at Tiffany's*

Bingo (1965), revolved around surfing, making out and dancing in bikinis.

It was down to four lads from Liverpool to really shake up screen comedy. The Beatles'

first film, *A Hard Day's Night* (1964; see Canon), not only captured the insanity of being the four most famous faces in the world, but also took the lessons learnt from realistic, kitchen-sink movie making and applied them to comedy. Here was a movie that revelled in its working-class origins, which wore them proudly on its well-tailored sleeves, and at the same time helped to define youth cinema – something that would become dominant later in the decade with movies such as *The Graduate* (1967; see Canon) and *Easy Rider* (1969). Director **Richard Lester**, an ex-pat American, perfectly captured the last days of post-World War II Britain, shooting in austere black and white a world that was about to break into full colour. America of course, was already in full colour, even when it was basing itself in London, Walt Disney's exuberant *Mary Poppins* (1964) providing a curious contrast to Lester's view of England (and **Dick Van Dyke** providing a curious contrast to anything resembling an English accent).

In the mid-1960s Richard Lester continued his comedic look at the Swinging Sixties with *The Knack . . . And How To Get It* (1965) and the second of his movies with the Beatles, the inferior *Help!* (1965); meanwhile, **Michael Caine** became a global star courtesy of the rather more bitter than bittersweet *Alfie* (1966).

In the USA, Norman Jewison's *The Russians Are Coming, The Russians Are Coming* (1966) used its comedy to take a wry look at small-town America and to make a sly comment on the Cold War. The same year, **James Coburn** made fun of both his leading man status and the Bond-led spy genre in the parodic *Our Man Flint*. Over in Europe, Czech director Milos Forman, meanwhile, emerged as a director of considerable note courtesy of his quirky *A Blonde In Love/Loves Of A Blonde* (1965).

Despite these highlights, more than anything there was a feeling of lost direction in mid-1960s cinema. That a new direction was to be found by a former stand-up comedian was no accident.

Breakfast At Tiffany's
dir Blake Edwards, 1961, US, 115m

A gorgeous Audrey Hepburn, a top notch George Peppard and Edwards' excessive style turned Truman Capote's tale of a flighty gold digger into one of the greatest romantic comedy films. Highlights include Mickey Rooney (as an offensive Japanese neighbour) the song "Moon River" and a desperate search for a cat in the rain.

Beach Blanket Bingo
dir William Asher, 1965, US, 98m

Annette Funicello and Frankie Avalon up to their usual sun-surf-and-sand gallivanting, singing, gyrating, parachuting and rescuing the gorgeous Sugar Kane (Linda Evans) from a motorcycle gang. Look out for Buster Keaton as an ageing lech and Beach Boy Brian Wilson as one of the boys on the beach.

The Russians Are Coming, The Russians Are Coming
dir Norman Jewison, 1966, US, 126m

Alan Arkin and American comic Jonathan Winters excel in this Cold War romp in which a small town in Maine thinks it's being invaded by the dreaded red menace when a Russian submarine pulls into port. Very reflective of its time, along with the satirical *Dr. Strangelove* and the more serious *Fail-Safe* (1964).

Alfie
dir Lewis Gilbert, 1966, UK, 114m

One of those 1960s movies that really hasn't aged well, despite a young Michael Caine's bravura performance as the Cockney rogue who loves and leaves a sequence of dollybirds before facing his downfall. A fascinating evocation of "swinging London" that leaves a nasty taste in the mouth.

Comedy graduates

Mike Nichols had performed improvisational comedy with his partner Elaine May in the late 1950s before graduating to the stage as a director. His movie debut was the taut and deeply affecting *Who's Afraid of Virginia Woolf?* (1966) but for his sophomore effort he went with a little-known book by Charles Webb called *The Graduate* (1967; see Canon). Concerning a recently graduated, deeply alienated young man named Benjamin Braddock, the film quietly redefined Hollywood. A satire about ennui, it discovered an audience that for the majority of the decade Hollywood had lost and/or ignored. Post-World War II, post-rock'n'roll, the young had come into their own. They looked for movies that spoke to them, movies that knew where Haight-Ashbury was as sure as they knew anything. *The Graduate* got that. It related to a disenfranchised audience, told them their point of view was relevant, and, ultimately, helped *define* their point of view. It may well have been seven years into the decade, but the 1960s had arrived

The remainder of the decade reads like a series of mid-life crises in the wake of the great youth revolt (admittedly cinema was much better at handling this in terms of its drama – *Easy Rider* et al – than it was its comedies) – witness an ageing Peter Sellers ill-advisedly swinging in anything that was going *(Casino Royale*, 1967; *The Magic Christian*, 1969; *There's A Girl In My Soup*, 1970). By the end of the decade, however, comedy was finding its feet again. *Butch Cassidy and the Sundance Kid* (1969), with the help of **Paul Newman** and **Robert Redford**, injected humour back into the Western, while, over in the UK, the satirical *Oh! What A Lovely War* (1969), Richard Attenborough's directorial debut, dished up pacifism with cynicism. In a lighter vein, Barbra Streisand emerged to remind the world that despite the advancements in youth culture, America still liked nothing more than a good old-fashioned Broadway musical, courtesy of her sprightly turn as Fanny Brice in *Funny Girl* (1968).

For the most part though, serious politics dominated the landscape of late 1960s filmmaking – be it the political tension of *In The Heat Of The Night* (1967), the political ambivalence of *Easy Rider*, the political metaphor of *Planet Of The Apes* (1967), or the political loss of direction of Lindsay Anderson's *If...* (1968).

Over in Europe, the Czech comedy *Daisies* (1966), directed by **Vera Chytilová**, a story of two monstrous girls on the rampage, fell foul of the censor (its audience weren't too impressed either), while Milos Forman continued to display exemplary form with *The Firemen's Ball* (1967), his last hometown movie before he decamped for the US.

Oh! What A Lovely War
dir Richard Attenborough, UK, 1969, 144m

Just about anyone who was anyone in the British film industry showed up for Attenborough's take on Joan Littlewood's satire on World War I – and indeed, all wars. A series of vignettes chronicle key events of the war, spotlighting the moment where opposing sides come together in no-man's-land at Christmas.

Butch Cassidy And The Sundance Kid
dir George Roy Hill, 1969, US, 110m

Deliciously wry comedy Western, the first and most successful outing for Paul Newman (Butch) and Robert Redford (The Kid). Their screen chemistry and comic timing, along with a strong script by William Goldman, have kept the movie fresh; Katharine Ross as the girl they both love helps, too.

The morning after: comedy in the 1970s

Cynicism and knowledge

It's often said that if you can remember the 1960s then you can't have been there – and when it came to the movies, the seventies certainly began as the morning after the night before. Accepted morals – often the bugbear of the comedy movie – had quite simply changed for many people, and in the light of this comedy could also do so. On one level it was as simple as saying that one generation's values differed from those of their parents. Thus where **Abbott and Costello** made the army look fun, now **Robert Altman**'s blackly

comedic *M*A*S*H* (1969; see Canon) painted it in all its true colours (and most of them were blood red).

More than anything, the cinema of the early seventies was defined by a group of directors finding their way by coming to grips with a society that had lost its way. Political paranoia was rampant (*The Conversation, The Parallax View*, both 1974), corruption added a huge sense of melancholy (*All The President's Men,* 1976) and the Mafia were about the most wholesome family unit you were going to get to see (*The Godfather,* 1971; *The Godfather Part II,* 1974).

In the shadow of this, a sense of negativity seeped into comedy cinema of the early 1970s. The impact and implications of all that 1960s promiscuity were felt in Mike Nichols's *Carnal Knowledge* (1971), written by Jules Feiffer, one of America's leading cartoonists). Altman followed up *MASH* with the enigmatic oddity *Brewster McCloud* (1970), while **Peter Bogdanovich** (who emerged as a filmmaker of ultimately minor note) made an attempt to counter this by harking back to the screen comedies of the 1930s with the screwball *What's Up, Doc* (1972); later, he went even farther back with his 1976 homage, *Nickelodeon.* There were lighter touches, too, in Hal

Harold And Maude (1971) – Hal Ashby's unconventional classic

Ashby's masterpiece *Harold and Maude* (1971), the touching tale of a young adult (Bud Cort) who falls in love with an eighty-year-old woman (the perfect Ruth Gordon), and in *The Sting* (1973), which, as in *Butch Cassidy And The Sundance Kid*, teamed **Paul Newman** and **Robert Redford** to brilliant effect, this time to revive the caper movie. As the decade wore on, however, America stayed pretty cynical. **Dustin Hoffman** took comedian Lenny Bruce to the masses with his portrayal of *Lenny* (1974) – achieving more success with the role than the comic ever managed in his own lifetime – while *Fun With Dick And Jane* (1976) followed the jollies of two would-be bank robbers.

The seventies were also a time of great productivity for many directors. **Mel Brooks** (see Icons) came back in blistering form, first by taking the Western for all it was worth in *Blazing Saddles* (1974; see Canon) and then by debunking Universal's dominance of the Horror movie with *Young Frankenstein* (1974) and taking an even bigger leap back by tackling the *Silent Movie* (1976). It was a feat bettered by his contemporary **Woody Allen** (see Icons), who hit the 1970s with all his comic juices flowing: *Take The Money And Run* (1969), *Bananas* (1971), *Sleeper* (1973), *Everything You Always Wanted To Know About Sex, But Were Afraid To Ask* (1974), *Love And Death* (1975), *Annie Hall* (1977) and *Manhattan* (1979) gave even the Marx Brothers' output of the 1930s a run for its money.

In the UK, comedy stuck with the basics, which – like the cockroach in a post-nuclear world – will always prevail. The *Carry On* movies reached their popular height, duly followed by the *Confessions Of A...* series (*Window Cleaner*, 1974; *Driving Instructor*, 1976; and so on), which took smut beyond *Carry On* levels while leaving the best humour behind. Things got more surreal

when Monty Python appeared on the big screen searching for the *Holy Grail* (1974).

Other Europeans were taking their comedy a tad more seriously, however. Luis Buñuel took Catherine Deneuve to a dark place in *Tristana* (1970) and then took a savage knife to the upper-middle-class in *The Discreet Charm Of The Bourgeoisie* (1972). Czech filmmaker Milos Forman relocated to America and satirized his newly adopted home with his first English-language comedy, *Taking Off* (1971). Over in Australia, meanwhile, Peter Weir alerted the world to the Australian film industry courtesy of his comedic groundbreaker, *The Cars That Ate Paris* (1974).

Harold And Maude
dir Hal Ashby, 1971, US, 92m

Ashby's best, and most subversive, film finds twenty-year-old nihilist Bud Cort falling for lively eighty-year-old Ruth Gordon. She educates him about life – and then, when he falls in love with her, dies on him. Blackly comic and extremely confident: in short, a work of genius.

Taking Off
dir Milos Forman, 1971, US, 92m

Lynn Carlin and Buck Henry play middle-class parents searching for their runaway daughter (Leannia Heacock). Very much a post-1960s generation-gap movie, it is far more akin to Forman's early non-English-language comedies (*Blonde In Love, Fireman's Ball*) than his later dramatic works (*One Flew Over The Cuckoo's Nest*, 1975, or *Amadeus*, 1984).

What's Up Doc?
dir Peter Bogdanovich, 1972, US, 94m

Former film critic Bogdanovich goes screwball by placing Ryan O'Neal and Barbra Streisand centre-frame as a befuddled musicologist and a kooky seductress respectively. The director's aim was to make something in the vein of *Bringing Up Baby* (see Canon); while it falls short of that mark, it offers plenty of innocent laughs.

Lenny
dir Bob Fosse, 1974, US, 111m, b/w

Dustin Hoffman was Oscar nominated for his performance as 1960s stand-up Lenny Bruce, a man who challenged not only American society's attitudes to what could be said on stage, but also its obscenity laws. Hoffman perfectly captures the acerbic comic, and Fosse's film in many ways gets his point across better than the comedian himself often did.

Fun With Dick and Jane
dir Ted Kotcheff, 1976, US, 100m

Aerospace engineer George Segal loses his job and, along with wife Jane Fonda, decides that robbing banks is a better bet. Soon they're loving their life of crime. A comment on American commercialism, and at times very funny, never more so than when Segal – one of cinema's great cursers – is given full reign.

Television joins in

In the 1970s Britain began to look to its own TV staples to supplant the *Carry On* output. So shows like *Rising Damp*, *Steptoe And Son*, *Dad's Army*, *On The Buses*, *Porridge* and *The Likely Lads*, all of them ensemble pieces set in predominantly working-class milieu, became fodder for cinema in the wake of TV success.

Back in America, where the combination of *The Exorcist* (1973), *Jaws* (1975), and *Star Wars* (1977) heralded the age of the blockbuster and forever changed the face of cinema, comedy movies also found themselves looking to television for a response. The advent of *Saturday Night Live* gave rise to a new generation of comic performers who would come to dominate big screen comedy for the next thirty years and beyond. Initially seen as programming for the undervalued countercultural viewer *SNL* aligned itself with the equally influential humour magazine *National Lampoon*, which had begun its life as a campus-friendly

rag at Harvard University. Upon graduation, its contributors quickly turned the magazine into a viable commercial publishing success, which, by 1977, was willing and able to make a leap into the movies; witness *National Lampoon's Animal House* (1978; see Canon), a film that took the mag, the *Second City* improv troupe/*SNL* star **John Belushi**, and the *Second City* writer Harold Ramis to create a winner. American cinema had found a new direction in comedy, and it had no intention of looking back. The R rating (no one under 17 admitted without adult supervision) came to dominate US comedy fare, unleashing a glut of sex, drugs and rock'n'roll – from *Meatballs* (1979) through *Caddyshack* and *The Blues Brothers* (1980) to that bastard Canadian cousin they called *Porkys* (1981).

In the late 1970s, outside the world of the TV-spinoff comedy, things were looking flabby. There were some bright spots: **Dudley Moore** finally emerged from the shadow of Peter Cook by replacing him with **Bo Derek** in Blake Edwards's quirky (and very much of its time) *10* (1979); **Burt Reynolds** assumed dominance at the English-language box office courtesy of a lot of movies about cars, starting off with *Smokey And The Bandit* (1977), while the arthouse was seduced by the drag-themed glory of *La cage aux folles* (1978; later sequelized twice and Americanized once with Mike Nichols's *The Birdcage*, 1996). Hal Ashby, who had seen the decade in with such style in *Harold and Maude*, saw it out with Peter Sellers in the haunting presidential satire *Being There* (1979), based on a short but wonderfully satirical novel by Jerzy Kosinski. None attained the heights of **Monty Python**, however, who reached their zenith with their own typically surreal take on religion, *The Life Of Brian* (1979; see Canon) – another highly successful move from the small screen to the movies.

Screenwriting comedy icon: "quiet man" Harold Ramis

In many ways, screenwriter **Harold Ramis** is the quiet man of modern American cinema comedy. Although in the mid 1970s he had begun to make a name for himself writing and performing alongside the likes of John Belushi, Gilda Radner and Bill Murray on the *National Lampoon* radio show, unlike his contemporaries he was not picked to join the cast of the nascent *Saturday Night Live* TV show. As a result, he headed off to Canada and took up a regular gig on *SNL*'s competitor, *Second City Television* (*SCTV*), alongside the likes of Rick Moranis and the late John Candy. He also opted to devote himself more to writing than performing, becoming one of the most successful screenwriters in modern comedy. His allegiances still held true to his old friends however – he co-authored *Animal House* (with Belushi on board), *Meatballs* (Murray's breakthrough vehicle) and *Caddyshack* (with Murray and Chevy Chase), which he also directed, and co-wrote (and costarred in). Teaming up with Dan Aykroyd, he was soon responsible for the global smash that was *Ghostbusters*

(1984; see Canon), with Murray – once again – stepping in for the departed Belushi. Since then, Ramis has had a remarkable track record, arguably peaking with 1993's *Groundhog Day*, which he wrote and directed, but also finding time to author and direct the likes of the Michael Keaton cloning comedy *Multiplicity* (1996), as well as *Analyse This* (1999) and its sequel *Analyse That* (2002) in which he teamed Billy Crystal with Robert DeNiro's neurotic Mafioso.

While some of his work retains the authenticity of autobiography – see *Animal House* for a re-examination of his own frat years – Ramis remains first and foremost an exponent of blatantly commercial cinema, something that has not always stood him in good stead, as the likes of *Caddyshack II* (1988) and his unwise reworking of Peter Cook's *Bedazzled* (2000) have proved. Nonetheless, his work as a director has proved largely successful and he still occasionally appears on screen as a likeable performer, most notably in the *Ghostbusters* films and James L. Brooks's *As Good As It Gets* (1997).

Meatballs
dir Ivan Reitman, 1979, Can, 94m

Hot on the heels of *Animal House*, Bill Murray made his first significant leap to the big screen in this piecemeal tale of summer camp. It doesn't always play to Murray's strengths, casting him for once not as a misanthrope, but he's always watchable, and Harold Ramis's (co-written) script provides plenty of laughs.

Being There
dir Hal Ashby, 1979, US, 130m

Peter Sellers' penultimate film, and in many ways his finest; he stars as a simpleton gardener named Chance, whose homilies get mistaken for brilliant political insights. The project was a long-held dream for Sellers, and he gets to walk on water at the end – a strange but appropriate ending to his career.

Action and heroes: the 1980s

Wall Street (1987) told us greed was good: everyone else called it the "me" decade. Admittedly, Live Aid attempted to make it the "them" decade, but, with the two most powerful people on earth being Margaret Thatcher and Ronald Reagan that was something of a struggle.

True there was the **Dudley Moore** and **Bo Derek** escapist romance *Arthur* (1981) to keep things light but in the early 1980s even Woody Allen was getting serious, and opened the decade by finding himself attacked by aliens (a metaphor for film critics) in *Stardust Memories* (1980). To be fair to Allen, the more he fell into the trap of his own non-comedic self-obsessions, the more interesting he often became as a filmmaker. *The Purple Rose Of Cairo* (1985) and *Crimes And Misdemeanours* (1989) representing something of a purple patch for the man (no pun intended). Martin Scorsese also took a different turn as a director in the 1980s, producing a brace of frightening comedies: *The King of Comedy* (1982), a film that was undervalued on its initial release, despite giving us De Niro at his complex best and a career-redefining performance from Jerry Lewis (see Icons), and the yuppie-in-peril paranoid nightmare that was *After Hours* (1985).

In the 1980s a pernicious edge of cynicism took hold of the way movies were produced. Sequels – generally a means of guaranteeing bums on seats for a series of either repeated gags and/or diminished returns – became the norm. There were high points – **John Hughes**, for example, who emerged as the most talented comedy film writer of his generation – but for every Hughes triumph like *Sixteen Candles* (1984) or *Ferris Bueller's Day Off* (1986; see

Canon) there was a *Porky's Revenge* (1985) or *Lethal Weapon 2* (1989).

Arthur
dir Steve Gordon, 1981, US, 97m

Dudley Moore was riding the crest of a wave when it came to *Arthur* after the surprise success *10*. Here as Arthur Bach he not only delivered his finest screen performance, but was the best cinematic drunk since W.C. Fields, a millionaire spoiled and in need of the love of a good woman, which he finds in working class Liza Minnelli. Writer/director Gordon died soon after, depriving cinema of someone who could have developed into a serious comic talent.

After Hours
dir Martin Scorsese, 1985, US 97m

Scorsese's darkest comedy, and one of his most engaging movies, as Griffin Dunne goes through a long dark night of the soul in New York, having met a girl, lost his keys and found himself in an escalating night time nightmare, including an ice cream truck-led mob out for his blood.

Sixteen Candles
dir John Hughes, 1984, US, 93m

Teen traumas by the dozen as Molly Ringwald as Samantha Baker hits sixteen. Hughes's intelligent and sympathetic treatment runs the usual gamut of high school crushes, geeky friends, flawed families and embarrassing situations but is much more affectionately remembered than most.

New kids on the comedy block

Richard Pryor teamed up with **Gene Wilder** for *Stir Crazy* (1980), a fairly average comedy fest, but one that did at least give a glimpse of

to be extremely influential and reflective of their time. First up was *48 HRS* (1982), which took the Butch and Sundance approach and helped define the modern buddy movie. It was rapidly followed by *Trading Places* (1982), a film that precedes *Wall Street*'s greed message and supplants it – greed is good, but getting even is even better. Murphy also heralded in another major new trend in comedy – the action adventure element. While humour had always played a strong role in that particular genre – one only has to look at James Bond's wry double entendres to see that – Murphy's *Beverly Hills Cop* (1984) changed the nature of the beast. It was now OK to spend an hour wisecracking followed by a final half hour shooting people in a totally non-comedic way. The comedy movie had officially been co-opted, and this cross-pollination was to dominate the genre for at least another decade.

After Belushi's death, Aykroyd and fellow *SNL* alumnus Bill Murray, plus *Second City* regular/*Animal House* scribe Harold Ramis (see p.41), also upped the ante with *Ghostbusters* (1984), showing that the humble comedy movie could also cross-pollinate with the all-out special effects blockbuster extravaganza. Though Peter Venkman was Murray's breakthrough role, he had already made a name for himself by turning in a delightful supporting role in *Caddyshack* (1980) and *Tootsie* (1982), a film that saw Dustin Hoffman pick up Jack Lemmon and Tony Curtis's man-in-drag gauntlet, thrown down so well with *Some Like It Hot*. The horror genre provided another popular comic crossover courtesy of **Joe Dante**'s *Gremlins* (1984), a movie intent on ripping to pieces Frank Capra's enduring, wholesome view of small-town America. Former Disney animator **Tim Burton** also took laughter to the dark side, consolidating a reputation built

Getting even – Eddie Murphy in *Trading Places* (1982)

a comedy team emerging for the first time in years. Sadly, it was a promise that was never really fulfilled, as was the case with the duo of **Dan Aykroyd** and **John Belushi**. A couple of *Saturday Night Live* alumni, they triumphed in 1980 with *The Blues Brothers*, but their partnership came to a sad end when Belushi overdosed in 1982.

In many ways the key comedy movies of the 1980s were defined by one star in particular – stand-up comedian **Eddie Murphy**. Murphy, young and hot as hell, was another alumnus from the prodigious *SNL* stable. His superstar status lent its weight to a handful of movies that proved

on his short films *Vincent* and *Frankenweenie*, first through his collaboration with comic Pee-Wee Herman (Paul Reubens) in the absurdist *Pee-Wee's Big Adventure* (1985), then by teaming with Michael Keaton for the altogether more ghoulish *Beetle Juice* (1988).

Another actor who made the leap from TV in the 1980s was **Tom Hanks**, who was to go on to become one of American cinema's most popular actors, well-steeped in both comedy and drama, leading many critics to view him as the Jimmy Stewart of his day. He had first emerged on *Bosom Buddies*, a cross-dressing TV sitcom that owed more than a passing nod to *Some Like It Hot*, before making an even bigger splash in the romcom-with-a-mermaid *Splash* (1984).

Proving that American cinema could still deliver beautifully crafted films, driven by intelligent witty scripts, former stand-up comedian (and one time Mel Brooks collaborator) **Barry Levinson** emerged as a filmmaker with *Diner* (1982), a semi-autobiographical tale set in 1950s Baltimore, and went on to make *Good Morning Vietnam* (see Canon) and *Tin Men*, both in 1987. The costar of the latter, **Danny DeVito**, not only proved to be a popular comic stalwart, but would also become one of mainstream American cinema's darkest auteurs with bitter, often uncommercial black comedies such as *Throw Momma From The Train* (1987) and *The War Of The Roses* (1989).

On the independent scene, shockhaired punk director **Jim Jarmusch** turned out three of the coolest dry comedies ever seen on screen – *Stranger Than Paradise* (1984), *Down By Law* (1986) and *Mystery Train* (1989) – setting the stage for a boom in independent movie-making that was to characterize the next decade.

Diner
dir Barry Levinson, 1982, US, 110m

Former comic and occasional Mel Brooks collaborator Levinson made a splash with this, the first of a warmly autobiographical trio (with *Tin Men*, 1987, and *Avalon*, 1990) set in his native Baltimore. Observational and very funny, following a group of male friends as they struggle to come to terms with life, love and growing up.

Gremlins
dir Joe Dante, 1984, US, 111m

A young boy (Zach Galligan) receives a cute furry "mogwai" that, if it gets wet, can become something altogether more nasty. Dante, a long-time Spielberg collaborator, crosses the small-town world of Capra's *It's A Wonderful Life* with 1950s monster movies and a Chuck Jones/Looney Tunes mentality to create one of his most successful films.

Down By Law,
dir, Jim Jarmusch, 1986, US, 107m, b/w

Jarmusch takes the noir beat of Waits' *Rain Dogs* album, adds the loucheness of John Lurie, the comic talents of Roberto Benigni, and throws them altogether in a jail cell. Richly inventive and very blackly comic in unexpected ways.

Tin Men
dir Barry Levinson, 1987, US, 112m

For the second part of his Baltimore trilogy Levinson moves from adolescents to middle-aged men – in this case warring aluminium sidings salesmen Richard Dreyfuss and Danny DeVito – struggling to keep things going. Levinson's best work remains his most personal, and this is no exception.

Beetlejuice
dir Tim Burton, 1988, US, 92m

Burton is easily one of the most imaginative visual directors in Hollywood today. *Beetlejuice*, an early movie, combines his love of extreme humour and the macabre in the form of Michael Keaton's ghoul, who helps a recently deceased couple (Alec Baldwin and Geena Davis) rid their beloved old house of its new (alive) occupants.

🎬 The War of the Roses
dir Danny DeVito, 1989, US, 116m

Having started out as an actor, DeVito emerged as one of Hollywood's best directors of black comedy. This sharp and insightful take on modern-day divorce, with married Michael Douglas and Kathleen Turner (the Roses of the title) battering their relationship into the ground, embraces extremes, both in character and its visual sense.

Parody and beyond

Parody played a dominant part in the comedy cinema of the 1980s, the decade having been ushered in by the Zucker-Abrahams-Zucker powerhouse of *Airplane!* (1980; see Canon). Finding themselves onto something (very) good, the team went on to debunk World War II movies with *Top Secret!* (1984) and the crime genre with *The Naked Gun* series (1988–1994; itself spun off from their short-lived TV series *Police Squad*). Realizing his market was up and running again, **Mel Brooks** got back in the saddle with *History of the World Part I* (1981) – which lambasts the Epic – and *Spaceballs* (1987) – which takes a swipe at *Star Wars*. In 1984 rock'n'roll got turned up all the way to eleven with *This Is Spinal Tap* (see Canon), a movie that more or less invented the mockumentary (although it did owe a debt to Eric Idle's TV-based spoof of The Beatles – *The Rutles* – from some years earlier).

Those 1980s crossover movies also had more than a hint of parody: **Robert Zemeckis**, a protégé of Spielberg, brought humour to the action adventure romp with *Romancing The Stone* (1984), before ramping up the science fiction genre with the *Back To The Future* trilogy (1985–90). Terry Gilliam turned comedy into nightmare with *Brazil* (1985), as well as becoming something of a *cause célèbre* with the wildly over-budget fantasy that was 1998's *The Adventures of Baron Munchausen* (the notion that a film that ran to $46 million could now be considered a disaster of major proportions pales in an age where Jim Carrey commands $25 million per movie).

As the 1980s drew on, a new breed of hard-edged comedies – comedy dramas, or "drama-dies" as they became known – emerged. None achieved this with greater aplomb than James L. Brooks's insightful *Broadcast News* (1987; see Canon), which took a long, hard look at the American media and became one of the most prescient films of its day. Meanwhile, the romcom was given a huge boost when, taking a nod from the New York stylings of Woody Allen, *This is Spinal Tap* director **Rob Reiner** (and writer Nora Ephron) ended the decade not so much on a bang but definitely with cinema's finest faked orgasm, courtesy of Meg Ryan (with a little help from Billy Crystal) in the touching *When Harry Met Sally...* (1989; see Canon).

🎬 History Of The World Part I
dir Mel Brooks, 1981, US, 92m

Having parodied numerous genres, Brooks now decided to take on history – or rather the way Hollywood had traditionally tackled history. Witness delirious digs at Kubrick (with a *2001* pastiche), Cecil B. DeMille (*The Ten Commandments*) and just about every sword and sandals epic ever. Scatological, to say the least.

🎬 Spaceballs
dir Mel Brooks, 1987, US, 96m

Here Brooks parodies *Star Wars* ten years after the original, with a hit-and-miss approach that defines much of his later work. Bill Pullman plays the hero, Rick Moranis takes on Darth Vader (Dark Helmet), The Force is renamed The Schwartz and the late John Candy plays a kind of dog – the best performance in the film.

Leslie Nielsen, master of parody in *The Naked Gun*

The Naked Gun: From The Files of Police Squad

dir David Zucker, 1988, US, 85m

Having comically reinvented the disaster genre with *Airplane!*, and the war movie with *Top Secret*, the Zucker-Abrahams-Zucker team now turned to spoofing police work. Leslie Nielsen is superb as Lt. Frank Drebin, an American Inspector Clouseau, and there are gags-a-plenty, even in the ad campaign – "You've read the ad, now see the movie!"

The international scene

In the 1980s the Finnish director **Aki Kaurismaki** put his home country on the map in terms of global filmmaking with a series of quirky movies, including *Ariel* (1988) and *Leningrad Cowboys Go America* (1989), that delighted in a deadpan approach worthy of his friend Jim Jarmusch. **Paul Hogan**, a former bridge painter and TV comedy star, did the same for Australia (briefly) with his likeable, and hugely successful, *Crocodile Dundee* (1986), while Yahoo Serious, with his lamentable *Young Einstein* (1988), all but undid Hogan's good work.

Jackie Chan brought the Hong Kong action movie to the masses by attempting to break every bone in his body for the delight of his audience, coming to prominence in such high-adrenalin comedies as 1985's *Police Story,* while Swedish filmmaker Lasse Hallstrom offered altogether gentler humour with the bittersweet and quirky *My Life as a Dog* (1985).

Meanwhile, **Pedro Almodóvar's** *What Have I Done To Deserve This* (1984) and *The Law Of Desire* (1987) introduced arthouse audiences to the considerable comic talents of actress Carmen Maura, and let the world know a deliciously subversive filmmaking presence was emerging in Spain. His dark comedies made waves, but it wasn't until *Women On The Verge Of A Nervous Breakdown* (1988) that Almodóvar really made his big international breakthrough. Bill Forsyth also introduced himself, and indeed the Scottish Film Industry (a hitherto unmentionable) with the uplifting football fantasy *Gregory's Girl* (1980) and the deftly made, Capra-esque *Local Hero* (1983; see Canon) before deserting his native Scotland for the US and going on to produce very little worth talking about.

In Britain, *Carry On* finally stopped carrying on. Young English actress Emily Lloyd announced herself loudly ("Up yer bum!") in David Leland's British comedy drama *Wish You Were Here* (1987) before, much like Forsyth, decamping to Hollywood and effectively disappearing. Former Python John Cleese strived to evoke the best of the Ealing comedies in his movie, *A Fish Called Wanda* (1988), which became a major international hit. British film comedy was once more a force to contend with.

Gregory's Girl

dir Bill Forsyth, 1980, UK, 91m

Bill Forsyth all but kickstarted the modern Scottish film industry with this whimsical tale of a teenager (John Gordon

Sinclair) obsessed with a girl football player (Dee Hepburn) but who finds love elsewhere (Clare Grogan). Quirky, and very much rooted in its own culture, it made a star out of Sinclair and remains a delicately comic coming-of-age delight.

Police Story
dir Jackie Chan, 1985, Hong Kong, 99m

Chan has mined a unique path for himself in cinema by blending his singular martial arts skills with a sense of the absurd. This, in which he plays a drug-busting cop who finds himself framed, is a vehicle for his remarkable, almost slapstick, stunt work and the movie that began his ascent in the West.

Crocodile Dundee
dir Peter Faiman, 1986, Aus, 98m

Paul Hogan starred in and co-wrote this fish-out-of-water story about a bush-based Aussie hunter who finds himself in New York. Full of jokes based around his ignorance of Big City ways, written and played with a good degree of charm, it was an unexpected global smash and spawned two (vastly inferior) sequels.

A Fish Called Wanda
dir Charles Crichton, 1988, UK, 108m

Former Python Cleese wanted to make the perfect English comedy and so harked back to Ealing and hired one of their key figures, codirector Crichton. Wise move. He also cast both British actors (himself and former Python Michael Palin) and American ones (Jamie Lee Curtis and Kevin Kline) in his story of a jewel heist gone awry. Cleese's stuffy uptight lawyer falls for Curtis's brash American – named Wanda (as was the beloved pet fish of the tale). A perfect delight, and very true to the spirit of Ealing in many ways.

Women On The Edge Of A Nervous Breakdown (Mujeres al borde de un ataque de nervios)
dir Pedro Almodóvar, 1988, Spain, 89m

Three women reach crisis points – a mistress dumped by her married lover, his new lawyer girlfriend and a friend hiding from the police. Events escalate but Almodóvarian excess is tempered by a certain restraint that feels like the hidden hand of classical farce.

Independents' days: the 90s

Last of the action comedies

As the 1980s closed the *SNL* players were at a low point; established directors such as John Landis had proved they only had so many good movies in them; former wünderkind Eddie Murphy took his turn behind the camera and produced the execrable *Harlem Nights* (1989), and John Hughes opted to become a mogul rather than make movies.

In just about every way the beginning of the 1990s was a confused period for Hollywood in general, with audiences looking more backward than forward, and filmmakers choosing to re-examine major cultural themes and notions. The black tragi-comedy *The Bonfire of the Vanities* (1990) looked back at the soulless eighties, while *Ghost* (1990), an unexpected blockbuster, returned to good old-fashioned romance, along with the hooker's fairy tale, *Pretty Woman* (1990), that made a star of **Julia Roberts**. Billy Crystal regressed to school – dude school – in *City Slickers* (1991) while Robert Altman (demonstrating a rare return to form) hit Hollywood back for all they had or hadn't done for him in his *The Player* in 1992 – which, much like Maurizio Nichetti's Italian curio *The Icicle Thief* (1989), referenced Vittorio De Sica's neorealistic classic *The Bicycle Thieves*.

SNL alumnus **Mike Myers** hit the big time by – firstly in 1992 with *Wayne's World* (the first direct *SNL* spin off since *The Blues Brothers*) and later with the even more successful *Austin Powers* cycle (1997–2002; see Canon). Meanwhile, the biggest child star since Shirley Temple emerged in the form of **Macaulay Culkin** courtesy of the *Home Alone* series, scripted by John Hughes – a definite sign that his talent had waned – between 1992 and 1997.

In many ways, however, conventional Hollywood had become as bloated as its established stars. For the first half of the 1990s Eddie Murphy would continue to star in a string of lame comedies (*Boomerang*, 1992; *Beverly Hills Cop III*, 1994) while 1993's **Arnold Schwarzenegger** vehicle *The Last Action Hero*, a film that followed firmly in the wake of Murphy's *Beverly Hills Cop*, promptly died a death commercially and critically. Audiences were hungry for something new.

Pretty Woman
dir Gary Marshall, 1990, US, 119m

Backed by Disney, this modern take on the Cinderella story – Julia Roberts's hooker is hired by rich businessman Richard Gere for a few days – is the quintessential 1990s romcom. Gere is the model of restraint, whilst Roberts simply let the world see what a superstar she would eventually be.

City Slickers
dir Ron Underwood, 1991, US, 112m

Billy Crystal starred in this reinvention of the comedy western with this story of three suburban guys (Crystal, Daniel Stern and Bruno Kirby) who hit the proverbial mid-life/mid-city crisis and thus sign up for a spell on a dude's ranch.

Crystal also had the good sense to secure the presence of self-parodying iconic western figure Jack Palance as their instructor who subsequently won an Oscar.

The Player
dir Robert Altman, 1992, US, 124m

Altman's film industry satire sees Tim Robbins excel as a studio executive who kills a struggling screenwriter. The toast of Hollywood (among them Julia Roberts and Bruce Willis) cameo in a movie that takes great delight in biting the hand that feeds it.

The indie scene

As the decade progressed, a shift occurred in American cinema that was to have a huge global impact. While many other countries had viewed their movies as one-off productions, historically the US had used the studio system as a conveyor belt for popular culture. Now, more than at any time in its history, Hollywood began to feel the impact of independent filmmaking. Spurred on by the Cannes-award winning success of Steven Soderbergh's *Sex, lies and videotape* (1989), US cinema was soon to fall under the spell of the "indie", giving rise to a new generation of filmmaker and giving an older generation of comedy performer reason to reassess what they were doing and who they were choosing to work with.

In 1994, Kevin Smith made the micro-budget comic classic *Clerks*. Small it may have been, but its impact was huge, helping to identify the American independent movie as the most important film art form of its day. Smith would also prove himself a writer and director of note, producing a body of work in the years that followed *Clerks* exploring similar themes and using recurring characters (Jay and Bob) and actors

Indie duo Jay (Jason Mewes) and Silent Bob
(Kevin Smith) in *Chasing Amy*

(Ben Affleck, Jason Lee) in movies like *Chasing
Amy* (1996), *Dogma* (1999) and *Jay And Silent
Bob* (them again!) *Strike Back* (2001). Smith was
by no means the only American independent
leading the charge – the Coen brothers (Joel
directing, Ethan producing, both of them writing) had started to carve out a unique niche for
themselves back in the 1980s, financing their
first film, the smart *noir Blood Simple* (1983),
on the credit cards of friends and family. Over
the years they quickly displayed a strong feeling
for comedy – with the likes of *Raising Arizona*
(1987; see Canon), the darkly absurd Cannes-
winner *Barton Fink* (1991), *Hudsucker Proxy*
(1994), *Fargo* (1995) and *The Big Lebowski* (1998)
– and were later to become one of the most
influential teams in Hollywood. By the mid-
1990s the independent movement in American
cinema was being co-opted by the studios, who
saw there was money in it and wanted a piece.
In 1993 Disney became sleeping partners with
Miramax, and indie movies were looking to the
likes of Fox Searchlight (as owned by Rupert
Murdoch's Twentieth Century Fox) for their
financing. Another movement was proving perhaps to be too successful for its own good.

Clerks
dir Kevin Smith, 1994, US, 90m

Essentially a day-in-the-life story about a handful of workers
hanging out in a New Jersey convenience store, filmed in
a matter of days with a handful of semi-professional actors
(Smith included, playing Silent Bob, one half of the soon-
to-achieve-cult-status team of Jay and Silent Bob) hanging
out – in a convenience store.

The Hudsucker Proxy
dir Joel Coen, 1994, US, 111m

The Coen brothers began writing this comic fable with
fellow indie favourite Sam Raimi, right back at the start
of their careers. It tells the tale of Norville Barnes (Tim
Robbins) a small town inventor who comes to the big city
to wow Hudsucker Industries (headed up by a superb Paul
Newman) and ends up inventing the hula hoop – "You
know, for kids," as he explains. It's really their take on
the screwball comedy of Howard Hawks, plus plenty of
corporate satire.

Chasing Amy
dir Kevin Smith, 1996, US, 111m

Having laid out his pop cultural obsessions with *Clerks* (and
taken a slight miss-step with *Mallrats*), writer/director Smith
returned on top form with a look at the nature of relationships.
Though he still made his two male leads (Ben Affleck and
Jason Lee) comic book writers and artists (and threw in
several *Star Wars*-based conversations), he also added
Joey Lauren Adams – as a lesbian love interest – by far the
smartest character, with the best dialogue. Smith himself also
returns as his on-screen alter-ego Silent Bob, and delivers the
film's most cogent argument on the nature of love.

The Big Lebowski
dir Joel Coen, 1998, US/UK, 127m

The wonderful Jeff Bridges plays Lebowski, a hapless
dopehead who gets caught up in a kidnapping case in this
typically brilliant, typically twisted Coen fantasy. As ever,
the casting is top-notch (John Goodman, Steve Buscemi,
John Turturro and Julianne Moore co-star), the art direction
exquisite, and the soundtrack is just cool as hell.

New comedy world order

With the increased profile of American independent cinema came an audience demand for a wider variety of movies from around the world. Previously, who would have thought that one of the decade's most delightful comedies would come from Taiwan? But it certainly did, courtesy of Ang Lee's *The Wedding Banquet* (1993), a movie that also announced the arrival of a major modern filmmaking force in its soft-spoken director Lee, who within a handful of years would be tackling everything from **Jane Austen** (*Pride And Prejudice*; 1995) to Marvel comics (*The Hulk*; 2003).

The Antipodeans got a look in with the international success of *Strictly Ballroom* (1992; see Canon), a movie that displayed both a prodigious talent in the shape of its director Baz Luhrmann and a prodigious line in camp humour. **Stephan Elliott**'s drag queen comedy/road movie The *Adventures of Priscilla, Queen of Desert* (1994) took up the gauntlet, and captured a worldwide viewing public. The world was also won over in 1995 by the sweetly funny live-action story of a small talking pig named *Babe*, produced in Australia from the unlikely source of *Mad Max* trailblazer George Miller. Over in New Zealand **Peter Jackson** (later a multi-Oscar winner for *The Lord of the Rings* trilogy) was focusing less on cute farmyard animals and more on flesh-eating zombies with the deliriously excessive – both in terms of its

The Curtis effect and new British comedy

It's very seldom that one studio, let alone one writer, can be said to dominate a nation's comedic output. Even Mack Sennett had Hal Roach for competition. But since the early 1990s, British cinema has bowed down to the might of Working Title pictures. Not only have the producing team of Eric Fellner and Tim Bevan proved themselves to have an almost faultless knack for making comic films with worldwide appeal, they've used their deserved clout to further the careers of such cult filmmakers as the Coen brothers, taking them to Oscar-winning success with the blackly comic *Fargo*, among others, and even shown they can turn their dab hand to drama with the harrowing likes of Tim Robbins's *Dead Man Walking* (1995).

And if one man can be said to have helped them along the way, then that would be **Richard Curtis**, who found success as a writer working alongside his old friend Rowan Atkinson initially in the performer's live shows and later on TV as a contributor to the satirical *Not The Nine O'Clock News* and the world-wide smash *Mr Bean* (1997). With Atkinson in tow, Curtis made the leap into movies with scripting *The Tall Guy* (1989), before finding himself another talismanic performer in the shape of **Hugh Grant**. The result was 1994's *Four Weddings and a Funeral*, a global smash that established what quickly became seen as the "Curtis style": a romantic comedy confection that pits earnest Britishness against American assertiveness, and throws a fair few comedy cuss words into the mix for good measure. These are star-studded affairs: American superstar Julia Roberts joined Grant for *Notting Hill* (1999) while a raft of big British names including Liam Neeson, Alan Rickman, Bill Nighy and Emma Thompson showed up for *Love, Actually* (2002), Curtis's directorial debut.

Curtis also found time to take over the writing chores on two movies derived from his ex-girlfriend Helen Fielding's extremely popular *Bridget Jones* books – once again for Working Title – while on his off days he founded the British branch of Comic Relief and set out to save the world. All in a day's work.

comedy and the amount of on-screen carnage – *Braindead* (1992).

In France, **Gerard Départdieu** took a leaf from Steve Martin's book and starred in the second-best ever cinematic adaptation of *Cyrano De Bergerac* (1990; Martin's *Roxanne*, 1987, still had the edge) – and the same year played romantic lead in the English-language smash *Green Card* (1990), directed by **Peter Weir** – while director Jean-Pierre Jeunet was forging a very distinctly whimsical view of his native Paris in *Delicatessen* (1990). Fellow Frenchman **Patrice Leconte**, who had positioned himself as a world-class filmmaker with such bittersweet movies as *Monsieur Hire* (1989) and *The Hairdresser's Husband* (1990),

now embraced farce with the crazed road movie, *Tango* (1993).

If Europe had a major breakthrough comedy star of the 1990s, it was undoubtedly the Italian **Roberto Benigni**, who made a name for himself, certainly with his home country's audience, by spoofing the Cosa Nostra courtesy of *Johnny Stecchino* (1991). Blake Edwards quickly co-opted him as a substitute Sellers in *The Son of the Pink Panther* (1993), a movie that did no one any good. Benigni's best work remains firmly based in his own country and language. His greatest success to date involved him taking his comedy into the concentration camps of World War II (something Jerry Lewis had failed to pull off years before

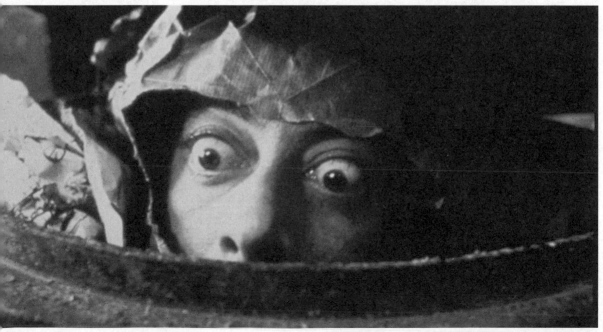

The surreal comic world of Jeunet and Caro's *Delicatessen* (1990)

with the largely unseen *The Day The Clown Cried*, 1972). *Life is Beautiful* (1997) saw Benigni win an Oscar – and climb over the chairs of many an American celebrity to pick it up.

Back in Britain, independence in cinema was becoming a matter of course. British filmmakers went to anyone and everyone to help get their films made: the witty comedy *Leon The Pig Farmer* (1992) being one of the most prominent early examples. Here was a movie with a noted cast, including **Bernard Bresslaw**, Janet Suzman, Brian Glover and Connie Booth, who mostly worked on the notion of deferred payment. The mid-1990s also saw **Jerry Lewis** appear as a has-been comedian and **Lee Evans** as an anarchic raw talent in the dark and dangerous *Funny Bones*, but ultimately British cinema comedy in the 1990s was dwarfed by two movies. In 1994, TV writer **Richard Curtis**, a university chum/collaborator of Rowan Atkinson's, moved from television onto the big screen and gave the world *Four Weddings And A Funeral* (1993; see Canon). While *Four Weddings…* very quickly seems to have become a British time capsule, it did serve three major functions at the time – firstly, it eclipsed Cleese's *Wanda* to become the most commercially successful British comedy ever; secondly, it made British cinema feel modern (despite the traditional range of posh characters, it was the first movie to open with the words 'Fuck, fuck, fuckity fuck!", surely a sign of the times), and thirdly it gave the world Hugh Grant. Previously the lost man of British drawing room drama, Grant was now revealed to be the finest screen comic this country had produced since his semi-namesake Cary.

This being Britain, it couldn't be too long before someone would come along and add a degree of social realism to the belly laughs – a few years later, screenwriter Simon Beaufoy did just that, and eclipsed *Four Weddings* at the box office with the male stripper delight that was *The Full Monty* (1997).

Delicatessen
dir Jean-Pierre Jeunet, Marc Caro, 1990, France, 90m

A local butcher takes in a clown as lodger with the firm intention of passing him on to his customers for dinner. Hugely inventive, visually and narratively, the film creates its own amusing, surreal and cannibalistic world with great panache.

Braindead
dir Peter Jackson, 1992, NZ, 104m

Twisted slapstick from *Lord of the Rings*'s Peter Jackson, featuring among other dark delights a mother-in-law from hell, bitten by a poisonous monkey and out for human flesh, along with a lawnmower-wielding, gore-splattered finale that's almost unwatchably sick.

The Adventures Of Priscilla, Queen Of The Desert
dir Stephan Elliott, 1994, Aus/UK, 102m

Elliott helped keep the Australian comedy movie industry alive with this road trip story of one transsexual (Terrence Stamp) and two drag queens (Hugo Weaving and Guy Pearce) that head off to a performance in Alice Springs aboard their tour bus named Priscilla. Along the way they break down, encounter hostility from some of the small town locals, but change a fair few attitudes along the way. Warm, winning and as camp as you can get.

The Full Monty
dir Peter Cattaneo, 1997, UK, 91m

Writer Simon Beaufoy claims this was never a comedy, being a film about destroyed industries, communities and mass unemployment. Yet there is great joy in the fact that Robert Carlyle, Tom Wilkinson and their colleagues choose to confront their strife by taking off their clothes. These most Northern of men – one on the brink of suicide – opt to take their fate into their own hands and become a band of male strippers. One of the most successful British comedies ever – and deservedly so.

Life Is Beautiful (La vita è bella)
dir Roberto Benigni, 1997, Italy, 116m

Fittingly, Roberto Benigni's divisive tragicomedy is very much a film of two halves. His courting of Tuscan teacher Nicoletta Braschi is charming. But the tone darkens, as Benigni and five-year-old son, Giorgio Cantarini, are transported to a Nazi concentration camp. Some considered Benigni's attempts to turn the experience into a game to prevent the boy from realizing the enormity of his predicament an insult to the Holocaust's countless victims. The Oscar electorate, however, viewed it as an uplifting tale of courage *in extremis* and gave Benigni the Best Actor award.

East is East
dir Damien O'Donnell, 1999, UK, 96m

The always excellent Om Puri leads the cast – and indeed the household – in this look at an Asian family living in 1971 Britain. Despite running a fish and chip shop, he increasingly wants offspring to respect their Asian background, but with an English wife, culture clash is inevitable. Often very funny, and sometimes very moving, this was one of the first movies to explore the Asian experience in the UK that crossed over to mass success.

Dumb animals

In the early 1990s, American animation was not so much having a resurgence as a total reinvention. Disney – now minus Walt and having languished in the wilderness of mediocrity for many years – finally found its saviours in the form of composer Alan Menken and lyricist Harold Ashman who gave the company *The Little Mermaid* (1989), *Beauty and the Beast* (1991) and *Aladdin* (1992). In the latter, **Robin Williams**, as the voice of the genie, put in a bravura performance that revolutionized the way in which animated movies were voiced; from now on cartoons were sold partly on the strength of star names. Thus **Woody Allen**, Dan

Aykroyd and Anne Bancroft would turn up as *Antz* in 1998, while *Shrek* (2001) "starred" **Mike Myers**, Eddie Murphy and Cameron Diaz. As the decade progressed and the technology changed, so did the animation it produced. *Toy Story* (1995; see Canon) combined great storytelling, cinematic invention and perfect vocal casting (**Tom Hanks**, Tim Allen and TV's John Ratzenberger, among others) to make computer-generated animation the new state of the art. The company it built, Pixar, became the first real challenger to Disney's crown in the entire history of cinema.

Suddenly the 1990s were looking like a cool place to be... and then, in the mid-1990s, along came the Farrelly brothers. There are two schools of thought on the Farrellys – either they "dumbed down" American cinema (a much over-used phrase which was essentially co-opted from the fact they made a movie called *Dumb and Dumber* in 1994), or they just threw back in some non-politically correct elements (witness *There's Something About Mary*, 1998; see Canon) that had run riot in the most outrageous screen comedies dating all the way back to the Marx Brothers.

Not directly in response to the Farrellys – though they certainly helped – political correctness reared its head in the last few years of the decade, as demonstrated when the National Federation of the Blind asked Disney pictures not to make a big-screen version of the nearsighted cartoon curmudgeon, *Mr. Magoo* (1997), claiming that it simply wasn't amusing to watch "an ill-tempered and incompetent blind man stumble into things and misunderstand his surroundings." They were right of course: there wasn't anything even remotely funny about the movie, despite the presence of the supremely talented Leslie Nielsen.

Aladdin
dir Ron Clements, John Musker, 1992, US, 90m

A peak of Disney's animated revival with Robin Williams cast as the genie and given free reign. Williams enjoys one of his funniest roles, mixing pop culture references into the classic Arabian Nights tale of the boy thief who falls in love with a princess.

Shrek
dir, Andrew Adamson, Vicky Jenson, 2001, US, 90m

A swamp-dwelling ogre (Mike Myers) is forced into becoming a hero. Full of visual and verbal puns – from *West Side Story* to Leonard Cohen – and heaps of inverted fairy tale references, the show is stolen by Eddie Murphy's voice work as the donkey.

The stars

Despite feeling the encroachment of its independent offshoots, Hollywood in the mid-to-late 1990s was managing to produce some of its finest comedy work in years. These were good times for comedy movie stars. **Bill Murray** hit a peak with *Groundhog Day*, and Tom Hanks, with some help from director **Robert Zemeckis**, managed to turn what was ostensibly the story of an idiot into one of the most satirical looks at America since *Dr. Strangelove* with the Academy Award-winning *Forest Gump* (1994). Eddie Murphy remembered how to be funny again, taking on multiple roles in *The Nutty Professor* (1996) in a *tour de force* that left Jerry Lewis jealous, while Canadian Jim Carrey broke all the rules – not only of performance (talking out of his backside in 1993's *Ace Ventura: Pet Detective*, for example) but also of the Hollywood business. He was the first actor to command and receive twenty million dollars a movie – for *The Cable Guy* (1996) – thus radically inflating the

average budget of any star vehicle. (It's worth noting that while Carrey asked for and got his twenty million, when John Travolta attempted to lampoon the very idea just a year or so later by demanding twenty million and one dollars, it is generally agreed by Hollywood-watchers that this action may well have cost him his Best Actor Oscar for *Pulp Fiction*! Don't these people get irony?) Carrey went on to broaden his range with **Peter Weir**'s brilliantly satirical and insightful *The Truman Show* (1998).

Other big names in this period include **Jackie Chan**, who crossed over to the US blockbuster market with the hugely successful *Rush Hour* (1998) – in which his physical prowess plays second fiddle to his considerable comic skills, pitted perfectly against those of African-American comedian **Chris Tucker** – and yet another *SNL* alumnus, **Adam Sandler** (see Icons). The latter's mixture of adolescent humour (rooted somewhere in the 1980s) and very real anger-management issues (rooted very much in the now) combined perfectly in movies such as the sports comedy *Happy Gilmore* (1996). Sandler was also canny enough to let audiences see his sweet side, finding his biggest hits in the soppier – but still rewarding – *The Wedding Singer* (1998), which is the only movie on record that treats you to the sight of **Steve Buscemi** singing Spandau Ballet, and *Big Daddy* (1999). Fellow *SNL* alumnus Eddie Murphy had put the guns away and was working the family ticket with a remake of *Doctor Dolittle* (1998), learning, it seems, from his contemporary **Steve Martin**, who had also been playing family man since 1989's *Parenthood* and 1991's *Father Of The Bride* (another remake) to the altogether more interesting *A Simple Twist Of Fate* (1994), based on George Eliot's novel *Silas Marner*. Who would have thought that the comedy stars once deemed to be "not ready for prime time" would become the moral guardians of family-oriented movies? **John Belushi** would surely be spinning in his grave. (Or possibly trying to snort it.)

🎬 Forrest Gump
dir Robert Zemeckis, 1994, US, 142m

With its homespun homilies and simple-minded hero (Tom Hanks), this gentle satire takes its cue from Woody Allen's *Zelig* to follow Forrest as he pops up in a number

of seminal historic moments in late twentieth-century America. Schmaltzy in the extreme, it swept the boards at the Oscars.

🎬 Rush Hour
dir Brett Ratner, 1998, US, 98m

Action-adventure comedy that teams Jackie Chan with Chris Tucker as a straight-laced Hong Kong detective and a rebellious LAPD cop respectively. The set-up is as old

Jack Nicholson turns to comedy and a dog (*As Good As It Gets*, 1997)

as the hills, but the charisma of the two leads and their undeniable chemistry made this a huge hit, spawning an equally successful Hong-Kong-set sequel.

As Good As it Gets
dir James L Brooks, 1997, US, 139m

As with all of Brooks' material he deals above all with characters, and with Jack Nicholson cast here as an obsessive-compulsive writer named Melvin, he has a doozie. When Melvin finds his gay neighbour – recently injured – has a dog that needs looking after, his love for the pooch leads to a genuine and unexpected friendship. But it's the Oscar-winning performance of Helen Hunt as a waitress they both befriend that sets the tone for the movie. Brooks is often accused of sentimentality, but, truth be told, his writing holds true to the people who populate his films.

The Truman Show
dir Peter Weir. 1998, US, 102m

Jim Carrey plays Truman, unknowingly adopted as a baby with the sole view of having his entire life filmed as the ultimate reality television show. The insights are sharp, Carrey downplays himself and Weir's direction reaches a career high with a remarkably poignant end.

Big Daddy
dir Dennis Dugan, 1999, US, 93m

Adam Sandler is Sonny, a slacker who, in an attempt to prove to his nagging girlfriend that he can be adult, adopts a troubled boy and vows to bring him up – on his own terms. Not one of Sandler's best movies, but one of the first in which he reveals a softer, more complex side.

The Noughties

A sideways view: comedy gets quirky

In comedy terms, the new millennium was dominated by one movie: *Bridget Jones's Diary* (2001), based on the hit novel by Helen Fielding, co-scripted by Richard Curtis, and with a great performance from **Renée Zellweger** as the lovable klutz of the title. The same year, Jean-Pierre Jeunet and **Audrey Tautou** brought the world a more offbeat but equally popular kooky French comedy heroine with *Amélie* (2001; see Canon). Curtis turned his hand to directing with *Love Actually* in 2003, another romantic US/UK ensemble piece, but as a whole the British film industry began to cast its eye beyond the romcom into other areas – from British–Asian society (*East is East*, 1999) to women's football (*Bend It Like Beckham*, 2002), and even to zombies (*Shaun Of The Dead*, 2004; see Canon).

A more reflective body of work was also being seen in the USA, where the devastating aftermath of 9/11 had as much of an impact on comedy movies as it did on everything else. Enter the popular documentary, which packs a serious punch by using a generous handful of irony and satire. The key proponent, of course, is Michael Moore, who became a spokesman for all things liberal by tackling American gun law in *Bowling For Columbine* (2002), and the entire structure of American politics in *Fahrenheit 9/11* (2004).

Family values for the 21st century – Wes Anderson's *The Royal Tenenbaums* (2001)

9/11 also made its mark on the career of actor/director **Ben Stiller**, who had come through as a major comedy player in the late 1990s, and found himself in the awkward situation of having his male fashion model opus *Zoolander* (2001) debut shortly after the event. To say the movie underperformed at the box office is an understatement, yet it was a deliciously-pitched stab at the modern obsession with celebrity, and a movie that in the years subsequent to its release is now being hailed

as "the new *Spinal Tap*." More than anything it also solidified Stiller's on-again, off-again, on-screen partnership with the broken-nosed **Owen Wilson**, a gangly Texan with a decidedly particular approach to comedy acting which has won him a broad range of admirers in recent years. The two of them have starred in other movies such as *Meet The Parents* (2000) and *Starsky And Hutch* (2004), and are as close to a comedy team as American cinema has produced in quite a while. They are joined – often in the same films – by **Will Ferrell**, *SNL's* more recent graduate who, despite successes like the Christmas-themed *Elf* (2003) and the should-have-been-funnier *Anchorman* (2004), has achieved star status without yet proving his comedy chops on the big screen (even standing in for Woody Allen in Allen's *Melinda & Melinda* in 2005 didn't really get him there).

Owen Wilson helped give rise (by both acting and co-writing with him) to **Wes Anderson**, probably the most exciting American comedy director since John Hughes. The likes of *Rushmore* (1998) and *The Royal Tenenbaums* (2001) remain two of the most potent, individual and beautifully realized slices of cinema in many a year, and can also take a bow for bringing Bill Murray back centre-stage. (Along with Sofia Coppola, whose delicately wry *Lost in Translation* [2003] earned Murray his first, well-deserved, Oscar nomination.)

Quirky, indie-flavoured movies such as these – arthouse/mainstream comedy crossovers – have characterized the 2000s, with sometimes surprising results. Adam Sandler pushed at the boundaries of comedy by playing the angry guy for real in a performance both disturbing and brilliant in the bittersweet *Punch-Drunk Love* (2002), before returning to mainstream form in *50 First Dates* (2004), with his *Wedding Singer* co-star Barrymore, and *Spanglish*, directed by James L. Brooks, also 2004. **Jim Carrey**, too, showed himself again to be an actor of great subtlety in the tragi-comic *Eternal Sunshine Of The Spotless Mind* (2004) scripted by **Charlie Kaufman**, who had also brought us the mind-bogglingly surreal *Being John Malkovich* in 1999. Arthouse director **Richard Linklater**, previously known for producing hip little movies like *Slacker* (1991), *Dazed And Confused* (1993) and *Before Sunrise* (1995), took a different and

wonderful direction with *The School Of Rock* (2003), a big-hearted romp through mid-life crises, pre-adolescent angst, and the redeeming power of 'Raaahk'. **Alexander Payne** gave us a couple of fine masculinity-in-crisis comedies with *About Schmidt* (2002), in which Jack Nicholson plays old and tired better than anyone, and the surprise smash *Sideways* (2004), a beautifully observed buddy movie set in the vineyards of southern California. The latter started the superb **Paul Giametti**, whose doleful presence was as spot-on here as it was in the previous year's *American Splendor*, a biopic about yet another anti-hero, the neurotic comic strip author Harvey Pekar.

Post-9/11, post-Iraq, post the re-election of George Bush, it was time for a new kind of hero. Enter **Trey Parker** and **Matt Stone**, the boys behind TV's *South Park*, who gave us Thunderbirds puppets and action adventure, political satire and out-to-shock humour in the outrageous *Team America: World Police* (2004). The musical story of a crack team who aim to fight the War Against Terror by disrupting a peace conference (and by blowing up the Eiffel Tower, the Sphinx, and the Panama Canal along the way), the subversive humour isn't limited to the Republican administration: American Democrats, including **Susan Sarandon**, Tim Robbins and Michael Moore, aren't safe, and even **Hans Blix** comes in for a ribbing. This is a politically daring movie made hilarious with (very) simple humour – and that's smart. Even if in the other highlight of the year, Ben Stiller's *Dodgeball* (2004; see Canon), all it took was a bunch of guys to throw big balls at each other for the world to roar with laughter. In comedy the basics don't change a great deal.

Meet The Parents
dir Jay Roach, 2000, US, 108m

The awkwardness of meeting potential in-laws is mined to full comic potential as male nurse Ben Stiller is taken to meet his fiancée's family. The mum (Blythe Danner) is fine, but the dad (Robert DeNiro) used to be in the CIA and doesn't trust anyone. Cat-hurting and dead mother's ashes-related farce ensues. De Niro finally had found his on-screen comedic feet following the previous year's *Analyse This*. (Although he was completely upstaged in this film's sequel, 2004's *Meet The Fockers*, by Dustin Hoffman.)

The Royal Tenenbaums
dir Wes Anderson, 2001, US, 110m

Anderson deals with dysfunctional people who form the most unlikely of families, never more so than here when he creates an almost mythical version of New York (note the white cabs instead of yellow) and tells a tale (inspired by Orson Welles' *Magnificent Ambersons*) of a family headed by Gene Hackman and Angelica Huston, and populated by child protégés, who really don't know how to function. Beautifully touching at times, extremely funny at others and perfectly sincere.

Bridget Jones's Diary
dir Sharon Maguire, 2001, US/Fr/UK, 97m

The smash-hit movie based on Helen Fielding's smash-hit novel, with Renée Zellweger demonstrating her fine comic abilities as the chubby heroine who wins the guy despite her big knickers and endless gaffes. Hugh Grant is a revelation as the charming cad, while Colin Firth puts in a likeable self-parody as stuffy Mr Darcy.

Zoolander
dir Ben Stiller, 2001, US, 89m

Stiller has quietly emerged over the last few years as one of American comedy's stealth bombers, a multi-tasker who really knows what he's doing. Witness this, his take on the self-satisfied fashion industry in which he plays the supreme male model, his intense vanity upset and thrown off-kilter by Owen Wilson's new pretender to the throne. Stiller satirizes the fashionistas to the hilt as the incredibly dumb – but always entertaining – Derek Zoolander.

About Schmidt
dir Alexander Payne, 2002, US, 125m

Cranky widower Warren Schmidt (a superb Jack Nicholson) takes to the road in a race to stop his daughter marrying a man he believes to be an idiot. Though he meets his match in his future sister-in-law (Kathy Bates, also superb), much of the delight in this movie is how unredeemable – and unredeemed – Schmidt remains.

Punch-Drunk Love
dir Paul Thomas Anderson, 2002, US, 91m

Almost unclassifiable in the way it bends genres, and totally wonderful to boot, with Adam Sandler giving a virtuoso, tense as hell, performance as a lonely man who finds a girl (Emily Mortimer), a harmonium (inexplicably abandoned one morning in LA), and an offer on desserts that results in thousands of free air miles.

Love Actually
dir Richard Curtis, 2003, UK, 135m

A multi-character piece, looking at the nature of love through a cross section of British society – from the Prime Minister and his tea girl, to a randy young man, to a frustrated author, to a recent widower and beyond. Using an all star cast – Emma Thompson, Liam Neeson, Laura Linney, his favourite on-screen muse Hugh Grant (as the PM) and the marvellous Bill Nighy (as an ageing pop star) – Curtis cleverly and subtly makes his point, that not only is love all around, but it also comes in many forms.

School Of Rock
dir Richard Linklater, 2003, Ger/US, 109m

Jack Black, no-hoper teacher and would-be rock star, puts together an unlikely band with a class of geeky fifth grade kids. They subvert the school system, enter a Battle of the Bands, and learn what's really important in the meantime. Hilarious, touching, and impossible not to like.

Eternal Sunshine Of The Spotless Mind
dir Michael Gondry, 2004, US, 108m

Shy, repressed Joel (Jim Carrey) finds his life changed inexorably after meeting blue-haired free spirit Clementine (Kate Winslet). The plot veers wildly – as do the visuals – but the whole thing is anchored by superb performances all round and a unique comic sensibility provided by screenwriter Charlie Kaufman.

Sideways
dir Alexander Payne, 2004, US, 123m

Director Payne takes to the wine country of northern California, with Paul Giamatti (Miles: uptight alcoholic) and Thomas Haden Church (Jack: irresponsible loose cannon), an odd couple who set off on a stag weekend there. Meltdown, mirth and mid-life crisis ensue.

Team America: World Police
dir Trey Parker, 2004, USA, 98m

Parker and Stone enjoy themselves with this "supercrappymation" (Stone's words), taking a pop at everyone and everything in an outrageous satire on world events. Swearing, violence and offensive songs (not least "Everyone Has AIDS"), along with the screen's first explicit puppet sex scene – Captain Scarlett must be turning in his box.

The Comedy Canon: 50 seriously funny films

A screwball for all seasons: Cary Grant and
Rosalind Russell in *His Girl Friday* (1939)

The Canon:
50 seriously funny films

Airplane!

dir **Jim Abrahams, David Zucker & Jerry Zucker, 1980, US, 87m**
cast **Robert Hays, Julie Hagerty, Lloyd Bridges, Leslie Nielsen, Robert Stack** *cin* **Joseph Biroc** *m* **Elmer Bernstein**

If movies were rated on a scale of gags-per-minute, **Airplane!** – from the team of Zucker-Abrahams-Zucker, affectionately known as ZAZ – would be way up there. Taking their inspiration from the 1957 melodrama *Zero Hour*, the **Zucker brothers** teamed up with the non-familial interloper **Jim Abrahams** to bring their penchant for parody to the 1970s *Airport* disaster movie series (which began with *Airport* itself, rapidly followed by fly-by-night sequels *Airport 75*, *Airport 77* and *Airport 79: The Concorde*).

The disaster movie premise was all they needed: *Airplane!* retains the sketchiest of stories whilst also managing to lay out a blueprint for all the genre parody movies that were to follow. Simply put, boy (flight-phobic ex-pilot **Robert Hays**) meets girl (air stewardess **Julie Haggerty**), loses girl (cue parodies from *From Here To Eternity* to *Saturday Night Fever*), then gets on a flight and has to save their relationship *and* everyone on board. But forget the token gesture of a plot — what matters here is the style (relentless) and the gags (punishingly relentless). Quite simply, *Airplane!* remains one of the funniest movies there is. For pure quotability, it rapidly became a standard-bearer. Classic exchanges include the immortal

No disaster - *Airplane!*, parody blueprint

"Surely you can't be serious?"

"I am serious … and don't call me Shirley."

But more importantly *Airplane!* defined two trends that would inform a great deal of cinematic comedy that followed – including ZAZ's own *Naked Gun* series and numerous others, from **National Lampoon**'s *Loaded Weapon Part I* (1993) to the **Wayans brothers'** 1990s *Scary Movie* cycle. For one thing, it revitalized genre parody, leaving **Mel Brooks** crying in its wake. But it also revived the career of a number of TV and character actors, who had been stymied by the roles that prime time US TV had heaped upon them over the years. Thus it was that **Robert Stack** (Elliot Ness of TV's *The Untouchables*) will now forever be known as the man who takes off one pair of sunglasses to reveal another pair underneath; **Lloyd Bridges** (former skipper of TV's *Sea Hunt*) found out exactly what happens when the shit hits the fan; *Mission Impossible*'s **Peter Graves** may never again choose to accept a mission without thinking of gladiator movies; and silver-haired stalwart **Leslie Nielsen** all but reinvented himself, discovering a heretofore unseen wealth of comic ability.

The ZAZ team were a product of the video generation. Making use of primitive VCR equipment, they began their career by shooting, editing and screening a series of comic sketches, which were played to enthusiastic audiences as part of their **Kentucky Fried Theatre Company** in the early 1970s. Soon these filmed interludes became the focus of the act and a move from their native Wisconsin to Los Angeles brought them to the attention of fledgling director John Landis (*National Lampoon's Animal House* (1978), *The Blues Brothers* (1980)), who remade the best of their material into the low-budget hit *Kentucky Fried Movie* (1977). Buoyed by this success, ZAZ wangled total creative control and a $3 million budget for *Airplane!*, which went on to gross over $80 million at the domestic box office. They would strive to ape their original success, as would others (the non-ZAZ *Airplane 2* (1982) is one to be avoided, **William Shatner**'s wig aside), but *Airplane!* remains both the epitome of the comedy parody movie and its finest example.

Mankiewicz's script and Bette Davis steal the show

All About Eve

dir **Joseph L. Mankiewicz, 1950, US, 138m, b/w**
cast **Bette Davis, Anne Baxter, George Sanders, Celeste Holm** *cin* **Milton Krasner** *m* **Alfred Newman**

"Fasten your seatbelts. It's going to be a bumpy night" is one of Hollywood's most iconic lines, uttered by one of its most iconic actresses, **Bette Davis**, and one that stems from one of its finest comedies. *All About Eve* is a film which explores jealousy with real honesty, a film for which the adjective "biting" might as well have been invented. And who "bites" better than Bette Davis? Very few.

The movie, which won **Joseph L. Mankiewicz** Oscars for Best Director and Best Screenplay, was based on a short story by **Mary Orr** entitled *The Wisdom Of Eve*, which first appeared in a 1946 magazine. **Anne Baxter** plays Eve, an ingénue on the make who, having won her attention in the guise of being a fan, eventually falls foul of the veteran Broadway actress Margo Channing (Davis, in a role that knowingly acknowledged her star status). Eve at first flatters the older woman before setting about usurping her in the bitterest, most spiteful of ways – in which director Mankiewicz's acerbic screenplay takes continual comic delight.

An air of cynicism pervades the film, but it's ably met by a script high on wit and observation, all of which seems to take its tone from Davis's accomplished performance, at once aggressive and vulnerable. In an ironic twist this was to be Davis' last major role until she re-emerged triumphant in the self-parodying *Whatever Happened To Baby Jane?* (1962).

George Sanders – another Oscar winner for his role as Addison DeWitt, Margo's favourite critic – is on splendid form as he struggles in vain to juggle the women in his life, while **Marilyn Monroe** makes an early appearance. Originally **Claudette Colbert** was cast in the Davis role (**Marlene Dietrich** was another early choice by Mankiewicz) but had to pull out due to back trouble, leaving Davis to step into the breach, despite the long-standing animosity between her and producer Daryl F. Zanuck. In 1970, the movie was adapted into a Broadway play called *Applause*, and, in yet another of the twists that seem to pepper its history, at one point during its run Anne Baxter found herself playing the role of Margo.

Rumour persisted at the time of the film that Margo was based on screen legend **Tallulah Bankhead**. When Ms Bankhead was confronted with the news she responded by saying that the next time she saw Bette Davis she would "tear every hair out of her moustache". Even Manciewicz himself couldn't have written a better line than that.

Amélie

dir **Jean-Pierre Jeunet, 2001, Fr/Ger, 123m**
cast **Audrey Tautou, Mathieu Kassovitz, Rufus, Yolande Moreau, Flora Guiet** *cin* **Bruno Delbonnel** *m* **Yann Tiersen**

A fly lands; glasses are disturbed by the breeze in an outdoor restaurant; a man is shown without context rubbing out his written name;

a child – Amélie – is conceived. On one level these are ordinary moments. The film that follows is anything but. Jean-Pierre Jeunet is that rarity amongst filmmakers – a striking visualist who knows how to tell a tale around the "look" of his film. *Amélie* may at times give the impression of being as serendipitous as the events surrounding the conception of its heroine, but that is its genius – this is a knowingly crafted work that blends beauty with black comedy, quirkiness with honesty, irony with love.

All grown up, Amélie Poulain (**Audrey Tautou**) is a waitress in a café in the picturesque Montmartre district of Paris, living a rather uneventful and unengaged existence. Following the death of Princess Diana, and then the discovery of a small box of old keepsakes, Amélie suddenly finds her vocation. She sets out to find the owner of the box and, having found him and returned it, realizes she has made him happy. She gets hooked on the idea of making the world around her a better place and in doing so, of course, she ends up making her own world a better place by finding true love.

It may sound odd to describe a film that has someone suicidally leaping off the top of Notre Dame in its first five minutes as being decidedly uncynical. But that's just what *Amélie* is. Jeunet swathes his vision of Paris in a heightened pattern of colours – green being to the fore – to let us know this is not the real world, but more the way the world should be. The director of the astonishingly inventive comedy *Delicatessen* (1990), fresh from his "Hollywood experience" on *Alien Resurrection* (1997), had started compiling the stories that make up Amélie's life as far back as 1974. Envisaging a sweetly whimsical beauty in the lead role, he originally wanted British actress **Emily Watson**, but she had to pass as she didn't have the French.

Audrey Tatou as Amélie

He had the good luck to discover newcomer Audrey Tautou, who is both gorgeous and unassuming, beautiful and able to blend in. She gives a finely judged performance, portraying a purity of spirit that never becomes mawkish. The scene in which Amélie goes to the movies simply to lose herself in the faces of the audience – who are losing themselves in the images on the screen – is almost unbearably poignant.

Jeunet's film is gentle but assured, and it has a humour that is peculiarly its own – deftly playing life's inexplicable randomness against the fairytale possibilities of human longing to create the most humane of comedies.

Annie Hall

dir Woody Allen, 1977, US, 93m

cast **Woody Allen, Diane Keaton, Tony Roberts, Carol Kane, Paul Simon, Shelley Duvall, Christopher Walken** *cin* **Gordon Willis**

For many people there are two kinds of Woody Allen movies: the "early, funny ones" (a notion Allen himself alluded to in his introspective *Stardust Memories*, 1980) and the later works, influenced by his love of **Ingmar Bergman** and other noted European auteurs, which combine his usual witty dialogue with a propensity for depression (even nihilism, in the case of *Crimes And Misdemeanours*, 1986).

Annie Hall, his most critically successful and popular movie, marked a kind of turning point between the two styles. It refined the witty, New-York-Jewish-intellectual self-deprecation Allen had mined since his days as a stand-up in the 1960s, and at the same time revealed more deep-seated anxieties he had evidently always been prone to. Only now, perhaps, did Allen feel confident enough as a filmmaker to give a mature voice to them, and in this regard the movie manages to be not only extremely reflective of its times but also endearingly timeless.

Allen plays neurotic comedy writer Alvy Singer, a man tussling with the travails of life in 1970s New York – dating, sex and psychoanalysis – and burdened by angst about love and death. Allen staunchly maintains that his films aren't autobiographical, but of course there are obvious parallels. Foremost among them is that between Alvy and Annie and Allen and his leading lady **Diane Keaton**, with whom he had a lengthy real-life relationship. Throughout the course of the movie Annie, who starts out as a Midwest wallflower with a fondness for the phrase "La Di Dah", blossoms into a sophisticated modern urbanite, outgrowing Alvy along the way. The film traces their time together, and in doing so comments on the impossibility of maintaining relationships in modern times.

It sounds like a downer – the movie was originally called "Anhedonia", the name of a condition in which someone is incapable of feeling any joy in life – but *Annie Hall* is actually a delight.

It's one of Allen's richest films, full of great lines ("Don't knock masturbation – it's sex with someone I love"); great filmic ideas (a conversation between Annie and Alvy uses subtitles to show what they are really thinking); and great performances, including a young **Christopher Walken**, splendid as Annie's psycho-in-the-making brother Duane. (Also watch out for a brief appearance from then-unknown **Jeff Goldblum**, as well as **Sigourney Weaver**'s non-speaking movie debut as "Alvy's Date Outside Theatre".)

On its release the movie certainly caught the zeitgeist, with Keaton's "Annie Hall look" – a mannish suit, waistcoat and tie, designed by **Ralph Lauren** – becoming a major fashion trend, and the film was hailed as the best of the year at the Oscars. It also picked up statuettes for Best Screenplay, Director and Actress. Sadly, Allen didn't win Best Actor, but then again he didn't show up anyway – the Academy Awards are always held on a Monday, and Monday is Allen's night for playing jazz clarinet (in those days at *Michael's Pub* in New York).

The Apartment

dir Billy Wilder, 1960, US, 125m, b/w
cast Jack Lemmon, Shirley MacLaine, Fred MacMurray, Ray Walston *cin* Joseph LaShelle *m* Adolph Deutsch

Billy Wilder could always find the humour in the darker side of American life. In *The Apartment* – made hot on the heels of his runaway hit *Some Like It Hot* (1959, see Canon) – he focused on a tale of seedy sex, infidelity and attempted suicide; its "hero" is a man who prostitutes his soul to his job and his apartment to his senior executives. Needless to say, this is one of Wilder's best and warmest comedies.

Beautifully shot in black and white but dwelling in shades of moral grey, the film introduces us to C.C. Baxter (**Jack Lemmon**), an insurance worker in a building of "31,259 drones", as he explains in the opening voiceover. But Baxter is different: he has ambitions to get on, and the key to doing so lies in his apartment, which he loans out to numerous executives as a venue to conduct their extra-

The compromised C.C. Baxter (Jack Lemmon)

marital affairs. Despite the immorality, for Baxter – a man whose life is dictated by figures and statistics – it is a reasoned straightforward transaction.

But then it gets personal, when married head of personnel J.D. Sheldrake (an impressively sleazy **Fred MacMurray**) takes the girl of Baxter's dreams, elevator operator Fran Kubilik (**Shirley MacLaine**) to his rooms for a fling. Her pre-Christmas attempted suicide in his apartment leads to Baxter and Kubilik finally spending some time together, but when Baxter secures his long-desired promotion, he realises he must now come to terms with the fact that he has sold himself for something he never really wanted.

One of the many successes of Wilder's tale is that, as much as the film is awash with dodgy married businessmen cheating on their wives with a pool of available and easy secretaries, it's clear that the most compromised person – the real sellout of the movie – is in fact Lemmon's Baxter. It's an idea that Wilder and co-writer

I.A.L. Diamond delight in playing to the hilt, the director having to squeeze out every ounce of Lemmon's charm to get the audience on his side and keep them there.

Wilder's film deftly walks a tightrope between warmth and cynicism. Surprisingly, the writer/director always claimed that *The Apartment* was inspired by David Lean's beloved weepie *Brief Encounter* (1945). Apparently, after seeing the movie he wrote himself a note that read "Movie about a guy who climbs into the warm bed left by two lovers". What he eventually created from that one line was a bittersweet, distinctly urban comedy, one of the great New York movies, in which **Joseph LaShelle**'s beautiful photography captures all the vicissitudes of the city. *The Apartment*'s story mirrors the fast-moving cosmopolitan life flowing through the metropolis, from the buzz of the office through the up-and-down of the elevator to the inescapable loneliness of the one-bedroom apartment.

Riding the crest of *Some Like It Hot*'s success the previous year, Wilder again did rather well come awards season, with *The Apartment* taking home a total of five Oscars, including Best Picture, Director and Screenplay. Lemmon and the radiant MacLaine (never better) were nominated for Best Actor and Actress but lost out, and had to make do with BAFTAs instead.

Austin Powers: International Man Of Mystery

dir Jay Roach, 1997, US, 95m
cast Mike Myers, Elizabeth Hurley, Mimi Rogers, Seth Green, Michael York, Robert Wagner *cin* Henri Alekan *m* Jean Ledrut

The big-screen success of *Wayne's World* (1992), adapted from a regular sketch on the TV show *Saturday Night Live*, led to Mike

Myers departing the show and developing his most successful movie alter-ego. Fuelled by Myers' love of British TV comedy, along with a fondness for Michael Caine and James Bond, *Austin Powers: International Man of Mystery* was born (described at the time by *Sight and Sound* magazine as "the swinging-London/Britpop-timeslip/easy listening-revival comedy we've all been waiting for"). Also inspired by his idol **Peter Sellers**, who excelled in playing multiple roles (see *Dr Strangelove*, Canon), Myers played not only Powers himself but also his arch-enemy Dr Evil (a nod to Blofeld, James Bond's nemesis as played by Donald Pleasance).

A great deal of the movie's humour comes from the fact that both Powers and Evil have been defrosted after thirty years of cryogenic freezing, thus placing their "swinging 60s" ways in sharp comic relief to the more conservative and worrisome 90s. Powers comes from a time when bad teeth were acceptable, sex was just good clean fun, and swinging was all; for his part the reanimated Dr Evil has failed to take account of inflation, farcically attempting to hold the world to ransom for a total of one million dollars.

Dr Evil (Mike Myers) with Number Two (Robert Wagner)

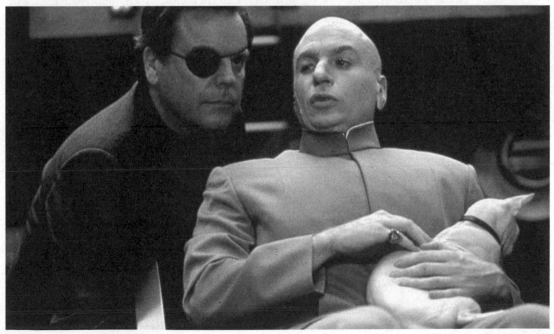

With its stereotypes in place, *Austin Powers* roars ahead. It's a brilliant, fast-paced gag-fest featuring go-go girls that transform into scary "fem-bots" with guns in their bikinis; Swedish penis enlargers; and camp catchphrases such as "bee-have!" and "shall we shag now or shall we shag later?" flying thick and fast. Even **Liz Hurley** suits her role – in a sub-Diana Rigg kind of way – as the glamorous Ms Vanessa Kensington.

Austin Powers had "cult hit" written all over it and, as with any good cult, it simply grew and grew. Only scoring moderate box office success upon its initial release, the film built a strong following via word of mouth, and its sequel, *Austin Powers: The Spy Who Shagged Me* (1999), became one of the most financially successful comic vehicles of all time. In the second movie Myers reprised his Sellers routine – this time with the aid of a vast amount of prosthetics, used to create a baby-eating, super-size Scottish villain by the name of Fat Bastard. A third film, *Goldmember* (2002), added the eponymous sub-1970s disco-dancing character to Myers' increasing list of on-screen roles. This time even Myers' hero **Michael Caine** showed up as Austin's equally swinging dad.

Throughout the trilogy, Myers also showed a sharp ear for a tune, revitalizing **Burt Bacharach**'s career and ensuring that **Quincy Jones**' immortal "Soul Bossa Nova" will now forever be thought of as "the *Austin Powers* theme".

Blazing Saddles

dir Mel Brooks, 1974, US, 93m

cast Cleavon Little, Gene Wilder, Mel Brooks, Harvey Korman, Madeline Kahn, Slim Pickens *cin* Michael Hertzberg *m* John Morris

No matter which way you look at it, cinema has never produced a funnier film written by a Jew, a dentist, a lawyer and a black stand-up comic than *Blazing Saddles*. Mel Brooks (the movie's cowriter and director) should take a large part of the credit. But, having worked as a staff writer on Sid Caesar's TV series *Your Show Of Shows* with

Brave and silly – Mel Brooks with Robyn Hilton

the likes of **Neil Simon** and **Woody Allen**, Brooks had a healthy respect for the notion of team writing. So when he was presented with a movie treatment for a comedy Western, courtesy of aspiring writer **Andrew Bergman**, he decided to hark back to the golden days of group writing.

Given the racial theme of the material – a black sheriff gets sent in to sort out the problems of an all-white town, thus addressing prejudices previously reserved for Native Americans in the Western – he looked first for a black voice, finding one in stand-up comic **Richard Pryor**. Sadly Pryor (who was soon to become a major star) was at the time considered to be too new to Hollywood to take the movie's lead role of Sheriff Bart, and it went to the altogether smoother and less interesting **Cleavon Little**. Then Brooks added the dentist (**Norman Steinberg**) and lawyer (**Alan Uger**) to the team and set about destroying all the myths of the Hollywood Western.

Also on board was, of course, **Gene Wilder**, a talented comedic actor who had found some degree of fame in Brooks' first outing as director, 1969's *The Producers* (see Canon). Brooks had kept Wilder up to speed with the script of *Blazing Saddles*, although he insisted the actor was too young to play the pivotal role of the Waco Kid, Sheriff Bart's unlikely right-hand man. Having been turned down by veteran cowboys **Dan Dailey** and **John Wayne** (who read the screenplay, loved it, but couldn't bring himself to tarnish an image he had spent a lifetime securing), Brooks finally cast **Gig Young**, only for Young to show up drunk on the first day. Wilder stepped in, and in doing so gave the film its heart.

There's a curious, not unlikeable, imbalance to *Blazing Saddles* that in many ways defines it: everyone seems to be playing in a completely different key. Brooks was clearly throwing everything at the wall just to see how much would stick. A lot does, but it's a style that works less well in his later work. Little plays it cool, **Harvey Korman** is all shtick, **Madeline Kahn** is superb as a Garbo facsimile ("the Teutonic Titwillow"), while Wilder (possibly channelling Dean Martin in *Rio Bravo*) is simply operating on his own internal rhythm, delightfully unaware of everyone around him – which works beautifully.

Ultimately *Blazing Saddles* not only attacks racism and destroys Western clichés, but also plays with the very nature of movie-making itself, as in its final reel where the action literally spills out into the street and into the local movie theatre (which is showing, of course, *Blazing Saddles*). It's brave, it's silly, it's very funny – and, incidentally, it includes more references to Nazis than any Western made before or since.

Bringing Up Baby

dir **Howard Hawks, 1938, US, 102m, b/w**
cast **Cary Grant, Katharine Hepburn, Charles Ruggles, Walter Catlett, Fritz Feld** *cin* **Russell Metty** *m* **Roy Webb**

Screwball – it's a word that describes a certain kind of baseball hit, and it defines a certain kind of comedy. Whatever its literal

Cary Grant, Katharine Hepburn and tame leopard: classic screwball ingredients

meaning – which is debatable – it has no better incarnation in screen comedy than Howard Hawks' perfect *Bringing Up Baby*. The film's unique skewed logic defies any attempt to clearly explain its plot – simply put, David Huxley (**Cary Grant**), a bespectacled zoology professor who puts dinosaur bones together for a living, is waiting eagerly for the delivery of an "interclostal clavicle" to complete his current pet project, which is the reconstruction of a brontosaurus skeleton. He's also due to be married to a respectable co-worker the following day. He inadvertently hooks up with a wisecracking society heiress, Susan Vance (**Katharine Hepburn**), whose brother has just sent her a tame leopard, Baby (admittedly to the wrong address). Susan decides that she fancies Grant's gangly scientist type so much that she must stop his impending wedding by any means possible – a plan that is aided by not only Baby but her dog, George, who steals and buries David's precious dinosaur bone. There's a case of mistaken leopard identity, and a spell in jail for David and Susan – and while love eventually conquers all, the chaos doesn't look like ending anytime soon. It sounds crazy, and of course it is: this is a fast-paced, head-spinning movie that delights in its absurdity.

It also shows off the irrepressible talents of Cary Grant. As Tony Curtis so tellingly observed in his hilarious homage to/pastiche of the great actor in *Some Like It Hot* (1959, see Canon), no one on earth sounds like that. And no one on earth delivers dialogue like him, either, which must have given scriptwriters **Dudley Nichols** and **Hagar Wilde** a field day – the debonair Grant juggles double entendres like a gentleman, at times to the point where no discerning audience could even notice there was any rudeness inferred.

Then there's Hepburn to contend with. Her perfectly judged performance as the anarchic Susan, who brings both chaos and class into David's previously staid life, is one of her best, balancing her androgynous, athletic beauty with her sharp intelligence to perfect effect. Ironically, and ridiculously, Hepburn, whom audiences hadn't yet taken to, was later blamed for the film's relative failure at the US box office, an ignominy she didn't get beyond until her success in *The Philadelphia Story* two years later. It has also been argued that *Baby*'s lukewarm reception was simply to do with its timing – Depression-era audiences were finally wearying of the screwball genre, concerned as it was with the misadventures of ditzy social-ites and the idle rich. However, from today's perspective, despite

Bringing Up Baby very much reflecting its era, it nonetheless remains timelessly, wonderfully ridiculous.

Broadcast News

dir **James L. Brooks, 1987, US, 132m**
cast **William Hurt, Albert Brooks, Holly Hunter, Joan Cusack** *cin* **Michael Ballhaus** *m* **Bill Conti**

Received wisdom has it that comedy is all about timing. Well, *Broadcast News*, James L. Brooks' newsroom-based comedy certainly bears that out. Not only was it timely in its political and industry-related observations, it also managed to stand as a brilliant dissection of romance and how it, too, is all about timing. When the romantic triangle at the heart of this film meets in its closing moments, accompanied by the subtitle "Seven Years Later", the characters find themselves meeting in a different world and a different time and realize their feelings for each other have changed. This is no casually tacked-on finale, but crystallizes the very point of the film. Timing is all.

Writer/director **James L. Brooks**, a TV sitcom veteran on shows such as *Mary Tyler Moore* and *Taxi* (and then later *The Simpsons*) wrote the most perfectly realized – and by default, perfectly pre-scient – media-based comedy since *His Girl Friday* (1939; Canon). *Broadcast News* dissects the very heart of modern journalism, using American TV news as its primary source with the basic notions of ethics and morality as its subtext (one somewhat to the fore). What *Broadcast News* does – more than possibly any other funny movie – is to recognize the moral responsibility that lies behind the heart of all great comedy. Comedy is here used to show us the best and equally the worst of ourselves. This takes the venerable institution of the press and puts it through the mill. All its central characters are asked to compromise their ideals and work out where they stand afterwards. This is brave filmmaking that never forgets it's supposed to be comedic first and foremost.

Set against the hyperactive milieu of a modern TV newsroom, much of the comedy comes from the beautifully played love triangle between the three main protagonists: Jane, a young female producer

(**Holly Hunter** in a career-defining role); Aaron, a really-good-at-his-job reporter hampered by his lack of star charisma (the always perfect **Albert Brooks**); and Tom, a handsome, vacuous anchorman in the making (**William Hurt**, who plays vacuous with his usual intelligence). It also contains what may well be one of the best written, best acted and best directed scenes in modern US cinema, in which Aaron tries desperately to explain his love for Jane by explaining that her media-friendly boyfriend may well be the devil. She replies by telling him he's the devil instead, to which Aaron replies that he can't be – "Because I think we have the kind of friendship that, if I were the devil, you'd be the only one I could tell."

Brooks' film remains as timely today as it was when it was made – if not more so. Although as a writer/director he isn't exactly prolific (five films in twenty two years) his movies are rarely less than brilliantly funny (1983's weepie *Terms Of Endearment* being the exception), and they are populated by some of the best realized movie characters of the age.

Caddyshack

dir **Harold Ramis, 1980, US, 98m**
cast **Chevy Chase, Bill Murray, Rodney Dangerfield, Ted Knight** *cin* **Stevan Larner** *m* **Johnny Mandel**

Having taken on the inner sanctum of the college fraternity in *Animal House* (1978, see Canon), screenwriters **Harold Ramis** and **Doug Kenney** decided to bring their outrageous brand of humour to the fairways, invading the sanctity of the golf course in a snobs-versus-slobs duel. The result was *Caddyshack* – "the comedy with balls", as the posters proclaimed it at the time.

Caddyshack brought together some of the major figures – Harold Ramis, Bill Murray and his brother, writer Brian Doyle-Murray – from *National Lampoon, Saturday Night Live* and *Chicago's Second City* troupe, and, unsurprisingly, it is reminiscent of all three. The movie is basically a series of vignettes, loosely held together by a plot involving young golf caddy Danny (**Michael O'Keefe**), who is in the process of deciding whether to go to college or not. Opposite

O'Keefe is Chevy Chase, back when he was still funny, giving a sublime performance as the golf pro Ty Webb, who ambles his way through the golf course of life in a Zen-heavy way, equally at home drinking champagne with the toffs or smoking a joint with the caddies. He is the man who straddles both worlds, the transcendental hero always there with a word of advice: "Don't be obsessed with your desires, Danny. The Zen philosopher Basha once wrote 'A flute with no holes is not a flute. And a donut with no hole is a Danish.' He was a funny guy."

Stealing Chase's thunder, however, is **Bill Murray** as groundskeeper Carl Spackler, a man who over the years has become a little too familiar with the turf and exists largely in a world of his own. Carl's constant battle with a puppet gopher is great fun, but it's his standalone scene, in which he takes a bishop out for one last round in a thunderstorm (and skulks off after the man of the cloth has been struck down by lightning), that remains one of the film's comic highlights. Another standout scene – in which Ty visits Carl in his quarters – was improvised at the last minute after the filmmakers realised they had no scenes in which Chase and Murray appeared together.

Anyone who has seen *Caddyshack* more than once (and if you have seen *Caddyshack* at all, you've probably done so several times – it's that kind of film) is apt to quote their favourite lines, of which there are many. This is "guy" humour par excellence, from "You're rather attractive for a beautiful girl with a great body," to **Rodney Dangerfield**'s nouveau-riche interloper at the club, addressing one overweight woman, "Hey lady – you wanna make fourteen bucks the hard way?"

Battling with the gopher

The film was followed eight years later by an inferior sequel, with none of the major cast returning, bar a brief cameo from Chase. But the original remains truly loved, even by its cast – Bill Murray went so far as to write a book based on his golfing memories, named after one of Carl's most memorable phrases – *A Cinderella Story*.

Being a good sport

Sport is essentially dramatic. Whether it be scoring a goal, winning a race, or sinking a putt – lives (and often a good deal of money) hang in the balance. Comedy movies, however, see the lighter side. What better place to find humour than in an arena in which everyone takes every move so seriously?

With such a wide variety of sports available to deflate, it's striking that the majority of sports-themed comedy movies have been devoted to a mere handful of the more popular sports, in particular football (largely American), baseball (largely American) and golf (largely American). Americans hold their sports in high regard but it seems are amenable to making fun of them.

Sport provides the perfect arena for physical comedy and slapstick. **Harold Lloyd**'s diminutive size on the field and distinctive glasses made fun of the notion of running with an armful of pigskin in 1925's *The Freshman*. Often sport licenses behaviour that would otherwise be seen as violent, in much the same way cartoons do – cue more comic potential. **Burt Reynolds** (a former pro-football player) motivated his fellow prisoners to use a football game as their one chance to beat the crap out of their sadistic prison guards in Robert Aldrich's caustic *Mean Machine* (1974), also known as *The Longest Yard*. **Adam Sandler** and a troupe of his ex-*Saturday Night Live* buddies (including Chris Rock) remade the movie under the latter title in 2004.

Indeed, Sandler's patented anger management shtick works well in the realms of the sports comedy; as a college football team's *Waterboy* (1998), he harnesses that suppressed rage to tackle men twice his size, and takes it all the way to the touchdown line. He also unleashed his fury on the golf course as the eponymous *Happy Gilmore* (1996), a pro hockey player forced to rethink his ways and swap his hockey stick for a nine-iron, as his rage-fuelled, crude power shooting is his only real skill. (If the golfing comedy can be said to have a classic, however, it is of course the inestimable *Caddyshack*, the comedy not only with balls, but with Murray, Chase and Dangerfield to boot.)

Kevin Costner is another star who repeatedly pops up in sports comedies, practising his swing against Rene Russo in romantic golf comedy *Tin Cup* (1996) and transferring his swing to the baseball field – that other beloved American sport that has proved good for a gag or two – in Ron Shelton's superb *Bull Durham* (1988), undoubtedly the best baseball comedy film to date. Kids got a look in courtesy of the popular *Bad News Bears* series of the 1970s: the first one being entertaining enough and starring Walter Matthau; the two sequels being dire schmaltz.

A more interesting example of the sports comedy genre was 1976's classic *The Bingo Long Travelling All Stars And Motor Kings*. Produced by Motown, it was a look at the Negro National League of the late 1930s, with a cast that featured **Richard Pryor** and *Star Wars* stalwarts-to-be **Billy Dee Williams** and **James Earl Jones**.

Le dîner de cons
(The Idiots' Dinner)

dir **Francis Veber, 1998, Fr, 80m**
cast **Jacques Villeret, Thierry Lhermitte, Francis Huster**
cin **Luciano Tovoli** *m* **Vladimir Cosma**

Ever since his stage success as the author of the breakthrough cross-dressing comedy *La cage aux folles* (1978) brought him to a wide international audience, **Francis Veber** has mined a distinctive career as a writer-director who explores two of the most striking aspects of French comedy cinema – farce and the comedy of manners. Veber is a master at taking a simple initial idea and allowing it to escalate out of all control: the very essence of comic misunderstanding and farce. Adapted from his own play, 1998's *Le dîner de cons* makes the transition from stage to screen a lot better than most attempts.

Pierre Brochant (**Thierry Lhermitte**), a well-to-do publisher, is a man who has yet to fully grow up, and he lives a cosseted enough life in his beautifully decorated apartment – with a lovely view of the Eiffel Tower just outside – not to have to.

To entertain themselves, he and his friends hold a weekly dinner party in which they indulge themselves at the expense of those less fortunate. Their game is to search high and low for idiots, people who they, with their supposedly sophisticated ways, find to be foolish, then invite them along and give them free reign to speak whilst feigning to be interested. The winner is the one who has brought the most ridiculous fool to the festivities. Apparently these occasions grew out of the "dog dinners" the circle held at university – to which each man would invite the ugliest girl he could find.

Pierre has been having a hard time finding a suitably idiotic subject this week, until he hears about lowly accountant François Pignon, a man who, since his wife left him, has devoted his life to building matchstick replicas of such landmarks as the Eiffel Tower. He seems like a prime candidate. However, on the day of the dinner, Pierre's wife leaves him and he throws his back out on the golf course, leaving him unable to leave his apartment. When the naïve

Jacques Villeret (middle) is one-man jinx François Pignon

Pignon shows up there, he proves to be not so much an idiot as a complete jinx. Pierre may be having a bad evening; but little does he know that it's going to get much worse. He is about to receive his just desserts for all of his actions over the years, with farcically painful repercussions involving a nymphomaniac girl friend, a case of mistaken identity and a crippling tax audit.

Veber works the classic farce structure with a small but perfectly formed cast of characters, all of whom the audience can (just about) identify with. None more so perhaps than the author Just LeBlanc (**Francis Huster**). LeBlanc and Pierre's now-estranged wife used to be an item, until Pierre moved in on her, and he simply can't help but laugh as the events spiral out of everyone's control. (His first name also provides a shamelessly *Airplane*-style pun/misunderstanding gag: "His name is Just LeBlanc"/"Oh, doesn't he have a first name?"). But it's Pierre and Pignon who are at the centre of everything – a classic movie "odd couple" in which the clever one proves to be the fool and the fool proves to be a catalyst for catastrophe.

Díner is undoubtedly a very "staged" movie but one which is incredibly well staged. (Jacques Villeret is said to have performed his role as Pignon live at the theatre no less than 900 times.) Near collisions, mistaken identities and the use of a phone to both change and intensify the plot not once but several times all add to a sense of a perfectly executed play on celluloid. The scheduled Hollywood remake (*Schmuck's Dinner*) starring **Sacha Baron Cohen** ("Ali G") will be an interesting one to watch...

Dr Strangelove: Or, How I Learned To Stop Worrying And Love The Bomb

dir **Stanley Kubrick, 1963, UK, 94m, b/w**
cast **Peter Sellers, George C. Scott, Sterling Hayden, Keenan Wynn, Slim Pickens** *cin* **Gilbert Taylor** *m* **Laurie Johnson**

In the early 1960s, **Stanley Kubrick**, like many others, was alarmed about the possibility of nuclear annihilation. In the light of this, he optioned a book by **Peter George** entitled *Red Alert*, determined to make a serious movie that would help bring the world to its senses.

But when he began writing the screenplay with George, the pair of them found they kept on getting sidetracked, their curiosity leading them astray, and they would frequently end up asking each other questions such as: "what do they do if they get hungry in the War Room?" They initially put such ideas aside and ploughed on dedicatedly, their project labouring under the earnest working title of *The Delicate Balance Of Terror*. But following the Cuban Missile Crisis of

1962, Kubrick decided the only way to properly address the sheer absurdity of the nuclear arms race was to attempt to out-absurd it altogether. Noted American humourist and novelist **Terry Southern** was drafted in to work on the script and the result was one of the most brilliantly incisive satires Hollywood has ever produced.

The film told the tale of renegade U.S. Air Force commander Jack D. Ripper (**Sterling Hayden**), an increasingly delusional man with his finger on the button, who succeeds in setting America's nuke-carrying B-52s on an irreversible course to Russia. As diplomats scramble to sort out the situation, it becomes apparent that the Russians have something even bigger up their sleeve – and time is beginning to run out.

To aid them in exposing the lunacy of such warfare, Kubrick enlisted British comic polymath **Peter Sellers**, who had recently worked successfully with Kubrick on *Lolita* (1961). Kubrick at first seemed to want the actor to play just about every role, but in the end he took three – US President Merkin Muffley, Royal Air Force Captain Mandrake, and the mysterious, wheelchair-bound, former Nazi scientist, Dr Strangelove himself. Never on better form(s), Sellers was even permitted by the notoriously obsessive director to improvise much of his dialogue. The actor was also slated to play cowboy bomber pilot Major "King" Kong but broke his leg while rehearsing a scene in which King is pictured riding a nuclear missile as it falls towards Mother Russia. Kubrick sorted out the situation by casting a real cowboy, turning former rodeo rider **Slim Pickens** into a star.

Alongside the film's verbal satirical wit, the film offers some genuine visual delights. Former fighter pilot **Ken Adam** (later to provide many of the biggest and best Bond sets) designed the famous war room with its 22-foot circular table, a set that proved so iconic that, so legend has it, **Ronald Reagan** asked to be shown the war room he'd seen in *Strangelove*, presuming it to be real, after he became President of the US. The film opens brilliantly with a shot of a B-52 being re-fuelled in mid-air, a sort of mechanical copulation, and ends with a series of nuclear explosions set to **Vera Lynn**'s "We'll Meet Again." It was in fact originally due to end with an all-out custard pie fight in the war room, a scene that saw the cast incapacitated by both custard and their own laughter. It was quickly dropped, with Kubrick later describing it as "a disaster of Homeric proportions."

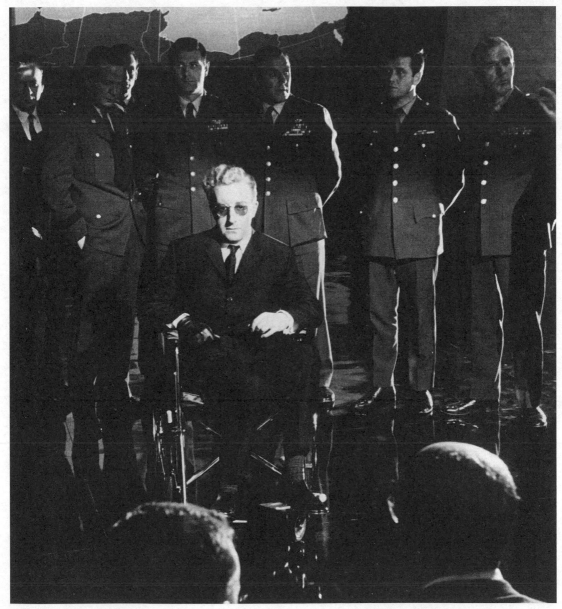

Peter Sellers as Dr Strangelove, improvising the absurd.

Dodgeball

dir **Rawson Marshall Thurber, 2004, US, 92m**
cast **Ben Stiller, Vince Vaughn, Rip Torn, Christine Taylor, Justin Long** *cin* **Jerzy Zielinski** *m* **Theodore Shapiro**

Dodgeball is a guilty pleasure, one of those movies where you go in expecting the worst – in this case, macho Americans throwing balls at each other's, well, balls... and not much else. But then it sucks you

Comedy from confrontation

in, and you end up experiencing so much more. In an era in which the phrase "dumbing down" has become a common complaint – levelled at everything from Jim Carrey movies all the way to the White House – here was a movie that proved just how clever you have to be to make a supposedly dumb comedy. The best comedy is rarely dumb: it just plays dumb. It nearly always knows what it's doing, and therein lies its appeal.

Dodgeball – subtitled "A True Underdog Story" – takes on the Hollywood sports movie, with all its supposedly heroic, uplifting highs and lows, and knocks it on its ass. Here we have the putative hero Pete La Fleur (a beautifully underplayed turn from **Vince Vaughn**) trying to save his local gym, full of losers, from the corporate buy-out threatened by White Goodman (**Ben Stiller**) and his mega Global Gym. So, of course, to deal with this issue they throw balls at each other's balls. It's a guy thing. If only all wars dealt with life's problems in the same way, the world would doubtlessly be a better place.

When the gauntlet is thrown down via the *Dodgeball* world championship (not *remotely* like the Superbowl at all, perish the thought), it inevitably comes down to a fight to the death between Stiller's macho men and Vaughn's ragtag collection of failed male cheerleaders and Steve the Pirate (**Alan Tudyk**), a weirdo who dresses and talks just the way his name suggests. A true underdog story indeed..

To add to the mix Thurber throws in genius comedy veteran **Rip Torn**, surely one of the American masters of cussing (and anyone who's ever seen him on HBO's deliciously dark *The Larry Sanders Show* can testify to that) as wheelchair-bound coach – and former Dodgeball champion – Patches O'Houlihan. His teaching methods involve throwing wrenches at prospective players on the grounds that "If you can dodge a wrench, you can dodge a ball." He will later extend his maxim to "If you can dodge traffic, you can dodge a ball."

Thurber pulls off another coup in getting an inspired cameo from Lance Armstrong, who really enters into the spirit of things with an "I can't believe he just said that" mock-heroic cancer gag. But there is more to the movie than snappy one-liners and celebrity appearances. This is a film that begins by attacking body image and our general obsession with the same. Ben Stiller's slimy to-camera advert about the merits of Global Gym opens the film, and comes complete with the wonderful line – "Of course, you'll still be you in a legal sense".

Dodgeball is representative of a new generation of performers, an almost post-SNL grouping that includes Stiller, Vaughn, Will Ferrell, Owen Wilson and more, who often appear in tandem or perform cameos in each other's films. Of this new era in American comedy, Dodgeball is its finest moment to date.

Duck Soup

dir Leo McCarey, 1933, US, 70m, b/w
cast Groucho, Chico, Harpo and Zeppo Marx, Margaret Dumont, Louis Calhern cin Henry Sharp m Bert Kalmar & Harry Ruby

It's difficult to pick a definitive Marx Brothers movie but as a 70-minute slice of jam-packed cinematic anarchy that manages to capture each of the Brothers doing what they do best, Duck Soup may just be the one. It does feature **Zeppo Marx** once again in a straight role, a supposedly handsome romantic lead, but he had the good sense to leave the troupe after this, their most frantic and funniest effort. And although it was followed by classics including A Night At The Opera (1935) and A Day At The Races (1937), Duck Soup sees the brothers at their zenith.

The Marx Brothers – in various familial combinations – started out in vaudeville, and made the leap to the movies in 1929's The Cocoanuts, an adaptation of their successful Broadway show, set in a hotel during the Florida land boom. Even as early as this, their screen personas were in place: Groucho, the quick-witted, fast-talking, ad-libbing, cigar-chomping opportunist; Chico, the pseudo-immigrant grifter; and Harpo, the horn-tooting physical comic of the group, nevertheless prone to the occasional sincere musical interlude. At times Marx Brothers movies appear almost free-form, the loosely structured plots often a contrivance for them to throw in bits of business to the bemusement of everyone around. **Margaret Dumont**, who appears here and in six more of their films, was more bemused than most, and thus made a perfect foil for Groucho.

Duck Soup sees Groucho playing Rufus T. Firefly, an itinerant con-man who, as a result of his attempts to seduce the wealthy dowager Gloria Teasdale (Dumont), finds himself leader of the fictional country Fredonia. Firefly is indeed the fly in the ointment for Trentino (**Louis Calhern**), the ambassador of the neighbouring country Sylvania, who had planned to marry Mrs Teasdale himself and seize control of her country. Disguised as lemonade salesmen, Chicolini (Chico) and Pinky (Harpo) spy for Sylvania. Insults – courtesy of Firefly – abound, and soon war is declared (after all, Firefly, as he puts it, has "already paid for the battlefield").

It's not much of a plot, admittedly, but the Marx Brothers fire on all cylinders here, twisting what little logic they can find well beyond the point of absurdity. Great scenes abound – one of the best sees Chico and Harpo disguising themselves as Groucho so they can steal Fredonia's plans, resulting in the classic (and often copied) "mirror scene" in which they ape Groucho's actions. The dialogue itself, pricelessly funny, comes thick and fast. At one point Firefly announces, "I suggest we give you ten years in Leavenworth, or eleven years in Twelveworth", to which Chicolini offers the inimitable response: "I tell you what I'll do. I'll take five and ten in Woolworth."

Surprisingly, perhaps, the film was not a huge hit for the Brothers. However, while audiences in general paid it little notice, one person certainly did. **Benito Mussolini** took umbrage at its comic depiction of small-time dictators, believing Groucho and his cohorts had someone specific in mind, and banned the movie in Italy.

Ferris Bueller's Day Off

dir John Hughes, 1986, US, 103m

cast Matthew Broderick, Alan Ruck, Jennifer Grey, Jeffrey Jones, Mia Sara *cin* Tak Fujimoto *m* Ira Newborn

"While the rest of us were just thinking about it, Ferris borrowed a Ferrari and did it all. In a day." So ran the tagline on the poster for *Ferris Bueller's Day Off*, the zenith of **John Hughes'** wonderful 1980s reinvention of the teen comedy. With *National Lampoon's Animal House* (1978; see Canon) already having laid claim to the college

Teen comedy comes of age,
kind of...

comedy, as the 1980s dawned, Hughes (a *National Lampoon* writer) decided to stake out the high school for a series of movies that not only found widespread fame and acclaim, but also brought a welcome, influential intelligence into the world of teen screen comedy. Despite being essentially a day-in-the-life of a confident, cocky, middle-class rich kid from the suburbs, whose biggest gripe in life is that his older sister got a car for her birthday when he only got a lousy computer, *Ferris Bueller* manages to be a remarkably likeable movie.

Hughes moved from magazines to movies as writer-director of the comedy *Sixteen Candles* (1984) with teen actress **Molly Ringwald** becoming his muse. He took her into drama with the kids-in-detention classic *The Breakfast Club* (1985), before finally allowing her to graduate into the big wide world of impending adulthood with the fairy-tale adolescent romcom *Pretty In Pink* (1986). During the same period, the prolific Hughes – he claimed it took him two days to write a screenplay, three if he was really putting a lot of effort into it – somehow found the time to deliver his teen masterpiece in the form of *Ferris Bueller*.

On the face of it, there's little to the plot. Having managed to fake his way into getting the day off school, the ingenious Ferris (**Matthew Broderick**, on superb form) spends his time not just goofing off but driving a quality car (his friend's dad's Ferrari); eating in the best restaurant in town; taking in an exhibition at the local art gallery; entertaining the crowd in a huge German parade (a real-life event which Hughes decided to take advantage of); and, more than anything, sorting out the problems of his uncool and uptight best friend Cameron (a great supporting performance from **Alan Ruck**).

Jennifer Grey delivers well as Ferris's (understandably) envious sister, while **Jeffrey Jones** ably chomps any scenery that comes to hand as Ferris's nemesis, the head teacher Dean Rooney, who is determined to catch him out. Watch out, too, for a great cameo from **Charlie Sheen**, as a truly wasted, spaced-out bad boy whose seriously considered response to the insult "blow yourself" is a classic. (Apparently Sheen stayed awake for two days straight to get a suitably frazzled performance.)

By the end of the decade Hughes had hung up his directing hat and, in his screenplays' subject matter, regressed from the teenage years back to childhood (he wrote *Home Alone,* 1990, which was then the highest grossing comedy of all time), then to infancy (*Baby's Day Out,* 1994). His refusal to direct is a huge disappointment and his ongoing commitment to such average family fare as *101 Dalmatians* (1996) and *Flubber* (1997) is a waste of a great talent. The *New York Times* once called Hughes "possibly the most influential creative force in films of the last twenty years", noting that he made his mark "by dramatizing his teenage cynosures while inflating their psychic wounds until they resounded with mythological overtones". All true. But they forgot one thing – he also used to make really cool, funny movies.

Four Weddings And A Funeral

dir Mike Newell, 1994, UK, 117m
cast Hugh Grant, Andie MacDowell, Kristin Scott Thomas, Simon Callow, Rowan Atkinson *cin* Michael Coulter *m* Richard Rodney Bennett

When *Four Weddings And A Funeral* came along, the British film industry was yet to be rocked by *Trainspotting* and was still largely dependent on the trusty dividends of **Merchant-Ivory** period dramas; *Four Weddings* was an unexpected breath of fresh air – and not just because it opened with a barrage of the F-word. It was a contemporary British film that *felt* contemporary – albeit in a completely different way from the realist working-class cinema of **Mike Leigh** or **Ken Loach**. Granted, the cosy upper-middle-class milieu of *Four Weddings* bore very little relation to everyday life in 1990s Britain, but had the simple virtue of being very, very funny, which won it its deserved phenomenal success.

Screenwriter **Richard Curtis** would go on to become a dominant figure in British comedy, with a handful of similar (and ultimately wearing) British romcoms: *Notting Hill* (1999), two instalments of *Bridget Jones's Diary* (2001 and 2004) and *Love, Actually* (2003). Prior to this he had worked his way up through British TV, partly through his association with comedian **Rowan Atkinson**, on topical sketch show *Not The Nine O'Clock News* and three of the four series of the splendid *Blackadder*, as well as the inferior *Mr. Bean* series. He'd also delivered a decent screenplay in *The Tall Guy* (1989), another Brit romcom, this time with **Emma Thompson** and **Jeff Goldblum** (on guest American duties).

With *Four Weddings* he found the perfect star in **Hugh Grant**, a handsome British toff with an adept comic timing and a finely-honed talent for saying the word "bugger". **Andie MacDowell** was brought in to hook the American audience – this was a movie clearly made to play as broadly across the board, and across the pond,

Classy comedy

as it could – and the cast was rounded out with a strong collection of British talent, among them Simon Callow, Kristin Scott Thomas and John Hannah.

The plot is simple enough. Over a course of a few months a group of friends attend, you guessed it, four weddings and one funeral, the story centring upon commitment-phobic Charles (Grant), who, at the movie's first wedding, meets Carrie (MacDowell) who captivates him and, eventually, changes his view on settling down. Even so, Curtis's film went through numerous drafts to make it the audience-pleasing beast that it became. At one point it was apparently titled *Four Weddings And A Honeymoon*, and partly took place in the Caribbean. But when it was felt that a touch of gravitas was needed, Simon Callow's flamboyant character was bumped off (and John Hannah, playing his lover, sent sales of W.H. Auden's *Selected Poems* sky-high thanks to his reading of "Funeral Blues" at the funeral). Another late addition was the photo montage at the end, created after test audiences found Grant and MacDowell's final scene (kissing in the rain) too mawkish. The final sight of Kristin Scott Thomas ending up with a most surprising groom made sure everyone went away on a big laugh.

Four Weddings gave the world a respectable comedy leading man, became the highest grossing British film ever, and launched a good few imitations (not least by Curtis himself). For its warmth, humour and intelligence – and its perfect ensemble cast – it remains at the top of its class.

The General

dir **Clyde Bruckman & Buster Keaton, 1927, US, 75m, b/w**

cast **Buster Keaton, Marion Mack, Blyde Bruckman, Al Boasberg, Charles Smith** *cin* **Dev Jennings**

When **Buster Keaton** made his masterpiece, *The General*, he took no prisoners – even going as far as driving a locomotive off the end of a burning bridge into a river-bed somewhere in deepest, darkest Oregon. Such brio is typical of this action-packed Civil War-set epic,

Death-defying Buster Keaton

the silent comedian's most ambitious, and in many ways his most accomplished, feature.

Working as director and writer as well as star, Keaton cast himself as a hapless, poker-faced locomotive engineer named Johnny Gray, eager to impress his girl by joining up with the Confederates, but rejected on the grounds that he's more use in the war effort working on the trains. His girl, not knowing the reason he isn't fighting, believes him to be a coward, but when the Union soldiers capture his beloved train, the *General*, with his girl on board Buster springs into comic action both death-defying and second-to-none.

The General is in many ways the ultimate chase movie. Keaton, his astonishing acrobatic skills stretched to the limit, pursues his dream loco and dream woman one way, then retreats to take them back another, playing both the pursuer and ultimately the pursued as they race for their lives. At the time it was his attempt to achieve the recognition he deserved as a serious comedy filmmaker. Among his own films, he always cited it as his favourite .

Keaton invested a lot in *The General*, making it one of the biggest-budget silent movies this side of **Cecil B. DeMille**'s. He strove for authenticity, basing much of its look on Civil War photographs, and set the action against a never-more-panoramic American landscape. Screen comedy had previously confined itself to less grandiose locations and backgrounds, and indeed here the rugged scenery could have overshadowed the subtlety of his comedy; Keaton, however, was always in control, and effectively made what could well be called the first comedy epic.

His efforts went unrewarded, by a poor showing at the box office – partly because in 1927 the Civil War was still in living memory, and not, it was believed, to be made fun of. The studio was so worried about that fact that it opened the movie in Japan first, under the improbable title *Keaton, Shogun*. But time has been kind to *The General*, which offers an opportunity to see a true comic legend at the peak of his powers, both in front of and behind the lens.

Ghostbusters

dir Ivan Reitman, 1984, US, 105m

cast Bill Murray, Dan Aykroyd, Harold Ramis, Sigourney Weaver, Rick Moranis, Ernie Hudson *cin* Laszlo Kovaks *m* Elmer Bernstein

Ghostbusters cleverly mixed three of the key ingredients that had defined Hollywood since the late 1970s – the blockbuster (as epitomized by 1975's *Jaws*); the special effects movie (as epitomized by *Star Wars*, which appeared in 1977); and the teen movie, as launched by *National Lampoon*'s comedy *Animal House* (1978; see Canon).

The first writer on the piece, *Saturday Night Live* regular Dan Aykroyd, took his initial inspiration from Walt Disney's cartoon film, the Mickey Mouse short *Lonesome Ghosts* (1937) – in which a trio of spook hunters (Mickey, Donald Duck and Goofy) explored a haunted house – which provided the basic ghost-hunting plot. Translated into the trio of oddball maverick scientists Venkman, Stantz and Spengler (played by **Bill Murray**, **Dan Aykroyd** and co-writer **Harold Ramis**), the 1980s team of ghostbusters set about taking on all things supernatural. Aykroyd's first stab at the script saw it set in the future, where an intergalactic team battle not only with the undead but also with a raft of rival ghostbusting companies. But budgetary constrictions – and common sense – prevailed, after fellow Canadian **Ivan Reitman** became involved. Reitman persuaded Aykroyd to relocate

Screamingly funny

In the 1930s, Universal Pictures introduced the world to a whole bestiary of monsters, creepy-crawlies and ghouls, often in their definitive cinematic version, with *Frankenstein* (1931), *Dracula* (1931) and *The Mummy* (1932). More than a decade later it introduced them to comedy team Abbott and Costello, in a series of *Abbott and Costello Meet...* movies: *Frankenstein* (1948); *The Killer, Boris Karloff* and *The Invisible Man* (1951); *Dr Jekyll and Mr Hyde* (1954); and *The Mummy* (1955) – featuring the likes of Boris Karloff, Bela Lugosi and Lon Chaney Jr. reprising their original ghoulish roles.

There has always been a fine line between what makes us scream and what makes us laugh. Many horror movies deliver laughs along with the chills – a phenomenon that has become more and more prevalent since **Freddy Kruger** insisted on dispatching teen after teen with a patented witty quip. But this, of course, hardly makes them comedies: in the laughter stakes he's not on a patch on the scarily funny **Marty Feldman** as the crazy, lumbering Igor in Mel Brooks' *Young Frankenstein* (1974).

Each cinematic horror icon gets its own treatment in the comedy genre. Ghosts are the most benign, as a rule, facing off against **Bob Hope** in *The Ghost Breakers* (1940), and against Bill Murray and the team in *Ghostbusters* (1984); leaving Scotland for America in *The Ghost Goes West* (1936); and saving Gene Tierney from a bad marriage in *The Ghost and Mrs. Muir* (1947). Vampires have more of a bite to them, and pop up everywhere – **George Hamilton** sent up both the genre and his perma-tanned playboy image in *Love At First Bite* (1979), while **Mel Brooks** got

the piece to modern-day New York, where the team of Ghostbusters fortuitously come together just as a demon decides to come to life and invade New York's Upper West Side. It was Reitman, too, who persuaded Aykroyd to take Ramis on board as cowriter and eventual costar. The lead role of Peter Venkman was earmarked for Aykroyd's erstwhile partner in comedy crime (and fellow Blues Brother) **John Belushi**, but his untimely death in 1982 led to fellow *SNL* graduate Bill Murray stepping into the soon-to-be-slimed boots.

It proved to be a great move: the team gelled perfectly on screen, aided by **Ernie Hudson**'s wisecracking fourth ghostbuster Winston Zeddmore (a role once mooted for Eddie Murphy). The movie knew from the off that it was bucking for iconic status, and certainly achieved it: lines such as "Who ya gonna call?" and "We came, we

into his usual parody act (as always, just a few years too late) seeking to send up 1992's *Bram Stoker's Dracula* with *Dracula – Dead And Loving It* (1995). Eddie Murphy proved his vulnerability more than his versatility when he tried to meld his comic instincts with his love for horror movies in Wes Craven's execrable *Vampire in Brooklyn* (1995).

Werewolves too have had their comic moments, never more so than in John Landis' seminal *An American Werewolf In London* (1981). **Michael J. Fox**'s high school outing as *Teen Wolf* (1985) was an altogether more disappointing affair. Zombies have also been well represented in the comedy crossover, never more so than in *Braindead* (1992), an early splatter-fest from Oscar-winning *Lord Of The Rings* director Peter Jackson, in which a domestic lawn mower became a thing of mass gore-emitting destruction. *Shaun of the Dead* proved both a sincere homage to the work of zombie-master **George Romero** and one of the best British comedies in years when it was released in 2004. Previous British horror comedies may well have peaked in the late 1960s and early 1970s with the likes of *Carry On Screaming* (1966) and *The House In Nightmare Park* (1973), the latter featuring the incomparable **Frankie Howerd** as a Victorian thesp trapped in a haunted house.

Sometimes it's movies, rather than creatures, that inspire the comedy-horror film – **Wes Craven**'s tongue-firmly-in-cheek *Scream* trilogy of the mid-1990s, for example, breathed new life into a form that was becoming static and begat the parodic *Scary Movie* series (2000), while *The Exorcist* (1973) was the prime inspiration for *Repossessed* (1990), which featured the source movie's **Linda Blair** among its cast, alongside veteran off the spoof **Leslie Nielsen**.

saw, we kicked its ass" became instant catchphrases, delivered as they were by these modern-day cowboys, guns in hand, riding in to save the town in a reconditioned souped-up ambulance. *Ghostbusters* became more than just a runaway comedy hit – it was a pop culture phenomenon, with the call-and-response of **Ray Parker Jr.**'s catchy theme song dominating radios across the world throughout the summer of 1984. At one point US TV started showing the Ghostbusters agency's own advert from the movie as the ad for the film, adding a real number to call – the line received a thousand calls an hour, 24 hours a day, for six weeks.

It's easy to view *Ghostbusters* as a cynical exercise in marketing – especially given the fact that various extras hold up T-shirts emblazoned with the movie's logo (a "No Ghosts" sign, complete with red line through the middle) in its climactic moments. The resounding success of *Ghostbusters*, however, is that it roots itself in reality. For all the expensive effects and the spectral goings on, we recognize the team as real people, and the romance that develops between Murray and the Ghostbusters client played by **Sigourney Weaver** feels natural. At heart, *Ghostbusters* is a rare comedy about heroism and friendship. It's also one of the great city movies, a homage to New York made by a group of guys from Chicago and Canada. As Winston says at the end "I love this town!" – and clearly they did.

The Gold Rush

dir **Charles Chaplin, 1925, US, 82m, b/w**
cast **Charles Chaplin, Mack Swain, Georgia Hale, Tom Murray, Henry Bergman** *cin* **Roland Totheroh & Jack Wilson**

For many people, *The Gold Rush* remains Charlie Chaplin's masterpiece – he certainly intended it to be so when he began making it in 1924. Inspired by a photo of a line of prospectors in the 1896 Yukon gold rush he had seen at **Douglas Fairbanks** and **Mary Pickford**'s house, Chaplin set out to find the humour in the arduous, life-threatening struggle these pioneers had endured. Chaplin was to play his usual tramp-like figure, renaming him the

"Lone Prospector" and relocating him to the wind and snow of the Chilkoot Pass, dodging bears and dealing with evil fellow opportunists, all of them snowbound and hungry.

Chaplin, who initially veered between calling the film *The Lucky Strike* and *The Northern Story*, quickly set about building the movie's elaborate sets, including the prospector's log cabin, which is balanced precariously on the edge of a ravine (it was operated in the studio by an elaborate system of pulleys), and adding bears and teams of dogs to the shoot. Perhaps the film's most memorable sequence – in which the starving Chaplin takes off and eats his boot, winding the laces up like the finest spaghetti, all to the consternation of the brutish **Mack Swain** – was indicative of Chaplin's meticulous approach to his work, taking as it did 63 takes and three days to film. (The shoe and laces were in fact made from liquorice, and Chaplin was taken to hospital with insulin poisoning after the shot was complete.) Another classic scene, the so-called "Dance Of The Rolls", in which the Tramp/Prospector character makes two bread rolls dance on the table top, was also painstakingly executed – despite *The Gold Rush* being a silent, Chaplin employed musicians on set so he could time his moves perfectly.

All told, Chaplin spent 15 months shooting the film, followed by nine frantic weeks holed up in the editing room putting together his longest movie to date. Although not the immediate box office hit he had hoped for, it slowly went on to become a financial success. What was more assured from the off was the criti-

Meticulously planned mirth - *The Gold Rush* (1925)

cal response, which was as unanimous in its praise as Chaplin felt it should be. When the movie was released in England, the BBC went so far as to stage a broadcast from the Tivoli Theatre in London's Strand of "the laughter of the audience ... during the ten most uproariously funny minutes of the new Charlie Chaplin film, *The Gold Rush*".

Good Morning, Vietnam

dir Barry Levinson, 1987, US, 108m
cast Robin Williams, Forest Whitaker, Bruno Kirby, Robert Wuhl, J.T. Walsh, Richard Edson cin Peter Sova m Alex North

Upon its release in 1987, *Good Morning, Vietnam* managed two impressive feats. Firstly, it brought humour to the subject of the Vietnam War, previously the province of such nightmarish jungle-bound cinematic psychodramas as *The Deer Hunter* (1978) and *Apocalypse Now* (1979). Secondly, after several years of unsuccessful attempts, here was a movie that finally knew what to do with **Robin Williams**.

There was no denying that Williams was an amazing comic talent. On his debut TV sitcom, *Mork & Mindy* (1978–82), he had been given

Robin Williams finds a vehicle

unprecedented free rein to improvise on camera before a live studio audience, a risky move for prime-time TV but the only way possible to capture his free-associating, hyper-kinetic abilities. Similarly, his stand-up work was just about the best in the business. But on film, he had floundered. By the mid 1980s, following such weak efforts as *The Best of Times* (1986) and *Club Paradise* (1986), Williams's cinema career looked like it could be over. Levinson knew just what to do, however: just turn on the camera and let Williams go.

Before he could do this, of course, he had to find the right vehicle, and he found it in the story of airman Adrian Cronauer. Though Mitch Markowitz's original screenplay transformed him into an anti-authority figure, Cronauer was an armed services DJ during the Vietnam war, and his wake up catch-phrase was indeed "Gooooood Moooooorning Vietnaaaahhm!" But according to Cronauer's own testimony, this was about as wacky as he ever got on air. The rest was pure Williams. Upon filming, Levinson covered his performer using several cameras, turned on the mic and let Williams roll. The result was a barrage of comedy expression, with Williams touching on everything from Nixon's testicles to Ho Chi Minh meeting the Wizard of Oz. It was, in short, a hell of a turn, and one that not only secured Williams's subsequently hugely successful film career but also landed him an Oscar nomination as Best Actor.

But there is more to *Good Morning, Vietnam* than Williams. In 1965, the year in which the film was set, the US presence in Vietnam was not yet the political albatross and international cause of protest it was to become. Few back home were really taking it very seriously – so why should Cronauer and co? But Levinson gives us constant signs that things are changing. The ever-present teletype machine keeps us abreast of the rising number of troops being deployed; Cronauer's meeting with a convoy of green infantry men on their way to battle reminds us of the human cost of these soldiers – and the youth; and a nascent romance between Cronauer and a local girl (Chintara Sukapatana) demonstrates that the Americans simply do not belong in this land.

By the time Cronauer ships out, he is a wiser man. He has been irrevocably tainted by his experiences in Vietnam, like America itself. The movie closes to the poignant strains of Louis Armstrong's "What A Wonderful World", a song which gains an added emotional punch from the irony the context gives it.

The Graduate

dir **Mike Nichols, 1967, US, 108m**
cast **Dustin Hoffman, Anne Bancroft, Katharine Ross, William Daniels** *cin* **Robert Surtees** *m* **David Grusin**

Comedy movies are often noted for their quotable lines, gags that become part of the popular lexicon. Strange, then, that *The Graduate*, one of the most influential satires in the history of American cinema, is often remembered for one word – "plastics" – uttered to its nominal hero Benjamin Braddock (**Dustin Hoffman**) at a party his parents host to celebrate his college graduation. It's barked at him by a family friend as career advice, but in the context of **Mike Nichols'** scathing look at his own middle-class culture in the late 1960s, it sounds more like some kind of prison sentence. Ben certainly takes it that way, leading him to turn his unfocused, alienated attention to the wife of one of his father's business partners – a certain Mrs Robinson (**Anne Bancroft**).

Mike Nichols began his stage career as part of a stand up/improvisational double-act with **Elaine May**, who would herself turn filmmaker and writer with such movies as 1972's *The Heartbreak Kid* (which shares many concerns with *The Graduate*) and 1970's *A New Leaf* (with a superb Walter Matthau). We won't mention *Ishtar* (1987).

The Graduate began life as a slender novel by **Charles Webb**, its protagonist Ben being something of a comic take on Salinger's disaffected Holden Caulfield. The book was decent enough, but the screenplay that Buck Henry and Calder Willingham derived from it was altogether stronger. This is a youth movie that not only deals with the disaffection of the young and the lost, but shows how that same loss of self permeates their families and their background. **Robert Redford** was an early choice for Ben, while **Doris Day** was considered for Mrs Robinson – after both turned him down, Nichols wisely opted for the sultry charms of Anne Bancroft and cast the then largely unknown Dustin Hoffman opposite. In reality there were only seven years between them – Hoffman was 29 (playing 21), and Bancroft 36 – but on screen he played the innocent and she played the temptress to perfection.

The Graduate was a radical film in many ways. Firstly, it identified a youth market that simply wasn't being catered for at the time in Hollywood. This was a movie that defined the generation gap before the phrase even existed. Nichols' visual style was bold and unusual for a comedy, influenced by the French *nouvelle vague* movies that had become a staple of the East Coast arthouse scene throughout the mid 1960s. Though it now looks very much of its time, that's largely because it was one of the movies which defined its time: its bright, glaring, saturated colours providing an expansiveness that parallels the distances between the movie's characters and the vacuums within them. The movie's closing shot (which *The Simpsons* neatly parodied at the end of an episode charting Grandpa Simpson's OAP fling: a very funny reverse-generation pastiche) has an uneasy ambivalence to it. The two lovers sit side by side, unspeaking, looking blankly ahead.

Finally, not content with a standard orchestral soundtrack, Nichols brought songwriter **Paul Simon** on board, to write songs tailor-made for the film, making *The Graduate* just about the first movie to be scored entirely to pop music. Serendipity lent a hand when Simon proved to be a slow worker – Nichols cut the movie to pre-existing Simon and Garfunkel songs including "The Sound Of Silence" and "Scarborough Fair"; then, realizing they captured Ben's feelings of loss and uncertainty, left them in. In the end the only original song Simon provided was "Mrs Robinson" itself, and even that he didn't finish on time, only a brief snatch of the chorus surfacing as Ben struggles to get to the wedding of Elaine Robinson (Katharine Ross) – Mrs Robinson's daughter – and the one he thinks he really loves.

Nichols and co gave the world a new star in Hoffman and an abiding older woman fantasy in Mrs. Robinson – giving a name to an archetype that has become common currency. He also radically changed the face of cinema while he was at it. There's not many comedy movies you can say that about; here's to you, Mrs Robinson indeed.

Groundhog Day

dir **Harold Ramis, US, 1993, 101m**

cast **Bill Murray, Andie MacDowell, Chris Elliot, Stephen Tobolowsky** *cin* **John Bailey** *m* **George Fenton**

Capraesque small town romance? Modern day morality tale? Buddhist parable? Arguably the best mainstream American comedy of the 1990s? *Groundhog Day* is all these things and many more. It begins with a very basic premise – what would you do if you could live the same day over again? Then it ups the stakes and asks what would you do if you could live the same day over and over and over... and over again ad infinitum. This is the fate that befalls cynical TV weatherman Phil Connors (**Bill Murray**) – the fact that it's a fate that is never explained only adds to the film's overall magic.

Groundhog Day itself is a real festival that takes place in the real town of Punxsutawney in Pennsylvania on the date of February 2 every year, and it involves a real groundhog. This is where the reality ends. Legend has it that if on this day the groundhog sees his shadow, winter will continue for several more months. Initially trapped in the town overnight by his inability to predict an incoming blizzard, when Phil awakes the next morning he hears the same radio broadcast, has the same conversations and finds himself having to do the same broadcast as the day before. Yet again, he is trapped by the same blizzard. The same thing happens the next day, and the next ... and so on.

Phil goes through a series of emotions that range from confusion and fear to smug delight in his new-found power (he learns over the course of the days just how to seduce the local women – and if it doesn't work one day, there's always tomorrow) to delusions of deity-level grandeur ("I'm *a* God ... not *the* God ... I don't think ..."). Soon desperation and denial set in – but when even suicide fails to rid him of the inexplicable curse, he is steadily forced into acceptance. Slowly he becomes part of the community and begins a series of daily chores – catching a boy who falls out of a tree the same time every day, saving the mayor from choking at dinner, and rescuing a destitute bum who dies in the cold that night. Along the way he becomes a master pianist and ice sculptor, all the while trying to woo his producer Rita (**Andie MacDowell**), the one thing he can never seem to get right.

What could have become bogged down in mawkish sentimentality is here kept continually fresh – partly by throwing Murray's essentially cynical urbanite into the milieu of picture-postcard small-town American life. It's a vicarious delight to watch Murray doing anything he wants to, knowing that there's no tomorrow: punching out irritating insurance salesmen, robbing the cash delivery at the local bank; and drinking, smoking and stuffing his face with every cake in the café.

Secondly, full marks must go to long-time Murray collaborator **Harold Ramis**, whose direction has never been better. Building up, and then showing variations on, the same scenes allows Ramis to offer a commentary on the nature of filmmaking itself, showing us what amounts to a number of subtly altered takes, much as Phil must work through how he feels about all the daily events of his newly cirumscribed existence in order to make his life work out. *Groundhog Day* remains one of the cleverest American comedies of recent years, and also one of the warmest; if this is indeed a nightmare Phil is living through, it's one you never really want to wake up from. Interestingly, on his DVD commentary, Ramis said that the original idea was to have Phil stranded in Punxsutawney for 10,000 years.

A Hard Day's Night

dir Richard Lester, 1964, UK, 85m, b/w
cast John Lennon, Paul McCartney, George Harrison, Ringo Starr, Wilfred Brambell, Norman Rossington, Victor Spinetti *cin* Gilbert Taylor *m* John Lennon & Paul McCartney

Few films capture a moment as well as Richard Lester's semi-fictionalized saga of the mop-tops' day-in-the-life, *A Hard Day's Night*. Full of energy from the outset, it has a brilliantly ridiculous opening: three of the four most famous men in the world run down the road to a train station, one of them falls flat on his face, the others laugh, all whilst being pursued, of course, by the obligatory hordes of screaming girls (plus a very young **Phil Collins**). **Alun Owen**'s screenplay, too, is a thing of beauty, highlighting each Beatle's individuality – John Lennon is acerbic, possibly dangerous, but still lovable, McCartney is Mr Nice Guy (a persona he still banks on), George is a little mysterious (probably "quiet but deadly" is the best way to sum him up), and Ringo is, well, Ringo, but ended up being touted by one critic as a natural heir to Chaplin.

Their force-of-nature irreverence is captured brilliantly in the moment when Lennon confronts a city gent in a first-class train carriage by cooing: "Give us a kiss!" It's right up there with George's real-life one-liners: his deadpan response to a facile journalist who asked him what he called his haircut was, famously, "Arthur".

The Beatles would follow up *A Hard Day's Night* the following year – once again with Lester – with the wackier, all-colour (though less satisfying) *Help!*, invent the psychedelic cartoon with 1968's *Yellow Submarine*, and implode in the anything but amusing falling apart documentary *Let It Be* (1970). But this is their best screen work, a film that not only perfectly captures the biggest band in the world, but also the world they lived in.

The fact that Lester shot his film in black and white was a necessity that plays in the movie's favour. It's a direct consequence of the film financiers deeming the Fab Four too risky to invest in the use of colour – unthinkable now, given that this was possibly the height of what was to become known as Beatlemania. But the black and white images seem emblematic of Britain at a moment of change – World War II was very much within living memory, rationing had recently ended, and the 45rpm pop single, along with a new-fangled concept called the "teenager", had entered the national consciousness.

Perhaps even more so than any of the celebrated British kitchen-sink dramas – *Look Back In Anger* (1959), *Saturday Night And Sunday Morning* (1960), *The Loneliness Of The Long Distance Runner* (1962) – this film shows Britain as it was at that singular, transitional moment. For young people at least, with minds of their own and a new spending power to put their ideas into action, this was a world just about to turn from black and white into colour. More than anything, Lester's film stands the test of time because it defines the era it stood in. And did we mention the music? That's pretty damn good too.

His Girl Friday

dir **Howard Hawks, 1939, US, 92m, b/w**
cast **Cary Grant, Rosalind Russell, Ralph Bellamy, Gene Lockhart, Porter Hall** *cin* **Joseph Walker** *m* **Morris W Stoloff**

Also known as the fastest talking movie in town. Somebody once clocked the dialogue between **Cary Grant** and his girl **Rosalind Russell** as running at an average of 240 words per minute. It doesn't

A word in edgeways?

even bear thinking about. What does bear thinking about is how splendid an example of the screwball genre *His Girl Friday* is. And while it's fair to say that the Hollywood movie industry does indeed dominate the world, this film suggests why that might be – because it offsets incredible cynicism with incredible warmth.

Reporter Hildy Johnson (Russell) and her ex-husband, editor Walter Burns (Grant), have been in the newspaper game for a long time, possibly longer than is good for the health of either of them. They see the world through unpleasantly coloured glasses, knowing how to sell a story and standing behind the notion that ethics are for the other guy. Yet when it comes down to it – in this case when covering a story of a man wrongly placed on Death Row – they both know that what's right is right, even if it won't sell more copies of their rag. And it's in that sentiment that this movie – adapted from the popular play *The Front Page* by **Ben Hecht** and **Charles**

MacArthur, which usually featured two male leads and was here given a gender twist courtesy of Russell – finds its soul.

It's a genuine romance. For all the subplots involving wrongly accused innocents and women down on their luck, what we most care about is whether Hildy and Walter will reunite. Their courtship has to move at a frantic pace because that's how the world around these characters moves. It's no coincidence that Ralph Bellamy, playing Hildy's dull fiancé, who hopes to take her away from all this, delivers his dialogue at a completely different speed – he's clearly not part of their hectic world, and as such can never really make an impact.

Hollywood lore has it that Hawks was originally planning on casting the film as the play had it, with two men. It was only the fact that he had auditioning actors read for their roles opposite his secretary that he noticed how well the dialogue worked with a woman. It was an inspired move, one which took a story about moral dilemmas and personal ethics, and turned it into a wonderfully original battle of the sexes. *His Girl Friday* is one of the genuine jewels in the screwball crown.

It Happened One Night

dir **Frank Capra, 1934, US, 105m, b/w**
cast **Clark Gable, Claudette Colbert, Walter Connolly, Roscoe Karns** *cin* **Joseph Walker** *m* **Louis Silvers**

In which Hollywood invents the road movie... A classic screwball picture, *It Happened One Night* features **Claudette Colbert** as spoiled heiress Ellie Andrews, on the run having just made a marriage deemed close to scandalous. She jumps off the family yacht to make it back to her new husband in New York, but along the way meets out-of-work reporter Peter Warne (**Clark Gable**) on the bus. He knows a story when he sees one and offers to help her, in return for a scoop on the tale of course. Together they hitchhike through

Depression-era USA and, inevitably, break down each other's well-maintained facades and fall in love. There's also a whole other thing about Clark Gable and vests, but we'll come back to that.

The movie triumphed at the Oscars. It was the first ever film to pick up the top five awards for Best Picture, Actor, Actress, Director and Screenplay: a real vindication, given how little faith many people had in it. Clark Gable was actually being punished in making it. Under contract at the time to MGM, who disapproved of his rather hectic off-screen activities, Gable was loaned out to the smaller Columbia studio in order to teach him a lesson. When he picked up his statuette, the joke, of course, was on them. (**Robert Montgomery** had originally turned down the role, saying the script was the worst thing he'd ever read. So he probably wasn't feeling too chipper that Oscar night either.) For her part, Colbert was so unenamoured of the film that she didn't even bother to show up on Oscar night – until word came through that she'd won, when she was rushed to the theatre.

Odd couple, Clark Gable and Claudette Colbert

That the principal talents behind this much-loved movie thought so little of it may well have been symptomatic of many actors' and directors' prejudice that screen comedy in general didn't have much to offer them. Thankfully, this was an attitude that **Frank Capra** never shared, and with *It Happened One Night* he rapidly established himself as one of the premier filmmakers of his day. Oh yes, and that vest – well, it is said that when Gable stripped off his shirt, revealing the fact he was not wearing one, sales of the undergarment plummeted. It's also rumoured that Gable's eating of a carrot while talking at the same time inspired **Bugs Bunny**'s trademark chomping style. All this from a film that no one seemed to want to make!

Kind Hearts And Coronets

dir **Robert Hamer, 1949, UK, 106m, b/w**
cast **Dennis Price, Alec Guinness, Valerie Hobson, Joan Greenwood** *cin* **Douglas Slocombe**

One of Ealing's most unusual but nonetheless exemplary films, *Kind Hearts And Coronets* takes its title from a Tennyson quote – "Kind hearts are more than coronets/And simple faith than Norman blood" – and introduces one of cinema's first serial killers to undermine the notions of nobility and inherited privilege that the film plays with. **Dennis Price** stars as the impoverished Louis Mazzini, who sees himself as the rightful heir to the Dukedom of Chalfont, and who sets out to claim it in a series of cold-blooded but often hilarious murders.

Eight relatives stand between Louis and his birthright, and director Hamer introduced the then-unprecedented notion of having **Alec Guinness** play all of them. His *tour-de-force* performance as every single member of the D'Ascoyne family – young and old, male and female – secured his reputation as one of Britain's finest screen actors. Some of these roles are extended character pieces, some register as little more than brief cameos – witness the Admiral who goes down with his ship – but each is separated from the another by Guinness's brilliant ability for characterization.

As versatile as Guinness is before the camera, he is well met by director and cowriter **Robert Hamer** behind it. Once described by Guinness as a man who "looked and sounded like an endearing but scornful frog", it is Hamer who makes this essentially morbid material comically macabre while also acceptable and even entertaining. He sets the tone instantly with the arrival of the hangman at the jail now holding Mazzini, debating whether to call his intended victim "your Grace" or not – this is after all a comedy of gentility, despite the venality of the man in question. The rest of the movie is then told in flashback as we chart Mazzini's early days ("In those days I never had any trouble with the sixth commandment"), rich in black comedy as he recounts that his father died in childbirth, while his mother was hit by a train. The young boy grows up and, still stung by the fact he had to bury his mother in a suburban public cemetery, sets about wreaking his revenge.

Kind Hearts And Coronets is a delicate balancing act between bad taste and good manners, and remains probably the only movie that can sell the death of two babies by diphtheria as a convincingly comic moment. It's also one of the best films produced on the finest comedy production line Britain ever saw (and yes, that does include the *Carry On*s). Ealing Studios would continue from strength to strength but, with the exception of *The Ladykillers* (1955), it would never dabble in such splendidly dark material again.

The Ladykillers

dir **Alexander Mackendrick, 1955, UK, 97min**
cast **Alec Guinness, Herbert Lom, Cecil Parker, Peter Sellers, Katie Johnson, Jack Warner, Danny Green** *cin* **Otto Heller** *m* **Tristram Cary**

The Ladykillers was in the same dark territory as its previous Ealing stable-mate *Kind Hearts And Coronets* (1949) and, in a typically knowing in-joke, the portrait of Mrs Wilberforce's husband that you can see is actually a picture of **Alec Guinness**'s Admiral from

Kind hearts? The many faces of Alec Guiness

that earlier film. In many ways it's a fine companion piece, and is certainly Mackendrick's best film (though his American-set *Sweet Smell Of Success* from 1957 is an arguable contender). What he came up with here was his swan song for Ealing – it was the last film he made before moving to America – a blackly perfect, brilliantly delivered comedy that more or less said goodbye to the finest, and most influential, comedy production house English cinema ever produced.

Five felons (Guinness, Lom, Sellers, Green and Parker) plan a robbery. Their cover is to rent rooms nearby from an elderly landlady called Mrs Wilberforce (**Katie Johnson**), posing as a respectable classical music quintet, using gramophone players to fake their practice while planning their heist. Unfortunately for them, the aged Mrs Wilberforce is by no means the fool they've taken her for, and when she discovers their true motives and demands they give themelves up, it's up to one of the gang to bump her off. Only they can't. None of them can bring themselves to do it: treachery and mistrust sets in, one by one their fates are comically sealed, and the gang eventually falls to pieces.

Mackendrick had previously set the benchmark for Ealing comedy with both *Whisky Galore!* (1949) and *The Man In The White Suit* (1951), and more than anything – as was always a trait of Ealing – the film is impeccably well cast. Johnson is a very British sort of daffy elderly lady, while **Herbert Lom** is brilliantly slimy. **Peter Sellers** is young and eager, welcoming, one senses, the chance to flex his notable acting chops alongside Guinness, who wisely underplays his role to convey, at times, a quietly unnerving sense of real threat. He is surely the only one in this motley crew who might stand up to the formidable Mrs Wilberforce.

William Rose's script was Oscar nominated. It failed to pick up a gong, but both he and Johnson did manage the trick at the BAFTAs of 1956. In 2004, the **Coen Brothers** teamed up to remake the film, relocating it to the Deep South and casting **Tom Hanks** in the Alec Guinness role. It had its moments, but it's a testament to the mordant strength of Mackendrick's original that it seemed rather toothless all in all.

Local Hero

dir **Bill Forsyth, 1983, UK, 111m**

cast **Burt Lancaster, Peter Riegert, Denis Lawson, Fulton Mackay, Peter Capaldi, Jenny Seagrove** *cin* **Chris Menges** *m* **Mark Knopfler**

By the time he came to make **Local Hero**, Scottish writer-director Bill Forsyth was something of a local hero himself. The previous year his breakthrough film, *Gregory's Girl*, the tale of a gawky teenage boy's love for a football-playing girl, had single-handedly awoken the world to the notion that such a thing as a Scottish film industry might actually exist. Buoyed by that success, Forsyth teamed up with newly Oscar-winning producer David Puttnam (fresh from the award-laden *Chariots of Fire*, 1981) and set about making a film that dealt with American interest in, and exploitation of, North Sea oil (Forsyth claimed he originally saw it as a Scottish *Beverly Hillbillies*). The result was a total delight, an instant classic that dealt with contemporary issues but also found a timeless sense of magic realism, echoing both the best of Ealing and a **Frank Capra**esque vision of small-town life transplanted from the USA to the Highlands.

Clearly relishing his role as an eccentric millionaire oil magnate, **Burt Lancaster** sets events in motion when he sends junior-exec-on-the-rise Mac (Riegert) off to Scotland to check out a large section of coastline they want to buy up to build a refinery. As Mac constantly reminds us, in a line that dates the film, he is a "telex man", and can at first see no point in having to go into the field to close the deal. But when he arrives in the small seaside town he is planning to buy, Mac's opinions slowly start to change and his personality transforms as the people and ways of this idyllic town start to win him over.

Owing more than a passing nod to the ensemble playing of Ealing's best comedies (1949's *Whisky Galore!*, with its Scottish setting, being the obvious example here), *Local Hero*'s town overflows with finely drawn characters and quirky detail: Urquhart (Lawson) the pub owner, cook and accountant; the bar regulars, always willing to cough up their ten-pence pieces so the American can phone home; the visiting Russian trawlerman who regularly jumps ship and shows up for a ceilidh; and the supposedly rebellious young motorbike rider (a cameo from **John Gordon Sinclair**, better known as Gregory in *Gregory's Girl*) who roars through the town streets, never seeming to get anywhere.

One of the great strengths of Forsyth's movie is undoubtedly the score by **Mark Knopfler** (then of Dire Straits), a mixture of local sounds and bluesy guitars, which culminates in the film's triumphant end theme "Going Home". Ironically, the film itself was not a great success on its initial release, but Knopfler's soundtrack was a big hit, outgrossing the movie it came from.

Forsyth's subsequent career has been something of a disappointment, with a move to America prompting the uninspired *Housekeeping* (1987) and *Breaking In* (1989), and a return to home leading to the erratic *Being Human* (1994), a failed epic look at life through the ages with Robin Williams, and the frankly disastrous *Gregory's Two Girls* (1999).

But *Local Hero*, his finest work by far, remains a film that determinedly sets its own pace and gives you a real sense of place. More witty than laugh-out-loud funny, it has moments of great sweetness. Its ending – as we return home with Mac to his empty city apartment, then cut to the town's phone box ringing (presumably Mac calling "home") – is one of the most perfectly poignant endings in modern cinema.

Manhattan

dir **Woody Allen, 1979, US, 96m, b/w**

cast **Woody Allen, Diane Keaton, Mariel Hemingway, Michael Murphy, Meryl Streep** *cin* **Gordon Willis** *m* **George Gershwin**

Both **Woody Allen** and **Steve Martin** have penned, in their own very different ways, hymns to their native towns, and both have found themselves awash in the romance that each disparate city evokes within them.

Mythological, romantic New York

Twelve years before Martin's *L.A. Story*, Allen did it old-school style, drenching the city he loved in a glorious sheen of black and white photography. **George Gershwin**'s *Rhapsody in Blue* was chucked in on the soundtrack for good measure. This was the New York that Woody Allen mythologized, a Runyonesque world in which people dined in great restaurants, met real characters and fell in love with women far too young for them. As one line puts it, "I'm 42 and she's 17. I'm older than her father, can you believe that? I'm dating a girl wherein I can beat up her father."

Manhattan was ostensibly his follow-up to the huge success of *Annie Hall* (if you don't count *Interiors*, and most people don't). In many ways, it may be Allen's most autobiographical film (although he'd deny that) in that by showing the soul of the city, it captures the soul of the man. He casts himself as yet another comedy writer riddled with existential angst: he's never got over the fact that his ex-wife (**Meryl Streep**) became a lesbian and left him for another woman, one he tried to run over. He sublimates such anxiety by romancing the inappropriately young, but radiant, **Mariel Hemingway**. **Diane Keaton** – a contemporary who is having an affair with Allen's married best friend – shows up to throw his notions of love into disarray, one of those scenarios that the romanticized streets of Allen's New York City typically engineer.

The standout moment comes when Allen lies alone on a couch recounting the things that he genuinely loves. The litany includes his jazz heroes, his sports heroes, **Groucho Marx**, the city (obviously) and the smile of the girl he realizes he really does care for. Her final line to him – "Everybody gets corrupted. You have to have a little faith in people" – makes this the most bittersweet of his movies.

At the time of completing the film, Allen was so disappointed with his work that he told United Artists he would give them another movie for free if they were to keep all existing copies permanently on the shelf. Thankfully they were smarter than that, and realized what they had here. Despite Woody's protestations this may well remain his enduring masterpiece, a film that not only captures all his usual obsessions – comedy, sex, death, younger women, neurosis and New York – but also finds the perfect balance for them. Woody was definitely wrong on that one.

M*A*S*H

dir **Robert Altman, 1970, US, 116m**
cast **Donald Sutherland, Elliot Gould, Robert Duvall, Sally Kellerman** *cin* **Harold Stein** *m* **Johnny Mandel**

Right from the off, it was clear that *M*A*S*H*, a film ostensibly about the Korean War of the 1950s, was really much more concerned with examining the Vietnam War that was still raging, dividing America and the world. Its scenes may have been set in a field hospital as opposed to the battlefield itself, but they were equally steeped in blood and carnage and the loss of young lives. However, hope was also present, in the form of the surgeons and nurses who populated the O.R. of the 4077th MASH (Mobile Army Surgical Hospital), who worked to save those lives. **Robert Altman** was determined not to glamorize the actions of these people: he concentrated instead on their disdain and hatred of being there, and their contempt and lack of respect for those who had put them there. As with just about every military comedy, it took the proverbial anti-authority stance, but *M*A*S*H* also thrived on the kind of modern black satire with which **Stanley Kubrick** had imbued *Dr. Strangelove* (see Canon) seven years earlier. The long-running TV series that followed the movie two years later may have taken a more humanist, liberal approach to proceedings, but that was not for Altman.

   *M*A*S*H* was adapted by screenwriter **Ring Lardner Jr**, blacklisted in the McCarthy era, from a novel (later a popular series of novels) by one Richard Hooker, which was a pseudonym for Richard Hornberger, himself a doctor who had served in a MASH unit in Korea. Lardner would pick up the film's only Academy Award for his troubles, although he claimed that very little of his script actually made

Serious laughs with the Mobile Army Surgical Hospital

it up on the screen – hardly surprising given Altman's penchant for improvisation.

At the time of production, 20th Century Fox was also working on the World War II epics *Patton* and *Tora! Tora! Tora!*, and *M*A*S*H* was very much seen as the poor relation. So much so, in fact, that initially it proved near-impossible to find a director, with everyone from Stanley Kubrick to George Roy Hill to Bud Yorkin turning it down. Altman, with very few credits to his name, was low down the list. In many ways he found his style with *M*A*S*H* before going on to become one of the 1970's most influential maverick directors. Here he displayed for the first time his fondness for grainy, grimy and often hand-held photography, coupled with his use of overlap-

Comedy on parade

When comedy meets authority, its first impulse is to lampoon it, hold it up to the world and point out its inherent flaws. It's a basic drive, and dates back beyond even the earliest days of film. There is just something innately comic about a well-oiled machine marching in perfect unison, all except for that one loose cog, as **Charlie Chaplin** knew well in *Shoulder Arms* (1918): the one private unable to keep up, going the wrong way and dropping his pack, gun and more. It's one of the fundamental tenets of comedy – chaos undermining order.

Given that the century in which cinema came to flourish featured two of the big ones (three, if you count Vietnam) – it's natural that World Wars I and II especially have had their fair share of comic abuse. Thus we find Depression-era comedy geniuses **Laurel and Hardy** donning uniform for *Great Guns* (1941), dealing with the child of a dead comrade in arms in *Pack Up Your Troubles* (1932), and even having a pop at the French Foreign Legion in both 1931's *Beau Hunks* and 1939's *The Flying Deuces*. Their somewhat inferior successors Abbott and Costello tackled the khaki pants of authority in 1940's *Buck Privates*, determined to prove to American audiences that this whole war thing was really gonna be a lot of fun. (They can probably also lay claim to inventing the cliché of the loud-as-hell and tough-as-old-boots drill sergeant.) Chaplin also tackled World War II during its run, with his altogether different and extremely brave broad swipe at Hitler in *The Great Dictator* (1940).

The British, meanwhile, have been less fond of making fun of our brave boys on the front lines (not counting 1968's *Carry On Up The Khyber*, of course). They have, however, delighted in the activities of those back home, from such classics as Ealing's 1949 comedy *Whisky Galore!* (the

ping, almost free-running dialogue. At times his cast weren't really sure he knew what he was doing, and the studio certainly didn't know what Altman was up to. But somehow he and his team managed to get away with it all: when *M★A★S★H* was released it became a huge box office success and, much to Fox's consternation, easily outstripped its other pair of war movies. The original tag line for the movie ran: "M★A★S★H gives a D★A★M★N". It turned out that its audience did too – in their droves.

M★A★S★H not only proved to be a significant influence on the nature of 1970s American cinema, but also spawned two other legacies: the long-running TV series, which saw **Alan Alda** step in for Sutherland's Hawkeye Pierce and **Wayne Rogers** fill the regulation

effects, during wartime rationing, of an unexpected discovery of crates of booze), to the big-screen adaptation of TV's eternally popular *Dad's Army* (daffy old geezers protect Blighty from the dreaded Hun).

WWII comedy movies have also been tinged with nostalgia, with many prominent comic writers recalling their salad days in the services – in the UK we had **Spike Milligan** with the mixed adaptation of his wartime memoirs, *Adolf Hitler – My Part In His Downfall* (1972), while in America, **Neil Simon** turned in the delightfully bittersweet *Biloxi Blues* (1987), featuring the by now regulation issue homicidal drill sergeant, played to perfection by **Christopher Walken**. Nostalgia was present too in **Roberto Benigni**'s hugely successful *Life is Beautiful* (1997; see p.53), which used comedy to deal with devastatingly serious material.

Vietnam has proved a harder war to make fun of, probably as it was the first one we got to watch from the comfort of our own homes courtesy of television. *Good Morning, Vietnam* (see Canon) had a go by looking at the build-up to the war, while *Air America* (1990), starring **Mel Gibson** and **Robert Downey Jr.**, seemed to reduce it to little more than a backdrop.

The ZAZ team let the navy have it with *Hot Shots!* (1991; which largely aimed at the overblown *Top Gun*), and *Hot Shots Part Deux* (1993; which did in fact have a crack at 'Nam, via its Rambo pastiche). The modern military has also been the butt of a good few movies, to varying effect. 1981's hugely entertaining *Stripes* saw **Bill Murray** and co as foul-up volunteers forced into genuine action, whilst 1984's thoroughly misguided Eddie Murphy/Dudley Moore vehicle *Best Defence* attempted to make fun of American arms manufacture and dealing. In terms of more recent wars, David O. Russell's exemplary and ambitious *Three Kings* (1999) remains the yardstick by which the others – and there will surely be others to come – must be judged.

issue boots of Elliott Gould's Trapper; and its enduring theme song, "Suicide is Painless", with lyrics by Altman's then fifteen-year-old son, Michael, which hit the number one spot in the pop charts.

Monty Python's Life Of Brian

dir Terry Jones, 1979, UK, 93m

cast Graham Chapman, John Cleese, Terry Gilliam, Eric Idle, Terry Jones, Michael Palin *cin* Peter Biziou *m* Geoffrey Burgon

Graham Chapman and Terry Jones tackle religion

It was during the the promotional tour for *Monty Python And The Holy Grail* that, when asked what the title of the Pythons' next project would be, Eric Idle quipped: "Jesus Christ, Lust For Glory". It was an off-the-cuff comment. At that point, the group was dividing

and each performer was moving on to their own projects: Cleese with *Fawlty Towers*, Idle with *Rutland Weekend Television*, Jones and Palin with *Ripping Yarns*, and Gilliam turning solo director with *Jabberwocky* (1977). But something about Idle's joke stuck, and when the team reconvened to try their hand at another movie, they decided to tackle religion head-on.

The Life of Brian was the group's most cohesive script and was all set to shoot on location in Tunisia (a step up from the rain-swept Scottish Highlands of *Holy Grail*) when, at the eleventh hour, their financing was pulled on the grounds that the movie was deemed potentially offensive and blasphemous. Ex-Beatle **George Harrison** stepped into the breach, raising the £4 million needed to make the film – largely on the grounds that he really wanted to see it (leading Idle to comment that it was "the most expensive cinema ticket in history").

Life Of Brian saw the team tackling a subject they all had strong views on. While **Jesus Christ** does make a brief cameo appearance giving the Sermon On The Mount, the film focuses on Brian (Chapman, again taking a relatively straight lead), an ordinary Judean man who ends up being mistaken for a Messiah. Using this framework the team railed against organized religion in a bitingly satirical and extremely funny way, creating another array of memorable characters: from the Ex-Leper (out of a job begging now that Jesus has healed him); Michael Palin's 'Big Nose'; the bickering People's Judean Front (or the People's Front Of Judea – they never *could* make up their minds), and of course the speech-impedimented Pontius Pilate and his friend Biggus Dickus, with their campaign to "Welease Woger". All are immaculately silly.

On its release, the film proved even more controversial than its original backers had feared, prompting banning and protests in many parts of both America and Britain, where much of the criticism seemed unable to distance the character of Brian from Jesus. The Pythons were of course delighted with the fervent debate the film created. While there's religious satire aplenty, the film is much more about human beings, crowds and their failings: human comedy in the truest sense. It's crystallized in the scene in which Brian tells the crowd to go away and stop hanging on his every word, reminding them that they're all individuals. They repeat it en masse – "We're all individuals". Except one who doesn't agree. It's Python at its most perfect.

From small screen to big

When TV first took off, in the early-to-mid-1950s, it was seen as the potential death-knell of cinema. After all, who was going to go out to see movies if they could watch them at home for free? However, on more than one occasion, television has proved to be cinema's saviour. Think back to the British film industry of the 1970s. Take away a handful of Bonds, a couple of Pythons and some of the weaker *Carry Ons*, and there was precious little else. Enter, to the rescue, the British sitcom. At this time the general perception of British film- and TV-makers was that if it worked on the small screen, it could work on the big screen. Sometimes they were right, and sometimes they were very, very wrong. Their maxim gave us one *Dad's Army (1971)*, one *Porridge (1979)*, one *Likely Lads (1976)*, one *Are You Being Served? (1977)*, one case of *Rising Damp (1980)*, three trips *On The Buses* (the first being in 1971), and one *Man About The House* (1973). Kids got a look in when Florence and co took *The Magic Roundabout* for a spin down at the local flea pit in 1970's psychedelic reel *Dougal And The Blue Cat*, and those "Keep Britain Tidy" campaigners of Wimbledon Common, **The Wombles**, took both the pop charts and the multiplex by storm with 1977's *Wombling Free*.

American moviemakers also realized there was money in this kind of branding. Enter such contenders as *The Addams Family (1991)*, *The Brady Bunch Movie* (1995; a postmodern, ironic take on what had been a traditional, safe, 1970s' family sitcom), *McHale's Navy (1997)*, *The Beverly Hillbillies (1993)*, *My Favourite Martian (1998)*, *Sgt Bilko* (1996) and *Bewitched* (2005), to name but a few. This is not to say that you

National Lampoon's Animal House

dir **John Landis, 1978, US, 109m**
cast **John Belushi, Tim Matheson, John Vernon, Tom Hulce, Donald Sutherland, Kevin Bacon, Peter Riegert** *cin* **Charles Correll**

Modern American comedy cinema really begins with *National Lampoon's Animal House*. Previously, 1970s Hollywood had been

need a sitcom to come up with a spin-off comedy. An increasing trend has developed for taking old drama shows and giving them a comic/ironic big screen turn: witness **Tom Hanks** and **Dan Aykroyd** spoofing the beat of Sgt Joe Friday in *Dragnet* (1987), **Eddie Murphy** and **Owen Wilson** stepping into the tennis shoes of **Bill Cosby** and **Robert Culp** in *I, Spy* (2002), and Wilson (again) alongside **Ben Stiller** in a pastiche of 1970s' cop favourite *Starsky And Hutch* (2004).

Saturday morning TV cartoons (never the high end of the art of animation) have also provided a wellspring of cinematic entertainment, although the transition from 2-D drawings to 3-D actors has not always been successful. **John Goodman** brought Fred Flintstone to life in *The Flintstones* (1994; replaced by Mark Addy in its equally dreadful sequel). **Brendan Fraser** "watched out for that tree" as the musclebound incompetent *George Of The Jungle* (1997), all-girl band *Josie And The Pussycats* (2001) rocked into life, while *Scooby Doo* (2002) became "real" by virtue of CGI. *The Adventures Of Rocky And Bullwinkle* (2000) beat the hybrid path by keeping our titular heroes as cartoons and placing them alongside the less-than-animated **Robert DeNiro**; **Robin Williams** meanwhile found his obvious talents smothered beneath vast amounts of latex – and the penchant of his director, **Robert Altman**, for oddball dialogue – in *Popeye* (1980), an altogether more interesting movie that found little favour with either critics or audiences.

While TV series have provided much fodder for cinematic comedy, few have gone as far as taking what began as a commercial to the big screen. The one exception was **Rowan Atkinson** in *Johnny English* (2003), a lame spy spoof derived almost entirely from a series of adverts the comedian had done for Barclays Bank.

awash with star vehicles, diminishing-returns sequels and hymns to genres past – a safe cushion of films only occasionally punctured by the likes of **Mel Brooks** and, of course, **Woody Allen**.

With *Animal House* a number of elements that had been brewing since the late 1960s came to fruition. *The National Lampoon* was a countercultural humour magazine that had grown out of the university publication *The Harvard Lampoon*. It was read by the young, the hip and, quite often, the stoned – the same audience that tuned into TV's comedy show *Saturday Night Live* when it landed on late-night television in late 1975. While things were happening in stand-up, fuelled by the political challenges of **Richard Pryor** and the surreal absurdism of **Steve Martin**, this challenging school of humour had yet to fully cross over to the mainstream. With *Animal House* it came crashing through.

John Belushi is (President–to–be) Bluto Blutarsky

When **Doug Kenney**, the over-worked editor of *Lampoon*, tried to leave his job in 1976, he was persuaded to stay by the prospect of the magazine empire expanding into movies (they had already done very well on radio). Teaming up with *Second City* alumnus and *Lampoon* contributor **Harold Ramis** (see p.41), he wrote a screenplay entitled *Laser Orgy Girls,* a high-school comedy full of swearing, drinking, drug taking and sex. The concept was supposedly **Charles Manson** in high school. They decided that the content didn't really suit high school but would work in a college setting, and the idea of the fraternity comedy was born.

John Landis, fresh from the anarchic *Kentucky Fried Movie* (see p.5) and deemed to be the perfect director for the project, set about assembling a cast of unknowns, which included the likes of Kevin Bacon, Karen Allen, Peter Riegert, Tim Matheson and Tom Hulce. Its writers, noting that every animal house needs an animal, brought John Belushi on board in the iconic role of human zit and later President of the United States, Bluto Blutarsky (typical line: "Was it over when the Germans bombed Pearl Harbour?")

A simple tale of one outrageous frat-house's battle to beat an unfair system and an insanely vengeful faculty Dean, *Animal House* struck a huge chord with its

The *Saturday Night Live* effect

When a late-night, 90-minute live television show debuted on the American NBC network back in late 1975, nobody had any idea that it would come to dominate screen comedy for the next thirty years and perhaps beyond. Canadian **Lorne Michaels** – himself formerly part of a stand-up double act – was the mastermind behind it. His premise was simple: ninety minutes of live television, combining rock 'n' roll music with a rock 'n' roll approach to comedy. He figured that by 11.30pm on a Saturday night, his target audience would be dragging themselves out of the local bar just in time to watch his self-proclaimed "Not Ready For Prime Time Players".

Chevy Chase was the show's first star – he left after one year for a Hollywood career in the comedy thriller *Foul Play* (1978) opposite **Goldie Hawn**. He found further success with *Caddyshack* (see Canon), the *National Lampoon Vacation* series of movies (from 1983), and the *Fletch* franchise (1985 onwards). He was replaced at *SNL* by a certain **Bill Murray**, himself no slouch in the funny department. A graduate of the famed *Second City* improv/theatre troupe of Chicago, Murray went on to have an even more successful film career than Chase, starring in such hits as *Stripes* (1981), *Ghostbusters* (1984; see Canon) and *Groundhog Day* (1993; see Canon). He is now the second *SNL* alumnus to have been nominated for an Oscar (in 2004 for Sofia Coppola's *Lost in Translation*), the other being his occasional co-star **Dan Aykroyd** (for *Driving Miss Daisy* (1989)).

Aykroyd himself, another graduate of the Canadian *Second City* troupe, remains one of the most successful of the original *SNL* team. Having starred in such movies as *The Blues Brothers* (taken to the big screen by director John Landis in 1980), *1941* (1979) and *Ghostbusters* (which he co-authored, along with its sequel), Aykroyd has established himself as a reliable character actor. In his *SNL* heyday he was often teamed with the late **John Belushi**, who died young in 1982 from a drug overdose and left behind only a handful of film performances, among them the iconic Bluto (*Animal House*) and Jake Blues (*Blues Brothers*).

Later *SNL* cast members were quick to follow the original team in making the transition to movies, among them **Eddie Murphy**, Mike Myers, Billy Crystal, Will Ferrell, David Spade and Chris Farley. Tim Lawrence, Gilda Radner, Randy Quaid and Robert Downey Jr. have all also passed through the revolving doors of *SNL*'s Studio 8H. The list just goes on, proving without doubt that *Saturday Night Live* has been American comedy cinema's most successful, and influential, breeding ground.

young audience, proving influential in many ways. It all but single-handedly invented the gross-out movie ("Food fight!"), revitalized many an old song on its soundtrack (would "Louie, Louie" ever be the same?) and proved *SNL* to be a rich breeding ground for young movie talent – which has remained the case ever since. More than anything else perhaps, *Animal House*, following in the wake of *Jaws* and *Star Wars*, brought the comedy movie into the age of the blockbuster, proving that funny could also mean money. (Indirectly, of course, its legacy has also meant that anyone attending university post-1978 must endure the inevitable "toga party".) *Animal House* actually improves with age, something that cannot be said for the likes of its shockingly inferior pretenders, such as *Porkys* (1982) and *Road Trip* (2000) which limply aped the formula of this true classic.

The Odd Couple

dir Gene Saks, 1967, US, 105m

cast Jack Lemmon, Walter Matthau *cin* Robert B Hauser *m* Neal Hefti

Like Woody Allen, Mel Brooks and Carl Reiner before him, **Neil Simon** served his writing apprenticeship on Sid Caesar's *Your Show Of Shows* during the early 1950s. But while his comrades graduated to stand-up and movies, Simon took to the New York stage, becoming over the last half century or so its most successful exponent. In his early work, his tales were sharply urban and contemporary. In the way they celebrate New York – the city he loves in all its glory and/or lack thereof – they predate **Woody Allen**'s cinematic paean to the same landscape, *Manhattan* (see Canon). But while Simon's writing deals with the same sophisticated urbanite characters as Allen, he paints them in broader strokes, less concerned with the neuroses and anxieties of city dwellers, and more with what it takes to live, love and survive in the Big Apple. These themes are never more evident than in what is probably still his best loved work, *The Odd Couple*.

This is a tale of marriage lost, and a curious kind of new marriage found. Sports writer Oscar Madison (**Walter Matthau**) and his pal Felix Unger (**Jack Lemmon**) are opposites: the former slobbish and unkempt, the latter uptight and prissy, a man who must bellow loudly at every public opportunity just to clear his sinuses. In any other city they would probably never meet, let alone be friends. But as their weekly poker games prove − they're also attended by a cop and an accountant, among others − New York is a place in which opposites not only function together, but must stay together to survive.

The two characters soon become united by one other thing: Oscar is divorced and behind with his alimony payments, while Felix's wife has just thrown him out. Felix's first response is to attempt to commit suicide, but he throws his back out while opening the hotel window he planned to throw himself from. Oscar's response is to offer him a place to stay. After all, it makes sense: his apartment is too big for a bachelor and it would save them both money, easing their mutual burden of alimony. Having both left behind one marriage, they enter into another − with each other.

Simon's play was originally staged in 1965 with Matthau as Oscar, **Art Carney** as Felix and **Mike Nichols** directing. The movie version rarely expands, cinematically, for the big screen, which is utterly appropriate − these two men are trapped within their apartment and trapped with each other. Lemmon and Matthau had worked together on Billy Wilder's excellent 1966 comedy *The Fortune Cookie*, and here they cemented what would become one of the best loved of all screen partnerships: Lemmon, "clenched of hair" and always torn between a wry smile and a look of exasperated bewilderment, contrasts beautifully with Matthau, jowly and unkempt. They clearly relish their performances, and the true measure of their genius and of Simon's brilliant script is that no matter how many times you watch this film it's hard to decide whose side you're on. Lemmon and Matthau would go on to make a further five films together, including the curmudgeons-are-us *Grumpy Old Men* series (1993), and their final film together, an unwise reunion in the disappointing *Odd Couple Two* (1998). The play itself would prove to be enduring, and Simon even rewrote it in the 1990s for two female leads. But Matthau and Lemmon remain the perfect Oscar and Felix and this movie is the best example of Simon writing at his peak.

The Producers

dir **Mel Brooks, 1968, US, 88m**

cast **Zero Mostel, Gene Wilder, Dick Shawn** *cin* **Joseph Coffey** *m* **John Morris**

Character comedy – a rarity for director Brooks

Before he found his niche parodying other movie genres, Mel Brooks penned his finest work, *The Producers* – easily one of the funniest films ever made. The movie's premise was highly original, impressively daring, and extremely close-to-the-bone. A failed Broadway producer, Max Bialystock (**Zero Mostel**), and a timid and naive accountant, Leo Bloom (**Gene Wilder**), have a few serious cashflow problems, and realize they can make more money on Broadway by over-financing a sure-fire flop. As part of their scam, they come up with the most tasteless musical in history, one *Springtime For Hitler*.

The whole thing would be just perfect as it stood. But *The Producers* had one more vital thing going for it, something Brooks often neglected in his subsequent films: properly-written characters. The protagonists seem like real, three-dimensional people, and are played by actors at the peak of their powers, giving what could arguably be called the performances of their lives. As a viewer you care about Bialystock, despite the repellence of some of his character traits – his cynical, pathetic seductions of elderly ladies to make his crust, for example. You also come to understand the significance of Leo Bloom's blue security blanket, and delight in Gene Wilder's unparalleled conveyance of comic anxiety.

The office-bound first half-hour of *The Producers* runs almost like a stage play (little wonder Brooks later adapted it into the most financially successful Broadway show in history). Max and Leo meet, face off, confront and connive and are, in some way, reborn – one (Max) as the man he once was and the other (Leo) as the man he always wanted to be. For all its undeniable laughs, it's actually a beautiful sight to behold. From that point on it's all systems go. Brooks switches back into gag mode, eschewing character development for wickedly observed stereotypes: the camp theatre director Roger De Bris (**Christopher Hewett**), the Nazi playwright Franz Liebkind (**Kenneth Mars**), the va-va-voom Swedish secretary Ulla (**Lee Meredith**) and of course the show-stopping actor Lorenzo St. DuBois (also known as L.S.D.), played to perfection by **Dick Shawn**.

In the film's final act, Brooks presents us with the glorious sight of his hated Nazis kick-dancing in swastika formation as they sing the immortal, catchy number "Springtime for Hitler and Germany/ Winter for Poland and France…" It is a perfect comedy scene, ably abetted by the excessive performance from Shawn which follows – and of course by the film's final twist, that their play is a stomping hit. Brooks himself had once written the libretto for a Broadway flop, 1962's *All American*. This is possibly the sweetest revenge in American comedy history.

Raising Arizona

dir Joel Coen, 1987, US, 94m

cast Nicolas Cage, Holly Hunter, Trey Wilson, John Goodman, William Forsythe *cin* Barry Sonnenfeld *m* Carter Burwell

Very few modern filmmakers can do screwball comedy; even fewer can make it their own. But then there are very few filmmakers like **Joel** and **Ethan Coen**. Having begun their careers in the early 1980s lo-fi American independent cinema scene – Joel worked on **Sam Raimi**'s *Evil Dead* (1982), and they financed their first movie, *Blood Simple* (1984), using donations from friends and family – the Coens were ripe to take on the mainstream with their second film, *Raising Arizona*. Even so, despite the increase in production values, they took the quirky road less-travelled with this marvellous film.

Nicolas Cage plays H.I. McDonnaugh, a recidivist petty crook who ends up marrying Ed (**Holly Hunter**), the female police officer who is there for him so often – to take his mug shot on arraignment. In a brilliantly sustained eleven-minute pre-credit sequence, the Coens set the scene for the film's own surreal world by showing us H.I. and Ed's repeated meetings, his treks back to prison, his pleadings to the parole board, and his inevitable return to crime.

The crazy world of the Coens

Having fallen in love, the couple find that Ed can't have children ("her insides were a rocky place where my seed could find no purchase", H.I. proclaims), while H.I. can't adopt because of his criminal record. Meanwhile, shady furniture salesman Nathan Arizona (**Trey Wilson**) has just become the proud father of quintuplets. With perfect Coen logic, career criminal and decorated police officer decide that the Arizonas have too many offspring, and that the only sensible thing to do is relieve them of one. And all this before the opening credits – with their accompanying Cajun yodelling – roll.

What follows is a series of set pieces, brilliantly shot by cinematographer **Barry Sonnenfeld** – the Steadicam up-the-ladder tricksiness of the kidnap bid; H.I.'s comic ineptitude when confronted with five infants in the nursery; and his recourse to robbing a convenience store when they find they need Pampers. Things only get weirder with the arrival of two of H.I.'s buddies (Goodman and Forsythe) freshly escaped from jail, and Tex Cobb's biker of the apocalypse, recruited by the Arizonas to reclaim their missing infant. The movie ends on a dream-like note that throws off the perspective of the whole film, with Cage recounting events as a possible fantasy, projecting into the future the family that may well be his one day.

As with the brothers' other work, there are lots of in-jokes in *Raising Arizona*. There are visual references to *The Evil Dead*; the name of a security company lifted from Sam Raimi's film *Crimewave* (1985), which the brothers cowrote with Raimi; and the sight of Cage in a uniform belonging to Hudsucker Industries, an anticipatory reference to their *The Hudsucker Proxy* (1994), once again written with Raimi. Jokes for the boys? Or the creation of a complete cinematic parallel world? It's a bit of both.

What *Raising Arizona* also has is a frantic, anarchic pace, and a sense of total individuality as a film which verges on the gestalt. It's one of the brothers' finest scripts and the cast is superb, too. The brothers wrote the role of Ed especially for Holly Hunter, who was at that time known primarily as a stage actress. Cage, perfect as the hapless H.I., took on the lead after **Kevin Costner** apparently turned it down. Even the babies are good – there were fifteen in total, but unfortunately one of them was fired during production when it recklessly showed no consideration for its future film career and learned to walk.

Roxanne

dir Fred Schepisi, 1987, US, 107m

cast Steve Martin, Daryl Hannah, Shelley Duvall, Rick Rossovich *cin* Ian Baker

Steve Martin, once America's premier stand-up comedian, began to devote himself to cinema in the late 1970s with a series of brilliant, fast-paced, gag-heavy movies such as *The Jerk* (1979), *Dead Men Don't Wear Plaid* (1982) and *The Man With Two Brains* (1983). He then turned towards romantic comedy, but *The Lonely Guy* (1984) proved to be a faltering misstep, despite being scripted by **Neil Simon**. However, Martin finally got it right with one of the greatest plays ever written about love, attraction and its potential duplicity.

In adapting **Edmond Rostand**'s *Cyrano de Bergerac* – a fictional-ized nineteenth-century play about a real-life seventeenth-century writer – to the modern age, Martin made the large-nosed protago-nist into a small-town fire chief named C.D. Bales. He's good at sniffing out fires, you see; he's also well-read, and possessed of a great wit and a sharp mind. In fact, he's just the kind of person you'd think new-in-town astronomer Roxanne (**Daryl Hannah**) would fall for – if only the nose didn't get in the way. Roxanne instead goes for the hunky but dim new fireman Chris (**Rick Rossovich**), thus leading to C.D. settling for the second best of wooing Roxanne by proxy: he writes the words, Chris desperately tries to remember them, and Roxanne falls for it.

Roxanne is something of a *tour-de-force* for Martin. It remains one of his best pieces of screenwriting, perfectly capturing the romance at the heart of the piece while never forgetting to deliver plenty of gags. He also puts in a fine performance, making great use of his physical comedy skills as well as his considerable verbal wit, never more so than in the movie's stand-out scene, in which C.D. offers twenty-five nasal insults to an obnoxious drunk who is taunting him in a bar, classifying them as he goes: "Obvious – 'scuse me, is that your nose or did a bus park on your face? Meteorological – everybody take cover, she's going to blow! Fashionable – you know, you could de-emphasize your nose if you wore something larger, like... Wyoming. Personal – well, here we are, just the three of us. Punctual – all right, Delman, your nose was on time but *you* were fifteen minutes late! Envious – Ooooh, I wish I were you! Gosh, to be able to smell your own ear! Naughty – uh, pardon me, sir, some of the ladies have asked if you wouldn't mind putting that thing away..." and the list goes on. Quite simply, this is Steve Martin at his very best.

Rushmore

dir Wes Anderson, 1998, US, 93m
cast Jason Schwartzman, Bill Murray, Olivia Williams,
Brian Cox *cin* Robert Yeoman *m* Mark Mothersbaugh

The teen movie has long lived in the domain of the comedy movie, but very few movies of any genre fully understand – or convey – just how *miserable* it is to be fifteen. For all its glorious humour, stand-out performances, great soundtrack and highly personal visual style, perhaps the most striking thing about *Rushmore* is that it gets across just how lousy it is to be in love and too young to do anything about it.

The movie tells the tale of Max Fisher (**Jason Schwartzman**), over-achieving student at the prestigious Rushmore Academy. He edits the school yearbook, runs the French club and the Kung Fu club, speaks on the debating team, teaches classes in calligraphy and is a chorale choirmaster. In between these and other school activities, he finds time to write, direct and star in plays. In short, Max has made Rushmore Academy his life – until two people enter this hallowed ground and change what Max thought his life was. One is jaded millionaire Herman Blum (**Bill Murray**), the other, widowed teacher Rosemary Cross (**Olivia Williams**), with whom Max falls in love.

Rushmore was the sophomore film from writer-director **Wes Anderson**, a Texan who has rapidly established himself as one of the brightest talents in modern American cinema comedy. His partner in writing the film's screenplay was fellow Texan **Owen Wilson**, an actor-writer who often appears in Anderson's films (in *Rushmore* he makes his presence felt visually in the photos of Rosemary's dead husband). Long-time friends, the pair first worked together on the idiosyncratic caper movie *Bottle Rocket* (1995) before graduating to *Rushmore*, the film that first defined Anderson's arch style.

In all his movies, Anderson creates a complete world that is just slightly

Jason Schwartzman salutes the arch style of director Wes Anderson

removed from the real one. He uses formal devices to emphasize this – in *Rushmore* a series of curtains open and close to introduce each act of his film and denote the passing of the months; in the equally wonderful *The Royal Tenenbaums* (2001) it is the pages of a book that tell the story of the scene to come. It's mannered, but it works.

Then, of course, there is the cast. One of the many things we should thank Anderson for is his rehabilitation of Bill Murray's career. Thought by many to be the most talented of the early graduates of *Saturday Night Live* (see p.67), by the mid-1990s Murray had lost his way on film. Few who saw him play opposite an elephant in *Larger Than Life* (1996) could have imagined this man could ever make a comeback. *Rushmore*, with Murray's perfectly jaded performance as Herman Blume, changed all that, paving the way for his celebrated mature performance in *Lost In Translation* (2003). The movie can also gain credit for the discovery of Jason Schwartzman as Max (though given the fact he is nephew to **Francis Ford Coppola**, and therefore cousin to **Sofia Coppola** and **Nicolas Cage**, the odds were he would end up in movies one day). His performance is perfect – touchingly funny, believably lost, and gently ridiculous (when he learns that Blume was in Vietnam, he tries to knowingly ask "Were you in the shit?") and completely convincing as a teenager in hopeless love.

Shaun Of The Dead

dir **Edgar Wright, 2004, UK, 99m**
cast **Simon Pegg, Kate Ashfield, Lucy Davis, Nick Frost, Dylan Moran, Bill Nighy, Penelope Wilton** *cin* **David Dunlap** *m* **Dan Mudford**

In 2004 the British comedy movie was in something of a rut. Screenwriter **Richard Curtis**, he of *Four Weddings And A Funeral* (see Canon), seemed to have his hand in every script that made money, and Working Title, the most successful production company in Britain, seemed to make a lot of movies by Richard Curtis. A cricket bat needed to be taken to British comedy. And a cricket bat is the singularly British tool our titular hero Shaun (**Simon Pegg**) uses to despatch the flesh-hungry legions of zombies in *Shaun Of The Dead*.

Pilfering – or paying homage to – several classic genre moments, writer/actor Simon Pegg and his cowriter and directing partner **Edgar Wright** took the romcom to the suburbs (in this case, leafy Crouch End in North London) and populated it with ordinary young people who spend half their lives sitting on the bus getting to and from their dead end jobs, and the other half vegetating in the

Romcom goes to the zombies

local pub with their mates. This is the real world, where a somewhat alienated Generation X, going about their daily business (dragging themselves out of bed, staring at the TV, queuing in a corner shop, and playing videogames), are all but indistinguishable from the undead – the film then explores what happens to such people when they come under attack from real, flesh-eating zombies. One of the movie's great skills is how it keeps the tone hovering expertly between the darkly horrific and the heartwarmingly humane.

Thus we are genuinely appalled when Shaun and his friends flee their undead pursuers by bashing their heads in with cricket bats, impaling them on spikes, and shooting their brains out. But we are genuinely touched when friendships, love affairs and family relationships are resolved, not without a great deal of loss, against the backdrop of this fast-paced gorefest.

Shaun Of The Dead combines an established cast (**Bill Nighy** and **Penelope Wilton**) with a raft of up-and-coming talent (Pegg, the always excellent Dylan Moran and Lucy Davis), and balances a sense of film history with a fresh, distinct irreverence to produce a genuinely original piece of work. To give them their due, it was in fact Working Title who bankrolled *Shaun* (albeit via their offshoot "WT2"). Having hit gold with *Four Weddings*, *Notting Hill*, *Love Actually*, *Bridget Jones* and so on, it appeared they now wanted to add a pun-heavy, **George Romero**-inspired, zombie romance to their CV. *Shaun Of The Dead* presented the British romcom with an extremely hard act to follow.

A Shot In The Dark

dir **Blake Edwards, 1963, UK, 101m**
cast **Peter Sellers, Elke Sommer, George Sanders, Herbert Lom, Burt Kwouk** *cin* **Christopher Challis** *m* **Henry Mancini**

Let's start by making one thing clear – the Pink Panther is the name of a diamond, the target of suave cat burglar **David Niven**, not the name of that cartoon feline that appears at the beginning of each of the movies in the series, and which had its own spin-off TV series.

The diamond which gave its name to the series did not feature in any of the sequels until 1974's *Return Of The Pink Panther*.

Director **Blake Edwards** had made his name with successes such as *Breakfast At Tiffany's* (1961) and *Days Of Wine And Roses* (1962). *The Pink Panther* was intended to be a stylish light comedy, putting **David Niven**'s elegant thief among the high society of Europe. The presence of Sellers changed all that.

The role of Clouseau had originally been accepted by **Peter Ustinov** but when he backed out at the eleventh hour Sellers was approached. Unhappy with being second choice, and with taking second billing to Niven, Sellers would have passed on the part had it not been for the fact that it was by far the biggest Hollywood movie he'd been offered to date. It was Sellers who developed the look and voice of **Peter Sellers**' anglophonically-challenged French detective, Inspector Jacques Clouseau, adding the bumbling, physical incompetence that would define the role; he found a like mind in Edwards, a filmmaker who also had a penchant for excess (witness **Mickey Rooney**'s jarring racist cliché of a Japanese neighbour in the otherwise elegant *Breakfast At Tiffany's*).

With the character of Inspector Clouseau, director and star realised they'd trapped lightning in a bottle and went for a sequel with more speed than Hollywood has seen before or since (it was released three months after the original). Straight after shooting *The Pink Panther*, Sellers was due to co-star with **Walter Matthau** in *A Shot In The Dark*. It was an adaptation of a stage play, to be directed by Anatole Litvak, and Sellers' part was a foolish magistrate. But buoyed up on what he (rightly) felt was a *tour-de-force* performance in *Panther*, Sellers felt he deserved better, and threatened to quit. He didn't have to – Matthau did. The studio brought in Blake Edwards as director to placate their troublesome star; he took one look at the material and decided that *A Shot In The Dark* would make a perfect vehicle for Clouseau.

Here, Edwards and writer William Peter Blatty created the Clouseau template. **Herbert Lom** came on board as Clouseau's long-suffering superior Chief Inspector Dreyfus, **Burt Kwouk** dropped in as the karate-chopping manservant Kato, and Clouseau got to say "beumb" (ie "bomb") for the first of many (some would say, too many) times. Edwards spent much of the 1970s developing increasingly dire sequels – *The Return Of The Pink Panther* (1974), *The Pink Panther Strikes Again* (1976) and *Revenge Of The Pink*

Panther (1978). It's more than likely that Sellers' involvement in them was in order to finance his dream project, the odd but inconsequential *Being There*, realised in 1979, shortly before his death.

It's hard to credit, but Sellers' demise didn't stop Edwards' *Pink Panther* production line. Using a mixture of old clips, unseen footage and outtakes, he cobbled together 1982's risible *The Trail Of The Pink Panther*, and then replaced Sellers with **Ted Wass** in *The Curse Of The Pink Panther* (1983). Never one to leave a dead horse unflogged, a decade later the director unsuccessfully tried to revive the brand name with **Roberto Benigni** as *The Son Of The Pink Panther*. And the franchise refused to die: **Steve Martin**, aided and abetted by **Beyoncé Knowles**, donned the Clouseau moustache in 2005's *The Pink Panther*. In many ways, *Austin Powers* has a lot to answer for.

Some Like It Hot

dir Billy Wilder, 1959, US, 120m, b/w
cast Marilyn Monroe, Tony Curtis, Jack Lemmon, George Raft, Pat O'Brien, Joe E. Brown *cin* Charles Lang Jr *m* Adolph Deutsch

With an opening scene depicting a hearse being pursued by gun-toting cops, using a near-as-damn depiction of Al Capone's St Valentine's Day Massacre to propel its plot, and throwing transvestism, sexual innuendo and jazz music into the mix, *Some Like It Hot* is one of cinema's unlikeliest but best-loved comedies. Its reputation over the years has grown to the point where the American Film Institute voted it the number one comedy movie of all time, a position it often occupies whenever such lists are drawn up.

A lot of that has to do with its director **Billy Wilder** and his long-time writing partner **I.A.L. Diamond**. Austrian-born Wilder had fled Germany when Hitler came to power in 1933, leaving behind a successful career as a screenwriter before establishing himself in Hollywood with dramas such as *Double Indemnity* (1944), *The Lost Weekend* (1945) and 1950's *Sunset Boulevard* (picking up Oscars for the latter two). He had also proved himself a dab hand at comedy with the script for *Ninotchka* (1939) and *Sabrina* (1954).

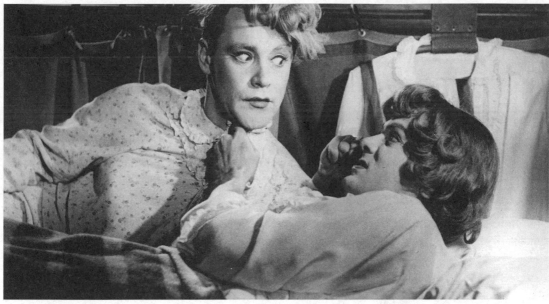

The ditzy and the demure (Lemmon and Curtis)

In 1958, Wilder was presented with an idea for a comedy by writers Robert Thoern and Michael Logan. The premise was to take two male musicians on the run from gangsters, whose only means of escaping is to dress in drag and join an all-girl band. Getting down to work with Diamond, Wilder located the story in Prohibition-era Chicago, and set about choosing his cast. First on the list was **Tony Curtis**, best known in Hollywood for his good looks and athletic ability in such movies as *Trapeze* (1956) and *The Vikings* (1958). Having considered Frank Sinatra, Wilder eventually then cast **Jack Lemmon** (relatively new in Hollywood but with an Oscar to his name for a supporting turn in *Mister Roberts* the previous year) and **Marilyn Monroe** as band member Sugar Cane. At the height of her fame – and the beginning of her fall from grace – Monroe was perfect in the role, although when Wilder later said "I knew we were in mid-flight, and I knew there was a nut on the plane", he wasn't referring to his male leads. Monroe's contract insisted that all her movies be shot in colour, but when make-up tests on the men left their features looking too green on camera, Wilder opted to shoot in black and white. It was an opportune decision, and Monroe never looked more luminous.

The movie is awash with in-jokes and film references – **George Raft**, having noticed a gangster flicking a coin (a visual echo of Raft's own performance in 1932's *Scarface*), asks "Where did you pick up that cheap trick?"; Curtis, when masquerading as an oil magnate who meets Sugar on the beach, pulls off a thinly veiled impersonation of Cary Grant; Raft's character is shot by Johnny Paradise, played by **Edward G. Robinson Jr.**, son of one of Raft's greatest on-screen rivals. Raft knowingly replies "Big joke!" before dying. It is also full of brilliant performances, not only from Curtis, who plays female as delicate and demure, and Lemmon, who goes for a ditzier style, but also from Monroe, who gives a delicately nuanced comic turn, and from a host of notable supporting players including **Pat O'Brien** and **Joe E. Brown**.

Strictly original, camp and comic

Strictly Ballroom

dir **Baz Luhrmann, 1992, Aus, 92m**
cast **Paul Mercurio, Tara Morice, Bill Hunter** *cin* **Steve Mason** *m* **David Hirschfelder**

If you can imagine *Footloose* sent "down under" with the camp and kitsch of, say, *Best In Show*, then you've got a pretty good idea of what **Baz Luhrmann**'s audacious cinematic debut is like. Scott Hastings (**Paul Mercurio**) is a potential big-time player on the Australian ballroom dancing circuit – greatness is within his grasp. But what he really strives for is originality – to be allowed to perform his own routines rather than the formulaic moves which win prizes. The judges be damned – he knows what's best! The aforementioned judges (led by **Bill Hunter**'s splendidly excessive and corrupt Federation President Barry Fife) are, of course, against such radical actions, and therein lies the fun in Luhrmann's garish but sincere film: that the supposedly staid world of ballroom dancing could ever be big enough, and dramatic enough, to engender such things as "radical actions."

Luhrmann's greatest skill in *Strictly Ballroom* is not in the way he plays a certain amount of it as a mock-newscast/documentary, reporting on the scandal and strife as if the whole thing were a major world event – though this is undoubtedly a major part of its comedic appeal. The film's real strength lies in the fact that, while it appears to parody its subject, it also manages to convey real admiration and affection for it. It's very much a feelgood movie, as testified to by the fact that this low-budget, humble Australian offering won universal acclaim and box office success much further afield than the country in which it was set.

Baz Luhrmann used to take part in similar ballroom dancing contests as a child, and he brings both a quizzical and satirical eye to the way he presents his film, but never – wisely – to the way he presents the dancing. There are moments when *Simply Ballroom* just soars – the song "Love Is In The Air" has never sounded so good as when Scott and his partner take to the floor and make it theirs. With its optimism and its intelligent use of music, this joyous little film feels almost like a musical without the songs, and paved the way for Luhrmann's triumphant *Moulin Rouge!* (2001) (about as big a musical as you could ever wish for).

It would be nice to be able to say that charismatic lead – and professional dancer – Paul Mercurio went on to bigger and better things having been discovered by his director but, sadly, he didn't. Essentially, the star of this movie is Baz Luhrmann himself, who, having previously established himself as a stage director, went on to triumph with his intelligently stylized *William Shakespeare's Romeo & Juliet* (1996), and, of course, the none-more-camp baroque extravagances of *Moulin Rouge*.

Sullivan's Travels

dir Preston Sturges, 1941, US, 91m, b/w
cast Joel McCrea, Veronica Lake, Robert Warwick,
William Demarest, Franklin Pangborne *cin* John F. Seitz *m*
Leo Shuken & Charles Bradshaw

What's the point of making comedies? They're cheap and easy, they offer no value to the world beyond a few laughs, and they have no real social value or relevance. So why bother? That's the question that filmmaker **Preston Sturges** and his fictional alter-ego, film-

Where art thou brother?

maker John Lloyd Sullivan (**Joel McCrea**), ask in **Sullivan's Travels**. The answer is one that writer-director Sturges clearly knows, but the more naive Sullivan must go on a journey into Depression-era America to find out.

Sullivan, a successful movie director, has made his career with light comedies such as *Ants In Your Pants*. But now he wants to make more challenging, significant work. He wants to be an important filmmaker, and hopes to achieve this by stripping away his wealth and success and turning himself into a hobo, wandering the highroads and byroads of America to get a real feel for "the common man". His dream project is to be a serious social piece named *O Brother, Where Art Thou?* (Which, of course, is a film the Coen brothers actually made, and made very funny indeed.) The fact that Sullivan picks his hobo outfit from the studio's wardrobe department is a sure sign that this is a journey he really needs to make.

Casting the studio system in a cynical light, Sturges has Sullivan's bosses send along a trailer full of publicists behind him, in order to get more mileage out of what they perceive as his folly in wanting to make a "serious" masterpiece. Sullivan's voyage into the poor and lost world outside his limo window sees him hooking up with the gorgeous **Veronica Lake**, playing a poor girl heading home from Hollywood having failed to make it in the movies. Sturges ups the ante in this journey of self-discovery when Sullivan is mistakenly thought to be dead – the publicists head back home, and his new-found life as a genuine hobo sees him shipped off to a prison work camp in the Deep South. Now he finally gets to see the real hardship he had been so nobly (but foolishly) looking to experience – and it's a lot tougher than he thought. He eventually learns his lesson by experiencing one of the inmates' few pleasures in life: they love the movies – Disney cartoons in particular – and very quickly Sullivan finds himself laughing along with them. Through this he finally realizes the true worth of what he has to offer the world: "There's a lot to be said for making people laugh. Did you know that's all some people have? It isn't much … but it's better than nothing in this cockeyed caravan."

At the time he came to make *Sullivan's Travels*, Sturges was one of the highest-paid comedy screenwriters in Hollywood. Some saw the movie as an attempt to bite the hand that fed him (or at least take a few lunges at it). The great and affirmatory irony, given the altogether grimmer nature of the third act of his movie, is that he did, of course, end up making his own *O Brother, Where Art Thou?* The critics hailed him (and continue to do so to this day), the public loved it, and *Sullivan's Travels* remains one of Hollywood's most unusual, ambitious and satisfying comedies.

There's Something About Mary

dir **Bobby & Peter Farrelly, 1998, US, 119m**
cast **Cameron Diaz, Ben Stiller, Matt Dillon, Lee Evans, Chris Elliott** *cin* **Mark Irvin** *m* **Jonathan Richman**

As a rule, in romantic comedies you don't seriously abuse small dogs. You rarely show a man's genitals painfully caught in his trouser zip.

And you never show your leading man feverishly masturbating, let alone having his bodily emissions accidentally ending up in your unsuspecting leading lady's hair. Or at least you didn't – until the Farrelly brothers brought their own unique vision of extreme, gross-out comedy to the romcom. That romcom was *There's Something About Mary.*

Former salesmen and aspiring writers, Peter and Bobby Farrelly hit the big time with their 1994 hit *Dumb and Dumber*, the good-natured tale of two total dimwits, played to perfection by **Jim Carrey** and **Jeff Daniels**. The outrageous lunacy of their movie seemed to fit the mid-1990s perfectly, the era in which the phrase "dumbing down" became one of the most overused (especially by politicians) of the whole decade. They also tapped into the much-maligned tradition of gross-out comedy, one that hadn't been that active since the glory days of *National Lampoon's Animal House* (see Canon) and *Porky's*. Bowing to commercial pressure and a trend for family-friendly movies, Hollywood simply hadn't been in the habit of making R-rated comedies in the previous few years. The Farrellys changed all that, and their impact can be felt in the slew of movies that followed, from *American Pie* (1999) to *Road Trip* (2000) to *Old School* (2003) and beyond.

They are also directors possessed of a real knack for coaxing fantastic turns from their actors. Cameron Diaz cemented her reputation as a bona fide star with her turn as Mary, the ditzy beauty who is also the object of every man's desire. For the role of Ted, the former geek who holds a torch for her from Prom night on, the Farrellys wanted **Ben Stiller**. He was already established as a TV comedian as well as a writer and director, but to the studios he just didn't seem like romantic leading man material. The Farrellys

The twisted humour of the Farrellys

suggested going for the then-unknown **Owen Wilson** instead, someone the studios were even less sure of – they eventually backed down in favour of Stiller. **Matt Dillon**, cast against type as the smarmy private eye, and British comic **Lee Evans** (in a curiously strained physical comedy act as a man on crutches) rounded out the cast. The singer **Jonathan Richman** was also on hand to provide an on screen wandering minstrel/Greek chorus act, as he had done on the Farrellys' earlier *Kingpin* (1996).

There's Something About Mary is by no means a perfect film. At times it feels like little more than a series of

THE CANON: 50 SERIOUSLY FUNNY MOVIES

comic set pieces strung together by a very thin plot: boy meets girl, gets testicles caught in zipper, tries to win girl, gets girl, loses girl, gets girl back. But at their best, there's a lot more to the Farrellys than dumb, sick, twisted and admittedly very funny gags. There's a warmth to their characters, who may not be the brightest sparks but are rarely malicious. Rather, the contending suitors of *There's Something About Mary* have peculiarly unfathomable drives and motivations, displaying all the unquestioning impulses of cartoon characters in their persistent attempts to out-manoeuvre each other and get the girl. It's as if the Farrellys, in their assault on the rom-com, consciously rejected any kind of traditional structure in favour of one disorientatingly like a game of snakes and ladders.

This Is Spinal Tap

dir Rob Reiner, 1983, US, 82m

cast Christopher Guest, Michael McKean, Harry Shearer, Rob Reiner, June Chadwick *cin* Peter Smokler *m* Christopher Guest, Michael McKean, Harry Shearer, Rob Reiner

Few bands have ever received a review along the lines of "they are treading water in a sea of retarded sexuality and bad poetry" – but then, there are few bands like Spinal Tap. Three men on stage and one behind the scenes created the Tap, one of Britain's loudest post-1960s heavy metal monsters. On lead guitar and vocals there's Nigel Tufnell (**Christopher Guest**), on guitar and lead vocals there's David St. Hubbins (**Michael McKean**), and on bass Derek Smalls (**Harry Shearer**). Off-stage there was actor, writer and director **Rob Reiner**. Together, they created the definitive mockumentary, *This Is Spinal Tap*.

Reiner should know a thing or two about comedy – his father was Carl Reiner (who wrote for Sid Caesar in the 1950s, appeared on and wrote *The Dick Van Dyke Show*, and was the other voice on **Mel Brooks'** legendary recordings of *The 2,000 Year Old Man*). Reiner Jr. began his career as an actor, finding fame as the unwanted son-in-law of couch potato bigot Archie Bunker in the hugely successful and influential US sitcom, *All In The Family*. In 1979, Reiner was offered a shot at a sketch show pilot called *The TV Show*. He recruited friends Guest (late of *National Lampoon*), McKean (late of TV's *Laverne and Shirley*) and Shearer (who would later play literally dozens of voices on *The Simpsons*), and formed Britain's finest rock band. (On this, their debut appearance, noted singer-songwriter **Loudon Wainwright III** was their keyboard player.)

The sketch rapidly morphed into a feature-length rockumentary. Kitted out with a Martin Scorsese beard and Spielberg baseball cap, Reiner introduces his own movie via the fictional persona Marty DiBergi, a documentary filmmaker who has set out to film the Tap's comeback tour of the US. *This Is Spinal Tap* takes up with the fictitious group of rockers, documenting their history (37 members in total – most of them drummers, who have a worrying habit of dying on the band); their subsequent falling apart; and their eventual reconciliation, all to the tunes of such classics as "Sex Farm", "Lick My Love Pump", "Big Bottom" and more.

Largely improvised by its cast, *This Is Spinal Tap* remains a tour-bus favourite for many a real-life rock band. For one thing, it's exquisitely observed: from the impossibly pretentious album cover for *Smell The Glove*, to the band's original mid-1960s names ("The Originals", "The New Originals", "The Thamesmen") to the fact that they can't even find the stage during one gig. For another, *Spinal Tap* works because, like the best comedy, it's true.

As this fictitious band starts to fall apart, you genuinely feel for them; the fact that the lifelong childhood friendship between Tufnell and St. Hubbins could be lost really matters. At its best, *Spinal Tap* not only captures the pomposity of overblown rock music, but wears its influences lightly – the low-key interviews and fly-on-the-wall observations echo the Dylan movie *Don't Look Back* (1967). **June Chadwick**, playing the domineering spiritualist girlfriend of the lead singer, teasingly parodies Yoko Ono's presence in The Beatles' *Let It Be*, and so on. While, sadly, such classic abums as *Intravenus DeMilo* and *Shark Sandwich* may not be available, we'll always have this mockumentary. The tagline on the original poster read: "Does for rock 'n' roll what *The Sound Of Music* did for hills", but those of us who have watched it (probably several times) know better. Rock on!

To Be Or Not To Be

dir Ernst Lubitsch, 1942, US, 99m, b/w
cast Carole Lombard, Jack Benny, Robert Stack, Felix
Bressart, Lionel Atwill *cin* Rudolph Maté *m* Werner R
Hayman

Few film comedies have tackled the subject of Nazism. Charlie
Chaplin trod dangerous ground lampooning Hitler while he was in
power in *The Great Dictator* (1940); Mel Brooks took the goosestep
and turned it into a high kick in *The Producers* (see Canon) – and
also remade *To Be Or Not To Be* in 1983; and **Roberto Benigni**
attempted to find what little humour he could in the concentration camps with *Life Is Beautiful*. **Ernst Lubitsch**, a filmmaker better known for such tender romantic comedies as *The Shop Around
The Corner* (1940), created one of the finest satires ever in *To Be Or
Not To Be*, a movie made during World War II and set around the
German occupation of Poland.

Actor, Sig Ruman – a lot funnier
than Hitler

In a hare-brained plot with
a cutting edge, Lubitsch's film
focuses on an egocentric Polish
acting troupe headed by the nar-
cissistic pair of Joseph Tura (**Jack
Benny**), the kind of actor who
likes a beer before he gives audiences his *Hamlet*, and his wife and
co-star Maria (**Carole Lombard**),
an actress who thinks wearing
a glamorous gown in a concentration camp scene elevates the
art. As the Nazis move in on
their native country, the pair find
themselves embroiled in an escalating series of events that involve
their troupe having to use all its
talents to stop vital information
intended for the Polish resistance
falling into enemy hands.

Cue the sight of Jack Benny disguised as a member of the Gestapo, a moment that caused Benny's own father to walk out of the film's premiere – until he was persuaded by his son that this was in fact satire. As indeed it was, at its very best. Lubitsch – a German Jew who had moved to the US in the 1920s – skilfully employed a combination of fast-paced physical comedy with a sharply clever script and superb performances to represent the seriousness of the situation in Europe as blackly and bleakly funny. That he was taking a risk was reflected in the movie's reception – many people were offended because they weren't prepared to see the Nazis ridiculed rather than demonized, and the film performed poorly at the box office.

To Be Or Not To Be appeared at a pivotal moment: shot in 1941 and released the following year, it came out just as America had entered the War. In addition, its star, Carole Lombard, had died before the film's release on a flight back from a war bonds rally. After this tragic accident her line "What can happen in a plane?" was cut from the final movie.

The famous "Lubitsch touch"- light, elegant, poised - was never better deployed than when faced with the tragedy of the Nazi occupation of Poland. It's a measure of the achievement of this unique film that it not only manages to be a wonderful satire of thespian vanity but that it also finds laughter and absurdity in the midst of the gravest subject matter – even as the war was taking place – without ever seeming trite.

Tootsie

dir **Sydney Pollack, 1982, US, 116m**
cast **Dustin Hoffman, Jessica Lange, Terri Garr, Dabney Coleman, Charles Durning, Bill Murray** *cin* **Owen Roizman** *m* **David Grusin**

Larry Gelbart has long been acknowledged as one of the great comedy writers in America, yet his body of work remains as sporadic as it is diverse. A product of Sid Caesar's *Your Show Of Shows* school (along with Woody Allen, Mel Brooks and Carl Reiner, among others), he was best known as coscriptwriter of the 1960s

Stephen Sondheim stage musical *A Funny Thing Happened On The Way To The Forum*, and for brilliantly adapting **Robert Altman**'s movie *M*A*S*H* into a successful, long-running TV sitcom. In 1982, with *Tootsie*, he hit comedy cinema paydirt. It was the tale of an unemployed actor, **Dustin Hoffman**'s Michael Dorsey, who resorts to pretending to be female in a radical attempt to get his acting career moving. The movie struck a chord with audiences in the early 1980s, with its straddling high farce and sexual politics, and juxtaposition of romance with soap-opera caricature.

With a nod to Hoffman's reputation for being difficult on set, his character, Dorsey, is a talented actor who, at the start of the film, has been reduced to dressing up as vegetables in commercials because no one agrees to work with him. His agent (a brilliant, high-energy cameo from director Pollack) tells him he's unemployable, so, taking the bit between the teeth, Dorsey sets out to get himself a job – as a woman. Auditioning for a daytime hospital soap in drag, renaming himself Dorothy Michaels, he lands the role that his casual girlfriend (**Terri Garr**) had failed to get. She wasn't woman enough – he, in a dress, appears to be just the thing.

What follows is a comedy of misunderstanding and mixed-up identity: Dorothy/Michael becomes a big star, falls for the show's love interest Julie (**Jessica Lange**), catches the eye of Julie's dad (**Charles Durning**), is chased by the show's lothario, loathed by its sexist director (**Dabney Coleman**), and begins to develop delusions of grandeur, grandly informing his near-apoplectic agent "I could play Eleanor Roosevelt". Amid all the humour, though, the movie manages to tackle a number of interesting and complex issues.

The movie takes on sexism in general – superbly embodied by the turn given by the comedy god that is character actor Dabney Coleman – but it is also seen in Michael himself, when he attempts to seduce Julie at a party. The course of the film charts Michael's journey towards being a better man, and it appears that the only way he's capable of it is by becoming a woman. Dorsey, at one point, relates the lot of the unemployed actor to that of the lonely single-ton – he knows what it's like to wait by the phone, hoping for it to ring. The movie even finds time to take a decent stab at the vagaries of celebrity in general (take a bow, **Andy Warhol**, seen briefly in cameo) and low-quality television soap opera specifically.

To prepare for his role, Hoffman went to his children's school, pretending to be a female relative, to see if he could pull off the part.

When social services weren't called, he was convinced he could get away with it, although the character's on-screen concerns that he wishes he could make Dorothy prettier stemmed from Hoffman's own off-screen feelings. And despite a slew of Oscar nominations (including Best Film, Best Director, Actor and Screenplay), *Tootsie* picked up only one gong – a supporting award for the luminous Lange.

Toy Story

dir John Lasseter, 1995, US, 80m
cast Tom Hanks, Tim Allen, Don Rickles, Jim Varney *m* Randy Newman

When industry insiders, film critics and the general public heard in the early 1990s that an unknown company, **Pixar**, was about to produce the first-ever fully computer-generated animated movie, they were all pretty sceptical. When they also heard that **Tom Hanks** and **Tim Allen** had signed up as the star voices, many thought "bad career move!" Then again, all of us sceptics would probably have said the same at the end of the silent-movie era when the "talkies" first came along.

As it turned out, **Toy Story** quite simply redefined the animated movie. And it did so not only with cutting-edge technology, but also with vast imagination, a huge degree of wit and – let's not understate it – a fair amount of genius. Perhaps Pixar's real masterstroke (and one that so many animation companies have failed even to consider) was to place story and characters always at the forefront, and to put the technology second.

Director – and Pixar founder – **John Lasseter** and his team began with something we could all understand – the appeal and importance of childhood toys. They then tried to visualize every child's dream – what would the toys get up to if they had a life of their own? Rather than ground this conceit in the modern age of PlayStations and Pokémon, they went back to the classics. And when it comes to movies, as well as toys, how much more classic can you get than the cowboy and the spaceman?

Tom Hanks, the Jimmy Stewart of his day, is absolutely perfectly cast as the voice of one-time cowboy Woody, struggling to maintain his place in the affections of his beloved owner, Andy, while painfully aware that Andy one day has to grow up and leave him behind. Enter new toy Buzz Lightyear (Allen), the space hero to beat them all, who threatens to take Woody's place in Andy's heart. Despite his design superiority, Buzz proves unable to make the existential leap that he's a toy in his own right and not the generic, pre-programmed hero he has been manufactured to be. This is a fully-fledged drama, not just an animated movie, and moves skilfully between tension (evil Sid next door), horror (evil Sid's mutant toys – like something straight out of **Tod Browning**'s 1932 *Freaks*), high comedy, parody, and one of the best action movie finales in cinema history. No matter how many times you see it, who doesn't have a lump in their throat as Buzz and Woody come together to save the day?

After the release of *Toy Story*, Pixar very quickly became the first name in animation to ever come close to equalling the branded pulling power of Disney. For many, and not just those of "the Pixar generation", they have even surpassed it – *Toy Story 2* (1999) proved that an animated sequel could be as good as its original, while *A Bug's Life* (1998), *Monsters, Inc.* (2001), *Finding Nemo* (2003) and *The Incredibles* (2004), each of them masterpieces, show that Pixar's run of beautifully made movies is not likely to slow any time soon.

Les vacances de M. Hulot (Mr Hulot's Holiday)

dir **Jacques Tati, 1953, Fr, 91m, b/w**

cast **Jacques Tati, Nathalie Pascaud, Michèle Rolla, Louis Perrault** *cin* **Jacques Mercanton & Jean Mousselle** *m* **Alain Romans**

Jacques Tati's best-loved film, *Les vacances de M. Hulot*, is set in a small coastal town in Brittany, and follows the guests of a seaside hotel during their annual week's holiday. And that is really all there is to the plot, a mere thread on which Tati hangs his unforgettable comic set-pieces.

A recurring theme in Tati's films is the oppressive regimentation of modern life. In *Les vacances de M. Hulot*, all the other guests are only too desperate to cling to the routines of their working lives. Hulot, however, is determined to have a good time. The film follows his enthusiastic attempts to join in various holiday activities including horse riding, canoeing, tennis and a fancy-dress ball, all the while inadvertently disrupting the rigid regimes of his fellow guests. In one revealing scene a student tries to impress a glamorous young blonde with his textbook talk of revolution; in the background, meanwhile, it's Hulot who is really upsetting the status quo, in this instance via his bizarre table tennis technique.

Hulot holidaying

Tati always acknowledged the influence of the great silent comedians on his work, giving particular credit to **Buster Keaton**. And just like Keaton, in his Stone Face persona, Hulot is a perennial outsider, removed from the rest of the world, yet apparently happy with his lot, or perhaps even unaware of any inadequacies in it. Unlike Chaplin's Little Tramp, Hulot never demands our sympathy. Gangling, clumsy, yet always well-meaning, he never consciously sets out to create anarchy, but unwittingly produces it nonetheless.

Tati was not only a great slapstick physical performer, but also a director who utilized the full comic potential of film. He was the master of what became known as the "transformation" gag, in which one object becomes something else before our eyes. In one scene, while Hulot is changing a wheel on his car, the spare tyre falls into a pile of sticky leaves. Hulot retrieves the tyre, only for it to be taken from him by a passing funeral cortege who have mistaken it for a wreath. Another example occurs during Hulot's attempt to use a damaged canoe, which breaks in mid-paddle – suddenly metamorphosing into a giant "beak" that swallows him whole.

Tati also delights in toying with audience expectations. In one delightful scene, a tiny child buys two ice creams from a street vendor, and totters back to the hotel via rickety stairs and difficult doors, barely balancing his prized cones along the way. At every obstacle we expect the ice creams to fall, but the long expected accident never happens, and finally the little boy triumphantly sits down to enjoy his frozen treat. The joke is on us. Tati was also well aware of the comic potential of sound, post-dubbing the soundtrack of his films with quirky sound effects, such as the weird boinging of the restaurant door that heralds the arrival of the grumpy waiters from the hotel kitchen.

At the end of the movie, an old gentleman who has spent the week quietly relishing the mayhem brought by M. Hulot thanks him for bringing some excitement and fun to his life. As the final credits roll, the audience owes Jacques Tati a similar debt of gratitude.

When Harry Met Sally...

dir **Rob Reiner**, 1987, US, 95m

cast **Billy Crystal, Meg Ryan, Carrie Fisher, Bruno Kirby**

cin **Barry Sonnenfeld** m **Marc Shaiman**

...Or the romantic comedy best remembered for a fake orgasm. When director **Rob Reiner** met screenwriter **Nora Ephron**, they asked one of those age-old questions – can a man ever truly be just good friends with a woman? (As Billy Crystal's Harry explains, even if sparks aren't flying, "You pretty much want to nail them [anyway]".) In attempting to answer this question they created *When Harry Met Sally...*, a smart, witty romantic comedy that explores the point male-female relationships appeared to have reached in the late 1980s, a time when career concerns and high aspirations vied with matters of the heart.

Relaxed, somewhat slob-like student Harry (Crystal) first meets uptight, none-more proper Sally (Ryan) when she gives him a lift home from university. Thus begins their journey through the years, as they set about establishing their adult lives, going through romantic relationships and slowly discovering that, despite it all, they have actually become good friends. Ephron, an essayist/novelist-turned-screenwriter does a tremendous job here, creating a dialogue-heavy movie that sparkles with wit but never undermines its characterization in favour of its gags. The script is handled with great panache by Reiner, who not only has a great ear for rhythm and timing, but keeps everything moving by setting his characters against a glorious series of Manhattan backgrounds – though the characters themselves don't seem to notice them, being more concerned with each other. The film's wistful charm is buoyed by **Harry Connick Jr.**'s retro stylings of a number of classics from the 1930s and 1940s (one of the film's working titles was *It Had To Be You*).

Billy Crystal had moved from stand-up to TV via the ironic soap-opera pastiche *Soap* (playing US primetime TV's first openly gay character) and had slowly developed into a fine movie actor, with an old-fashioned but perfectly formed, New York, comic delivery. Meg Ryan emerged as a fine comic actress in this film and crystallized her persona (one that she worked hard to shake off) as America's latest sweetheart, a total darling who also knew how to fake it in bed.

The fake-orgasm-in-the-restaurant scene dominates the movie, and it's worth noting three things about it: the woman who says "I'll have what she's having" after Sally finishes is Reiner's mother, Estelle; the line itself was apparently contributed by Billy Crystal; and, after the shot was finished, the crew presented Ryan with a salami in honour of her performance.

By creating an old fashioned movie – the music, the images of New York, the eternal theme of the struggle to find love – Reiner and Ephron created a very contemporary romantic comedy, one that has been copied several times (Ephron even tried it herself with 1993's *Sleepless In Seattle* and 1998's *You've Got Mail*) but one that has rarely been equalled, and never bettered.

Withnail & I

dir Bruce Robinson, 1986, UK, 107m
cast Richard E. Grant, Paul McGann, Richard Griffiths, Ralph Brown cin Peter Hannan m David Dundas, Rick Wentworth

No movie has criticized an era and its ideology as savagely, as effectively and as humorously as Bruce Robinson's pacan to the dog days of the 1960s. From the opening sax-led blast of King Curtis' take on Procol Harum's "A Whiter Shade Of Pale", *Withnail & I* walks the tightrope between being beautifully sad and tragically funny with more finesse than could be imagined possible. It is also, quite possibly, the greatest hangover movie of all time.

This death knell on the sixties dream arrives in the form of two would-be actors who use the atmosphere of the times to reconcile themselves to the fact that underachievement is their primary talent. This point is brilliantly observed, and all the more biting for having been made in Thatcher's Britain. The movie follows their seedy lives in Camden Town, London, and their failed attempt to escape from themselves in the countryside. It ends on a bittersweet note as the unnamed "I" of the title gets to a position where he can move on, leaving Withnail isolated and left behind, an anachronism rooted in the closing decade.

Much like his protagonists, director-writer **Bruce Robinson** had been a struggling actor (his glory days of playing Benvolio in Franco Zeffirelli's 1968 *Romeo And Juliet* long behind him) who had turned to screenwriting (including 1984's Oscar-nominated *The Killing Fields*) while facing endless days of unemployment. Wanting to direct the movie himself, he secured the patronage of ex-Beatle **George Harrison**, whose production company Handmade Films – originally set up to salvage *Monty Python's Life Of Brian* (see Canon) – became a beacon of hope during the 1980s in the shadows generally referred to as the "British Film Industry".

Casting, of course, was crucial. **Paul McGann** – then making his film debut – was quickly cast as "I"; Withnail proved harder to find, although when Robinson came across Richard E. Grant he knew he had found a star in the making. Grant, a teetotaller, threw himself

Hangover humour- *Withnail and I*

into the boozy role with emphatic abandon, leading Robinson to comment that "Grant's ability to convey drunkenness as simultaneously tragic and funny makes this film what it is". Other characters are equally memorable, most notably **Ralph Brown**'s Danny, the man who knows how to roll a "Camberwell Carrot" – the role was such a hit that **Mike Myers** hired Brown to more or less repeat it, as a roadie, in 1993's *Wayne's World 2* – and of course **Richard Griffiths** as Withnail's eccentric, predatory and lonely Uncle Monty.

On its release, the movie was critically lauded but did little at the box office. But, courtesy of video, it developed an afterlife of its own, and over the next decade became a major cult movie, *Withnail* understands the sordid and the grim better than most comedy films, which perhaps accounts for its enduring status as a student classic. Along the way it has fostered a number of sideline activities, notably the Withnail drink-along game, in which players try to keep up with the beverages consumed on-screen (note to the wise – avoid the lighter fluid).

"Comedy is tragedy ... plus time"

First and foremost, let's put this in perspective – the above quote stems from Woody Allen's nihilistic masterpiece *Crimes And Misdemeanours* (1989). It is uttered by Alan Alda's character – a vacuous filmmaker – and is intended to illustrate his vacuity. Allen is clearly disdainful of this man and all he represents, but the quote nonetheless touches on something significant – the fine line between comedy and tragedy.

Allen has walked the line between comedy and tragedy in many of his best works. *Crimes And Misdemeanours* is a movie in which one character gets away with murder (literally), one woman is shat upon (literally) and the only character who represents morality – a priest – is struck blind. This is a comedy movie that seems intent on disproving the existence of a moral universe. Though, as Allen points out at the end, morality does have a place – only it's in the movies. Not the real world.

And Allen is by no means alone in this. While there is a deluge of comedies that simply set out to make you feel good about the world, or, even more simply, to make you laugh (could anyone come out of *Blazing Saddles* feeling worse about the world?), there is often a great deal more resonance to the movies we tend to think of as being funny and sad at the same time. Everyone thinks of Frank Capra's *It's A Wonderful Life* (1946) as being the quintessential feel-good hunk of holiday cheer, but it's also an intensely bleak film about a suicidal man; *Broadcast News* (1987; see Canon) brilliantly satirizes the state of the world's media, but never fails to show us just what a parlous state it's in; *Being There* (1979), regarded by many as Peter Sellers' finest hour, is a grim, dour film that throws us a curve ball in its closing minutes. And these movies are not alone at dealing with the dark, while frothing it up with the light – hell, even *Four Weddings* had a funeral in it.

The Icons: comedy legends

Two icons of comedy – a bawdy Mae West and a
sly W.C. Fields in *My Little Chickadee* (1940)

The Icons

Abbott and Costello

Bud Abbott Performer, 1895–1974
Lou Costello Performer, 1906–1959

While no comedy team could match Laurel and Hardy in terms of ability, **Bud Abbott** and **Lou Costello** came close to matching them in popularity during the 1940s and early 1950s. With Bud playing the tall, skinny, straight man and Lou the plump, lovable clown, their act was steeped in the routines of vaudeville, burlesque and slapstick – forms of "low" comedy that made them phenomenally successful during World War II and beyond. As fan Jerry Seinfeld put it, "they were giants of their time, who truly immortalized burlesque forever".

Neither man set out to be in showbusiness. Abbott always claimed that, after growing up on New York's Coney Island, he was shanghaied at the age of fifteen and forced to serve as crew on a ship bound for Norway. A slightly more plausible story has it that he was working as a theatre cashier one night in 1931 when he was asked to go on stage in place of Lou Costello's straight man, who was unable to appear that night due to a mystery ailment. Whatever the truth, the duo didn't know each other before that fortuitous encounter in 1931. Costello, eleven years Abbott's junior, had kicked around in a string of dead-end jobs before heading West to break into the movies. Failing to secure anything better than labouring and minor stunt work, he turned to vaudeville.

The two men instantly clicked – Costello's innocent, bumbling, oversized humour offset by Abbott's hard-edged, cynical exasperation. After headlining on the vaudeville circuit and establishing themselves on radio, the leap to Hollywood was an obvious – and easy – one, the boys signing to major comedy studio Universal in 1939. They scored quickly with their second movie *Buck Privates* (1941), which, while providing a comic look at the war that the US was about to enter, could also lay claim to all but inventing the now standard comedy movie character of the unforgiving, tough-as-nails drill sergeant. The string of movies they made in the 1940s provides the best examples of their particular form of vaudeville, particularly *The Naughty Nineties* (1945), which shows for the first time on screen their classic baseball routine, *Who's On First,* which the pair performed literally thousands of times live on the radio.

Costello: Who's on first?
Abbott: Yes.
Costello: I mean the fellow's name.
Abbott: Who.
Costello: The guy on first. . .
Abbott: Who is on first!
Costello: I'm asking *you* who's on first.
Abbott: That's the man's name.
Costello: That's who's name?
Abbott: Yes!
– and so on . . .

In the late 1940s the pair shifted into an increasingly bizarre and laboured series of *Abbott*

And Costello Meet... movies: their first encounter was with *Frankenstein* in 1948, followed by meetings with *Boris Karloff* (1949), *The Invisible Man* (1951), *Dr Jekyll And Mr Hyde* (1954), *The Mummy* (1955) and even the Keystone Kops (1955). They also explored the distant reaches of space in *Abbott And Costello Go To Mars* (1953). After a stint on television and continuing to work on the stage, their final movie together was 1956's *Dance With Me Henry*, a move from vaudeville skits and into comedy drama, in which they struggle to recapture their earlier chemistry. Abbott retired soon after, but Costello did have one solo venture – *The 30 Foot Bride of Candy*

Rock – before his death in 1959.

Buck Privates
dir Arthur Lubin, 1941, USA, 84m, b/w

Abbott and Costello hit the big time with their slick vaudeville routines and high energy tomfoolery in this tale of two men who join the army to avoid jail – only to find the cop who wanted to run them in in the first place has been made their drill sergeant.

Abbott And Costello Meet Frankenstein
dir Charles Barton, 1948, US, 83m, b/w

The best of the *Meet...* series, in which Bud and Lou team up with the Universal Pictures horror franchise to reinvent Frankenstein's monster, along with Dracula and the Wolf

Another encounter for Abbot and Costello – meeting the *Mummy*

Man, as figures of fun. The pitting of horror screen legends Bela Lugosi and Lon Chaney against Bud and Lou's capering has assured it cult status.

Woody Allen

Actor, Screenwriter and Director, 1935–

It's testament to the talent of this diminutive, bespectacled, freckled, red-headed neurotic that on more than one occasion during his career he has been voted one of the sexiest men alive – proof, if any were needed, that laughter is indeed a great aphrodisiac. This may well be something that **Woody Allen** (born Allen Konigsberg) has known since the age of fifteen, when, still in high school, he started selling gags to newspapers and comedians. Having decided to make comedy writing his career, Allen dropped out of New York University and ensconced himself in the writing team on Sid Caesar's classic *Your Show Of Shows* along with Neil Simon, Mel Brooks, Carl Reiner and others.

Despite his performance anxiety, Allen started to perform his own material and soon found great success in both nightclubs and on TV. It was here that Allen perfected what would become his on-screen persona – he took a whole wealth of history of Jewish comedy and adapted it for the modern age, seeding it liberally with contemporary concerns and neuroses. He soon found himself in demand as a screenwriter, making his debut on those typically 1960s mish-mashes *What's New, Pussycat?* (1965) and James Bond spoof *Casino Royale* (1967).

Frustrated by these over-inflated productions, Allen took control of his work. He began by buying the rights to a Japanese thriller, dubbing it into English and creating a comedy, *What's Up, Tiger Lily?* (1966), another 1960s curiosity. In *Take the Money And Run* (1969) he wrote and directed, and also took the lead role of an inept bank robber. Although patchy, it contained a wealth of great gags and showed the beginnings of a major filmmaking talent. Allen would soon refine his abilities behind the camera, making on average a movie a year, creating one of the most prolific and strongest bodies of work in American cinema.

The early 1970s were Allen's golden period, producing a string of movies that still rank amongst his funniest. *Bananas* (1971) tackled South American politics, *Sleeper* (1973) parodied science fiction, while *Love And Death* had a field day with gloomy Russian literature. With 1977's *Annie Hall*, however, Allen offered a more serious side. Exploring the problems of finding, and holding on to, love, it saw Allen break through into the mainstream, landing a handful of Oscars along the way.

This success gave the ever-wilful director his first chance to alienate his audience. Long an admirer of such European filmmakers as Ingmar Bergman and Federico Fellini, in 1978 Allen made *Interiors*, a drama that proved to be a major flop. He followed this with a return to comedy – the sumptuous hymn to his home town that was *Manhattan* (1979) and *Stardust Memories* (1980), a sometimes savage look at a filmmaker who has lost his passion for his work, trapped by the demands of an audience who only want to see the "early funny ones". It was clear that this side of things now interested Allen less, but as his work became more esoteric, so it became more interesting. Thus a warm homage to the movies such as *The Purple Rose Of Cairo* (1985) could be followed a couple of films later by the breathtakingly downbeat *Crimes And Misdemeanours* (1989), which singlehandedly sets out to disprove the existence of God and gets away with it.

Allen, who insists that his films are never

Woody Allen's comedy musical: *Everyone Says I Love You* (1996)

Allen had always scored his movies to his own record collection – a mix of jazz and classical, from Armstrong to Gershwin, Porter to Berlin. With this movie he finally decided to put the music firmly in the foreground and make a musical. So what if none of his cast could carry a tune? There's still delight in watching Julia Roberts, Ed Norton, Drew Barrymore, Tim Roth and Allen himself make their way through an array of classics as the delicate romance moves from Allen's native Manhattan to Venice and Paris, two of his other favourite cities. For the movie's final act, Allen dressed everyone as Groucho Marx and staged a magical dance number with Goldie Hawn on the banks of the Seine, surely one of the most perfect and bizarre moments in any of his films. *Everyone Says I Love You* has an innocence and charm, often missing from his more acerbic later works, and remains one of his finest and most underrated movies. Plus it's a great opportunity to watch Hollywood royalty as their voices crack.

autobiographical, has nonetheless produced one of the most deeply personal bodies of work in American cinema. Relationships are chronicled in all their beauty and ugliness, his love of the movies and jazz meticulously documented, and, if his later films are anything to go by – *Deconstructing Harry* (1997), *Hollywood Ending* (2002) – he has been slowly detailing the most protracted nervous breakdown in cinema history.

Bananas
dir Woody Allen, 1971, US, 81m

Allen tackles South American politics in a way that is both hit and miss, as his nebbish alter-ego Fielding Mellish finds himself embroiled in a political overthrow south of the border (complete with requisite Castroesque beard). Often very funny, with distinct echoes of the Marx Brothers' *Duck Soup* (see Canon).

Sleeper
dir Woody Allen, 1973, US, 88m

Allen, cryogenically frozen in the 1970s, awakes more than two hundred years later to discover that sex takes place via a machine called the "orgasmatron" and the emperor of the country is little more than a nose. The director's most slapstick film, in many ways a homage to the comedians of his youth.

Love And Death
dir Woody Allen, 1975, US, 85m

Woody takes on classic Russian literature in what may well be his funniest film. He is Boris Grushenko, a Russian peasant, dealing with the imminent invasion of his land by Napoleon and trapped by endless philosophical conversations on the meaning of love and death and his desire for Diane Keaton. And he says he doesn't make autobiographical films!

Crimes And Misdemeanours
dir Woody Allen, 1989, US, 104m

Allen in nihilistic mode, as one man (Martin Landau) gets away with murder while another (Allen) compromises his art by making a documentary about a facile TV producer (Alan Alda). In many ways this movie is the perfect synthesis between his "early funny ones" and his often more challenging later work.

Roscoe "Fatty" Arbuckle

Actor and Director, 1887–1933

One of the first truly big – in every sense – Hollywood stars, **"Fatty" Arbuckle** is predominantly remembered today for giving Tinseltown one of its first truly big scandals. In 1921, when 320-pound Roscoe Conkling Arbuckle, affectionately known the world over as "Fatty", was charged with the manslaughter of young starlet Virginia Rappe (she died from a ruptured bladder, alleged to be the result of a sexual assault during one of Arbuckle's drunken parties), the Hollywood community, and the world, was rocked to its core.

Kansas-born Arbuckle began his professional life as a plumber's assistant before branching out into vaudeville and pantomime. His combination of baby-faced looks and huge – though agile – girth soon singled him out, and he began to get work as an extra in movies. In 1913 he became one of Mack Sennett's Keystone Kops, and was soon costarring in a variety of shorts alongside famed comedians including Mabel Normand, Chester Conklin and Charlie Chaplin. As with his peers, Arbuckle had

He Did And He Didn't (1916) – Arbuckle and Normand

the savvy and ability to take control of his own on-screen work, and by 1916 was writing and directing his own films. By 1917 he was doing the same for others, including Buster Keaton, and had set up his own production company, Comique Film Studios. One of his biggest successes was 1921's *Brewster's Millions*, the second telling of this popular tale (it's been filmed seven times to date), in which he plays a man who stands to inherit ten million dollars if he can spend two million in one year – and not fall in love and get married along the way.

Although Arbuckle was unsuccessfully tried no less than three times over Rappe's death – the jury was hung twice, Arbuckle acquitted on the third occasion – the scandal still put paid to his acting career. Forced off the screen, Arbuckle remained behind the camera, directing under the pseudonym William B. Goodrich (the story goes that his loyal friend Buster Keaton encouraged him to take the name "Will B. Goode"). He travelled to Europe in a failed attempt to resume his previous work, but eventually returned to America. In 1931, after pleading in Hollywood paper *Photoplay* "Just let me work", he appeared in a couple of shorts, took to heavy drinking and died broke in 1933. Meanwhile, swayed by the vehemence of public opinion in the wake of this and other Hollywood scandals, and in an attempt to prevent being crippled by censorship from outside forces, in 1922 the major Hollywood players invited Postmaster General Will Hays to become president of the newly formed MPPDA, the Motion Pictures Producers and Distributors of America. Enforcing Hollywood self-regulation, with a list of "Don't"s and "Be Careful"s, Hays eventually created the famed Production Code, a censorship body that was enforced, with varying success, on Hollywood until 1952.

Today the events and implications of the Fatty Arbuckle scandal far outweigh the actor's reputation as a talented comedian. They formed the basis for James Ivory's 1974 film *The Wild Party*, in which James Coco plays Arbuckle in everything but name.

The Butcher Boy
dir Roscoe "Fatty" Arbuckle, 1917, USA, 30m, b/w

A classic piece of slapstick set in a general store and a girl's boarding school. Arbuckle does what he does best, juggling slabs of meat and cleavers, chucking pies and cross-dressing as America's Sweetheart, Mary Pickford – it's also notable as being Buster Keaton's first movie.

John Belushi

Actor, 1949-1982

Coming as it did just two years after the assassination of John Lennon, the sudden drug-induced death of **John Belushi** in 1982 helped define the nature of celebrity in that era. Here was a child of the 60s who came into his own in the 70s, and was no longer around by the 80s – the very definition of live fast, die young, and (at least in Belushi's case) leave a not-so-healthy-looking corpse.

Of Albanian descent, Belushi was born and raised in Chicago (his younger brother James

also became an actor), and made his way into Chicago's famed Second City improv theatre by the early 1970s. His manic energy, rough edge and sheer physicality (despite his fluctuating weight, he remained a nimble and able physical comedian) singled him out, along with his uncannily accurate Joe Cocker impressions, and he was soon poached by *National Lampoon*, the satirical magazine that was expanding its empire into theatre and radio. Belushi was picked to head the cast of *Lemmings*, a parody of the Woodstock music festival, and played the on-stage announcer in a cast that included Christopher Guest and Chevy Chase.

By 1975, when producer Lorne Michaels was casting a new TV show called *Saturday Night Live*, Belushi was already a fairly big fish in the relatively small pond that was the New York comedy scene, and was a natural catch. Many at the time – Belushi included – expected him to be the star of the show, but, much to his annoyance, Chevy Chase stole everyone's thunder that first year. Yet Belushi soldiered on, winning audiences with surreal characters such as an aggrieved killer bee a and nonsense-spouting Samurai warrior. *SNL's* writing team – Belushi included – won an Emmy award that first year and, after the departure of Chase, Belushi began to assume pole position.

Lampoon decided to make 1977 the year of the movie. *Animal House* (see Canon) was their first project and Belushi was cast as the iconic Bluto Blutarski, thus breaking him into the mainstream. Back on *SNL*, he was by now working closely with Dan Aykroyd and by the start of the show's third season they introduced a pair of characters who became known as the Blues Brothers. Originally put together as a warm-up routine, Jake and Elwood Blues found themselves backed by a sterling cast of 1960s soul musicians, and in 1980 made the leap to the big screen (with a little help from John Landis). Thus it was that two comedians became million-selling rock stars.

Belushi also wanted to be taken seriously as an actor, and his performances in old-fashioned comedies such as *Old Boyfriends* (1978) and his final film *Continental Divide* (1981) certainly indicate that he had a great deal to offer. All this was curtailed, however, one night in a bungalow on the grounds of LA's famous Chateau Marmont. Both Robert DeNiro and Robin Williams visited him there that night – Belushi was preparing to play a junkie in an upcoming movie and reportedly asked DeNiro if he thought it was a good idea to shoot up live on camera for the sake of verisimilitude. Yet it was never to be. One speedball of cocaine and heroin later, Belushi was no more.

The Blues Brothers
dir John Landis, 1980, US, 133m

Jake (Belushi) gets out of jail, teams up with his brother Elwood (Dan Aykroyd), dons his shades, dark suit and pork pie hat and sets out on a "mission from God" to get their old blues band back together, ostensibly to save the orphanage they both grew up in. A delirious – and often excessive – example of what *SNL* had to offer the big screen. Great music, too.

The brilliant Belushi (right)

The other Blues Brother: Dan Aykroyd

Canadian born Dan Aykroyd has had a far lengthier and more successful career than his erstwhile partner John Belushi, but his mainstream status has meant he has never really enjoyed the same kind of cult celebrity. Like many of his peers, Aykroyd started with the Second City theatrical troupe (the Canadian branch in Toronto in his case) before finding fame on *Saturday Night Live*. He followed Belushi into the movies, first in Spielberg's military comedy *1941* (1979), then with *The Blues Brothers* (a long-time blues devotee, he later opened a string of successful nightclubs called

The House of Blues). Over the years he has worked in a variety of genres, from successful comedies with fellow *SNL* alumni – *Trading Places* (1983), *Ghostbusters* (1984; see Canon) – through dramas, including *Driving Miss Daisy* (1989) for which he was Oscar nominated, to animation voicework (*Antz*, 1998). He remains a Hollywood stalwart, and, when he's not busy hosting TV shows on unexplained psychic phenomena, makes the best of a steady stream of so-so comedies including 2004's *Christmas with the Kranks*.

Robert Benchley

Screenwriter and Actor, 1889–1945

Robert Benchley was an acerbic, fast-talking wit – famed for the quip "Let's get out of these wet clothes and into a dry Martini", among many others – who took the pace and the voice of his own journalism (he wrote for the *New Yorker* in its late-1920s heyday) and turned it into terrific on-screen dialogue. He found great success on radio, in witty stage revues and as a supporting player in a number of features, but is perhaps best

remembered for the hilarious series of *How To…* shorts he made in the 1930s and 1940s, which cast his dry humour over a number of modern-day conundrums.

Following his graduation from Harvard in 1912, where he had developed a popular skit as a drunken after-dinner speaker that he was to repeat numerous times over the course of his career, Benchley moved into advertising. He served as associate editor of the *New York Tribune's* Sunday magazine before becoming managing editor of *Vanity Fair*, where he worked with

Robert Benchley (centre) in *I Married a Witch* (1942)

Dorothy Parker and Robert E. Sherwood, fellow members of the so-called Algonquin Round Table, an elite group of New York intellectuals and wits. He later became drama editor for *Life* magazine from 1920 until 1929, and theatre critic for the *New Yorker*. By 1928 he was taking his essays to the screen, with such wonderful pieces as the small but perfectly formed *The Sex Life Of The Polyp* (1928), in which he delivers a surreal lecture on said subject to a genteel ladies group.

Benchley's comic insights in another cinelecture, 1935's *How To Sleep*, were greeted with an Academy Award. Other classics in the series included *How To Behave*, *How To Vote*, *How To Become A Detective* (all 1936), *How To Figure Income Tax* (1938), *How To Sub-Let* (1939), *How To Eat* (1940) – "We must be careful of what we eat. We must eat a balanced diet. By a balanced diet I mean no bread, no butter, no potatoes, no meat, no vegetables, no solid food – just a handful of old lettuce now and then or a few dried beans is all we'd better try to take care of" – and *How To Take A Vacation* (1941), as well as offering a few pointers on *The Trouble With Husbands* (1940). He also appeared in numerous features, including *Bedtime Story* (1941), *I Married A Witch* (1942), and alongside Bing Crosby and Bob Hope in *The Road To Utopia* (1946).

All in all, Robert Benchley wrote and acted in 38 feature films and contributed to scores of others. His grandson is the novelist Peter Benchley, author of *Jaws*.

The Sex Life Of The Polyp
dir Thomas Chalmers, 1928, US, 11m

Benchley's trademark mix of eruditeness and confusion as a lecturer is in full mode here, taking an already ridiculous subject and making it more so. This impish piece set the template for his numerous short movie "lectures" that followed, as well as establishing Benchley as a movie character.

Mel Brooks
Director, Actor and Screenwriter, 1926–

There are three talented writers who, more than anyone else in cinema, define the modern image of New York Jewish humour. Woody Allen focuses on the anxiety, Neil Simon on the romantic, and **Mel Brooks** on the downright wacky. By far the loudest of the trio, Brooks acts most often like a comedy tornado: writing, producing, directing and performing in a never understated manner, he has amassed a body of work that moves from the sublime to the ridiculous, sometimes within the same moment.

Born Melvin Kaminsky in Brooklyn, Brooks had a precocious gift for impersonations and an ear for music that led him, after completing service in World War II, to find his way to the Catskills – the home-from-home for New York's vacationing Jewish community. Brooks worked at the Grossinger's resort, becoming the club's social director and resident comic. More than any of his peers, his rapid-fire comedy is rooted in these clubs – the fast-paced patter, the slow build capped by the one-liner.

Having hooked up as a writer and occasional performer with Sid Caesar on 1950s television shows including *The Admiral Broadway Revue* and *Your Show Of Shows*, Brooks began working with another writer-performer, Carl Reiner, and honing his Jewish shtick. Brooks made a name for himself with their 1960 album, *The 2000 Year Old Man*, in which he played said man, eager to offer his insights on all the major historical events. The success of this character kept Brooks in the public eye, making appearances on numerous US talk shows. In between he cowrote and developed the popular spy parody TV show *Get Smart* with Buck Henry, and also wrote an Oscar-winning cartoon, *The Critic* (1962), in which he provides

Mel Brooks with Cleavon Little on the set of *Blazing Saddles*

a scathing "New Yoik" voiceover for the pretentious images shown on screen.

Brooks was, of course, headed towards movies, and when he got there, he peaked right away with 1968's *The Producers* (see Canon). The brilliant tale of a musical show, *Springtime For Hitler*, starred Zero Mostel and the then largely unknown Gene Wilder, and became an instant classic. He stumbled somewhat with his next feature, *The Twelve Chairs* (1970) and it wasn't until 1974 that Brooks got back in the saddle with the much-loved Western parody *Blazing Saddles*.

He followed this with a parody of Universal Studio's 1930s horror classics, *Young Frankenstein* (1974, again with Wilder), and the delightfully silly *Silent Movie* (1976).

Brooks may well have displayed a talent for breaking with tradition and taboo, but his films have always been typified by excess, by their creator's inability to hone a single gag when three would do. After *Silent Movie*, a lack of care began to dominate his work, which became both lazier and mired in parody – *High Anxiety* (1977) did Hitchcock, *Spaceballs* (1987) did *Star Wars*, *Robin Hood: Men In Tights* (1993) did *Robin Hood: Prince*

Of Thieves, and *Dracula: Dead And Loving It* (1995) was no *Young Frankenstein*. Brooks's one attempt at an original screenplay, 1991's *Life Stinks*, sad to say, stank. As a producer however – as head of Brooksfilms – he was indirectly responsible for such great movies as David Lynch's *The Elephant Man* (1980) and David Cronenberg's *The Fly* (1986).

Young Frankenstein
dir Mel Brooks, 1974, US, 108m, b/w

A homage to the cinema of director James Whale and Universal Studios with Gene Wilder as the doctor and Peter Boyle as his creation – never better than when proving his inherent civility to society by performing the song and dance number "Puttin' On The Ritz".

Silent Movie
dir Mel Brooks, 1976, US, 87m

Brooks is Mel Funn, a Hollywood filmmaker who tries to sell the first new silent movie in over forty years. A homage to Sennett-influenced slapstick, it rounds up Brooks regulars Marty Feldman and Dom DeLuise alongside Paul Newman, James Caan and Liza Minnelli cameoing as themselves. Marcel Marceau gets the best role, however, with the only line in the film – "No!"

High Anxiety
dir Mel Brooks, 1977, US, 94m

Brooks tackles Hitchcock, from *Vertigo* to *Psycho*, with several stops in between, starring as a psychologist working at an institute for the "Very, Very Nervous." It's a pastiche more than a narrative, but full of fun moments – although a working knowledge of Hitchcock probably aids enjoyment.

Frank Capra
Director, 1897–1991

Alongside Hitchcock and Spielberg, **Frank Capra** remains one of the most emblematic of American filmmakers. The word "Capraesque"

has fallen into common parlance, describing a movie that echoes the quintessentially American images and virtues that the director sought to convey through such classics as *Mr. Smith Goes To Washington* (1939) and *It's A Wonderful Life* (1946). Possibly more than any other Hollywood director, Frank Capra created a vision of America that defined that nation for the world, the echoes of which can still be felt today in everything from *Gremlins* to *Groundhog Day*.

Not bad for a Sicilian immigrant who graduated with a degree in Chemical Engineering. Finding no work in his chosen field, in the early 1920s Capra drifted and gambled. Down to his last nickel (so legend has it), he talked his way into directing a one-reel adaptation of Rudyard Kipling's *Fultah Fisher's Boarding House* (1922). Realizing he knew nothing about film, Capra spent the next year working in a small film lab, printing, processing and splicing amateur films. He then moved on to work for the Hal Roach studios, providing gags for the popular *Our Gang* series of shorts. From there he leap-frogged over to Mack Sennett, and in 1926 and 1927 found his first success writing and directing three vehicles for the hugely popular comic Harry Langdon.

But it wasn't until 1928, when he was put under contract to Columbia Pictures, that Capra really came into his own as a filmmaker. He made more than twenty films at the studio over the next decade, starting with two snappy comedies, *Platinum Blonde* (1931), with Jean Harlow, and *American Madness* (1932), starring Walter Huston, before finding enormous success with *It Happened One Night* (see Canon, 1934), the first movie to scoop all of the top five Academy Awards (Best Picture, Director, Screenplay, Actor and Actress). Capra's Columbia movies blended screwball comedy with earnest idealism, often focusing on the triumph of the individual over

Quintessentially Frank Capra

both the odds and the world around him, and struck a major chord with Depression-era audiences. Even when he turned his hand to wartime propaganda documentaries such as 1942's *Prelude To War*, it seemed that Capra could do no wrong, winning yet another Academy Award.

Ironically, it was only when he chose to make one of his most heartfelt films, the Christmas story *It's A Wonderful Life* – in which Capra regular Jimmy Stewart plays one of his defining roles, as a suicidal man who reassesses his life with the help of a friendly angel before realizing quite how important he is, and has been, to those around him – that he finally came unstuck:

the movie was a critical and box-office disappointment. After the film fell into public domain ownership in the 1970s, however, it became a staple of Christmas television, often broadcast in the States several times a day, and rapidly rose to its position as one of the best loved movies of all time. Capra, meanwhile, followed the movie with a series of lesser works, culminating in 1961's leaden *A Pocketful Of Miracles*.

 Mr Deeds Goes To Town
dir Frank Capra, 1936, US, 115m, b/w

This restrained screwball movie finds a small town idealist adrift in the big city following an unexpected inheritance and ultimately states that money isn't everything. Gary Cooper is splendid as Longfellow Deeds, and Jean Arthur matches him scene for scene as the reporter out to get his story. A classic Capraesque take on Depression-era America.

You Can't Take It With You
dir Frank Capra, 1938, US, 127m, b/w

Jimmy Stewart is Tony Kirby, the wealthy son of a munitions manufacturer who falls for Alice Sycamore (Jean Arthur), apparently the only sane person in a house of eccentric, poor-but-happy inventors. Capra delights in taking the American family and turning it on its head, while Stewart plays bemused better than just about anyone in town.

Jim Carrey

Actor, 1962–

It's not surprising that people who knew Canadian-born **Jim Carrey** as a child remember him as an extrovert. After all, this is the man who made his name by, literally, speaking out of his arse, and who has almost single-handedly redefined the word "manic" – a crown that has clearly been passed to him via Danny Kaye, Jerry Lewis, Robin Williams, and possibly all three of the Marx Brothers combined. He grew up (in part at least) in a trailer park – a young, slightly disaffected kid who knew from an early age that his family needed him to pay his way. Thankfully for many of us, he chose the comedy route to do so.

In comedy terms, he practically embodies the word precocious – he sent his resumé to top-rated US variety series *The Carol Burnett Show* when he was ten, having been allowed a few minutes at the end of each school day to stand up and entertain his classmates. He then, however, went on to pay his dues. Starting out as a janitor, he decided to go with the comedy thing, concentrating initially on honing his celebrity impressions. A gig at the Comedy Store in LA brought him to the attention of the late "no respect" maestro Rodney Dangerfield, who booked him for a season at his New York club as his own opening act. Early movie roles, including a furry alien alongside Jeff Goldblum in the lamentable *Earth Girls Are Easy* (1988), were inauspicious, but he did manage to become a favourite of Clint Eastwood, who cast him in both *Pink Cadillac* (1989) and the *Dirty Harry* opus *The Dead Pool* (1988).

On TV Carrey starred in a lame sitcom called *The Duck Factory*, which quickly died a death. However, those lucky enough to have caught him on the 1990s comedy sketch show *In Living Color* – in which he stood out, not just as the only white guy but also as the show's most original performer – knew that something good was forming. When his next movie, *Ace Ventura, Pet Detective* (1993), went through the roof, the rest of the world caught up, and Carrey experienced a rise to global fame that practically redefined the word "meteoric". He was the first actor to demand – and receive – $20 million for a single movie (*The Cable Guy*, 1996), something

that everyone from Tom Cruise to Tom Hanks quickly took note of.

Carrey's ascent helped put CGI (and Cameron Diaz) on the map as he turned human cartoon for *The Mask* (1994), gave the world the Farrelly brothers (*Dumb and Dumber*, 1994), established Ben Stiller as a director (*The Cable Guy*, 1996), helped ruin the Batman franchise (*Batman Forever*, 1995) and proved that poor sequels could still make shedloads of money (*Ace Ventura – When Nature Calls*, 1995).

Despite his crazy whirlwind energy, throughout Carrey somehow retains a certain dignity, and has successfully turned to serious acting. Peter Weir's *The Truman Show* (1998) was a provocative and intelligent film that Carrey's presence alone turned into a milestone in modern cinema. Likewise, his earnest attempt to convey the confused wonder (and malice) of obscure comedy god Andy Kaufman in *Man On The Moon* (1999) was a nuanced and sensitive performance, as was his work in *Eternal Sunshine of the Spotless Mind* (2004), which showed that, sometimes, less really can be considerably more.

Ace Ventura, Pet Detective
dir Tom Shadyac, 1993, US, 86m

Having all but stolen the Wayans brothers' sketch TV show *In Living Colour*, Carrey got his first big-time, big screen role as a larger-than-life private eye who specializes in animal-related theft and has to track down a kidnapped dolphin. A very effective vehicle for Carrey's array of physical humour.

The Mask
dir Charles Russell, 1994, US, 101m

Carrey's elastic, over-amped features make him perfect for computer-generated caricature; he gives a sublime performance in this tale of a man who discovers an old mask that transforms him into a Looney Tunes lothario. His green-faced alter-ego wreaks revenge, robs a bank and wins the girl (Cameron Diaz), taking in a lot of lavish musical numbers along the way.

Jim Carrey dumbing it up!

🎬 Dumb & Dumber
dir Peter Farrelly, 1994, US, 107m

Two absurdly slow-witted friends become caught up in a kidnapping scheme in this naive, good-natured comedy. Belying the silliness of the content, the movie has some brilliantly sustained moments of comic tension, while Carrey stands back and becomes a star before our eyes.

🎬 The Cable Guy
dir Ben Stiller, 1996, US, 96m

Stiller's decidedly unsettling directorial piece is something of a curiosity. Carrey, in dark mode, is the Guy in question, an obsessive and increasingly dangerous figure in the life of a hapless Matthew Broderick. A fine on-screen confirmation of Carrey's insanity and his daring.

The Carry On team

Born: 1958

Current Status: Appears still to be alive

With some thirty one films – to date – the **Carry On** series is the most popular comedy series in British cinema history. And it all came about by accident. Peter Rogers was a screenwriter who turned to producing and based himself at Pinewood studios in Buckinghamshire in the early 1950s. Here in 1958 he teamed with former editor-turned-director Gerald Thomas to make what was a small comedy film entitled *Carry On Sergeant*, featuring an ensemble of British comedy talent of the day, including the likes of Charles Hawtrey, Kenneth Connor, Hattie Jacques and Kenneth Williams, many of them already established performers via theatre and radio. It was intended as a one off, but audiences fell for its quick-moving, gag-heavy approach – and the nascent beginnings of what would become its team – and Rogers very quickly found himself making a sequel, *Carry On Nurse*, released that same year.

As the *Carry On*s progressed, the series opportunistically parodied specific movies – 1964's *Carry On Cleo* was quick to poke fun at the previous year's overblown and over budget Burton-Taylor vehicle, *Cleopatra* – and sometimes they simply went for whole genres. *Carry On Spying* (1964) was a direct response to the newly launched James Bond series, while *Carry On Cowboy* (1965) sent up the Western years before Mel Brooks did the same. *Carry On Screaming* (1966), of course, took on the Hammer horror movies. British history also took a pounding in the *Carry On* hands, most notably the British Raj in *Carry On Up The Khyber* (1968), one of the most popular in the series.

The movies, which proved to be enduringly popular for the best part of two decades, are often remembered for their smut and British postcard humour. While it's true there was a fair amount of young women in short skirts bending over and being ogled by dirty old men, these 1960s movies retain a degree of innocence. What's striking is how the series reflected its times: so, as British cinemas became dominated by the sex comedy in the 1970s, so the team moved onto toilets (*Carry On At Your Convenience*, 1971), and beauty contests (*Carry On Girls*, 1973), culminating with

1978's *Carry On Emmanuelle*, an attempt to cash in on the then-popular soft core porn series, something that was quite new to mainstream British cinema at the time.

As well as the producing/directing team of Peter Rogers and Gerald Thomas, the series' key element was its regular collection of performers. Alongside those mentioned above, the team would often be joined by the likes of *Hancock* veteran Sid James, the busty Barbara Windsor, Bernard Bresslaw, Joan Sims, Jim Dale and others. *Sgt Bilko* star Phil Silvers was one of the few non-British – or internationally known – actors to ever sign up, for *Carry On Follow That Camel* in 1967.

In 1992 Rogers unwisely revived the brand with the megaflop *Carry On Columbus* (an attempt to ride the coat tails of two movies that year dealing with Christopher Columbus) and in 2005 plans to do the same again with *Carry On London*, in which a host of soap stars attempt to step into the shoes of giants.

Carry On Sergeant
dir Gerald Thomas, 1958, GB, 83m, b/w

The movie that started it all, with a stellar British comedy cast – Kenneth Connor, Kenneth Williams, Charles Hawtrey and Hattie Jacques, of course, but also Bob Monkhouse and Dora Bryan, with William Hartnell (who was soon to become TV's first Doctor Who) as the requisite bellowing sergeant.

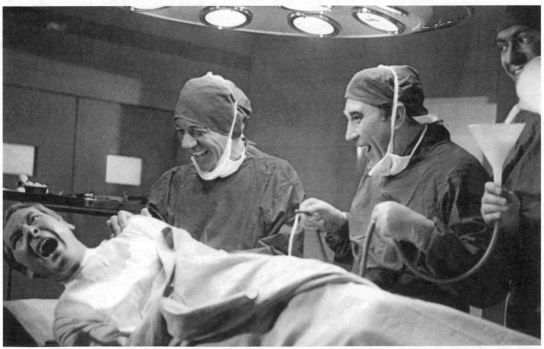

Ensemble comedy in *Carry on Doctor* (1968). Kenneth Williams screams

Carry On Cleo
dir Gerald Thomas, 1964, GB, 92m

One of the Carry On team's finest hour-and-a-halfs, with Amanda Barrie spoofing Elizabeth Taylor's Cleopatra from merely months before. The regular repertory company includes Sid James as an (unlikely) Mark Antony and Kenneth Williams as Caesar – "Infamy! Infamy! – They've all got it in for me!"

Charles Chaplin

Actor and Director, 1889–1977

Born in London to music-hall entertainers, **Charles Chaplin** became not only one of cinema's first global stars, but also one of its most iconic performers, as well as a hugely innovative and influential force behind the camera. His beginnings were tough – his father left soon after Charles's birth, eventually dying of alcoholism, and his mother struggled to raise her sons. He first performed on stage at the age of five, thrust into the spotlight to cover for his mother when her singing voice failed. Soon after, she had a complete breakdown and was hospitalized, forcing Charles and his older brother Sydney into an orphanage. From here, Charles found himself part of a travelling dance act, The Eight Lancashire Lads, and by the age of seventeen had joined his brother in Fred Karno's pantomime troupe. Karno was the leading theatrical impresario of his day and his company, which also included the young Stan Laurel, toured the States in 1910 and 1912. There Chaplin was spotted playing a drunk by movie mogul Mack Sennett, who promptly signed him to Keystone.

Charlie's performance in his first film, *Making A Living* (1913), was adequate, but by his second outing, *Kid Auto Races At Venice* (1913), he had found the outfit and image that would become the Little Tramp – baggy trousers, bowler, cane, moustache – and which would soon become known the world over. Supporting roles alongside Fatty Arbuckle (see Icons) and Mabel Normand followed, and by his thirteenth short, *Caught In The Rain* (1914), Chaplin had set up behind the camera, writing and directing himself. He made 35 films in his first year at Keystone, and became so popular that he left and signed to Essanay for a then staggering $1250 a week. Chaplin perfected his trademark combination of sadness and slapstick in 1915's *The Tramp*, and thus began the remarkable series of movies that became popular all over the world.

Offered a then unprecedented degree of creative control, Chaplin made fewer and fewer films for more and more money, taking time to polish his work rather than just churning it out. His movie character was always physically dexterous, quick-witted and even abrasive at times, but with his first feature in 1921, *The Kid*, Chaplin began to rely more heavily on the sentimentality that would come to dominate his work – and which ensured the film was a huge hit. Charlie Chaplin was now the biggest star the movie world had ever known.

Throughout the 1920s Chaplin delivered what many consider to be his masterpieces – 1925's *The Gold Rush* and 1927's *The Circus* (winner of a special award at the first ever Academy Awards) among them. The advent of sound curtailed his work somewhat, although he flew in the face of fashion with *City Lights* (1931) and, later, *Modern Times* (1936), which are both effectively silent movies made in the talkie era.

He made only a few more features, all of them interesting, including *The Great Dictator* (1940), which lampooned Hitler's Germany when most other American-based filmmakers were running scared from what was happening in Europe at

Chaplin – the cog in the machine of *Modern Times*

the time. *Monsieur Verdoux* followed in 1947, in which Chaplin plays a villain, and *Limelight* in 1952, which, despite offering the on-screen pairing of Chaplin with Buster Keaton, displayed an old-fashioned sentimentality that received a mixed reception.

Subpoenaed by the House Un-American Activities Committee to testify on his alleged Communist leanings, Chaplin found himself denied re-entry to the US when he travelled to London to attend the opening of *Limelight* in 1952. Settling in Switzerland, he vowed never to return to his adopted home, and did so just once, to pick up an honorary Oscar in 1972. A British knighthood followed in 1975.

The Kid
dir Charles Chaplin, 1921, US, 50m, b/w

Chaplin's first full-length feature shows him at both his most sublime and most cloyingly sentimental as the Little Tramp struggles to save Jackie Coogan's impoverished Kid from his inevitable future. In transcending the knockabout of Sennett and the Keystone Kops, Chaplin here elevates the comedy movie to an art form all its own.

The Circus
dir Charles Chaplin, 1928, US, 71m, b/w

A perfect example of Chaplin at his cleverest – if not always his most heartfelt, or even at times comedic – this sentimental tale of circus life and love gone wrong gives his character the opportunity to face off against lions, high wires and a hall of mirrors.

City Lights
dir Charles Chaplin, 1931, US, 87m, b/w

The Little Tramp falls for a blind flower seller, hoping to pay for an operation to restore her eyesight. Quintessential Chaplin, blending the two defining sides of his character as a filmmaker – the man with his heart on his sleeve and the comic who knows better.

Modern Times
dir Charles Chaplin, 1936, US, 85m, b/w

Chaplin's a cog in the machine – literally so, when he falls into, and travels through, an assembly line – and goes slowly insane, dragged down by the relentless monotony of "progress". Take it as a metaphor – the director's response to the age of the talkies – or just enjoy comic genius at work.

The Great Dictator
dir Charles Chaplin, 1940, US, 128m, b/w

Possibly Chaplin's most mature film, tackling the rise of fascism in Europe, with his little moustache coming in very handy in his direct take-off of Hitler. Here the filmmaker embraces both political polemic and the coming of sound in the movies, while never, of course, forgetting his art.

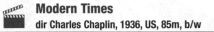

The Coen brothers

Joel Coen Director and Screenwriter, 1954–
Ethan Coen Director and Screenwriter, 1957–

Along with their friend and contemporary Sam Raimi, the **Coen brothers** virtually established modern American independent cinema on a global scale. (Jim Jarmusch also lent a hand.) Raimi first assaulted people's senses in 1982 with the groundbreaking horror movie *The Evil Dead* (on which Joel worked as an editor); a year later, the Coens announced themselves to the world with the extremely stylish film noir *Blood Simple* – directed by Joel, produced by Ethan, and written by them both. Both Raimi and the Coens found unique ways to finance their debut movies,

calling on local doctors, grandparents and friends to max out their credit cards to aid them. Their benefactors clearly made the right choice.

Blood Simple was a striking, blackly comedic debut that one would have thought was to define things to come. But from the very beginning the Coens sought to defy expectation, bringing their own unique style to a wide variety of genres and filmic styles, more often than not peppered with a delightfully twisted comic sensibility. Their follow-up was to move into anarchic, almost screwball comedy with *Raising Arizona* (1987), a sweetly touching *tour de force* that brought best-ever performances from Holly Hunter, Nicolas Cage and John Goodman. From there they delved in Irish gangster mythology with the labyrinthine *Miller's Crossing* (1990) and dark devilish existentialism with *Barton Fink* (1991), which picked up the Palme d'Or at Cannes. *The Hudsucker Proxy* (1994), cowritten by Raimi, was a flop, despite its big budget, but was followed by one of their biggest successes to date, the snowy white dark comedy of *Fargo* (1995), which collected an Oscar. In general, however, while their films have proved to be hugely influential and critically lauded, they have rarely crossed over to a mass audience. Their biggest success to date, other than *Fargo*, was the all-out Southern period comedy of *O Brother, Where Art Thou?* (2000), starring an exuberant, self-mocking George Clooney. (The title of the movie alludes to the deep and meaningful picture that Joel McCrea longs to make in Preston Sturges's classic *Sullivan's Travels*; see Canon.) Even the foray into straight(ish) romantic comedy *Intolerable Cruelty* (2003), despite the presence of heartthrob George Clooney, failed to ignite the box office, its sharp cynicism too close to the surface for comfort. While Raimi went on to win audiences round with the *Spiderman* franchise, the Coens never really strayed from their quirky path.

In 2004 they chose to remake the Ealing classic *The Ladykillers* with Tom Hanks, setting it in the Deep South and bringing complicated issues of race into the mix. It was not a big success. The influence of the Coen brothers on American independent cinema, however, cannot be under-estimated. Incidentally, though Joel is usually billed as the director of the films and Ethan as the writer, in truth there has never been any delinea-tion – they both write and they both direct, and are often referred to as "the two-headed director." Joel, however, tends to edit most of the movies, under the pseudonym Roderick Jayne.

Fargo
dir Joel Coen, 1995, US, 98m

As ever, the brothers get phenomenal performances from their cast in this off-beat, very snowy, character-based comedy. William H. Macy plays anxious as only he can when a plot to kidnap his wife goes drastically wrong, while heavily pregnant police chief Marge (Frances McDormand) ruminates, investigates and makes certain that good will prevail.

O Brother, Where Art Thou?
dir Joel Coen, 2000, US, 102m

The overblown Depression-era movie – inspired either by *The Odyssey* or Preston Sturges (or both) – in which

George Clooney has a lot of fun in *O Brother*

George Clooney dons a shaggy beard and becomes an instant comic legend. The crackling dialogue and surreal plot are both pure Coen; the soundtrack, an impeccable collection of American roots music, became almost as big a hit as the film.

The Ladykillers
dir Joel Coen, 2004, US, 104m

The brothers made an audacious – and some said unwise – move taking this beloved Ealing classic, dragging it down to the Deep South, and overwriting it with their trademark surreal sensibilities. The result is patchy but fascinating, with Tom Hanks enjoying himself as the murderous "professor" (a role that Alec Guinness had made his own).

Gérard Depardieu

Actor, 1948–

Since the mid-1970s the prolific **Gérard Depardieu** has become one of the most recog-nizable of all European performers both in serious drama and in an increasing number of comedies, both at home and abroad. Depardieu's childhood was spent on the streets, wandering, gang-running, and, according to a press interview that has haunt-ed him ever since, committing a violent sexual crime by the age of nine, something he dismissed later. (Then again, he also said he drank seven bot-tles of red wine each and every day and – let's be honest – while a big man, he's not that big.) In the late 1960s Depardieu attempted to leave his delinquent past behind by joining the travelling theatre company Café de la Gare – the actress Miou-Miou was a contemporary – and first came to international acclaim (after a few smaller roles in French cinema in the early 1970s) in Bertrand Blier's semi-comic *Les Valseuses* (*Going Places*, 1973), a delinquents-on-the-run movie in which he was perfectly cast.

He turned to comedy again in a series of films with director Francis Veber, with *La Chèvre* (1982), *Les Compères* (1983) and its sequel *Les Fugitifs* (1986). The last two were subsequently remade for America minus Depardieu (the former as *Father's Day* and the latter as *Three Fugitives*), so when another collaboration, *Mon père, ce héros* (1991), was remade as the Disney movie *My Father The Hero* (1994), the actor made sure he was cast. Unfortunately, it was nowhere near as successful (or nowhere near as good) as his previous English-language movie, Peter Weir's *Green Card* (1990), a tale of love-after-faked-immigration, with Depardieu cast as the lovable giant against Andie MacDowell's apartment-hunting horticulturist.

Back home in France, Depardieu had been finding acclaim in comic collaborations with director Bertrand Blier, including *Tenue de soirée* (1986), which sees the actor in his most outrageous role, and *Trop belle pour toi* (1989), in which he plays a businessman married to a beautiful woman (Carole Bouquet) who falls in love with his far more ordinary secretary. He also directed and starred in his own version of Molière's *Tartuffe* (1984).

In English-language cinema, however, Depardieu remains an underused force, with turns such as an overweight Musketeer in *The Man In The Iron Mask* (1998) and a wicked couturier in *102 Dalmatians* (2000) hardly adding up to much. And although further international acclaim followed after he brought to life the classic comic book sidekick Obelix in *Asterix & Obelix Mission Cleopatra* (2002), perhaps his finest performance to date remains that of the tragi-comic hero in Jean Paul Rappeneau's *Cyrano de Bergerac* (1990), a role that the larger than life – and to be frank, big nosed – Depardieu was surely born to play. The actor agreed – he

wouldn't shave the facial hair off for months after the film wrapped.

Tenue de soirée (Evening Dress)
dir Bertrand Blier, 1986, Fr, 85m

One of Depardieu's most extreme roles, as a bisexual burglar who seduces both a wife (Miou-Miou) and her husband (Michel Blanc), after leading them into a life of crime. Depardieu is at his most charismatic, just as his frequent collaborator Blier is at his most outrageous – a solid combination.

Trop belle pour toi (Too Beautiful For You)
dir Bertrand Blier, 1989, Fr, 91m

Blier keeps Depardieu in check in one of the director's most restrained films and one of the actor's biggest successes. The various and varied relationships on display are explored from a number of angles, sometimes hilarious, sometimes missing the point, and occasionally unbalanced.

Green Card
dir Peter Weir, 1990, US, 107m

Depardieu's first serious attempt to conquer the American market has him as an illegal immigrant needing to marry Andie MacDowell in order to stay in the US. Australian Peter Weir casts an outsider's eye on American life, while Depardieu delivers a gentle giant of a performance in every sense.

W.C. Fields
Actor and screenwriter, 1880–1946

W. C. Fields, born William Claude Dukenfield, talked often about his difficult childhood. And though there is some debate about quite how true the traditional story is, it is, without doubt, a good story: four years of schooling in Philadelphia were cut short when a series of violent arguments with his father, a vegetable peddler who hit his son with a shovel, led young William to leave home at the age of eleven to

W.C. Fields's distinctive comic style

life.) Performing around the world, Fields topped the bill on the Ziegfeld Follies from 1915 to 1921, the period when, allegedly, he started the heavy drinking that was to become an integral part of his comedy persona. After headlining in the Broadway show *Poppy*, a melodrama set among circus folk, he was cast by director D.W. Griffith to star in his movie based on the show, 1925's *Sally of the Sawdust*. Fields plays the typically daftly named Eustace McGargle, a juggler and con artist, and although he puts in a great comic performance, this film, and the few that followed, made little impact.

Fields's film career really took off with the advent of sound, and a run of classic movies such as *The Dentist* (1932), 1934's *The Old Fashioned Way* and, the same year, the hilariously irritable commentary on modern marriage, *It's a Gift*. In each movie he hones his distinctive comic style: a misanthropic, drunken and beleagured persona that combines physical agility with acerbic wordplay, all delivered in Fields's distinctive mumbling drawl. In 1935, he offered a quintessential Mr Micawber in David Selznick's *David Copperfield*, a role he was practically born to play. Beset by alcohol abuse, however, Fields soon found the film work dropping away, though he continued to enjoy popular acclaim on the radio. In 1940, after the surprise success of a bizarre collaboration with Mae West, *My Little Chickadee* (see Icons), Fields was able to take total creative control of his work, and wrote his freewheeling masterpiece *The Bank Dick*. A year later, *Never Give a Sucker an Even Break*, the skewed account of a hopeful screenwriter's journey to get his film made, resembles nothing so much as the vision of a drunken, wildly erratic mind. This was his last major movie. Unfashionable and ailing, W.C. Fields was dropped by his studio and died of alcohol-related pneumonia a few years later.

live on the streets. Fighting to get by (and thus developing his famed swollen nose), he hustled pool and learned to juggle, struggling his way to the top of his game in a string of carny shows and vaudeville theatres. (His sister's story, that her brother led an ordinary life, living at home and employed in a number of ordinary jobs before turning to juggling and vaudeville, is far less compelling.)

Whatever the truth, without doubt Fields worked the carny shows, and during some time in his teens got his first vaudeville gig; it took him no time at all to establish himself on the circuit. A virtuoso juggler and a hard and determined worker, he vowed he would never return to the poverty of his childhood, and as he developed his juggling act into a broader comedy revue, he demanded, and received, huge sums for his performances. (A hard-nosed attitude to his work that he was to demonstrate throughout his

The Bank Dick
dir Eddie Cline, 1940, US, 72m, b/w

Fields at his misanthropic best, drunkenly meandering (and often ad libbing) through what almost amounts to a story – that of a man, "Souse", who starts off as a film director, foils a bank robbery and ends up working for the bank in an attempt to scupper his daughter's impending marriage.

Never Give A Sucker An Even Break
dir Edward Cline, 1941, 70m, b/w

Fields made a career out of being cantankerous – beautifully demonstrated in this oddity, in which he plays a largely drunken screenwriter pitching his latest opus. It encapsulates the best of the man, but also captures him on his last legs, varying between inspired comic flights of fancy and almost tragic moments of reason.

Cary Grant

Actor 1904–1986

Cary Grant may well be the suavest man to have ever graced a screen: equally adept in light comedy and high drama, handsome, engaging, and always, above all, debonair. It's a testament to his fine and unique abilities as a performer, and to his iconic status, that Tony Curtis cheekily stole his distinctive vocal stylings in order to seduce Marilyn Monroe in *Some Like It Hot* (1959; see Canon), while John Cleese, in another homage, adopts Grant's real name (Archie Leach) to take on the role of romantic leading man in *A Fish Called Wanda* (1988). Even the man himself was not averse to a bit of self parody – there is one moment in the immortal screwball classic *His Girl Friday* (1939; see Canon) in which Grant, in a virtuoso performance as fast-talking newspaper man Walter Burns, states menacingly "The last man who messed with me was Archie Leach."

Born in Bristol, Archibald Leach arrived home at the age of nine to find his mother had "gone off to the seaside", his family's euphemism for her having been committed to a mental asylum. He left school at the age of fourteen to join an acrobatic troupe, where he learned a variety of performing skills and got his first experience of working on a stage. He also began working on his accent, passing Bristolian over in favour of London Cockney and refining it further in 1920, when his acrobatic troupe toured the States, to create his trademark phrasing. When the rest of the troupe went home, Archie stayed, and after a decade doing odd jobs and some theatre work re-christened himself Cary Grant.

In 1933, Mae West cast him as the male lead in *She Done Him Wrong*, where he made the perfect straight man foil for her sassy Diamond Lil character. (He said later that he learned more from West than any person he'd worked with.) After his impressive performance as a Cockney rogue in *Sylvia Scarlett* (1936) – the first of his movies with Katharine Hepburn, with whom he always displayed a tangible chemistry – he went on to star in the first of the sophisticated screwball comedies in which he excelled, *The Awful Truth* (1937). He was soon taking the lead in a string of classic comedies including *Bringing Up Baby* (1938), *The Philadelphia Story* (1940) and *Arsenic And Old Lace* (1944), displaying a broad range of comic performances from coolly sardonic through flustered to just plain beleaguered.

Much of Grant's unique charm is down to his slightly ambiguous, almost mercurial quality. As well as his unplaceable, if not downright peculiar, accent he also had an unerring ability to appear quintessentially masculine while displaying the silly side of machismo at the same time, and often his suave manner suggested mysterious, not always benign, hidden depths. Perhaps unsurprisingly, then, he became something of a muse to Alfred

Tangible chemistry with Katharine Hepburn

Hitchcock, who brought his wry ambiguity to some of his most successful films, including *To Catch A Thief* (1955) and, most notably, the classic *North By Northwest* (1959). Wisely, Grant knew when to call it a day and retired in 1966, despite receiving subsequent offers of work from the likes of Billy Wilder and Stanley Kubrick. He died in 1986, in Iowa, shortly before a performance of his one man show *An Evening With Cary Grant*.

The Awful Truth
dir Leo McCarey, 1937, US, 91m, b/w

Grant is effervescent as one half of a divorcing couple who don't really want to separate, most certainly don't want their exes to end up with their new partners, and do whatever they can to make it all go wrong. Screwball at its finest.

My Favourite Wife
dir Garson Kanin, 1940, US, 88m, b/w

Delightful slice of screwball in which Grant plays a

remarried widower whose first wife – who's been marooned on a desert island – returns. Complete with the man she's been marooned with! What's a guy (or indeed a gal) supposed to do? Grant plays flustered to perfection, while costars Irene Dunne and Randolph Scott bring up the rear.

I Was A Male War Bride
dir Howard Hawks, 1949, US, 103m, b/w

Setting the benchmark for gender-bending in comedy movies, this farce sees Cary Grant at his disarming best as an army officer trying to consummate his marriage to Ann Sheridan but having to go through hell and high water – and masquerading in drag – to do so.

Katharine Hepburn

Actress, 1907–2003

With her haughty cheekbones and athletic, androgynous body, her clipped vocal style and no-nonsense New England demeanour, **Katharine**

Hepburn was not your typical movie star. In her first film, *A Bill of Divorcement* (1932), director George Cukor – who was to become one of her favourite comedy collaborators – wove in a number of shots of the young actress's face, simply to inveigle her quirky beauty into the audience's consciousness. The gambit succeeded, and Hepburn, until then a theatre actress, was set for movie fame.

Brought up in a progressive Connecticut family, Hepburn had a rebellious streak and a fierce intelligence that was often taken for arrogance in Hollywood circles. Never afraid to make her feelings about her scripts and her directors known, she also chose her roles with care. Sometimes she got it wrong – hillbilly faith healer Trigger Hicks in the bizarre melodrama *Spitfire* (1934) comes to mind – but mostly her choices were spot on. Spanning genres from frothy comedy to high drama, she cornered the market in strong women and made every role her own, from the sharp-talking would-be actress in smart ensemble comedy *Stage Door* (1937) right up to the cantankerous wife in *On Golden Pond* (1981).

Though it means little to talk of a "heyday" when referring to an actress whose career spanned five decades, twelve Oscar nominations and four Oscars (none of which she turned up to accept), Hepburn's 1930s screwball heroines are among her most memorable, and timeless, roles. These women were a modern breed – active, vivacious and irreverent, and more than a match for their leading men. Hepburn's spiritedness, comic timing and wiry physicality made her an ideal screwball heroine, as did her generosity as an actress. Always at her best when pitted against other gifted comic actors, she shone especially bright with the debonair Cary Grant (see Icons), with whom she was first teamed in the curious *Sylvia Scarlett* (1935) – she as a cross-dressing girl, he as a Cockney chancer. Sharing a genuine affection based on a mutual sense of mischief and wry intelligence, the two actors went on to set the bar for comedy partnerships in the classic screwball *Bringing Up Baby* (1938, see Canon), and in the sparkling comedies *Holiday* (1938) and *The Philadelphia Story* (1940), both directed by Cukor.

Hepburn's most important sparring partner, however, was Spencer Tracy, with whom she had a discreet affair – he remained married – for more than twenty years until his death in 1967. Tracy's gruff manliness was the perfect foil for her mercurial femininity, playing to great effect in sprightly two-handers such as *Woman Of The Year* (1942), *Adam's Rib* (1949) and *Pat And Mike* (1952).

Hepburn continued working into her seventies, playing meaty dramatic roles but also, as she aged, creating a series of dryly comic, eccentric spinsters. *The African Queen* (1951) pits her buttoned-up missionary against Humphrey Bogart's boozy river trader to wonderful effect, while as lonely Jane Hudson in *Summertime* (1955, aka *Summer Madness*) she reprises her screwball days by tumbling into a Venice canal – a comedy moment both knowing and knockabout that perfectly captures the spirit of this unique actress.

Holiday
dir George Cukor, 1938, US, 95m, b/w

Few banter better than Cary Grant and Hepburn, and here they're on top form: Hepburn as a rich girl with no direction, Grant a rather well-off rebel who chooses to holiday rather than work and finds himself more attracted to Hepburn than to the younger sister he is due to marry (Doris Nolan).

The Philadelphia Story
dir George Cukor, 1940, US, 112m, b/w

Hepburn, in a reprise of her Broadway role, plays socialite Tracy Lord, recently divorced and about to remarry in the society wedding of the year. Teaming her with Cary Grant as her ex and James Stewart as a reporter covering the marriage for a magazine, Cukor created one of cinema's greatest comic ensembles.

🎬 Adam's Rib
dir George Cukor, 1949, US, 101m, b/w

Hepburn and Spencer Tracy play opposing lawyers – married to each other – opposed to opposing each other, but forced to do so during a murder case on which they find themselves on opposite sides. A battle of the sexes, certainly, a battle of ideology, also certainly, and more than anything a meeting of minds with a flair for comedy.

Bob Hope

Actor, 1903–2003

Hard to imagine that an English boy born in the quiet London suburb of Eltham could grow up to become one of America's best loved entertainers. But not so hard, perhaps, when you consider that he won a Chaplin imitation contest at the age of ten – **Bob Hope** was clearly intent on emulating Chaplin in more respects than one.

Leslie Townes Hope arrived Stateside at the age of four, shipping up in Cleveland, Ohio. As a teenager he tried his hand at boxing, and was even a "soda jerk" for a while, before taking to the boards in an amateur fashion with what he later labelled a selection of "song, patter and eccentric dancing" – the very definition of an all-round entertainer. Adding comedy to his obvious talents, the rechristened Bob Hope found himself working the vaudeville circuit, displaying a comic timing (of sorts) by arriving in New York in 1929, just as the Wall Street Crash hit. Even so, by 1933 Hope had landed a role in the musical *Roberta* on Broadway and, over the next two years, he made the leap to movies with a series of comedy shorts. Having already developed his trademark persona

– the fast-talking, quick-witted coward – he was also finding his greatest success on radio, which led to a Hollywood invitation to join the cast of the movie revue *The Big Broadcast of 1938*. Here he sang "Thanks For The Memory", the song that was to remain his theme tune for the next 66 years.

Hope made it quickly in the movies, both as a solo act (1938's *The Cat And The Canary* established him as a comic lead), and also as part of a duo – beginning with 1939's *Road to Singapore*, the first of seven *Road To. . .* movies made over a twenty-two year period that teamed him with crooner Bing Crosby and against Dorothy Lamour. The popular series was characterized by the chemistry of the two male leads, invariably cast as hapless saps, stuck somewhere bizarre with no control over their destiny.

Throughout the 1940s and 1950s Hope remained a popular box office star, but as his film career began to dwindle, he wisely repositioned himself in the marketplace. Embracing television, his regular TV specials became national events. Having entertained the troops during World War II, Hope continued to do so in later years, moving through Korea and Vietnam and beyond. Should the global audience ever forget about him for a moment, he could be regularly seen plying his patented, topical one-liners as a regular host of the Academy Awards. In the process he became one of the world's wealthiest entertainers, with a personal fortune reckoned to run into hundreds of millions. Naturally, in his spare time, he golfed – once again turning this into an international television event, courtesy of countless pro-celebrity charity tournaments. Having won five honorary Oscars (for humanitarian work and contribution to the industry), he remained one of the world's most beloved entertainers up until his death at the ripe old age of 100.

Paleface Bob Hope – for once stuck for words

Road To Morocco
dir David Butler, 1942, US, 83m, b/w

Bob and Bing are washed ashore, finding themselves in a city where Hope is sold as a slave to the local princess, played by the third member of the *Road to. . .* team, Dorothy Lamour. Bing sings, Hope gets scared and – as ever with the *Road* films – everyone looks as if they're having a good time.

The Paleface
dir Norman Z. McLeod, 1948, US, 91m

Hope was never better as on-screen coward – "brave men run in my family!" – than in this comedy Western, which saw his hapless dentist, "Painless" Peter Potter, inadvertently teamed with Calamity Jane (Jane Russell) in a bid to find out who's been selling guns to the local Indians.

Chuck Jones

Animator and Director, 1912–2002

Charles Martin Jones – **Chuck Jones** – once said he always wanted to be Bugs Bunny, but knew he was more like Daffy Duck. He also had more of an affinity with Wile E. Coyote over the Road Runner, seeing the former as a perfect example of man's eternal, and futile, struggle. And, as he animated most of them, he knew what he was talking about. He took as his lead the anarchy of animator Tex Avery – very different from the "safeness" of Walt Disney – and made it his own in a series of short animated movies for Warner Brothers that redefined the cartoon art form.

Jones started as a cel washer and then a general animator before graduating to director. Warner Brothers' *Looney Tunes* cartoons benefited greatly from his, in many ways, defining vision, with Jones adding such unforgettable characters to the roster as Wile E. Coyote and Road Runner, along with stalwarts Marvin the Martian and Pepé Le Pew; he also helped further define the

characteristics of Bugs, Daffy and Porky Pig by foregrounding their smallest, and most distinctive, gestures. He even brought opera to the cartoon pantheon and won an Oscar to boot – with Bugs and Elmer Fudd's 1957 take on Wagner's *Ring Cycle*, *What's Opera, Doc?*

But then redefining the animated form was always one of Jones's strengths, as he showed with *Duck Amuck* (1953), in which Daffy is literally undrawn and the whole nature of the cartoon thus deconstructed. Much of his best work was done in collaboration with writer Michael Maltese, including his futuristic take on Daffy as *Duck Dodgers of the 24½th Century* (1953), a timeless classic, as well as *One Froggy Evening* (1955), in which he introduced the character of Michigan J. Frog.

As the late 1950s rolled around, and the animated short became something of a rarity, Warner Brothers stopped producing cartoons. Jones moved to MGM, where he became director on the 1960s run of *Tom and Jerry* shorts; these may not have been his best work, but his trademark innovation was still present in his other work of the same period. Once again he deconstructed the cartoon with an adaptation of the book *The Dot And The Line* (1965), in which a straight line falls in love with a dot; he also struck up a friendship with children's book author Dr. Seuss (aka Theodor Geiscl) that resulted in the classic TV adaptation of Seuss's *How the Grinch Stole Christmas* in 1966 (narrated by Boris Karloff), and the subsequent *Horton Hears A Who!* (1970). Jones made one move into live action movies (although still mixed with a large degree of animation) with 1970's *The Phantom Tollbooth*. Adored by the filmmakers that followed him, in the early 1990s Jones attempted to revive the Warner Bros cartoon franchise with a new Road Runner cartoon titled *Chariots Of Fur*, a notion that was sadly abandoned. In his later years he appeared in Joe Dante's *Gremlins* (1984), and animated a sequence for the otherwise forgettable film *Stay Tuned* (1992).

What's Opera, Doc?
dir Chuck Jones, 1957, US, 7m

Chuck manages to condense (and rewrite) Wagner's *Ring* from twelve hours to seven minutes to create one of Bugs's (and Elmer Fudd's) finest moments. Mel Blanc, *the* voice of Warner Brothers Cartoons, provides the voices – singing, this time. A deserved Oscar winner for Best Animated Short.

The Phantom Tollbooth
dir Chuck Jones, Abe Levitow, Dave Monahan, 1970, US, 90m

A young boy, Milo (the TV *Munsters'* son, Butch Patrick), finds a tollbooth in his room and is transported from the real world into a unique animated world. By no means as succinct as Jones's best work, this is still a prime example of the man's eccentric genius, and he is reunited with Mel Blanc, who provides many of the voices.

Buster Keaton

Actor and Director, 1895–1966

Along with Charlie Chaplin and Harold Lloyd, **Buster Keaton** was one of the great innovators of silent comedy cinema. Legend has it that young James Keaton and his parents, itinerant medicine show performers, were staying at a boarding house when the boy took a tumble down the stairs and came up all smiles. Famed escape artist and illusionist Harry Houdini, also in residence, was duly impressed and nicknamed him "Buster", testament to a physical dexterity that came to dominate Keaton's on-screen canon. (That and his remarkably deadpan face, which seemed incapable of registering expression, no matter whether he was being chased by a runaway train or about to be crushed by a collapsing house.)

Buster soon joined the family act, graduating from falling down stairs to the role of "The Human Mop" – his father would literally hold him upside down and wipe the floor with him. The Three Keatons, as they were known, continued to perform throughout Buster's childhood, with the young boy developing his abilities as an acrobat and physical comedian. (Popular history has it that he was so skilled that people refused to believe he was a child, taking him for a midget in disguise.) The act broke up in 1917, when Buster opted to leave vaudeville behind for supporting roles in a series of Fatty Arbuckle comedies, beginning with 1917's *The Butcher Boy*. Following a brief stint in the army, having been stationed in France during the last days of World War I, Keaton returned to the US and a new movie deal that saw him headlining his own shorts, quickly followed by his feature film debut, *The Saphead*, in 1920. Buster was by now a bona-fide star, and also started directing, moving away from shorts into features.

Abstract comic ideas found fruition in Keaton's inventive direction and his use of emerging film technology – thus multiple exposure allowed him to play every member of the audience, along with the orchestra, the actors, the stage hand and so on, in *The Playhouse* (1921), while in *Sherlock, Jr.* (1924) the hapless projectionist (Keaton) finds himself caught up in the events he is screening. Other acknowledged classics from this period include 1924's *The Navigator*, his Civil War epic *The General* (1927; see Canon) and 1928's *Steamboat Bill, Jr.*. Keaton's career took a turn for the worse, however, when he opted to give up his own independent production company and sign up to work for MGM. His private life soon followed his career, with the actor battling alcohol and depression before entering a psychiatric clinic in 1937. Yet Keaton did eventually battle his demons, and even returned to work quietly in film as an uncredited gag writer and assistant director.

But it was his live appearances at the Cirque Medrano in Paris in 1947 that led to his body of work being revived and reappraised, and was followed by his only appearance on screen with Charlie Chaplin in 1952's *Limelight*. His final film appearance was as Erronius in 1965's *A Funny Thing Happened On The Way to the Forum*. In the end, Keaton was lucky enough to see his own revival in his own lifetime, the breadth, innovation and influence of his work being acknowledged by a whole new generation of filmmakers and audiences alike. They even made a movie about him – 1957's *The Buster Keaton Story* (although admittedly Donald O'Connor makes a poor substitute for the real thing).

Sherlock, Jr.
dir Buster Keaton, 1924, US, 44m, b/w

If one aim of film is to pull the audience into the story, Keaton reckoned the projectionist should be dragged along for the ride – literally. *Sherlock, Jr.* remains one of his most innovative films as Keaton's projectionist turns himself into the famous Sherlock Holmes in order to solve a crime. Imaginative and technically brilliant.

Steamboat Bill, Jr.
dir Charles F Reisner, 1928, US, 71m, b/w

As ever with Keaton, the plot – a young man turns up to help his father run their ailing steamboat company – is overshadowed by the comic's incredibly varied and ambitious stunts; the climax, involving a small town and a big storm, is a perfect, beautifully protracted example of his unique comic art.

Limelight
dir Charles Chaplin, 1952, US, 140m, b/w

Chaplin's last American movie, a bittersweet paean to his past, offers the opportunity for him to share a scene – for the one and only time – with former screen rival Buster Keaton. A rare and touching opportunity to see two of cinema's greatest geniuses at the tail end of their careers.

Laurel and Hardy
Stan Laurel Actor, 1890–1965
Oliver Hardy Actor, 1892–1957

Born Arthur Stanley Jefferson at Ulverston in northwest England, Stan Laurel, the man who would become one half of cinema's greatest comedy double act, **Laurel and Hardy**, was the son of an actress and a theatrical impresario. Surprisingly, given this background, Arthur didn't set foot on a stage until the age of sixteen, when he debuted in music hall in Glasgow. For the next four years he toured, performing comedy routines in music halls up and down the country, before joining Fred Karno's troupe in 1910. Here he was assigned to understudy one Charles Chaplin, and followed him and Karno's gang to America on their first tour there later that year. He was also a featured player alongside Chaplin in one of Karno's major attractions, *A Night In An English Music Hall*, and later, like many comics of the time, developed a Chaplin impression that proved a mainstay of his act.

After Karno's second tour of the US in 1912, Arthur opted to stay and try his hand at the American vaudeville circuit. It was then that he changed his named to Stan Laurel, and, as a member of the Three Comiques, was brought to the attention of Adolph Ramish, owner of the Los Angeles Hippodrome. Ramish was so impressed with the comic performer's talent that he rented studio space and financed Laurel's film debut, *Nuts In May* (1917). The film, picked up for national distribution, was seen by Laurel's old friend and colleague, Chaplin, who, planning to set up his own company and studio, invited Laurel to come on board. Yet confirmation never arrived, and Laurel went off to make a series of (now lost) movies for Universal before finding himself forced to return to vaudeville. As he struggled to find his movie persona, this was the pattern his life took over the next few years – sporadic film work with periods on the stage to pay the rent.

By 1926 he was behind the camera, writing and directing comedies for Hal Roach. Then he was persuaded to step back in front of the lens to star with an actor who had been making a living playing a series of screen heavies. The other man's name was Oliver Hardy, and the legendary team was born in 1927, with *The Second Hundred Years*, *Hats Off*, and *Putting Pants On Philip*. (In fact these weren't the first films the duo had appeared in: that honour goes to the long-lost *Lucky Dog* of 1921, in which Laurel took the lead and Hardy merely a supporting player.)

Oliver Hardy, known affectionately as "Babe", hailed from Harlem, Georgia, and took his first steps on a stage at the age of eight, singing in a minstrel show. He later toured the Southern states with his own singing act, and even opened a small movie theatre in 1910. In 1913 he became one of the repertory players in the Lubin movie production company, and was soon playing the heavy in a number of comedy one-reelers. He worked opposite many comedians, including the hugely popular clown Larry Semon, who had also used Stan Laurel as a sidekick (and allegedly fired him when he found Laurel was getting more laughs). In the early 1920s, Hardy graduated to the occasional feature, and also worked as a gag writer and comedy director. By the mid-1920s he found himself under contract to Hal Roach, where his natural comic abilities were sidelined by his size, forcing him into another string of forgettable roles.

It was director Leo McCarey at Roach's studios that saw beyond this when he suggested that Hardy and Laurel be teamed together. The combination they brought to the screen was always deceptively simple: Ollie appeared to be the big one, the fat guy in charge who pushed around the weedy, quiet Stan. In reality, though cantankerous, Ollie was the bashful sweetheart of the duo, while Stan was the one "with the temper" – and who often, despite his apparent simpleton persona, came up with the better ideas (echoing the fact that Laurel was usually calling the shots on-set, largely writing and directing their films, albeit unofficially).

Their visible chemistry worked well in silents, but really blossomed after the arrival of the talkies, when their characters became more fully defined. Deceptively simple gestures – Ollie bashfully playing with his tie, Stan fiddling with his bowler hat or crying – combined with catchphrases such as Ollie's "Here's another fine mess you've got us into" – became recognized and loved throughout the world. Two traits separated them from their contemporaries: dignity and an elegant simplicity. Although they invariably played down-at-heel saps trying to get by, they always held their heads high and kept their bowler hats on. The simplicity of their approach can be witnessed in just about all their classic shorts, where a basic comic situation is developed over and over again – the continued attempts to get that piano up the stairs in the Oscar-winning *The Music Box* (1932), the increasingly desperate attempt to pack the car for a day out in *Perfect Day* (1929), and so on. They were also aided by a number of talented supporting players, most notable among them Scottish-born James Finlayson, the moustachioed stooge, and the duo Charlie Hall and Mae Busch, another pair of great foils.

Laurel and Hardy made over 100 films, 27 of them features, although the latter, despite one or two exceptions – *Sons Of The Desert* (1933), *Our*

Great Laurel and Hardy shorts

The joy of watching a Laurel and Hardy short is to see two comedy geniuses take just one simple idea and extrapolate it over the course of a few minutes into comic magic. For many, the Oscar-winning *The Music Box* (1932) is the best Laurel and Hardy short there is. And true, their relentless, frustrating saga of trying to get a piano up one of the longest staircases in Hollywood is a gem. But not to be overlooked are two tales in which they appear with the fine supporting actors Charlie Hall and Mae Busch, who play husband and wife. In *Them Thar Hills* (1934) Ollie's gout leads to a trip to the mountains. Eager to get healthy, Stan and Ollie drink copious amounts of water from a local well, enthusiastically discussing its virtues and not realizing that bootleggers have just offloaded a ton of hooch down it minutes before. They, and Busch, get remarkably sloshed, much to the consternation of her husband. When they next encounter the couple, in *Tit For Tat* (1935), they set up an electrical store next to Cross's grocery. Things, naturally, get out of hand as they slowly destroy each other's livelihoods.

The Music Box – falling over yet again

Relations (1936), *Way Out West* (1937) – never proved to be their forte. A break from Hal Roach in 1940 to gain more creative control proved to be a mistake and, as times moved on, these two Depression-era souls lost their way, finishing what had been a glorious career with the appalling *Atoll K* (1951), which combined an overweight Ollie, ill and underweight Stan, a host of poor supporting actors and terrible direction to make an ultimately depressing experience.

Yet this wasn't to be the end of Laurel and Hardy. Loved worldwide, the pair toured Britain in the late 1940s and 1950s. This success encouraged them to consider a new series of colour movies, but a stroke Hardy suffered heralded the end of their joint career. Hardy died in 1957, and Laurel vowed never to perform again, though he received a special Academy Award in 1960 for his contribution to cinema comedy.

Sons Of The Desert
dir William A Seiter, 1933, US, 69m, b/w

The Sons of the Desert is a fraternal organization, and both Mr Laurel and Mr Hardy wish to attend their upcoming convention. Their wives aren't too happy with them going on a boys' night out, however – so comic subterfuge is the only solution. Mae Busch (as Mrs Hardy) lends excellent, feisty support.

Our Relations
dir Harry Lachman, 1936, US, 74m, b/w

One of the duo's finest features, with Laurel taking charge behind the scenes. The two play both themselves and their rather disreputable twin brothers (Alf and Bert respectively), allowing both performers to show another side to their stock characters. Various cases of mistaken identity ensue, in typically brilliant comic style.

Way Out West
dir James W Horne, 1937, US, 65m, b/w

Stan and Ollie head off to the Wild West to unleash their unique brand of comic mayhem – which also involves doing a soft shoe shuffle while singing "On The Trail of the Lonesome Pine" (later a number one hit record in the UK). The always reliable James Finlayson provides support.

Jerry Lewis
Actor and Director, 1925–

Joseph Levitch (as he was born) claims that he was thrown out of high school when he punched his principal for making an anti-Semitic remark. Whether that's true or not, high school's loss was vaudeville's gain, and the newly christened **Jerry Lewis** honed his skills as a performer, developing a mix of extraordinary physicality and high-energy verbal silliness.

Along the way he hooked up with crooner Dean Martin. They were never friends, but their double act worked – Martin brought good looks and style to the mix, with a subtle humour that both offset Lewis's manic pace and permitted him to be even more absurd. They quickly became a nightclub sensation, soon moving to radio and the movies. Starring in films such as *Sailor Beware* (1951), *You're Never Too Young* (1955) and *Hollywood Or Bust* (1956), they rapidly became one of the biggest box office draws of the 1950s. While some claim that their movie work was merely a watered-down version of the live show, it nonetheless established both performers – Martin as the louche heartthrob, Lewis as the endearing idiot savant. Mutual animosity led them to split in 1956.

Martin continued acting, singing, and hosting his own TV show, while Lewis created a successful solo movie career. From 1957 until the mid-1960s hits like *The Delicate Delinquent*, *The Patsy* and *The Disorderly Orderly* saw him play more or less the same character he had with Martin. In 1960 he shot *The Bellboy*, which was, essentially,

The Nutty Professor (1963) – a Lewis-directed classic

a series of gags connected only by location – a hotel lobby – and Lewis's hapless bellboy character. This was not only a huge success but also marked the actor-comedian's first stab at directing. From now on, he would concentrate on turning himself into a comedy auteur rather than a funny man for hire.

This was to prove both his making and ultimately his failing. With masterpieces such as *The Nutty Professor* (1963) under his belt, he was hailed as a genius in France, but for others the movies appeared increasingly self-involved and ego-led. History has it that Lewis's indulgence reached

its peak with 1972's *The Day The Clown Cried*, the story of a clown interned at Auschwitz death camp, but the movie has so seldom been seen that this has become a matter of conjecture.

By the 1970s, audiences had fallen out of love with Lewis, and he resigned himself to appearing on TV, collecting awards (he was awarded the French Légion d'honneur in 1984, and nominated for the Nobel Peace Prize for charity work in 1977), and teaching: George Lucas and Steven Spielberg were among his students in the 1970s.

Ostensibly in retirement (rumours persisted that he was simply having a fit of pique), Lewis spent years overcoming an addiction to prescription painkillers for a damaged back, the result of a mistimed pratfall on a 1965 edition of TV's *The Andy Williams Show*. He began a comeback with Martin Scorsese's caustic *The King of Comedy* (1983), which saw him playing an aggressively cynical version of a performer not a million miles from himself. Years later he gave another stand-out turn in the sorely undervalued *Funny Bones* (1994), a meditation on the nature of comedy and the darkness that lies beneath it. He also returned to the Broadway stage, playing the Devil in a revival of *Damn Yankees* – and became the highest paid performer in Broadway history into the bargain.

Hollywood Or Bust
dir Frank Tashlin, 1956, US, 95m

The final Lewis/Martin collaboration finds the two winning a convertible and heading off to Hollywood, in part to satisfy Lewis's longings for leading lady Anita Ekberg. Plot gets thrown out of the window in favour of some rather ridiculous but thoroughly entertaining gags. Martin and Lewis were rarely better as a team.

The Nutty Professor
dir Jerry Lewis, 1963, US, 107m

Lewis's nerdy, heavily bespectacled, Professor Julius Kelp invents a serum that turns him into the ultra-smooth ladies' man Buddy Love. Many saw the alter ego as a stab at ex-partner Dean Martin; if so, the film can be read as a combination of bitter resentment, earnest desire and borderline schizophrenia. In short, the stuff of comedy genius.

The King Of Comedy
dir Martin Scorsese, 1982, US, 109m

Scorsese's blackest of black comedies, an examination of American society's fascination with media and celebrity. Lewis plays, not against type, a successful and egotistical comic, while Robert DeNiro – never better – co-stars as Rupert Pupkin, a wannabe who never was. Lewis's brilliant,

brutal performance is open and honest, one of the best of his career.

Funny Bones
dir Peter Chelsom, 1994, UK, 128m

Lewis is cast as what he is – an ageing American comic whose greatest successes lie many years behind him – and here he wisely lets British comic Lee Evans steal the show. Chelsom's film brilliantly explores the notion that sometimes being funny isn't all that funny, never more so than in its difficult but faultless finale.

Harold Lloyd
Actor, 1893–1971

The bespectacled **Harold Lloyd**, often known for his "thrill comedies" (in which he would hang off a tower clock, balance precariously on the roof of a bus – that kind of thing), took some time to find his way in the movies. His first part was an extra role as a near-naked Indian in a 1912 short for the Edison company, and he took more extra work at both Keystone and Universal before meeting and befriending producer-to-be Hal Roach. When Roach inherited $3000 months later, he formed his own production company and cast his pal Lloyd in a series of one-reelers featuring a character named Willie Work. Willie Work didn't really work with audiences, however, so Lloyd attempted to ply his trade back at the Keystone studios, run by comedy giant Mack Sennett.

A falling out with Sennett drove Lloyd back to Roach in 1915, and their mutual creation "Lonesome Luke", a character patterned in part on Chaplin's Tramp (as was the fashion of the day), was both. Luke proved popular with audiences, and more than a hundred shorts were made, although neither Roach nor Lloyd were that enamoured of the character. It wasn't until

1918, with the movie *City Slicker*, that Roach came up with the inspiration both had been looking for: instead of giving the comic lead the comedy costume (as was the norm), he dressed Lloyd in a young man's Sunday best, complete with straw boater and horn-rimmed glasses – an ensemble which offset perfectly Lloyd's moon-like, expressionless face (a visage bettered in the silent era only by Keaton's deadpan), and emphasized his normality, rather than his outsider status. Appearing in movies that foregrounded story and character development over slapstick, this new persona caught on with 1920s audiences, who warmed to the increasingly inventive Lloyd. An ordinary middle-class fellow, not inherently funny in himself, the character, once described as a "zanily optimistic Everyman", was funny in a fresh, new way – responding to the sequence of comic events that happened to him, rather than creating them, and thus easy to identify with. Audiences loved this upbeat hero, and Lloyd soon became the highest paid actor in Hollywood, appearing in a series of hit titles from *A Sailor-Made Man* (1921) to *Speedy* (1928).

Stunts to take the breath away in *Safety Last* (1923)

Always more athletic and physically adventurous than his contemporaries Chaplin and Keaton, Lloyd was struck by a grim accident during the filming of 1920's *Haunted Spooks*, when a bomb prop went off in his right hand, destroying his thumb and forefinger and leaving the hand itself partially paralysed. Nevertheless, wearing a glove to cover his injury, Lloyd went on to perform an increasingly impressive array of physical stunts and sequences, perhaps best typified by the famous scene in *Safety Last* (1923), which sees him hanging from the hands of a clock atop a New York skyscraper.

Lloyd left Roach in 1923 and was soon making features. Though his popularity waned during the Depression, Lloyd, tearing a page out of Chaplin's book, had ensured that he owned the rights to his films, and eventually made his fortune by their later rerelease. He also introduced his work to a whole new generation with the 1962 compilation *Harold Lloyd's World Of Comedy*, which was greeted with a standing ovation when it debuted at Cannes that year.

Safety Last
dir Fred Newmeyer, 1923, US, 77m, b/w

Lloyd's small-town boy, determined to make a success of himself in the big city, suggests that someone climb the facade of the department store he is working for. Eventually he is forced to do it himself – resulting in breathtaking stunts aplenty and culminating in the iconic sequence in which he dangles off the clock hands atop a skyscraper.

The Kid Brother
dir Ted Wilde, J.A. Howe, 1927, US, 82m, b/w

Unusual for a Lloyd movie, in that it is set in the countryside, this time the bespectacled one plays the kid brother of the title who must prove himself to his bullying family. A string of high-octane set pieces follows, with a breathtaking finale set in an abandoned ship.

Steve Martin
Actor, Screenwriter and Director, 1945–

At a time when comedy was becoming a serious business – post-Watergate America was wall-to-wall with topical satire – **Steve Martin** appeared in the mid 1970s like a hero in white suit and told everyone it was all right to be silly again. In doing so, he brought stand-up to new heights and also to new audiences: in a reversal of the show-business tradition that comics opened for rock bands, Martin's run of shows at LA's Universal Amphitheatre opened with the recently formed Blues Brothers, while the comic himself entertained upwards of 16,000 people a night.

Having already bagged an Emmy as a TV writer (for Sonny and Cher among others), Martin decided in the late 1960s to perform his own trend-bucking material. Here was a man who, when everyone else was growing their hair, cut his (and it was prematurely grey); who donned a white suit when jeans were *de rigueur*. And where other comics opened their acts with sharp one-liners about Nixon, Martin put an arrow through his head, danced crazily with his trademark "happy feet", juggled cats and played the banjo. In doing so he rapidly became the biggest stand-up comedian in America, partly through his alignment with the emerging *Saturday Night Live* TV show, which he guest-hosted many times.

Martin's film career began in earnest with 1979's *The Jerk*, a wonderful rag-bag of gags, many of them derived from his stand-up act, not least the film's basic premise – Martin's assertion that he was born "a poor, black child". The movie was a smash and established Martin as a screen comic of the first order. It also established a relationship with Carl Reiner as director: the two would collaborate on a string of brilliantly inventive com-

The early manic Steve Martin of *The Man with Two Brains* (1983)

edies that, for all-out laughs, equal Woody Allen's first run of movies. 1982's *Dead Men Don't Wear Plaid* (a spoof *noir* that cleverly intercut pre-existing footage of classic stars, from Bogart to Davis to Cagney) was followed by 1983's *The Man With Two Brains*, a modern-day variation on the Frankenstein myth, itself followed by 1984's sublime *All Of Me*, which gave full rein to Martin's prowess as a physical comedian.

Martin often had a hand in writing these early movies, as he did with the two films that remain his finest big-screen work. *Roxanne* (1987) was a modern retelling of the Cyrano de Bergerac story that saw Martin move beyond gag comedy and into romance, while *L.A. Story* (1991), which works as a companion piece to Woody Allen's *Manhattan*, built on this theme, creating a wonderful slice of magic realism that paid tribute to his then wife, Victoria Tennant. In later years, Martin established himself as an accomplished straight actor in movies like *Grand Canyon* (1991) and David Mamet's *The Spanish Prisoner* (1997), and, unexpectedly, a leading family man (*Parenthood*, 1989; *Father Of The Bride*, 1991; *Cheaper By The Dozen*, 2003).

A philosophy major, off-screen Martin remains something of an intellectual. His play, *Picasso At The Lapin Agile* (1993), is a brilliant discourse on what might happen if two of the twentieth century's most important figures – Picasso and Einstein – met in a bar in Paris in 1904. Elvis Presley also shows up for good measure. Turning his hand to the novel, Martin has also excelled with the touching *Shopgirl* (later made into a film with Martin and Winona Ryder) and the superb *The Pleasure Of My Company*.

The Jerk
dir Carl Reiner, 1979, US, 94m

Born a "poor black child", Navin Johnson (Martin) seeks his fortune, ends up in a circus and invents a device for spectacles that turns everyone cross-eyed. This is very much a first film, using a lot of Martin's stand-up material, but when the gags are this good, you can forgive it its few flaws.

The Man with Two Brains
dir Carl Reiner, 1983, US, 93m

Martin is on great form as the wonderfully named Dr Michael Hfuhruhurr, leading brain surgeon and originator of cranial screw-top surgery, who falls in love with Kathleen Turner's body and Sissy Spacek's mind – the latter in the form of a brain in a jar. Martin would never be this relaxed – or just plain daft – again.

All of Me
dir Carl Reiner, 1984, US, 93m

Playing a lawyer whose difficult client (Lily Tomlin) literally possesses half of his body, Martin gets the chance to show off his considerable talent for physical comedy. Both actors are at their best, and it's a fine example of cinematic slapstick, although sadly it did mark the end of Martin's work with director Reiner.

Parenthood
dir Ron Howard, 1989, US, 124m

Marking the moment that Steve Martin became the movies' family man, this well-handled domestic tale features Martin as the guy who has a wife and kids but has to work out how to deal with them. Director Howard is a master at handling ensemble casts, and Martin knows exactly the right moment to bring out the comedy victory dance.

The Marx Brothers

Actors and Director (Groucho)
Chico (Leonard), 1886–1961
Harpo (Adolph), 1888–1964
Groucho (Julius Henry), 1890–1977
Zeppo (Herbert), 1901–1979

The **Marx Brothers**, very simply, mark the pole position at which cinema meets anarchy. Between the three of them (straight man and occasional crooner Zeppo doesn't really count) they presented a plethora of comedy styles – Groucho the wordsmith, Harpo the pantomime idiot savant, and Chico the worldly wise hustler, complete with comedy accent. Throughout the 1930s the Marxes attacked cinema and took it hostage, like it was their godgiven comedy right – which of course, it was.

The product of a stage-struck mother who was determined to live out her dreams of fame through her offspring, the Marx Brothers were trained early on to be a lean, mean entertaining machine. Early variations on a musical act stood them in good stead, but it was only when the boys' own personalities and abilities started to come to the fore – and when they adopted their nicknames, around 1914 – that they gelled as a unit. First and foremost among the group was young Julius (Groucho), who took to wearing a greasepaint moustache, brandishing a stogie cigar, adopting a comedy walk and developing an ability for the one-liner that has often been aped but seldom bettered. Adolph (Harpo) knew he couldn't compete with Groucho's verbal dexterity, so he opted to keep his mouth shut and go the way of mime. (He was so successful, legend records that when he got up to make a speech at an awards ceremony in the early 1960s, he opened with the line "Unaccustomed as I am to public speaking…" and drew an ovation so long that he never got around to the rest of his carefully prepared speech.) And then there was the wild card – a man who was wild about cards. Leonard (Chico) – never Italian, but always with an Italian accent – played the piano (he once filled in for George Gershwin in a local New York cinema) and played attitude as much as Groucho. While the latter played clever, the former played dumb – which, in the context of the ensemble, turned out to be just as clever.

From vaudeville they hit the big time on Broadway in the show *The Cocoanuts*, based in a Florida hotel; in 1929 it was produced as a movie, making for something of a stilted, if still hilari-

ous, debut. Although they continued to road-test their movies as stage shows in front of a live audience, it was only when the Marx Brothers gained confidence in the medium of film that they really came into their own. Realizing that, unlike in a live show, they were not dependent on timing their delivery to leave room for the audience's laughs, they created an anarchic mix of personality, gags and events that has seldom been bettered. If comedy is talked about in terms of delivery, the brothers were into assault – witness the rapid onslaught of such classics as *Horse Feathers* (1932) and *Duck Soup* (1933), breathtaking and bizarre ensembles which border on the surreal.

The brothers' unique style found a mass audience early on, although it proved increasingly difficult to maintain their momentum. Their careers dwindled in the 1940s, with only Groucho finding a second career later in life with the TV quiz show *You Bet Your Life* (1947–1961) and, latterly, as a memoirist and the performer of a one-man show in the early 1970s at Carnegie Hall.

The Cocoanuts
dir Joseph Santley, 1929, US, 96m, b/w

The Marx Brothers' first film has all the characters in place, along with their regular foil Margaret Dumont, in a

The other Marx Brother: Margaret Dumont

The statuesque Margaret Dumont proved the perfect comedy foil for the anarchic Marx Brothers. Generally the recipient of Groucho's come-ons and put-downs ("Well, that covers a lot of ground. Say, you cover a lot of ground yourself. You better beat it – I hear they're going to tear you down and put up an office building where you're standing. You can leave in a taxi. If you can't get a taxi, you can leave in a huff. If that's too soon, you can leave in a minute and a huff. You know,

you haven't stopped talking since I came here? You must have been vaccinated with a phonograph needle" – *Duck Soup*), Dumont argued that her saving grace as a performer opposite Julius Henry was that she didn't really know what he was going on about. Whether that be the stuff of legend is unimportant now; what counts is her wonderfully deft ability to diffuse any quip Groucho throws her way, therefore doing what all great comedy "feeds" do – forcing the player to raise their game.

A Night At The Opera: Marx Brothers mayhem with music

Florida hotel full of jewel thieves. It's not their finest work, betraying its theatrical origins and a relative insecurity with the new medium, but it's packed with gags, and sets the groundwork for their later masterpieces.

Horse Feathers
dir Norman Z. McLeod, 1932, US, 70m, b/w

The brothers really begin to hit their stride here as they take on university life – a university of which Groucho is president (which gives a pretty good indication of the academic standards therein). A classic, in which a great

comic team throws everything at the wall to see what sticks. Most of it does.

A Night At The Opera
dir Sam Wood, 1935, US, 94m, b/w

Although this movie marks the point where the brothers' career went downhill – the mayhem halted every few minutes for a musical number (Allan Jones stepping in for the recently departed Zeppo) – there's still some brilliantly inventive comedy here, with a script by George S. Kaufman and Morrie Ryskind backing up the classic routines.

Marilyn Monroe

Actress, 1926–1962

Few individuals have come to represent so much as **Marilyn Monroe**. Norma Jean Baker was the small-town girl who made it big in Hollywood, the epitome of glamorous, feminine beauty, the raw talent that needed nurturing and was often wasted, the sassy girl who told us diamonds were her best friend, the complex woman who sang "Happy Birthday" to the President, and the fragile woman who died tragically young and alone – making her, in the light of rumours linking her with President John F. Kennedy, as well as his brother Bobby, the ultimate conspiracy theory pin-up girl. More than any other star in Hollywood history, perhaps, she is cinema's most luminescent, enduring idol; continually emulated yet never matched. She was also, of course, a fine comedienne.

Raised by an unstable mother, who spent most of her daughter's formative years institutionalized, Norma Jean spent her youth in a series of foster homes, discovering she was illegitimate at the age of sixteen. She married soon after, and was discovered by an army photographer in 1944 while working in a parachute plant. Modelling work followed, her strawberry brown hair dyed platinum blonde, and in 1946 she was snapped up by 20th Century Fox, where she changed her name to Marilyn Monroe.

Determined to make it as an actress, she paid for her own acting classes while landing a succession of walk-on roles that grew into bit parts: she can be seen in a good few turkeys, not least *Love Happy* (1949), the Marx Brothers' last film, but also made her mark in a handful of classic movies including bitchy comedy *All About Eve* (1950; see Canon), John Huston's *The Asphalt Jungle* (1950), and the delightful screwball *Monkey Business*

A fine comedienne in *Gentleman Prefer Blondes* (1953)

(1952) alongside Cary Grant and Ginger Rogers. In 1953 came her first starring role, an uneasy performance as a scheming wife in the steamy drama *Niagara* (1953); more interesting are the comedies *Gentlemen Prefer Blondes* (1953) and *How To Marry A Millionaire* (1953), bright, frothy slices of comic perfection that rely on Monroe's compelling performance and portray her earthy sexuality as a source of power rather than vulnerability.

Acting talent aside, it was Monroe's mixture of sensuality and guilelessness, her breathy voice and her unselfconscious, curvaceous body that combined to make one of Hollywood's most glamorous stars. She was the most talked-about celebrity of her day, adored and also dismissed – derided for both her "unlikely" marriages to baseball hero Joe DiMaggio and, later, playwright Arthur Miller. Frustrated by the limitations of being typecast as a dumb blonde, in 1954 Monroe – mocked by many for having ideas above her station – moved to New York to study at Lee Strasberg's Actors Studio before forming her own production company and turning in a subtle performance as a nightclub singer in *Bus Stop* (1956). Her next production, *The Prince And The Showgirl* (1957), was less impressive, and she soon became beset by illness, emotional instability and professional unreliability. Her last great comic role was in Billy Wilder's *Some Like It Hot* (1959; see Canon), where she gives a characteristically natural performance as the fragile Sugar, ukulele player in an all-girl jazz band. For all the mythology that has sprung to life since her untimely overdose in 1962, this is how she should be remembered and valued.

Gentlemen Prefer Blondes
dir Howard Hawks, 1953, US, 91m

Splendid musical comedy that brings us the classic number "Diamonds are a Girl's Best Friend". The deliciously light comic tone belies numerous darkly ironic takes on female sexuality, and Monroe and co-star Jane Russell were never better, revelling in their roles as gold-digging cabaret artistes on their way to Paris.

How to Marry A Millionaire
dir Jean Negulesco, 1953, US, 95m

Shot immediately after Marilyn Monroe had all but redefined the blonde bombshell in *Gentlemen Prefer Blondes*, this features her, Lauren Bacall and Betty Grable on the lookout for the next available and extremely wealthy man. Dated the sexual politics may be, but Monroe's performance remains timeless.

Let's Make Love
dir George Cukor, 1960, US, 118m

Monroe is the best thing in this frothy comedy, iconically warbling "My Heart Belongs to Daddy" and romancing Yves Montand. Winning cameos from Milton Berle, Bing Crosby and Gene Kelly, with the always reliable Tony Randall and Wilfred Hyde White a delight in support.

Eddie Murphy
Actor, Screenwriter and Director, 1961–

When he was growing up, **Eddie Murphy**'s heroes were Richard Pryor and Elvis Presley. When he grew up, he fused the two and became a phenomenon. More than any other comic before or since, Murphy brought sex appeal to stand-up. By the time of his mid-1980s arena tour (captured in the movie *Eddie Murphy Raw*,1987) he was getting as many orgasmic screams as laughs as he handed out scarves to the ladies, Presley-style.

Raised in reasonably affluent Long Island, New York, Murphy began performing comedy routines inspired by Pryor's albums when he was in his early teens. By sixteen he had a manager and was playing bars that he still wasn't old enough to drink in. He soon progressed to Manhattan's comedy club circuit, and, aged nineteen, was the youngest ever cast member of NBC's *Saturday Night Live*. Murphy instantly became an audience favourite, creating characters such as pimp Velvet Jones, a grown-up Buckwheat (from the *Our Gang* comedy shorts of the 1930s), and numerous others, including spot-on impersonations of several music icons from James Brown to Stevie Wonder.

Rapidly becoming too big for TV, in the early 1980s Murphy headed for Hollywood. On screen, Murphy's blend of youthful good looks and sex appeal, macho attitude and comic chops initially worked extremely well – *48 HRS* (1982) saw him steal the action adventure show from Nick Nolte, while his next movie, John Landis' *Trading Places* (1983), teamed him with *SNL* graduate Dan Aykroyd for one of the best received comedies of the 1980s. The Murphy formula reached its zenith with his next film, *Beverly Hills Cop* (1984), which marked a shift in the position of comedian as movie star – here was a comic with a gun, who wasn't a hapless Bob Hope-type trying ineptly not to shoot off his own toe, but a tough guy who knew how to handle himself. Though it was billed a comedy,

Bowfinger (1999) – a comic twist on Murphy's public persona

there were precious few laughs in the movie's high body count finale. Many would try and follow the formula – himself included, in such later weaker efforts as *Beverly Hills Cop II* (1987) and *III* (1994) and *Metro* (1997).

By 1988 Murphy had conquered TV, the comedy album, live tours, the concert film (*Raw* significantly out-grossed *Richard Pryor Live In Concert*) and the movies. Now he wanted to show range – cue *Coming To America* (1988), the first film in which he takes a number of heavily latex-disguised roles – in this case, four of them. If *Coming To America* was a *tour de force*, hubris got the better of him with his next feature, *Harlem Nights* (1989), a gangster spoof that he not only starred in – alongside comedy heroes Pryor and Redd Foxx – but also wrote, produced and directed. On every level a disaster, this overblown production saw the beginning of the still young comic's fall from grace.

The early 1990s earned Murphy some redemption in 1996's remake of Jerry Lewis's *The Nutty Professor*, where, with the help of make-up and digital effects, he plays five family members. For once the Murphy ego was on hold, and the sheer joy he took in playing off his numerous creations radiates from the screen. Since then, however, his career has proved erratic, finding occasional box office success with a succession of kiddie movies – *Dr. Dolittle* (1998), *The Haunted Mansion* (2003) – but seldom, except in the clever *Bowfinger* (1999), revealing the raw talent that made him a star.

🎬 Trading Places
dir John Landis, 1983, US, 116m

Here we see two generations of *SNL* players – Dan Aykroyd ably passing the torch to Murphy – in an updated fairytale/commentary on Reaganite America. A bet by two millionaires leads to a life swap for Murphy's itinerant street hustler, Billy Ray, and Aykroyd's Wall Street dealer, Louis:

it's *The Prince And The Pauper* writ large, and no less funny for that.

🎬 Beverly Hills Cop
dir Martin Brest, 1984, US, 105m

The smash movie that practically created the comedy action genre. Though it was originally conceived as a vehicle for Sylvester Stallone, it's hard now to imagine anyone but Murphy, fresh from *SNL*, playing Axel Foley, the foulmouthed, streetsmart Detroit cop who ends up in La-La land while investigating the death of a friend.

🎬 Bowfinger
dir Frank Oz, 1999, US, 97m

Steve Martin's delightful script pitches Murphy as a self-centred movie star surrounded by yes men and still suffering from profound insecurity. Murphy offers a brilliant variation on his public persona, and also plays the movie star's younger, hapless brother. A pungent look at Hollywood that showed Murphy could still deliver the goods under the right circumstances.

Bill Murray
Actor, 1950–

More than just about any modern screen comedy performer, **Bill Murray** has remained distinctly contemporary. With his urbane, hipster wit and his cynical, know-it-all sarcasm, his ability to offer up with just a look more than many actors manage in a lifetime, he has become not only one of comedy cinema's coolest players, but also (as age catches up with him), one of Hollywood's most interesting and accomplished actors.

Murray was born into an Irish Catholic family in a Chicago suburb, the fifth of nine, and, by all accounts, the "difficult one". Like many comics who come from big families, he found his first audience around the dinner table, playing to a tough audience and against stiff competition (his brother Brian would also later make his

The Bill Murray "look" visible even under clown make-up in heist comedy *Quick Change* (1990)

name in comedy movies). Bill spent his teenage years working as a caddy at the local golf course – something that stood him in good stead for one of his early hits, *Caddyshack* (1980; see Canon) – and after a series of dead-end jobs, followed brother Brian into Chicago's famed Second City improvisational theatre troupe, where contemporaries included John Belushi and Harold Ramis, and, in the Canadian branch of the company, one Dan Aykroyd. Murray quickly found success at Second City and was recruited to join Aykroyd, Belushi and Gilda Radner on radio (in *The National Lampoon Radio Hour*) and on stage in New York (*The National Lampoon Revue*). Some of these performances would find their way onto albums, most notably 1976's *That's Not Funny, That's Sick*, but when his colleagues got the call to sign up for TV's *Saturday Night Live*, Murray didn't make the grade. He replaced Chevy Chase on the show a year later, however, and very slowly a star was born.

More than any of his *SNL* contemporaries, Murray has handled the transition to the big screen with aplomb. He started with the teen gross-out comedy *Meatballs* (1979), a year later teaming with *SNL* friends to play the clown in *Caddyshack* and then playing famed gonzo journalist Hunter S. Thompson in *Where The Buffalo Roam*. By 1981's *Stripes*, Murray had found his screen persona – the cynic who could also play lovable, and who could certainly command the screen. He built this persona into a well-judged career, taking a supporting role in *Tootsie* (1982; see Canon) for the chance to work with Dustin Hoffman, and stepping up a gear when Belushi's death opened up the lead opposite Aykroyd in *Ghostbusters* (1984; see Canon). Legend has it that by the time he came to make *Scrooged* in 1988 one studio executive referred to him as "the most bankable white man in town."

The 1990s, however, held less box office success, although Murray was still delivering some of his best work, often in supporting roles – *Mad Dog And Glory* (1993) and *Ed Wood* (1994), for example. He also made his codirectorial debut, in the undervalued heist movie *Quick Change* (1990), and delivered one of his finest ever performances in one of the decade's best movies, *Groundhog Day* (1993; see Canon).

At a time when Murray was forced to work opposite an elephant (*Larger Than Life,* 1996) and a poorly drawn Bugs Bunny (*Space Jam,* 1996), he was offered a lifeline by writer-director Wes Anderson with the role of Herman Blume in *Rushmore* (1998; see Canon). A superb piece of casting, Blume embodied a middle-aged version of Murray's patented cynicism, a man offered one last chance at saving himself. It was a fantastic part and a fantastic performance that revealed real depth. Murray continued his successful collaboration with Anderson on *The Royal Tennenbaums* (2001) and *The Life Aquatic With Steve Zissou* (2004); in between he took the time, and a serious pay cut, to star in Sofia Coppola's exquisite *Lost In Translation* (2004), for which he netted his first Oscar nomination as Best Actor.

Stripes
dir Ivan Reitman, 1981, US, 106m

Prototypical, delightfully subversive 1980s comedy that blends *SNL* (Murray) with *Second City* (co-star Harold Ramis) and sets out to kick some ass. In this case it's that of the American army, as Murray and Ramis join up largely because they can't think of anything else to do. John Candy and veteran Warren Oates lend able comic support.

Quick Change
dir Howard Franklin, 1990, US, 88m

A love letter to all that's bad about the Big Apple. Murray (dressed as a clown) and cohorts Geena Davis and Randy Quaid rob a bank so they can finally get away from this terrible place. The robbery is easy, but getting to the airport is all but impossible – everything they despise about the city conspiring against them.

Lost In Translation
dir Sofia Coppola, 2003, US/Jap, 102m

Peerless performances from Murray and Scarlett Johansson in this bittersweet tale of two lost souls who connect in a strange land – in this case, Tokyo. For those that remember Murray as "Nick the lounge singer" on *SNL*, the karaoke scene is simply splendid (and poignant).

The Life Aquatic With Steve Zissou
dir Wes Anderson, 2004, US, 118m

Continuing his fine work with director Wes Anderson, Murray is perfect as an ageing ocean explorer with a vendetta against the shark that killed his partner. As with all of Anderson's work, it's fundamentally about dysfunctional families – this time under the sea, complete with some wonderfully bizarre marine life from stop-motion animator Henry Sellick.

Mike Myers
Actor and Screenwriter, 1963–

Although Canadian by birth, **Mike Myers** is something of an Anglophile, his parents originally hailing from Liverpool. Having established himself as a stand-up performer in the Toronto branch of the *Second City* comedy troupe, Myers based himself in England during the mid 1980s, where he quickly became a fixture on the London cabaret circuit (most notably as a regular at the then burgeoning *Comedy Store*) alongside his partner, the Brit Neil Mullarkey. Myers eventually graduated to the inauspicious role of playing second fiddle to British television's Timmy Mallett on the turbo-charged children's show *The Wide Awake Club*, before heeding the call to return to North America, where in 1988 he fulfilled a childhood dream and joined the *Saturday Night Live* cast.

In an era that featured such stellar performers as Chris Farley, Chris Rock, Phil Hartman, Adam Sandler, Rob Schneider and Will Ferrell, Myers quickly became one of the show's more popular players, producing characters such as Lothar of the Hill People and Linda Richman, based on his mother-in-law. One of his earliest and most successful characters was that of Wayne, heavy metal-loving and amiably sexist cohost (along with "Garth", played by Dana Carvey) of cable access TV's *Wayne's World*. With its plethora of catchphrases ("NOT!" "schewing!") the sketch spun off into two hit movies, Penelope Spheeris's *Wayne's World* (1992) and the equally successful, and funny, *Wayne's World 2* (1993).

With these, and the delightfully daft *So I Married An Axe Murderer* (1993) under his belt, Myers left *SNL* behind and further developed his career by creating British 1960s super spy Austin Powers. Powers he claimed to be an affectionate homage to his British dad, who had been a great fan of Peter Sellers and Monty Python.

Despite a slow beginning at the box office, the Powers trilogy – *Austin Powers: International Man Of Mystery* (1997; see Canon); *Austin Powers: The Spy Who Shagged Me* (1999); *Austin Powers In Goldmember* (2002) – turned out to be one of the most successful ever, with Myers, Peter Sellers-style, constantly adding more and more characters to his range. Thus, in the original movie he plays not only the goofy, groovy Powers but also his bald arch nemesis Dr. Evil (his favourite role); in the second he adds the aptly named Scottish security guard Fat Bastard, and in the third comes itchy-skinned Goldmember himself, the Dutch roller-disco sensation. It also, like the *Wayne's World* movies, gave birth to a number of enduring catchphrases, among them "Oh be-have..."

A concerned Mike Myers in *So I Married an Axe Murderer*

and "yeah, baby, yeah!", repeated ad nauseam around student campuses worldwide.

As the voice of the ogre in animated block-busters *Shrek* (2001) and *Shrek 2* (2004), Myers once more displayed his felicity with accents, but another cartoon-related work, his turn beneath fur as the titular feline in the dismal *Dr Seuss' The Cat in the Hat* (2003) – proved to be a disappointment for all those who had ever read the classic book.

So I Married An Axe Murderer
dir Thomas Schlamme, 1993, US, 92m

Myers plays Charlie, a beat poet who suspects his butcher girlfriend (Nancy Travis) is out to kill him. Lots of silly jokes, and a raft of great performances – not only from Myers, who also plays his own insane Scottish father, but also

from the likes of Charles Grodin, comedian Steven Wright, Alan Arkin and Phil Hartman.

Wayne's World
dir Penelope Spheeris, 1992, US, 95m

Dana Carvey and Myers, who also cowrote, have great fun with their slacker heavy metal dude personas, lampooning everything from cable TV to pop culture – and ensuring along the way that listening to Queen's "Bohemian Rhapsody" will never be the same again.

Mabel Normand

Actress, 1894–1930

Playing an integral part in the career of Charles Chaplin and in the success of her long time partner, Mack Sennett – who called her "the most gifted player who ever stepped before a camera" – **Mabel Normand** was one of the screen's first great comediennes. Growing up in a vaudeville family and arriving in New York in 1908, by the age of thirteen Mabel was modelling for local artists and photographers. Three years later she was appearing in one-reel comedies such as *Indiscretions Of Betty* (1910) and *How Betty Won The School* (1911) and, under the direction of Sennett, soon became one of Biograph's biggest stars. When Sennett left to form his Keystone production company in 1912, Normand promptly followed. They planned to marry on several occasions but the event never materialized.

Normand, who often codirected with Sennett, directed alone, too – then unheard-of for a female star – writing, directing and starring in numerous movies including *Mabel's Married Life* (1914), *Mabel's Busy Day* (1914) and *Mabel's Bare Escape* (1914). She also directed many of the early works of Charles Chaplin – with whom she costarred in *Mabel At The Wheel* (1914), *Caught In A Cabaret* (1914) and the first ever feature comedy, *Tillie's Punctured Romance* (1914), and who always recognized her as an influence – and Fatty Arbuckle, her partner in a number of *Mabel and Fatty. . .* movies (1915 onwards). Recognized as one of the leading comedy actresses of her time, Normand had a knack for knowing what movie audiences would like. Much loved for her rumbustious stunt work – not only was she tied to railway tracks, but also drenched and soaked, and literally dragged through hedges backwards – she also had a good line in direct looks to camera, allowing the audience to identify with her instantly and whatever calamity was befalling her or whichever plot she was hatching. In 1916, in order to give her more control over her work, Sennett and his partners set up the Mabel Normand Feature Film Company.

Mickey (1918), the rollicking story of a poor girl who finds her way into the upper classes, was her first feature under that banner and was met with great acclaim. In 1918, however, Normand left Keystone for a five-year contract with Goldwyn films. Though she went on to make some twenty features with the studio, she was now proving to be something of an unstable character, with her all-night parties becoming the stuff of legend and her alleged drug abuse becoming fodder for Hollywood gossip. In 1922, following swiftly on the heels of the notorious Fatty Arbuckle scandal (see Icons), Normand became embroiled in the murder of director William Desmond Taylor, with whom she had been romantically involved. Shortly after that event, her chauffeur was accused of shooting dead Cortland S. Dines, a Hollywood millionaire; the gun he used was said to belong to Mabel.

This double scandal ruined Normand's career in Hollywood. Her movies were boycotted, and in 1924 she disappeared from the screen. In 1926 she returned to movie-making, this time for Hal Roach, but ill-health and depression dogged her to the end of her life, when she died from a combination of pneumonia and tuberculosis aged 36.

Tillie's Punctured Romance
dir Mack Sennett, 1914, USA, 86m, b/w

Chaplin, pre-Little Tramp, plays a cad who, with Normand as his partner in crime, is set on conning wealthy Tillie (an ageing Marie Dressler) out of her cash. Lots of trademark Keystone slapstick in this first ever comedy feature, and finely tuned comic performances all round.

Richard Pryor
Actor and Writer, 1940–

For many people – certainly those that followed him – **Richard Pryor** is the greatest stand-up comedian that ever held a mike. Emerging in the shadow of pioneering black stand-ups Bill Cosby and Dick Gregory in the late 1960s, Pryor certainly benefited from their influence – stylistically, however, he opted to take his lead from contemporary Lenny Bruce instead, and, like Bruce, eschewed straightforward Borscht-belt one-liners in favour of brutally honest routines based around himself, his life and his racial and political posi-

Richard Pryor – pioneering and brutally honest

tion in his own country. It was a quiet act of comic revolution, and one whose influence has been singled out since by performers from Eddie Murphy and Chris Rock to Robin Williams and Eddie Izzard.

When Pryor decided to co-opt his own life for his act, he certainly had plenty of material to work with – raised in his grandmother's brothel, he spent his young life with hookers and pool-hall hustlers, pimps and murderers, in the none-too-salubrious surroundings of Peoria, Illinois. Two years in the army seemed like a way out, and when Pryor returned to civilian life in 1960 he turned to stand-up comedy, soon becoming a regular face on such 1960s TV classics as *The Ed Sullivan Show* and *The Tonight Show*. Soon after, Pryor found himself playing clubs in Las Vegas before heading to Berkeley, where, politicized through reading the works of Malcolm X, his act became more close to the bone, portraying the realities of his life and the people he knew – junkies, whores and winos. He also recorded a number of albums with titles such as *That Nigger's Crazy!* (1974), *...Is It Something I Said?* (1975) and *Bicentennial Nigger* (1976). (Although he is often attributed with taking the n-word back from racists, after a visit to Africa in 1979 Pryor changed his views on this reappropriation of language, and vowed not to use it in his act any more.)

Away from the stage, Pryor made his movie debut in a straight role opposite Diana Ross in the Billie Holiday biopic *Lady Sings The Blues* (1972), won an Emmy for writing a 1974 TV special for Lily Tomlin, cowrote *Blazing Saddles* (1974) with Mel Brooks, and began a successful screen partnership with Gene Wilder in *Silver Streak* (1976) and to even greater effect in 1980's *Stir Crazy*.

Despite these successes, Pryor remained a performer who never really lived up to his maximum potential in the movies. He simply had too much to offer to be shoe-horned into a character that played off someone else (as with Wilder) or was merely played with – *The Toy* (1982), in which he plays a rich boy's plaything, was replete with sub-racist overtones. His best work remained on the stage, chronicled through three stand-up movies – *Richard Pryor Live In Concert* (1979), *Live On The Sunset Strip* (1982), and *Here and Now* (1983, also his directorial debut). In 1980, however, Pryor's lifelong battle with his demons literally went up in smoke – while freebasing cocaine one evening he set fire to himself and ran down the street aflame. This near-fatal accident became the crux of his movie *Live On The Sunset Strip*. After this, his act and his career both went into a lower key, and the onset of multiple sclerosis a few years later all but put an end to his movie work. He remains wheelchair-bound as a result of the disease.

Richard Pryor Live In Concert
dir Jeff Margolis, 1979, US, 78m

Pryor excels himself in one of the greatest stand-up shows ever captured in any medium: he lets loose on everything, from American race relations to boxing, from his impoverished upbringing to his kids and his heart attacks. Brilliantly incisive, caustically self-deprecating and simply very funny.

Richard Pryor Live On The Sunset Strip
dir Joe Layton, 1982, US, 81m

Pryor bravely returned to the stand-up arena after the freebasing incident that inadvertently made him more famous than ever. For Pryor this was grist to the mill, as he recycles his near-death experiences – and his history of addiction – into brilliant comedy moments. All pretenders, start here.

The Pythons
Actors, Writers and Directors
Graham Chapman, 1941–1989
John Cleese, 1939–
Terry Gilliam, 1940–
Eric Idle, 1943–
Terry Jones, 1942–
Michael Palin, 1943–

Three of the **Monty Python** team hailed from Cambridge University, two from Oxford University and one – Gilliam the American – from Occidental College in California. Raised in the wake of such innovative theatrical events as the famed *Beyond The Fringe* review (which launched Peter Cook, Dudley Moore, Alan Bennett and Jonathan Miller) and such British TV breakthroughs as the satirical weekly *That Was The Week That Was* (*TW3*), which gave the world David Frost, the six men who would be Pythons worked their way through a variety of stage and television shows before serendipity landed them around a table with a remit to write thirteen shows filled with anything that took their fancy.

Chapman and Cleese, both members of the *Cambridge Footlights*, had toured with its spin-off, the *Cambridge Circus* troupe, in New Zealand and New York before being invited by David Frost to work on the *Frost Report* along with British comedy stalwarts-in-the-making Ronnie Barker and Ronnie Corbett. Frost later gave Chapman and Cleese their own comedy show, *At Last The 1948 Show*, with Marty Feldman.

Over at Oxford, Palin (studying history) and Jones (English) had written and performed together in university reviews. After graduation they tried to get a foot in television's door wherever they could, Palin going so far as to host a TV pop music show called *Now!* Eager to perform as well as write, they took up an offer to make a children's comedy show entitled *Do Not Adjust Your Set* – where they were joined by Eric Idle, fresh from the *Footlights* – as well as a spoof documentary series, *The Complete And Utter History Of Britain*.

Hailing from the States, where he co-edited a humour magazine *Help!*, Gilliam arrived in England with a handful of his unique cartoons and a drive to break into television and movies. The producer (and former *Footlight*er) Humphrey Barclay introduced him to Palin, Jones and Idle, and soon he was providing a series of bizarrely brilliant animations for *Do Not Adjust Your Set*.

When the BBC invited Cleese to make a series of his own, they got more than they bargained for. Cleese, Chapman in tow, wanted to work with Palin and his team; thus, in 1969, was *Monty Python's Flying Circus* formed. It rapidly became a phenomenon – a sketch show that defied convention, revelled in its own surrealism, and abandoned notions of comic structure, given a unique visual quality by Gilliam's increasingly inventive and outrageous animated segments.

Having produced a series of sell-out stage tours and hugely successful comedy albums during and after the show's four-year run, the Pythons looked to the movies. Their first attempt was 1971's *And Now For Something Completely Different* (named after a regular catchphrase on the TV show). A collection of the best sketches from the first two seasons of *Monty Python*, reshot for the big screen, the movie was intended to break the Pythons in the States; it failed to do so but, much to their embarrassment, became a big hit back in the UK, where everyone had already seen the material.

By the time the series was drawing to a close in 1974, the team decided to have another stab at the big screen, hoping to find a means of adapting their style to a full-length consistent narrative. The result was *Monty Python And The Holy Grail* (1974), a retelling of the legend of King Arthur and the Knights of the Round Table. Although essentially sketch-based – each knight gets his own sequence – it still worked as a whole, and opened the Pythons up to a whole new audience, finally establishing them in the US and beyond. It went on to become one of the most commercially successful comedies of the 1970s.

Their follow up, *Monty Python's Life of Brian* (1979), the tale of Brian, a Judean mistaken for the Messiah, courted vast amounts of controversy with its comical dissection of organised religion. For many it remains their finest hour and a half. The Pythons' last big-screen outing was the Cannes award-winning *The Meaning of Life* (1983). Lacking the narrative consistency that defined *Brian*, this was a step back to the sketch format. Much of it worked well, but by now it was clear that the team had moved on. The untimely death of Graham Chapman in 1989, one day before the Pythons were due to celebrate their twentieth anniversary, signalled the end of this innovative and influential screen team.

And Now For Something Completely Different
dir Ian MacNaughton, 1971, GB, 88m

A sketch movie that combined the best of the Pythons' TV work, refilmed partly in an attempt to crack the American market. While the TV show benefited from having a live studio audience, this collection – which includes The Parrot Sketch and The Upper Class Twit of the Year – feels a touch sterile. A good Python primer, though.

Monty Python And The Holy Grail
dir Terry Gilliam and Terry Jones, 1974, GB, 90m

This wonderfully anarchic take on the legends of King Arthur (Graham Chapman) and his Knights of the Round

Table (the rest of them) is the team's first real attempt at narrative. From the opening, when Gilliam bangs coconuts together to make up for the fact they can't afford real horses, they have a lot of fun with a limited budget.

🎬 Monty Python's The Meaning Of Life
dir Terry Jones, 1983, GB, 90m

Python takes on the seven ages of man, from birth to death, in a series of sketches both diverse and diverting. Some sketches work better than others, including the songs "Every Sperm Is Sacred" (plus epic production number) and "Christmas in Heaven". Not their most satisfying work, but still brimming with wonderful comic ideas.

Adam Sandler

Actor and Screenwriter, 1966-

Adam Sandler, on first appearances, looked like he might be one of *Saturday Night Live*'s least promising big screen crossovers. The TV show itself never used him to his fullest potential, often linking him with such musical skits as *Opera Man* (who sang news stories) and playing him as "cute" far more often than edgy. His main success before he took charge of his own career was the hit record "The Chanukah Song". But thanks to a combination of innate comedy intelligence and a nose for what the public wants, Sandler has since become one of the biggest stars *SNL* has ever produced.

A native New Yorker, Sandler first discovered his affinity for comedy when he got up on stage in a comedy club in Boston at the age of seventeen, with no prepared material, and completely won over the crowd. He took this as a good sign, and was soon performing stand-up on a regular basis, often to university crowds, and more often than not co-written with his college roommate Tim Herlihy.

Dennis Miller, then the news anchorman on *SNL*, recommended Sandler to series producer Lorne Michaels, and, suitably impressed, Michaels invited Sandler to join the show's cast in 1990. A few movie appearances – supporting roles in films such as the dismal *Airheads* (1994) – could have signalled a disappointing costar career to match that of his friend and *SNL* contemporary Rob Schneider, but Sandler was smarter than that. Surrounding himself with old friends – like Herlihy, who wrote many of his early successes, including, with Sandler himself, the sports movie *Happy Gilmore* (1996) – Sandler rapidly and skilfully began developing his particular shtick: the gentle puppy-dog guy with a serious anger management problem that unleashes itself at the drop of a hat. Unsurprisingly, one of his biggest hits was *Anger Management* (2003), in which he more than holds his own against Jack Nicholson's considerable comic chops.

Sandler had enough sweetness – plus a pure, almost childlike delight in big, silly, and generally innocent jokes – to ensure that he was rapidly taken on by the mainstream. He refined his angry guy formula by using his considerable charms to turn himself into a romantic leading man in such frothy hits as *The Wedding Singer* (1998) and *50 First Dates* (2004), both with Drew Barrymore, as well as the less appealing *Mr Deeds* (a 2002 remake of Frank Capra's 1936 original), opposite Winona Ryder. His career has certainly not been without its slip-ups, particularly when over-indulging his penchant for grotesques and dummies – the execrable *Little Nicky* (2000) being an example – but Sandler has also developed as a fine dramatic performer, taking his natural affinity for playing slightly disturbed young men into new and rewarding territory in Paul Thomas Anderson's brilliantly off-centre love story, *Punch-Drunk Love* (2002). At bottom, however, Adam Sandler's heart

Jack Nicholson and Adam Sandler take a course in *Anger Management*

is still firmly rooted in the comedies he develops by and for himself. He remains an audience favourite and, at his best, one of contemporary cinema's funniest guilty pleasures.

 ### The Wedding Singer
dir Frank Coraci, 1998, US, 97m

The movie that brought Sandler to a mass audience. As the eponymous wedding singer he dons big hair, romances the delightful Drew Barrymore and while still producing those trademark manic moments – witness his furious, broken-hearted rendition of "Love Stinks" – creates an audience-pleasing homage to all that was kitsch about the 1980s.

 ### Happy Gilmore
dir Dennis Dugan, 1996, US, 92m

Sandler patents his angry-but-good guy persona in this tale of a major-league hockey player who ends up taking up competitive golf, and bringing all his violent on-ice tactics to the fairway. A highpoint of the actor's early career, where plots played second fiddle to gags.

Anger Management
dir Peter Segal, 2003, US, 105m

The perfect title for a Sandler movie, and a concept tailor-made for him. Here he attends classes to manage his explosive temper, only to be horrified when his teacher – Jack Nicholson (another mercurial screen presence)

– decides to move in with him, in order to really get to the heart of the problem.

Peter Sellers

Actor, Screenwriter and Director, 1925–1980

Years after his death, **Peter Sellers** remains one of Britain's most celebrated screen comedians, and one of its most perplexing. A performer with a natural gift for comic characterization, he appeared at times to be consumed by his own creations, haunted by his most famous and profitable role, and, certainly in his personal life, an aloof and often disdainful soul. There's no denying the impressive body of work he left behind – characters as indelible as Dr Strangelove, Inspector Clouseau, Chance the gardener – while at the same time the need to keep working and a desire for the fame and wealth it brought left a swathe of mediocre movies in its wake. His final two films sum up this paradox – 1979's *Being*

Peter Sellers as Fred Kite – one of his many classic comic characters

There, Sellers's long-dreamed-of adaptation of Jerzy Kosinski's satirical novel; followed by *The Fiendish Plot Of Dr. Fu Manchu* (1980), the kind of movie that not even his mother could love.

A child performer in his parents' unsuccessful vaudeville act, Peter displayed his impressive command of impressions, funny voices and characters at an early age. He was drafted into the RAF at eighteen, and after World War II joined up with fellow demob-ees Harry Secombe, Michael Bentine and Spike Milligan who, like Seller, had done time on the RAF entertainment circuit. In 1949, these talents were combined by the BBC for what was to become the most successful and influential radio comedy of its day: *The Goon Show*, an anarchic melange of insane plotting, daft voices and colourful characters largely written by Milligan.

Sellers was impatient to move into the movies, however, where he created a series of unforgettable characters in such hits as Ealing's *The Ladykillers* (1955; see Canon), *The Mouse That Roared* (1959), *I'm All Right, Jack* (1959) and prison comedy *Two-Way Stretch* (1960). *The Millionairess* (1960), in which he played an Indian doctor opposite Sophia Loren, gave him his biggest audience yet, along with a hit single, "Goodness Gracious Me". Impressed by Sellers' dramatic performance as the mysterious Clare Quilty in his 1962 *Lolita*, Kubrick then cast him in his era-defining Cold War satire, *Dr. Strangelove* (see Canon; 1963). Sellers played three roles – US President Merkin Muffley, RAF Captain Mandrake, and the eponymous mad ex-Nazi scientist himself. They were virtuoso performances, but it was his next movie, diamond robbery caper *The Pink Panther* (1963), that defined his career. Sellers played the bumbling French detective Inspector Clouseau as a supporting role to David Niven – armed with comedy moustache and

vowel-challenged accent, he stole the show and created his most popular screen character (one he would play five more times).

By the mid-1960s, Sellers, married to Swedish bombshell Britt Ekland, was living the "swinging 60s" life – something sadly reflected in his choice of movies, top-lining such unfortunate US/Euro puddings as *What's New Pussycat* (1965), or looking his age in lame stabs at youth culture like *There's A Girl In My Soup* (1970). There was still the sporadic flash of genius – a retread of his Indian character for Blake Edwards's *The Party* (1968) – but by the end of the decade, Sellers was something of a spent force in screen comedy.

Meandering through the 1970s in a series of Clouseau sequels, he made no attempt to hide the fact that he was only in it for the money – and in order to realize his dream project, *Being There* (1979). A man who always said he had no personality, Sellers loved the idea of playing an innocuous figure (Chance) propelled to political power through no agency of his own, and was Oscar-nominated for his efforts. He died a year after its release from the latest in a long line of heart attacks.

I'm All Right, Jack
dir John Boulting, GB, 1959, 105m, b/w

Brothers John and Roy Boulting dominated British movie comedy post-Ealing, and this tale of a battle between factory workers and bosses was their best work. Sellers, extolling the wonders of Mother Russia – all "cornfields and ballet in the evening" – is superb as by-the-book trade unionist Fred Kite, married to some slightly implausible communist ideals.

The Millionairess
dir Anthony Asquith, 1960, GB, 90m

Sellers was known for his variety of voices – in this case he's Indian – and his penchant for beautiful women – in this case Sophia Loren. The combination of her glamour and his self-loathing makes for a delightful double-header, as his doctor attempts to deal with her attempts to find a husband.

The Party
dir Blake Edwards, 1968, US, 98m

Sellers more or less replays his Indian character from *The Millionairess* in Edwards's dig at Hollywood, playing an accident-prone out-of-towner who inadvertently ends up at a studio head's party. The dated swinging sixties humour is augmented by Sellers' talent, hidden as ever behind an accent and a very specific character.

Neil Simon
Writer, 1927–

"When it's 100 in New York, it's 72 in Los Angeles. When it's 20 in New York, it's 72 in Los Angeles. However, there are six million interesting people in New York – and 72 in Los Angeles." **Neil Simon** is very much a New York kind of guy. Not only that, he is also the most financially successful playwright in the history

Trouble in store for Jack Lemmon and Sandy Dennis, *The Out-of-Towners* (1970)

of American theatre, to the point where he now has his own theatre on Broadway and finances his plays himself. He is unique among playwrights in having had four Broadway productions running at the same time, and has had more of his plays adapted for the screen than any other playwright in America.

Simon began his comic career in the 1950s by penning sketches for nightclubs and revues before moving on to TV, joining several of his peers, including Woody Allen and Mel Brooks, to write for the *Phil Silvers Show* and Sid Caesar's *Your Show Of Shows*. He took these events as the basis for his play *Laughter On The 23rd Floor*, which was later adapted for television starring Nathan Lane and Mark-Linn Baker. His first play was 1961's *Come Blow Your Horn*, which two years later became the first of his many screen adaptations, starring Frank Sinatra and Lee J. Cobb. His next theatrical success, *Barefoot In The Park*, also hit movie screens, this time with Robert Redford and Jane Fonda in 1967.

Simon's work invariably dealt with life and love in New York, and he produced plays at an alarming rate, even finding time to pen the book for the musical *Sweet Charity*, later produced as a movie (1968) starring Shirley MacLaine. *The Odd Couple*, originally begun by his brother and fellow writer Danny, was a huge hit both theatrically and as a movie starring Jack Lemmon and Walter Matthau (1967); it won Simon an Oscar nomination for Best Screenplay.

More followed, many of them quickly finding their way from stage to screen. Some dealt with hotels (*Plaza Suite*, 1970; *California Suite*, 1978), some with showbiz (*The Sunshine Boys*, 1975; *I Ought To Be In Pictures*, 1982), some with his own marriages (*Chapter Two*, 1979, which written as a play two years earlier was considered to be one of his finest pieces to date), some with his own

city (*The Prisoner Of Second Avenue*, 1975), and some with his early life, in particular his wonderful trilogy of his journey to becoming a writer – *Brighton Beach Memoirs* (1986), *Biloxi Blues* (1987) and *Broadway Bound* (1991). *Lost In Yonkers* (1993), meanwhile, saw him add the Pulitzer Prize for Drama to his many honours.

When Simon wasn't dominating the New York stage, he turned out such original screenplays as *The Out-Of-Towners* (1969), *Murder By Death* (1976) and *The Goodbye Girl* (1977). His 1991 *The Marrying Man* was something of a disaster, notorious for just about everyone clashing with the movie's leads, then real-life husband and wife Alec Baldwin and Kim Basinger. Simon found the whole experience so unpleasant that he vowed never to work in the movies again.

Barefoot In The Park
dir Gene Saks, 1967, US, 105m

Robert Redford and Jane Fonda are New York newlyweds struggling to deal with the fact they're young, married and have little idea how to cope. An autobiographical piece from Simon, and his first major success (both on stage and screen), its slightness is saved by witty dialogue and winning performances from its charismatic leads.

The Out-Of-Towners
dir Arthur Hiller, 1969, US, 67m

If Simon's work stands as a long-standing love letter to New York, then this borders on hate mail. Jack Lemmon and Sandy Dennis play a husband and wife trading in their life in Ohio for a shot at glory in the Big Apple. But the Apple doesn't want them, and disaster ensues. Caustic comedy, beautifully played.

The Goodbye Girl
dir Herbert Ross, 1977, US, 110m

Richard Dreyfuss won a Best Actor Oscar for his portrayal of a struggling actor who thinks he's the best. Simon's then-wife, Marsha Mason, becomes his inadvertent flatmate when it transpires that he's rented the same apartment at the same time as she and her daughter. This is Simon: light, but sweet.

Biloxi Blues
dir Mike Nichols, 1987, US, 107m

This middle and, in Nichols's capable hands, best, segment of Simon's autobiographical trilogy focuses on his days in the army at the tail end of WWII. Mathew Broderick, splendid as Simon's alter ego, Eugene Jerome, is ably met by Christopher Walken as a mean drill sergeant. Touching, bittersweet and full of great lines.

James Stewart

Actor, 1908–1997

Possessed of a striking everyman quality, **James Stewart** spent his lengthy screen career moving effortlessly between intense drama, Westerns, and some of the best-loved comedy movies of all time. His performances in each genre were always personality-led, and never less than convincing and compelling.

Stewart's rise to stardom was relatively painless. Although he had planned to go into architecture, a friend persuaded him to join a summer stock theatre company in Cape Cod called the University Players. Here, alongside the likes of Henry Fonda, he made his theatrical debut in *Carry Nation*, which transferred to Broadway. Although it flopped, Stewart shortly found himself in a hit, *Goodbye Again*. Within a year – and six more shows – MGM debuted him in a Spencer Tracy movie, *The Murder Man* (1935).

Numerous dramatic roles followed, although his part as a Parisian sewer worker in 1937's *Seventh Heaven* seems the very definition of miscasting. He cut his comedy chops as a professor opposite Ginger Rogers' showgirl in *Vivacious Lady*, followed by a similar turn with former University Player Margaret Sullavan in *The Shopworn Angel*,

both in 1938. It was his next movie, however, that really cemented Stewart's reputation as a comedy player. *You Can't Take It With You* (1938), his first collaboration with director Frank Capra, saw the easy-going, always affable Stewart in love with Jean Arthur and getting to know her somewhat unconventional family. It won the Oscar for Best Picture of that year. Stewart himself received a nomination from the Academy the following year for his next movie with Capra – the satirical comedy/drama *Mr. Smith Goes To Washington*. The role of Smith cemented the actor's image as the moral hero, prepared to crusade against cynicism and corruption, winning over the powers-that-be through the brute force of his good nature and optimism. It marked the moment that he went from actor to full-blown movie star.

He continued to demonstrate his natural comic abilities on screen, whether in the Wild West (*Destry Rides Again*, 1939) or a Budapest bookshop (Ernst Lubitsch's charming *The Shop Around The Corner*, 1940). He finally won his Oscar teaming with Cary Grant and Katharine Hepburn in 1940's effervescent *The Philadelphia Story*. After a spell in the Air Force during World War II, he returned to cinema, again with Capra, in what has become his best-loved film. *It's A Wonderful Life* (1946), a sometimes dark take on Christmas and small-town America, has Stewart as a decent working man in crisis who gets to see how the world would have been had he never lived. Although not the hit expected at the time, it has over the years become a seasonal fixture. Stewart later took the lead role of the town drunk with a large invisible rabbit for a friend in the Broadway run of *Harvey*; he repeated the role in the 1950 movie, delivering one of his most touchingly funny performances.

Stewart's career now began to move in different directions. Working with director Anthony

Mann on *Winchester 73* (1950) led to several more collaborations and firmly established him in the Western genre. He also worked with Alfred Hitchcock in *Rope* (1948), *Rear Window* (1954) and *Vertigo* (1958), and added biopic to his repertoire with *The Glenn Miller Story* (1953) and as Charles Lindbergh in *The Spirit Of St. Louis* (1957).

Pivotal movies followed – *Anatomy of a Murder* (1959), *The Man Who Shot Liberty Valance* (1962) – but the best of Stewart's work was behind him. A supporting role opposite old friend John Wayne in the latter's final film *The Shootist* (1976)

should have seen Stewart bow out gracefully. But while subsequent star turns in the lamentable *Airport '77* (1977) and *The Magic of Lassie* (1978) may have proved to be mistakes, they did nothing to tarnish the actor's glorious reputation.

Destry Rides Again
dir George Marshall, 1939, US, 94m, b/w

Stewart takes his everyman persona to the wild west to great comic effect. Marlene Dietrich's bar singer does all she has to do – while Stewart, with his intuitive knowledge of what the camera sees in him, takes a back seat and admires. A perfect parody that pays respect to its source.

James Stewart waxes whimsical as Elwood P. Dowd in *Harvey* (1950)

Harvey
dir Henry Koster, 1950, US, 104m, b/w

The role of Elwood P. Dowd, a gentle town drunk who finds pleasure in the company of his best friend – an invisible six-foot rabbit – suited Stewart to a tee and won him an Academy Award for Best Actor. A tale of whimsy, eccentricity and bar-room philosophy – and the fine line between sanity and insanity.

Preston Sturges
Director and Screenwriter, 1898–1959

Preston Sturges led a colourful life. Born into a wealthy family, his mother had a somewhat bizarre claim to fame – her company, *Maison Desti*, made the scarf that strangled Isadora Duncan, formerly a family friend. Sturges himself served in World War I and returned to his mother's company, where he invented a kiss-proof lipstick. He carried on inventing – everything from a ticker-tape machine to cars and planes – and began writing stories, penning his first play, *The Guinea Pig*, in 1929. By 1932 this had led him to Hollywood, where he worked as a screenwriter, but feeling a lack of control over his work he was soon looking to direct as well. Already the highest paid screenwriter in town, he got his shot behind the camera with the self-penned *The Great McGinty* in 1940 (he had to lower his writing fee considerably – to $1, legend has it – to get the director's chair). The movie brought him an Oscar for Best Screenplay.

Sullivan's Travels (see Canon), a satirical, big-hearted look at Hollywood and the Great Depression, followed a year later and secured his reputation. He left the more reflective tone of Sullivan behind with the screwball delight *The Palm Beach Story* (1942), followed in almost shamelessly rapid succession by such classics as *The Miracle of Morgan's Creek* (1943) and *Hail the Conquering Hero* (1943). All of this work had been for Paramount, but Sturges' increasing critical and box office achievements (and the arrogance that seemed to come with both) began to alienate the studio, while Sturges became increasingly dissatisfied with the way he was being treated. This came to a head when Paramount recut and delayed by two years the release of his 1942 film *The Great Moment*, a serio-comic tale about the man who invented anaesthesia. Sturges elected to leave the studio and finally claim the independence he felt was his right. It would prove to be his undoing.

His first move was to team up with the increasingly eccentric multi-millionaire Howard Hughes. They made only one film together, a late vehicle for Harold Lloyd entitled *The Sin of Harold Diddlebock* (1947), which Hughes kept out of theatres for a further three years, then released as the heavily recut *Mad Wednesday*. Sturges then relocated to 20th Century Fox, becoming one of the highest paid men in America. The black comedy *Unfaithfully Yours* followed in 1948, but the dark nature of its humour failed to ignite the box office. His next work, a zany Betty Grable vehicle entitled *The Beautiful Blonde From Bashful Bend* (1949), was such a flop that the writer-director, who only a few years before was seen as Hollywood's comedy genius, found himself unemployed and all but broke. He retreated to Europe, where he made 1956's *The French, They Are A Funny Race* (also known as *The Diary of Major Thompson*), another flop that effectively ended his run as a filmmaker.

Sturges died in New York at the famous *Algonquin* hotel three years later, having almost finished his autobiography, *The Events Leading Up To My Death*. It was published posthumously in 1990, by which time Sturges had been rightly re-evaluated as one of the most original and brilliantly funny filmmakers ever to work in Hollywood.

The Great McGinty
dir Preston Sturges, 1940, US, 81m, b/w

Sturges' first film as writer and director is a typically fast talking and satirical tale of a down-and-out (Brian Donlevy) who becomes state mayor and more. It's really a tale of corruption – both personal and political – and like the best of Sturges' movies manages to mix cynicism with heart.

Hail The Conquering Hero
dir Preston Sturges, 1943, US, 101m, b/w

A triumphant satire about jingoism made in the middle of a world war. Eddie Bracken stars as a Marine who gets sent home due to hay fever. Desperate to avoid the shame, he is flummoxed when his hometown mistakes his condition for jungle fever, makes him a war hero and asks him to run for mayor.

The Miracle Of Morgan's Creek
dir Preston Sturges, 1943, US, 99m, b/w

Here Sturges' trademark satire is directed towards both motherhood – Betty Hutton is a girl left pregnant after a drunken night out with a group of soldiers: she married one of them that night, but just can't remember which one – and the hypocrisy of small-town life.

Unfaithfully Yours
dir Preston Sturges, 1948, US, 105m, b/w

Rex Harrison's Sir Alfred De Carter – a noted classical music conductor – suspects his wife (Linda Darnell) of infidelity. Thus begins a comedy of ill manners as he elects to do away with her in a variety of ways. Sturges at his most formulaic but, as ever, always a genius with words.

Frank Tashlin
Animator and Director, 1913–1972

In the powerhouse of American animation that Warner Brothers dominated from the late 1930s onwards, three men loom large. Tex Avery helped set the benchmark and Chuck Jones scored the touchdown, but it was screenwriter **Frank Tashlin** that took this group's comic artistry into the real world. Like his colleague Avery (and very unlike their Disney contemporaries), Tashlin pioneered the extreme vision of animation that came to define Warner Bros cartoons – brilliantly anarchic characters coupled with skilful editing, extreme angles and a sense of fast-paced, unique action. His best work for Warners was with Porky Pig and a crazed Daffy Duck in titles such as *Porky's Poultry Plant* (1936), *Porky's Romance* (1937), *Scrap Happy Daffy* (1943) and *Swooner Crooner* (1944). He rarely got to work with studio mainstay and megastar Bugs Bunny, though they did team up for a few movies including *The Unruly Hare* (1945) and *Hare Remover* (1946).

More than any of his contemporaries, Tashlin wanted to move into the real world – but he also wanted to mess around with what real-life cinema could do in the same way that he had done with animation. He found a natural companion in Bob Hope (see Icons), whose quickfire patter and overblown character were reminiscent of some of the director's earlier animated stars. Having penned *The Paleface* (1948) for Hope, Tashlin finally got into the director's chair for *Son Of Paleface* (1952), the perfect arena for him to express his anarchic view of what cinema could be. He found another like-minded soul in the comic actor Jerry Lewis (see Icons), with whom he developed a strong working relationship, beginning with *Artists And Models* (1955), and continuing through such works as *The Geisha Boy* (1958), *Cinderfella* (1960) and *The Disorderly Orderly* (1964), all of which he wrote as well as directed. Actress Jayne Mansfield also proved susceptible to Tashlin's unique eye, bringing her own brand of dumb blonde anarchy and pneumatic excess to the rock'n'roll movie *The Girl Can't Help It* (1956) and the garish, biting *Will Success Spoil Rock Hunter?* (1957), nominally based on a play by George Axelrod.

More than anything, what Tashlin did with these movies was to take the sensibility of a cartoon and put it amongst real people. Daffy Duck and co worked brilliantly for eight minutes at a time; Tashlin's genius was to be able to sustain some of the same insanity over feature length. As with his friend Jerry Lewis, French cineastes, including Jean-Luc Godard and François Truffaut, lauded him as an original *auteur* and a genuine subversive. Since his death, the director's influence has continued to be felt and celebrated by numerous filmmakers, and can be seen in such movies as Robert Altman's live-action *Popeye* (1980), starring another anarchic comedian, Robin Williams, and, more obviously, in much of Joe Dante's work – most notably *Looney Tunes Back In Action* (2003), a seriously underrated homage to Warner Brothers and their inventive animators.

Artists And Models
dir Frank Tashlin, 1955, US, 109m

Tashlin brings his cartoon sensibilities to the fore, with all his trademark touches – garish colour, crazy pacing, sight gags and some gorgeous blondes. Jerry Lewis's vivid dreams help Dean Martin create a successful comic book, until eventually he dreams up a formula for rocket fuel, and the government gets involved.

Will Success Spoil Rock Hunter? (aka Oh! For A Man!)
dir Frank Tashlin, 1957, US, 94m

Tashlin was behind the only two Jayne Mansfield movies that anyone remembers (the other is *The Girl Can't Help It*); big, blonde and self-parodic, the voluptuous star forms the heart of this camp, fast-paced and glossy satire on the advertising business. Tony Randall also excels as the neurotic, put-upon guy of the title.

The Disorderly Orderly
Dir Frank Tashlin, 1964, US, 89m

Jerry Lewis and Tashlin have pretty much honed their formula in this, their final movie together. A high-adrenalin string of slapstick sight gags and verbal hysteria centring on Lewis's chaos-inducing medic, it veers between anarchic all-out destruction and difficult-to-swallow sentimentality. Exhausting and exhilarating in equal measure.

Jacques Tati
Director, Screenwriter and Actor, 1909–1982

Jacques Tati was a cinematic *auteur* in the truest sense of the word, writing, directing and starring in his films, a perfectionist who went to enormous lengths to ensure his unique comic vision reached the screen exactly as he intended – and who almost bankrupted himself in the process. But more than anything else, Tati is remembered as one of the great screen clowns, and his comic alter ego Monsieur Hulot ranks alongside the classic creations of Chaplin and Keaton.

Originally a Parisian music hall performer, with an act based on miming various sporting activities, Tati progressed to film acting with a number of small parts in the 1930s, before directing and starring in the short film *L'école des facteurs* (*School For Postmen*, 1947), parts of which were later to be recycled in his feature debut, *Jour de Fête* (*Holiday*, 1948). However, it was his second full-length directorial outing, *Les Vacances de M. Hulot* (*Mr Hulot's Holiday*, 1953; see Canon), that brought Tati international recognition, and gave cinema audiences around the world their first chance to see his immortal comic creation, the inadvertently anarchic Monsieur Hulot. *Les Vacances de M. Hulot* may lack the darker edge, or the critical and artistic plaudits, of his later works *Mon Oncle* (1958) and *Playtime* (1967), but it is the most accessible and complete of the director's films, and works as a wickedly skilful satire on, among other things, the regimentation of modern life that was to be a preoccupation for Tati throughout his career.

Always crediting the influence of the great silent clowns, especially Buster Keaton, Tati relied strongly on visual humour; not only in the comedic appearance (a straight-faced beanpole in raincoat and too-short trousers) and exaggerated stride of Monsieur Hulot himself, but also in various "transformation" gags, in which one object appears to become something else, and in a raft of sly visual jokes that play with and undercut audience expectations by delaying or withholding the expected punchlines. At the same time, his films are punctuated by ridiculous and incongruous sound effects, using just plain daft noises at just the right moment to raise a laugh.

These are technically complex, many-layered comedies, and Tati's painstaking attention to detail and almost obsessive desire to have absolute control meant that he produced only six of them in three decades. He followed *Vacances* with *Mon Oncle* in 1958, which placed M Hulot in a nightmarish automated house (courtesy of his brother-in-law), and won Tati an Oscar for Best Foreign Film and the Grand Jury Prize at Cannes. Then, in 1967, came another ambitious view of soulless modern life, *Playtime*, a surreal vision of Paris that appeared at times to be a complicated intellectual exercise. The filming of *Playtime* was to drive Tati to the point of financial ruin, and after which he was never to regain full artistic control of his films. *Cours du Soir* (1967) and *Traffic* (1971), a study in frustration set in a traffic jam, marked the final screen appearances of his famous creation.

Mon Oncle
dir Jacques Tati, 1958, Fr, 116m

Tati is the uncle of the title, playing with his M. Hulot character to the full, and offering many examples of his unique take on mime and slapstick. Episodic in nature – which inevitably means certain sequences are stronger than others – but certainly one of the French master's best.

Playtime
dir Jacques Tati, 1967, Fr, 152m

The genius director hits his indulgent period, taking his signature character Hulot and pitting him once more against the technology of the modern world, this time in the form of a bizarre, modern day Paris – replete with a party of American tourists. It's a complicated work, sometimes more clever than funny.

Traffic
dir Jacques Tati, 1970, Fr/It, 96m

Hulot's final cinematic outing finds him stuck in traffic and Tati not stuck for ideas but bogged down in minutiae. Devoid of plot, but heavy on observation, it has moments that work beautifully and moments of pure tedium.

Terry-Thomas
Actor, 1911–1990

Terry-Thomas adopted the use of a hyphen between his first and last names (itself a stage name) as he believed it would help people to remember him, reminding them of the gap between his two front teeth. Born Thomas Terry Hoar Stevens in Finchley, North London, he began his entertainment career by playing the ukulele in a jazz band that he also conducted. It was while working as a meat salesman in London that he joined an amateur dramatic society and decided to make performing his career. Also proficient in dancing and vaudeville, he soon found himself on the music hall circuit. Some radio work followed, with Thomas making his

The magnificent Terry-Thomas – the ultimate cad, with horse and flying machine

film debut as an extra in *This'll Make You Whistle* (1932). Some more extras work followed in such movies as *When Knights Were Bold* and *Things to Come* (both 1936) but this side of his career was curtailed by World War II. In the 1940s he turned to stand-up comedy and became a popular live act, also making further appearances on radio. By the end of that decade he had firmly developed the persona that would define his career – that of the ultimate English cad, likely to be seen with a cigarette holder in one hand and a cocktail in the other. This was mined to perfection in his immensely popular BBC Television series of the early 1950s, *How Do You View?*

This and further television work allowed Thomas to form the other key relationship in his career, with the Boulting Brothers, who first took his cad character onto the big screen with *Privates' Progress* (1957). This was followed by a string of big screen successes (often pitching Thomas against the likes of Peter Sellers and Ian Carmichael) in such British classics as *Lucky Jim* (1957) and *I'm All Right, Jack* (1959). Thomas also found great success alternating between playing the cad and the comic villain in *Too Many Crooks* (1958) and *School For Scoundrels* (1963).

By now Thomas' unique English toff was being noted by Hollywood and he was recruited as a wicked villain in the big scale fantasy *Tom Thumb* in 1958. In the 1960s he would become a regular feature of that decade's curious run of long-titled, star-heavy race/chase movies in such features as *It's A Mad, Mad, Mad, Mad World* (1963), *Those Magnificent Men in Their Flying Machines* (1965) and *Monte Carlo or Bust* (1969).

By the mid 1960s Thomas had all but relocated to the US, where the Hollywood glitterati delighted in his posh persona. He became a regular on the Hollywood party circuit, living the very life off screen that he emulated so well on

film. He returned to England to appear in a few movies that, while they didn't develop his persona, occasionally placed it in another context, such as the 1974 horror anthology *Vault Of Horror*. His last screen appearance was opposite Peter Cook and Dudley Moore in their comic take on *The Hound Of The Baskervilles* (1978). There were still many offers coming his way (including one from Derek Jarman to play Prospero in *The Tempest*) which Thomas was forced to turn down as he was by now suffering from Parkinson's Disease, from which he died in 1990.

Carlton-Browne Of The F.O.
dir Roy Boulting, 1958, GB, 88m, b/w

Terry-Thomas plays the dimwitted son of an ambassador, given a Foreign Office diplomatic job that becomes a little too hot to handle. A great British comedy cast, including Peter Sellers as corrupt Prime Minister Amphibulos, but in the end it's Terry-Thomas, as the quintessential upper-class twit, who steals the show.

Those Magnificent Men In Their Flying Machines, Or How I Flew From London To Paris In 25 Hours And 11 Minutes
dir Ken Annakin, 1965, GB, 133m

Another of those multi-starred, fast-paced and overlong comedies so beloved of the mid-1960s, and another posh twit role for Terry-Thomas. This time he's aviator Sir Percy Ware-Armitage, a cad and bounder who, along with his stooge Courtney (Eric Sykes), hatches fiendish plots in order to win the cross-channel race.

Mae West
Actress, 1892–1980

In a time of increasing cinematic conservatism, **Mae West** put sex firmly back on the agenda. A comedienne like no other – brash and buxom, not one to suffer fools gladly, and never afraid to ask a man "Is that a gun in your pocket, or are

A most memorable 'partnership' – Mae West and W.C. Fields in *My Little Chickadee* (1940)

you just glad to see me?" – she was a breath of fresh (if not exactly clean) air in 1930s cinema.

Clever as West was with a saucy quip, she was also a savvy businesswoman. Knowing she wasn't built like the skinny flapper starlets of the day, she used her sturdy, curvy figure to create a raunchy persona that was as much a product of the naughty nineties as the roaring twenties. Having established herself as a teenage performer in the

risqué worlds of vaudeville and burlesque, in the mid 1920s she took her act to the more respectable Broadway, writing (under the name Jane Mast) and performing a series of hit plays. The first was simply called *Sex* (1926), while the second, which dealt with homosexuality, was entitled *Drag* (1927). Both were raided by the police; she was jailed for ten days on obscenity charges for *Sex*, while *Drag* was eventually banned, ensuring West the kind of notoriety she knew how to build on. Two more plays, *Diamond Lil* (1928) and *The Constant Sinner* (1931), ensured her reputation as a skilled wordsmith and performer, and the movies quickly came calling.

She hit Hollywood running, appearing with George Raft in 1932's comedy drama *Night After Night*, and was soon firmly in control of her movie career. She co-authored her scripts, wrote most of her own dialogue and, by the mid-1930s, had earned herself the distinction of being the highest earning woman in America. (There were many other distinctions in her career, not least of which was having a life jacket named after her during World War II.)

For her second film, *She Done Him Wrong* (1933), adapted from her play *Diamond Lil*, West invited rising star Cary Grant to join her and broke all box office records in the process. Audiences couldn't get enough of her racy and witty characters, her sexy drawl and wry smiles, in this and other movies such as *I'm No Angel* (1933) and *Belle Of The Nineties* (1934). Pretty soon, however – and partly in response to West herself – censorship reared its head in the form of the Hays Office and the rigorous Production Code, and West found her scripts being reined in and her popularity dwindling. An inspired double act with W.C. Fields in *My Little Chickadee* (1940) was one of her last successes.

In her fifties, realizing Hollywood was losing interest, Mae West returned to the stage. She revived *Diamond Lil* and in 1944 starred in a Broadway revue she had originally written as a movie, *Catherine Was Great*. Allegedly turning down the role of Norma Desmond in Billy Wilder's *Sunset Boulevard* (1950), she remained an iconic figure, something aided later in life by her outrageous nightclub act. In 1961 she wrote and toured another play, *Sextette*, before

briefly returning to the screen in 1970's *Myra Breckinridge*, rewriting her role and all her dialogue herself. She hit the big screen one last time in 1978, aged 86, when *Sextette* was made into a movie; she was ailing by then, however, and the movie made little impact.

🎬 I'm No Angel
dir Wesley Ruggles, 1933, US, 87m, b/w

A curious movie, written by West, in which she stars as a circus girl who takes to lion taming, while using a fortune teller to help her find the man of her dreams. West double entendres and wiggles her way through the outlandish plot, while costar Cary Grant enjoys himself considerably.

🎬 My Little Chickadee
dir Edward Cline, 1940, US, 83m, b/w

A memorable double act. W.C. Fields and Mae West were both credited with the screenplay, but West claimed to have written most of this tale which finds the two unlikely partners out West – Fields propping up the saloon bar, and West marrying him for his money (their wedding night makes for memorable viewing).

Billy Wilder

Director and Screenwriter, 1906–2002

Billy Wilder was that rare filmmaker – a master of both drama and comedy, and as good a director as he was a screenwriter. In short, if Wilder couldn't do it (and generally he did it better than anyone else), it probably wasn't worth doing.

Originally intending to study law, and enrolling at the university of his native Vienna to do just that, after a year Wilder gave his studies up to become a junior reporter for a leading Austrian newspaper. This led him to Berlin and his big break as a screenwriter, collaborating with director Robert Siodmak on *Menschen am Sonntag* (*People On Sunday*) in 1929, a semi-documentary piece that used ordinary people to tell the story of an ordinary day. He continued to collaborate on other projects until Hitler came to power, after which Wilder, along with a number of other Jewish movie players, fled to Paris, followed by Mexico, and eventually the US.

Arriving in Hollywood with little money and even less English, Wilder scraped by as a co-screenwriter until he teamed up with Paramount staff writer Charles Brackett in 1938. Their twelve-year-long partnership produced sparkling comedies such as Ernst Lubitsch's *Ninotchka* (1939), in which Garbo, famously, laughs, and

Howard Hawks' *Ball of Fire* (1941), which pits a smart-talking Barbara Stanwyck against seven straightlaced professors. Disappointed with the way their screenplays were handled, after 1942 the team branched out into directing (Wilder) and producing (Brackett) their own scripts, moving into dark drama with the classic film noir *Double Indemnity* (1944) and *The Lost Weekend* (1945), a grim account of an alcoholic nightmare which hooked Oscars for best picture, actor (Ray Milland), director and screenplay. Their work together culminated in 1950's noir drama *Sunset Boulevard*, for which they won another

Billy Wilder on the set of *The Apartment* with Jack Lemmon and Shirley MacLaine

screenwriting Oscar. While the dramas continued, Wilder increasingly turned his hand back to comedy, beginning a long-term association with the writer I.A.L. "Izzy" Diamond. The results were some of the finest screen comedies ever produced, many of them imbued with Wilder's own biting cynicism, and including such gems as the cross-dressing *Some Like It Hot* (see Canon) and cynically romantic *The Apartment* (see Canon), both Oscar-winners, as well as *Sabrina* (1954) – an ostensibly light tribute to Wilder's hero, director Ernst Lubitsch, that was derided by its star, Humphrey Bogart, as a "crock of crap" – and *The Seven Year Itch* (1955), his first movie with Marilyn Monroe.

Though Wilder's career floundered somewhat in the later 1960s and 1970s, punctuated by a string of undistinguished movies, he did bring Jack Lemmon and Walter Matthau together on screen for the first time in 1966's *The Fortune Cookie* – teaming them again in *The Front Page* (1974), and, less successfully, in his last movie before retirement, *Buddy Buddy* (1981).

Ninotchka
dir Ernst Lubitsch, 1939, US, 110m, b/w

Wilder made his first big mark in Hollywood by writing, along with Brackett and Walter Reisch, this slyly comic movie about an uptight Russian emissary (Greta Garbo) on secondment to Paris. Here she meets Melvyn Douglas, who represents everything she's against, and then of course the ice maiden melts. Fellow emigré Lubitsch, Wilder's hero, directs.

Sabrina (aka Sabrina Fair)
dir Billy Wilder, 1954, US, 114m, b/w

A young, effervescent, Audrey Hepburn stars as a European-schooled girl who becomes the object of desire of two rich American brothers – William Holden (the rake) and Humphrey Bogart (the stiff). The light tone doesn't hide Wilder's usual acerbic observations on America, Capitalism and romance.

The Fortune Cookie
dir Billy Wilder, 1966, US, 124m, b/w

Scripted with I.A.L. Diamond, and embodying Wilder's trademark cynicism, it's the first movie that teams Jack Lemmon with Walter Matthau. Lemmon plays a TV sports cameraman who is knocked down by a football star while shooting a game. Enter his unscrupulous lawyer and brother-in-law (Matthau), who decides to sue the network for millions.

Robin Williams
Actor, 1951–

When only child **Robin Williams** was left alone to play in his vast family home (his father was a well-to-do executive with the Ford motor company) he turned to his army of toy soldiers. Not only would he stage mock battles with them, he would provide all the voices as well. It was a gift that was to stand him in good stead: a comic Tasmanian Devil in human form, this classically trained actor turned wildly improvisational stand-up comedian brought a fresh, unpredictable presence to American comedy in the late 1970s.

Following dramatic training at Juilliard (one roommate was the late Christopher Reeve) and after trying his hand as a street mime artist, Williams took to stand-up with apparently effortless ease, rapidly establishing a name for himself on the club circuits of the west coast. This led to a one-off spot on then popular sitcom *Happy Days*, somewhat bizarrely (yet aptly) appearing as alien visitor/observer Mork from Ork. Given unprecedented free rein to improvise before the studio audience, Williams went wild on air and was promptly spun off into his own smash hit series *Mork And Mindy* (1978–82).

Eager to make the move to movies, Williams at first faltered in a series of underachieving vehicles including Robert Altman's *Popeye* (1980), *The Survivors* (1983), which unsuccessfully pitched him opposite Walter Matthau, and the misjudged sports comedy *The Best Of Times* (1986). Only *The World According To Garp* (1982), based on John Irving's novel, brought Williams any cinematic kudos. He continued to thrive on stage, however, and when director Barry Levinson teamed his stand-up genius with his straight acting savvy Williams finally found a way to do what he does best on the big screen. The result was *Good Morning, Vietnam* (1987; see Canon), for which Williams's *tour-de-force* performance – involving a considerable amount of improvisation – earned him an Academy Award nomination. Not insignificantly, perhaps, Williams's success on the big screen coincided with a stable period in his personal life when his much-publicized dalliance with booze, cocaine and the wild Hollywood lifestyle came to an end. More success followed, both straight and comedic, with hits such as *Dead Poets' Society* (1989), in which Williams scored another Oscar nomination for skilfully handling a classic "rogue teacher" role that hovers just this side of sentimentality, and *Mrs Doubtfire* (1993), a cross-dressing farce that evokes Dustin Hoffman's similar gambit a decade earlier in *Tootsie* (see Canon). Williams's unique comic dynamo was also fused to animation in his – largely improvised – role of the Genie in Disney's hugely successful *Aladdin* (1992).

As the 1990s progressed, Williams continued to successfully shift between comedies (*The Birdcage*, 1996), dramas (he finally secured his Oscar for another sincere straight-man role in *Good Will Hunting*, 1997) and a continued love of stand-up. More recently he has stayed closer to drama, in a prolific range of roles from the pseudo-spiritual stinker *What Dreams May Come*

(1998) to finely nuanced psycho performances in movies like *One Hour Photo* and *Insomnia* (both 2002). However, his voicework in Pixar's *Robots* (2005), and a triumphant stand-up tour of the US in 2002 are encouraging signs that he will never abandon his comic roots entirely.

Popeye
dir Robert Altman, 1980, US, 114m

Much maligned on its release, Altman's take on the spinach-guzzling sailor is actually an erratic and eccentric gem: a live action movie that actually resembles a cartoon. This was Williams's big-screen breakthrough, playing opposite Shelley Duvall's splendidly gawky Olive Oyl. It's also a musical, with a score by Harry Nilsson.

A darker Robin Williams in *Death to Smoochy*

Mrs Doubtfire
dir Chris Columbus, 1993, US, 125m

Williams plays a father denied access to his children after his divorce, who comes up with a unique way to remian int hteir lives. Drag. When his ex wife needs a child minder, he uses his acting skills, prosthetics and a Scottish accent to transform himself and get hired as their nanny. Close at times to being overly sentimental, but Williams is on top comedic form.

Death To Smoochy
dir Danny DeVito, 2002, US/GB/Ger, 109m

The blackest of black comedies, dividing both critics and fans alike. Having lost his job to purple dinosaur Smoochy (Ed Norton), TV show host Rainbow Randolph (an on-the-edge Williams) gets drunk, crazy and out for revenge. A mean-spirited, foul mouthed exercise in caustic satire and sidesplitting hilarity from director and costar DeVito.

Funny World: international film comedy

Offbeat international comedy makes it to the USA
– *Leningrad Cowboys Go America* (1989)

Funny World: international film comedy

As with other genres, American comedy movies tend to have the most success in the largest number of overseas markets. But while Britain and the rest of the world may hang on Hollywood's coat-tails, it's a mistake to think this reflects a lack of comic competence, or even financial success, in those other countries – at least in their own backyards. What follows is a brief tour of some of the very best comedy movies available to Anglo-American audiences from other parts of the world.

With the happy conjunction of the Internet and the advent of cheap DVD subtitling, the opportunities to check out what makes the world laugh on celluloid have never been greater, and look set to grow still further. So – with apologies to Latin America, Japan and many major comedy-making nations not represented here because of space and other constraints – here is a quick snapshot of global comedy. In all but a few cases, the films discussed are either English-language or can be found on video or DVD with English subtitles. (see pp.288–90).

Africa

If you manage to find any African films at all in your local video store you're doing pretty well. And beyond a few rare outings at specialist film festivals, the Internet is pretty much your only bet for tracking down African comedy.

The first stop has to be *Xala* (1974), one of the best known of all African movies. Legendary Senegalese director **Ousmane Sembene**'s satire of an impotent polygamous government official punished by a *xala*, or curse, is reckoned to be one of his best films.

The French connection, in terms of production finance and hard currency markets, has been vital to the development of African film. Another movie taking post-colonial Africa as its comic subject is *Black And White In Colour* (*Noirs et blancs en couleur*, 1976), a French Ivory Coast production, directed by French auteur **Jean-Jacques Annaud**, in which comedy is mingled with the tragedy of war.

One surprise success on first release was *The Gods Must Be Crazy* (1980), in which a Coke bottle descending from the sky into the life of a traditional African tribesman leads to comic mayhem. The film was a major box-office hit: the US foreign language box-office number one in 1981, and number one in Japan in 1982. It inspired a sequel and three Hong Kong movies featuring the lead character, N!Xau. The film has also proved controversial, however, deemed by many to be an apologia for South Africa's apartheid regime and even a cause of further exploitation in the person of its star **Xixo** who was plucked from obscurity to play N!Xau.

African music has also featured heavily in comedies. World music superstar **Papa Wemba**

from the Congo, in what was then Zaire, fronted *La Vie est Belle* (*Life Is Rosy*, 1986) a charming tale of a musician moving from a village to the big city. Its central plot device – older man takes on a new younger wife – is common to many African comedies, including *Xala* and films like *Bal poussière* (1988), in which the village chief decides to take a sixth wife. In each of these movies the arrival of the new wife disturbs the existing domestic equilibrium as the older first wife (and usually second and sometimes subsequent wives too) adjusts to the new situation, and puts pressure on the male protagonist to "perform". Rich with comic potential, this is a plotline unlikely to go away any time in the near future.

The Internet is opening up opportunities to locate African films on DVD, such as *Jit*, a 1990 Zimbabwean romcom, and *Faces Of Woman* (Ivory Coast, 1985), though legendary regional successes like the Ghanaian *Love Brewed In The African Pot* (1981) remain out of easy reach for African and western audiences alike. However, the booming video film industry in Nigeria is spawning scores of comedies. So maybe a crossover success on the scale of *The Gods* is closer than it seems?

Xala
dir Ousmane Sembene, 1974, Senegal, 123m

There is lots to intrigue and amuse in this satire, whose message is still worryingly relevant. Corrupt politician and businessman El Hadji Kader Beye (Makhouredia Gueye) finds himself impotent after his marriage to his third wife. All efforts to remedy the situation, including a visit to a local healer/witch doctor, backfire as the mood darkens and Sembene (who adapted this from his own novel) conjures up a stinging, shocking finale.

The Gods Must Be Crazy
dir Jamie Uys, 1980, Botswana, 109m

An annoying (not to say hugely patronising) documentary voice-over mars much of the beginning of the film which then mutates agreeably into slapstick, gauche romcom and and even action comedy as N!Xi the bushman helps his new white friends rescue a school trapped by a small band of renegade guerrillas. Stunning landscapes and the sheer surprise of there being such an unlikely film still attracts fans, just as its critics still lament the crude contrast of outback black innocents with over-sophisticated white city folk.

La Vie est Belle (Life Is Rosy) dir Benoît
Lamy and Mweze Ngangura, 1986, Zaire, 80m

Papa Wemba was the headline attraction, but it is the women, particularly the scary (but ultimately sympathetic) figure of Mamou (Landu Nzunzimbu Matshia), wife of club-owner Nvouandou, that steal the show. Nvouandou wants to take another wife, Kabibi, but she has fallen for penniless musician Kourou (Wemba). Gentle and amusing, the comedy is the treat here; fans of Wemba's music would be better sticking to the CDs.

Australia

Raymond Langford's 1919 laddish comedy drama *The Sentimental Bloke* was an important but isolated landmark for Australian cinema. But for much of the twentieth century there wasn't much to laugh about down under when it came to competing with Hollywood. Blokeiness did however come to the rescue in the 1970s with the rise of the so-called "ocker" comedies, the most famous being *The Adventures Of Barry Mackenzie* (1972).

Scripted by and starring **Barry Humphries** (of Dame Edna fame), the film also featured Spike Milligan and Peter Cook, and was directed by **Bruce Beresford** who was later to have a hit with *Driving Miss Daisy* (1989). The vulgar but innocent Barry visits London and is subjected to a host of humiliations starting with an expensive taxi ride from Heathrow to Earl's Court (via Stonehenge) and culminating in a disastrous TV interview. It was to have a big impact. *Alvin Purple* (1973) and its successors took the ocker comedy into *Confessions Of...* territory with nudity and innuendo, while still maintaining one of the central ocker characteristics: the innocent abroad, fish-out-of-water hero. An altogether more stylish affair was cult director **Peter Weir**'s *The Cars That Ate Paris* (1974) which used rural Australia as the setting for a meeting of comedy with a number of other genres.

In the 1980s former Sydney bridge painter and TV comedian **Paul Hogan** became an international star (and a very rich man) courtesy of Mick Dundee. His old fashioned outback, out there, gator-wrestling hunk of easy charm made *Crocodile Dundee* (1986) one of the most unexpected global hits of the decade. Its sequels inevitably fared less well, and eventually Hogan chose to all but retire on his laurels.

By the early 1990s Australian comedy was moving into its next phase, relying on black urban and suburban satires and battles of the sexes. *Death In Brunswick* (1991) was one good example of the former, starring Sam Neill as a cook out of his depth when he becomes involved in a drug-dealer's death at the nightclub where he works.

A dating couple switch bodies and genders in *Dating The Enemy* (1996) featuring ex-*Neighbours* star **Guy Pearce**, while *Thank God He Met Lizzie* (1997) creates tension with a groom torn between his wife-to-be and a whackier ex. There were forays into more unlikely territories, including a clinic for the treatment of sexually transmitted diseases (*The Clinic*, 1983), while *Young Einstein*

A lot of laughs for Toni Collette in *Muriel's Wedding*

(1988), directed by **Yahoo Serious**, posited the allegedly comic notion that Albert Einstein (an Australian, naturally) invented rock 'n' roll. (Yahoo has not been so much in the limelight lately.)

The Adventures Of Priscilla, Queen Of The Desert (1994) fared far better. A road-movie comedy of three drag queens (Guy Pearce, **Terence Stamp** and **Hugo Weaving**) escaping Sydney's gay ghetto for Alice Springs won huge critical acclaim including (appropriately enough) an Oscar for costume design. Delirious costumes also feature heavily in **Baz Luhrmann**'s deftly choreographed 1992 hit *Strictly Ballroom* (see Canon). Luhrmann was followed by writer-director **P.J. Hogan** who struck comic gold with *Muriel's Wedding* in 1994 – a movie that reinforced Oz's abiding love for all things camp (Abba in particular) – before heading to America and, among other things, directing a stunning live-action version of *Peter Pan* in 2003.

In 1997 **Rob Stitch**'s tale of a working class family fending off an airport development (*The Castle*) won many plaudits. *The Night We Called It A Day* (2003) intriguingly cast **Dennis Hopper** as Frank Sinatra igniting problems with Australian unions and media. But neither ocker comedy *Strange Bedfellows* (2004) – Paul Hogan as one half of a fake gay couple in a tax dodge scam – or quirky romcom *Danny Deckchair* (2003) with **Rhys Ifans** floating in the sky besieged by the Australian media, broke any major new barriers.

The Adventures of Barry Mackenzie
dir Bruce Beresford, 1972, Aus, 114m

Starting life as a comic strip based around the boozy antics of an Aussie in London, this could well be (as creator Barry Humphries claims) the first ever gross-out movie. There's certainly enough urination, vomiting and broad humour for it to have alarmed those concerned with Australia's image at home and abroad. With cameos from the British comic aristocracy and a distinctly 1970s feel, *Adventures* also looks forward to the more sedate *Crocodile Dundee*.

The Cars That Ate Paris
dir Peter Weir, 1974, Aus, 91m

Peter Weir announced himself as a world class filmmaker with this anarchic tale of a rural outback town (the Paris of the title) and a spike-heavy Volkswagen that cannibalizes the vehicles of passing travellers, and leaves a few bodies in its wake. Weir mixes and matches his genres, veering from light horror to small town thriller to teenage rebellion flicks, always keeping things moving at a brisk pace, which makes it hard to be pinned down. Witty and stylish, and ultimately very influential.

Death In Brunswick
dir John Ruane, 1991, Aus, 109m

There's a limit to the pleasure of seeing Sam Neill (of *The Piano* fame) hapless and bemused for just over ninety minutes. But a down-to-earth grimy feel, some nice light touches and what is now period flavour will appeal to those wanting a holiday from slicker Hollywood stuff.

Muriel's Wedding
dir P.J. Hogan, 1994, Aus, 106m

Extremely kitsch, this landmark film was credited with launching the revival of Swedish supergroup Abba, It sees a breakthrough performance from Toni Collette as the eponymous Muriel, overweight but desperate to escape her small Aussie town, get married, and become a "Dancing Queen". A feel-good world-wide success that followed very quickly on the heels of the equally kitsch Antipodean hit *Strictly Ballroom*.

Canada

Where would we be without the likes of Jim Carrey, Mike Myers (see Icons) and Dan Aykroyd, all of them born and raised somewhere directly above the USA? That said, many argue that the film industry in Canada (and not just comedy) has suffered from the usual malady of non-US cinema: striving on the one hand to be distinctive and on the other dreaming of succeeding in and on Hollywood's terms. In terms of the latter it triumphed spectacularly with *Porky's* (1981) and *Meatballs* (1979). Many critics winced but both were big smashes and something of an achievement: it takes a lot of chutzpah to outgross (in both senses) Hollywood!

Canada has also produced a number of locally popular franchises such as *Les Boys* (1, 2 and 3; 1997, 1998, 2001) – in which comedy does ice-hockey. These have battled it out with the most recent success story of its kind, *Men With Brooms* (2002), in which ordinary guys find liberation through the sport of curling. French-language cinema in Canada has achieved a certain visibility through the more rarefied films of **Denys Arcand** – *Decline Of The American Empire* (1986) and, more recently, *Barbarian Invasions* (2003) – very much at the opposite end of the filmic spectrum to *Porky's*. But with a country that has given the world such distinctive cinematic talents as arthouse maestro Atom Egoyan and the warped genius of David Cronenberg (not to mention Myers and Carrey), it can only be a matter of time before movie comedy gold emerges again from north of the American border.

Porky's
dir Bob Clark, 1981, Can, 98m

Canada's paean to American 1950s high school teen nostalgia made for a more explicit, post-*Animal House* affair, specifically focusing on a group of young boys and their inability to make time with the opposite sex, unless they can crash the local night club/whore house, the titular Porky's. Ultimately, it was all fairly modest stuff with more emphasis on comedy than sex, and was in many ways a formative movie for the "gross-out" teen comedies that followed it (not to mention its own numerous sequels, and latter day movies such as *American Pie*, and its ilk.)

Decline Of The American Empire (Le Déclin de l'Empire américain)
dir Denys Arcand, 1986, Can, 101m

"Lets talk about sex, Professor" would be a more accurate title for this one-note comedy drama. Randy, bored (and not particularly attractive) Canadian academics muse out loud about the only topic of the day. Smug to the core and yet strangely compelling.

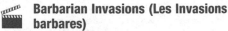

Barbarian Invasions (Les Invasions barbares)
dir Denys Arcand, 2003, Can, 99m

Critics viewed Arcand's return to the protagonists of *Decline Of The American Empire* as an inferior movie. But this time the story has more bite. Rotund libertine Professor Rémy Girard is dying of cancer and his friends gather for last rites and reminiscences. The humour is less dependent on pretentious dialogue, and the subplot involving Rémy's son and a heroin addict nurtures richer ironies.

Czech Republic (Former Czechoslovakia)

In the 1960s, Czechoslovakia's domineering political regime spawned a prolific school of Czechoslovakian filmmakers. Chief among them was Miloš Forman, who quickly went on to become a major filmmaker in the US (*One Flew Over The Cuckoo's Nest*, *Amadeus*, *Man On The Moon*). However, it's his early Czech comedies that remain some of his most delightful work. One of his first, *Black Peter (Cerny Petr*, 1964*)*, is enjoyable for some sly character acting and its slow, almost real-time documentary style, but far more accomplished are *A Blonde In Love* (1965) and *The Firemen's Ball* (1967) where the canvas is etched more broadly and with more colour.

Miloš Forman's contemporary, Jiří Menzel, also found international recognition with 1966's *Closely Observed Trains*, where the mirth displayed in Forman's work is replaced with a muted charm and a focus on adolesecent sexual longing that in cinematic terms seems ahead of its times. From the same year, Vera Chytilová's *Daisies*, a satirical tale about girls behaving badly, is probably more of interest to historians than comedy addicts.

A Blonde In Love/Loves Of A Blonde (Lásky jedné plavovlásky)
dir Miloš Forman, 1965, Czech, 82m, b/w

The Czechoslovakia portrayed here seems like another world now. Elements of kitchen-sink drama abound in this tale of a couple with different expectations of their relationship. A scene in which the male protagonist's family (reluctantly) shares a bed is truly hilarious and the performances are great.

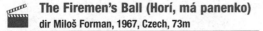

The Firemen's Ball (Horí, má panenko)
dir Miloš Forman, 1967, Czech, 73m

Amiable tale of a drunken fireman's social gathering which focuses on the ill-fated firemen's ball beauty contest. If you want to look for it, you'll discover a social satire of the ailing Communist regime (which Forman was on the verge of fleeing) along with much character comedy. Perhaps for most contemporary tastes, it's maybe all served up at just too leisurely a pace.

East Asia (China, Hong Kong and Taiwan)

Comedy is big in East Asia with active traditions in China, Hong Kong and Taiwan. The comedy movie tradition has been bolstered not only by the extraordinary exuberance of Hong Kong popular filmmaking but also by shared elements of a common cultural heritage. Major comic topics in all of these regional industries include food, family and fathers (the Taiwanese *Eat Drink Man Woman*, for example, released in 1994, has all three), the film industry itself (parody is big), kung fu and the trials of modern urban life. There are also several subgenres not found widely outside the region: gambling comedies, vampire comedies (which peaked in the 1980s after the success of 1985's *Mr Vampire*, made in Hong Kong), prodigal son comedies and comedies based around the lunar new year.

For audiences outside the region, it was the kung fu and police/thriller action comedies of the 1980s that provided many people's entry point to the comedy traditions of East Asia. Beginning with *Laughing Time* (1981), pioneer producer-director **Karl Maka** assembled a series of kung fu hits which repackaged martial arts comedy for a new generation. These included the *Aces Go Places* series of slapstick spy spoofs, complete with martial arts stunts, much gadgetry and a frenetic pace. Maka's Cinema City studio was even reputed to operate a joke quota, requiring that all the movies deliver a certain amount of gags per minute. Typical of the series is *Aces Go Places 5: The Terracotta Hit* (1989) – whose A-list cast includes the arthouse and action legend **Leslie Cheung** – in which Beijing's famous terracotta army are stolen and a typically comedic bunch of misfits have to recover them.

Outside Hong Kong, **Jackie Chan** is the most famous of the action comedy filmmakers. In the 1970s he seemed to be the obvious successor to kung fu legend **Bruce Lee**, but his career since then has made him somewhat harder to pigeonhole. In the 1980s he rode the worldwide wave (propelled also by Hollywood) of action-orientated comedies, including the fast-food funfest *Wheels On Meals* (1984). Most of Chan's films don't take themselves too seriously but nor do they go out and out for comedy, with the action often outdoing the acting. (His inclusion of outtakes at the end of his films being a revealing signature trait.) Some have also seen Chan as heir to Buster Keaton and particularly Harold Lloyd in his revival of stunt comedy – for which he is unrivalled. For most of the 1990s and beyond, his career has boomeranged between Hong Kong and Hollywood, achieving huge success in both. One of his more appealing recent appearances was in the comedy western *Shanghai Noon* (2000), in which he is teamed with Hollywood/indie darling **Owen Wilson**.

Chan's exuberant blend of slapstick and action would seem to be almost beyond parody. Not so in Hong Kong. *High Risk* (1995), a pastiche of Hollywood and Hong Kong movies, and in particular of Chan's work, caught fire at the local box office (and is rumoured not to have greatly pleased Chan himself). Other cinematic institutions to have come under fire include supercool art auteur Wong Kar Wai who, together with Wong Jing (a mainstream crowd-pleasing director), is mocked in *Whatever You Want* (1994). Topping that, *Those Were The Days* (1997) devoted something not far short of an entire feature to teasingly satirizing Wong Kar Wai. The gangster-cum-gambling movie *God Of Gamblers* (1989), a blockbuster starring **Chow Yun Fat**, was spoofed a year later in *All For The Winner*, which starred comedy legend **Stephen Chow** as a village naïf in possession of extraordinary gambling powers. Not only did the parody gross more than the original, it spawned many successors.

A sleazier sector of the local film industry was under the microscope in *Viva Erotica* (1996), which rather clumsily used the soft porn film to satirize the industry as a whole. More recently, hit Chinese director **Feng Xiaogang**'s *Big Shot's Funeral* (2001) sees an ailing film director, played

Stephen Chow – Hong Kong's King of Comedy

Take a look at Hong Kong's comedy canon and you will find **Stephen Chow** – prolific actor, sometimes director and writer – everywhere. (You may also find him listed under no fewer than eight names, including Xingchi Zhou and Stephen Chiau Shing-Chi.) Born in 1962, Chow's range is as bewildering as that of Hong Kong cinema itself. First showcased in the **gambling movie** spoof *All For The Winner* (1990), he took on Hollywood movies with the James Bond parody *From Beijing With Love* in 1994 and played a brilliant chef in *The God Of Cookery* (1996). He has also appeared in urban comedies, **historical fantasies** (as Joker/Monkey King in *A Chinese Odyssey*, 1995), and as a lawyer in a series of legal comedies. He even offered his services as narrator in *Crazy Safari* (*Fei zhou he shang*; 1991), a bizarre mix of Hong Kong **vampire comedy** (as epitomized by 1985's *Mr Vampire*) with the African bushman hit *The Gods Must Be Crazy* (see p.239). (The filmmakers must have been crazy, too.) Early Chow was typified by whacky characterizations, some toilet humour (no rarity in Hong Kong cinema) and a mangled way with language – a style that became known as *molaitau*, a kind of **nonsense comedy** that often embodies the defiant gibberish of the underdog. More recently, he has added directorial credits to his formidable CV, with *The King Of Comedy* (1999) about the humorous trials of a struggling actor; the well-received soccer-meets-kung fu feelgood romp *Shaolin Soccer* (2001); and 2004's *Kung Fu Hustle*, which, set in 1940s Canton, brings together the kung fu movie, gangsterism and social observation in a typically eclectic combination. *Kung Fu Hustle* has not only enhanced Chow's reputation, but even been credited with providing much-needed hope for an otherwise beleaguered Hong Kong film industry which since teaming up with the mainland has struggled to match the glories of the best years of the 1980s and 1990s. It is a fair bet that **Quentin Tarantino**, who has described Chow as the best actor working in Hong Kong, will be keeping a close watch on what Chow does next and be taking notes.

Stephen Chow and co-star at the premiere of *Kung Fu Hustle*

Asian film calendar. Some of the common components also appeared in Taiwanese director **Ang Lee**'s justly admired *Eat Drink Man Woman*: clashing families, food as a source of conflict, and misunderstandings between generations and genders. The films range from purely formulaic to gentle social critique, with happy endings in which couples get back together and wish audiences good luck for the forthcoming year direct to the screen. **Raymond Wong**, a major producer on the lunar comedy scene, produced and acted in the *All's Well That Ends Well* series and another lunar comedy that has been translated as *It's a Wonderful Life* (1994), although it is more accurately rendered as *Big Rich Family*.

by **Donald Sutherland**, stage his own mock funeral. There have also been Triad movie parodies, for example the famous Triad Olympics scene in **Wong Jing**'s *Boys Are Easy* (1993), a Stephen Chow James Bond parody *From Beijing With Love*, and farce set in the distant past with *A Chinese Odyssey* (1995) and its successor *A Chinese Odyssey 2002* (2002), in which the Ming dynasty setting is home to comedy of the broadest kind but exudes a polish that appealed to western audiences too. Taking things one stage further, *The Eternal Evil Of Asia* (1995), a low taste *tour de force* (of sorts), features **Elvis Tsui**, bald-pated king of HK porn, kitted out as a man-sized penis.

Families and friends

Since the 1990s, lunar year movies or New Year movies, screened during the celebration of the Chinese New Year (late January and early February), have become part of the East

Some movies took a more adventurous look at family and gender relations. Ang Lee's *The Wedding Banquet* (1993), about a gay couple, was one, as was **Peter Chan Ho-Sun**'s *He's A Woman, She's A Man* (1994) about a woman posing as a man so as to break into showbiz who becomes the object of desire for both halves of a couple. The film, focusing on a group of yuppies, spawned a sequel and started a trend for comedy dramas based on relationship and gender complications. Renowned Taiwanese arthouse director **Edward Yang** also looked at media types and modish mores in the highly rated and screwballish Taipei film *A Confucian Confusion* (1994). Satirical drama of a more conventional kind included the Chinese *Back To Back, Face To Face* (1994), a telling commentary on the absurdity of the Chinese system and way of doing things. There has also been *Platform* (2000), the bittersweet tale of a rural opera company changing with the times.

Though Hong Kong cinema has been ailing a little of late there has been no sign of the comedy urge abating. With Taiwan and Chinese films continuing to make a mark in the film festival circuits, there's a lot more still to look forward to.

Eat Drink Man Woman (Yinshi Nan Nu)
dir Ang Lee, 1994, Taiwan, 124m

Many have heralded the wonderfully framed shots of luscious Chinese food as the highlight but the main course is really director Lee's deft handling of the family dynamic of three very different sisters and their widower father keen for them to leave home.

Wheels On Meals (Kuai-can Che)
dir Sammo Hung, 1984, Hong Kong, 102m

Fast food jockeys, Jackie Chan and Yuen Biao, team with bumbling shamus Sammo Hung to prevent heiress Lola Forner from being cheated out of her inheritance by her scheming stepbrother. This is chop-socky slapstick at its most frantic and athletic, with car, bike and skateboard chases enlivening action already studded with audacious comic stunts.

Mr Vampire (Jiangshi Xiansheng)
dir Lau Kun Wai, 1986, Hong Kong, 92m

Lam Ching-ying became the Van Helsing of the Orient with this cult comedy chiller, as a priest bungling the Feng-shui reburial of a ravenous vampire in the early days of Republican China. The showdowns between Lam's incompetent acolytes and the hopping undead are hilarious, while Moon Lee's gorgeous ghost adds a touch of romance. Four sequels followed, along with countless inferior imitations.

All For The Winner (Du sheng) dir Jeffrey
Lau and Corey Yuen, 1990, Hong Kong, 101m

Lampooning the Chow Yun-fat vehicle, *God Of Gamblers* (1990), this confirmed the prolific Stephen Chow as a major comedy talent. Duped by his uncle into using his x-ray vision to score at major gambling tournaments, Chow plays

the Mainland bumpkin to the hilt and the humour is often shamelessly juvenile, even after his gangster girlfriend is kidnapped.

The Wedding Banquet (Xiyan)
dir Ang Lee, 1993, Taiwan, 108m

Wai-Tung has yet to explain the reason he hasn't married to his concerned parents. He's gay. Cue contrived marriage with his tenant, his Mum and Dad making a surprise visit from Taipei to New York, and stress with boyfriend Simon. A very fine family farce.

From Beijing With Love (Guo chan Ling Ling Qi)
dir Stephen Chow and Lik-Chi Lee, 1994, Hong Kong, 94m

A breakneck Bond spoof. As the retired superspy who leaves his job as a pork butcher to track down a dinosaur skeleton, Chow is spiritedly supported by Law Ka-ying's inept Q and Anita Yuen and Pauline Chan as his glamorous adversaries. It's scattershot and occasionally gory, but the Wong Kar Wai pastiche is a gem.

Back To Back, Face To Face (Bei kao Bei, Lian dui Lian)
dir Huang Jianxin, 1994, China, 138m

Huang Jianxin is the slyest critic of Chinese bureaucracy, as this satire on office politics proves. The power games that ensue after Niu Zhenhua is overlooked for promotion are both sitcomic and ironic and say as much about the national character as the socio-economic transformation that was just beginning to bite. Astute and amusing.

A Chinese Odyssey (Xi you ji di yi bai ling yi hui zhi yue guang bao he)
dir Jeffrey Lau, 1995, Hong Kong, 175m

The classic Chinese novel, *Journey To The West*, is reworked in this Stephen Chow two-parter. In *Pandora's Box*, Chow plays a bandit named "The Joker", who is lured into misadventure by a pair of evil sisters, who need to find both the Monkey King and the Longevity Monk to secure immortality. *Cinderella* pits Chow 500 years into his past and into his original guise of the Monkey King in order to rescue the captured Monk and defeat the Bull King. A true comedy epic

Big Shot's Funeral (Da Wan)
dir Feng Xiaogang, 2001, China, 100m

Director Feng Xiaogang and votoran actor Ge You are among the mainstays of Chinese film comedy. But there's an international flavour to this farce, in which Donald Sutherland arrives from Hollywood to shoot a costume drama in the Forbidden City, only to be fired and Ge's incomprehending cameraman sets about organizing his comedy funeral. Lowbrow, but brisk.

Shaolin Soccer/Kung Fu Soccer (Shaolin Zuqiu)
dir Stephen Chow, 2001, Hong Kong, 112m

Seen one kung fu soccer film, seen 'em all? Of course, the unfit novices and deadbeats rise to the challenge of beating the evil sneering opposition, but the zest and sheer energy of this otherwise fairly predictable action comedy should win you over

Kung Fu Hustle (Gong fu)
dir Stephen Chow, 2004, China/Hong Kong, 95m

Having choreographed the fight scenes in *The Matrix*, Yuen Wo-ping teamed with Stephen Chow for this cartoonish kung-fu comedy, in which a petty hustler finds himself caught between the warring Crocodile and Axe gangs in pre-Communist China. Packed with SFX shtick and Chow's trademark blend of cinematic spoof and *moleitau* wit, this busy period romp confirmed Chow's burgeoning international reputation..

France

Critically ignored internationally, French comedy has always been big box office domestically and has much to offer the DVD viewer. In the early days of cinema, before the Great War and the arrival of sound, suave superstar Max Linder (see p.6) ruled the comedy roost, not only at home but also overseas.

With the arrival of sound, French comedy turned to the avant garde, music hall and theatre for inspiration with directors **René Clair** – *Un chapeau de paille d'Italie* (*An Italian Straw Hat*, 1927) and *À nous la liberté* (*Liberty For Us*, 1931) – and the now terminally unfashionable **Sacha Guitry**, renowned for his innovative narration and historical fantasy romances, leading the way. Clair also made *Le million* (*The Million*, 1931), a lottery-ticket-goes-missing caper which successfully bridged comedy styles from the silent and sound eras.

In the 1930s, as in England and the USA, music hall and musical comedy were very much to the fore. Stars included **Arletty**, who was also famous for appearing in a range of musical romances. Other traditions blossomed too. **Jean Renoir**'s great dramas *La grande illusion* (1937) and particularly *La règle du jeu* (*Rules of the Game*, 1937) have many fine moments where drama and comedy shake hands, whereas the dark satire *Le crime de Monsieur Lange* (1935), in which a worker's collective murder their publisher boss, flags up a continuing satirical vein in French filmmaking that also packs a political punch. **Marcel Pagnol**'s *La femme du boulanger* (*The Baker's Wife*, 1938) captured for comedy the charm of Provençal settings and the director's ordinary realism in a tale of a lovestruck baker played by early French comedy star **Raimu**.

Postwar comedy auteur **Jacques Tati** (see Icons) entered the pantheon of comedy heroes with a visual comedy style harking back to Linder and the silent period. Tati's heyday was in the early 1950s; his main rival at the time was the prolific **Fernandel** (Fernand Contandin) who made over forty films in the 1930s before peaking in popularity as the priest Don Camillo, who talked to God and fought battles with the local Communist mayor. Five films, starting with *Le petit monde de Don Camillo* (*The Little World Of Don Camillo*, 1952) directed by **Julien Duvivier**,

Farcical tanglings in Clair's *An Italian Straw Hat*

charmed audiences in many countries, as did *L'auberge rouge* (*The Red Inn*, 1951) in which he played a monk. These are the only two Fernandel films to have received widespread distribution to English-speaking audiences.

In the 1960s French cinema made waves with the experiments of the *nouvelle vague*, a different kind of self-consciously experimental cinema that satirized the bourgeoisie from a leftish point of view. In the midst of all this, traditional comedy fare still fared well at the box office. 1964's *La grande vadrouille* (aka *Don't Look Now, We're Being Shot At*), directed by **Gérard Oury** and starring English comedy legend **Terry-Thomas** as an RAF pilot shot down over France, proved to be one of the most popular French comedies ever. Oury also directed the smuggling caper film *Le corniaud* (*The Sucker*, 1965) starring the popular comedy performer **Louis de Funès**, who is remembered for many movies, not least *Les aventures de Rabbi Jacob* (*The Mad Adventures Of Rabbi Jacob*, 1973), where he played a factory owner forced to impersonate a Rabbi after being kidnapped by an Arab leader – a film unlikely to see a Hollywood remake in the current political climate!

The early 1970s also saw French cinema playing host to Spanish surrealist **Luis Buñuel** whose satire *La discrète charme de la bourgeoisie* (*The Discreet Charm Of The Bourgeoisie*, 1972) has three couples meeting up for a meal they never actually get to eat. Nominated for an Oscar the film was more of a piece with the great director's other work than a new direction in French film comedy. It wasn't until the *nouvelle vague* began to ebb that a new French comedy emerged, its roots firmly fixed in the theatre and the café-théâtre. This new breed of naturalistic social comedy, with an emphasis on the battle of the sexes, was partly anticipated by the 1978 worldwide cross-dressing hit *La cage aux folles*. The movie was derived from a Francis Veber play and directed by **Edouard Molinaro** – by the 1980s, however, Veber and others were directing themselves, and a series of new comedy names emerged.

New masters of comedy

Modern French comedy is truly an industry, well supported not only by the usual government initiatives but also by a healthy and hungry home audience. As a genre many would argue it has become more reliable in quality than arthouse drama, which is what most international audiences expect of French cinema. The industry is supported by not only a large crop of big-name directors but also a stable of talented comedy actors such as Daniel Auteuil, Michel Serrault, Jean-Pierre Bacri and of course **Gérard Depardieu** (see Icons). The current crop of French auteurs include almost too many to mention, but particular note should be taken of the directors Bertrand Blier, Jean-Pierre Jeunet, Patrice Leconte, Francis Veber, Coline Serreau, Josiane Balasko and Jean-Marie Poiré.

Francis Veber became a playwright and then later a filmmaker who, following the huge global success of the gay-themed farce *La cage aux folles* (*Birds Of A Feather*, 1978), has found both himself and his work in huge demand, often in the form of providing Hollywood with material for remakes – no less than eight of his films have been either made or optioned. *La cage aux folles* became Mike Nichols' *The Birdcage* (1996), while Billy Wilder (a hero of Veber's) adapted one of his plays for his last film, 1982's *Buddy, Buddy*. Many more Veber scripts have seem themselves reincarnated for an English-language audience (or are currently in preparation), including the Tom Hanks vehicle *The Man With One Red Shoe* (1985), *Three Fugitives* (1989), *My Father The Hero* (1994; starring Veber regular Gérard Depardieu) and *Le placard* (*The Closet,* 2001), the comical tale of a man who tries not to get himself fired by pretending to be gay. Perhaps the pick of Veber's French films is 1998's *Le dîner de cons* (see Canon), in which an escalating series of misadventures demonstrates Veber's brilliant theatrical timing and mastery of farce.

Also noted in Hollywood was the success of **Jean-Marie Poiré**'s *Les visiteurs* (1993), a 13.6 million-ticket sale hit on home ground. Poiré's other films have not had quite the same impact, but were successful nonetheless. The well-received *Le Père Noël est une ordure* (*Santa Claus Stinks,* 1982), about a stressful Christmas, was remade as *Mixed Nuts* (1994) starring Steve Martin. Poiré's version was much the more favoured. The director continued his success in the 1990s with a string of hits including the bizarrely titled *L'opération corned-beef* (1991), in which Jean Reno (a Poiré favourite) is asked by the President of France to uncover a security agency mole.

Jean-Pierre Jeunet is a striking visualist who first found international success in 1990 with the brilliantly inventive *Delicatessen*. Since then he has continued to make striking movies such as *La cité des enfants perdus* (*The City Of Lost Children,* 1995) and even *Alien Resurrection* (1997*)* for Hollywood. Hovering between drama and a playful sense of humour, in 2001 he once again scored big with the worldwide success of the delightful *Amélie* (see Canon), which introduced **Audrey Tautou** as a major French star. The pair continued their collaboration in 2004's war-themed *A Very Long Engagement*, in which Jeunet leavens the tragedy with his wry, playful touch.

Patrice Leconte first came to universal prominence with his superb thriller *Monsieur Hire*

(1989) before revealing a fondness for absurdist comedy. *Le mari de la coiffeuse* (*The Hairdresser's Husband*, 1990), a knowing period piece, fared well internationally, while *Tango* (1998), a blackly comic road movie featuring three disparate men who go off in search of a wife that one of them must murder, remains one of his strongest works.

Another director drawn to the darker side of humour, **Bertrand Blier**, makes even more determinedly deadpan movies, often with a provocative undertone, that divide critics and viewers. *Trop belle pour toi* (*Too Beautiful For You*, 1989), starring Gérard Depardieu, is one of the lightest; darker efforts include *Préparez les mouchoirs* (*Get Out Your Handkerchiefs*, 1978), featuring a young Depardieu, and the following year's *Buffet froid* (Depardieu again), a film which is indeed cold, and only by some extraordinary extension of the copywriter's art could be called a comedy. In this respect Blier can be seen as perpetuating a strain of mordant amusement to be found in parts of the French *nouvelle vague* director **Jean-Luc Godard**'s films. An altogether gentler connection with the *nouvelle vague* of the 1960s were the films of veteran **Erich Rohmer** whose "comedies and proverbs" series of the 1980s represent an intimate and very human type of drama inflected with humour. In one of the best of his many intelligent and subtle comedies of manners, *Les nuits de la pleine lune* (*Full Moon In Paris*,1984), one half of a couple decides to see her partner weekends only. Complications inevitably ensue.

Much more in the comedy mainstream is **Josiane Balasko**, who has worked extensively as a comedy actress with lead roles in *Trop belle pour toi* and in the two sex comedies which she directed in the 1990s: the lesbian-themed *Gazon maudit* (*French Twist*, 1995) and *Ma vie en enfer*

Camp capers in the classic *La cage aux folles*

(*My Life in Hell*, 1991) starring the ubiquitous **Daniel Auteuil** as her lover-demon. Both movies received international recognition.

Trained trapeze artist **Coline Serreau** hit box office gold with *Trois hommes et un couffin* (*Three Men And A Cradle*, 1985), which was remade in Hollywood as *Three Men And A Baby* (1987). She followed this in 1989 with *Romuald et Juliette* (company director falls for a black cleaning lady) and more recently *Chaos* (2001) in which a bourgeois couple attempt to help a beaten-up prostitute.

The variety and quantity of French comic fare goes well beyond these big names, however. Recent highlights include **Étienne Chatiliez**'s delightful *Le bonheur est dans le pré* (1995) in which **Michel Serrault**'s businessman relocates

to a new life and a new wife in the countryside and meets Manchester United soccer legend **Eric Cantona** in one of his first cameo roles. Another delight is *Ma femme est une actrice* (2001), with director **Yvan Attal** enjoying playing himself hugely. Other treasures have been the unlikely stop-start musical comedy, *On connaît la chanson* (*Same Old Song*, 1997), **Sylvain Chomet**'s award-winning, super-stylish comedy noir animation *Les triplettes de Belleville* (*Belleville Rendezvous*, 2002) and **Francois Ozon**'s Almodovarish farce *8 femmes* (*8 Women*, 2002), in which an astonishing cast of three generations of France's finest actresses assemble to complete the line-up in the title.

Un chapeau de paille d'italie (An Italian Straw Hat)
dir René Clair, 1927, Fr, 60m, b/w

A horse, carrying Fadinard to his wedding, eats the straw hat of a married woman who is meeting her lover. A replacement must be found to avoid dishonour, and a whole series of unlikely events are set in motion. Based on a classic farce by Labiche, this anarchic satire of bourgeois hypocricy is one of the greatest of all silent comedies.

A nous la liberté (Liberty For Us)
dir René Clair, 1931, Fr 104m, b/w

Delightfully acted curiosity which merges slapstick, social comment and superb cinematography. Two cons escape from prison – one becomes a capitalist company boss who strikes it rich, while the other is recaptured. One day they meet again. . . Dystopian satire foreshadowing Chaplin's *Modern Times*, with real heart and class performances.

La cage aux folles (Birds Of A Feather)
dir Edouard Molinaro, 1978, Fr 108m, b/w

Nothing terribly subtle about this rather dated high camp farce when the son of a gay couple shocks his parents by deciding to marry the daughter of a family values politician. Drag, deception and comic delirium are the ingredients of a memorable finale.

Trois hommes et un couffin (Three Men And A Cradle)

dir Coline Serreau,1985, Fr, 106m

More high concept comedy in the film that started the Hollywood remake phenomenon in which irresponsible men face up to the challenges of infant care. Not as slick as *Three Men And A Baby*, the film still serves up the same message. Bachelors be warned!

Trop belle pour toi (Too Beautiful For You)

dir Bertrand Blier, 1989, Fr, 91m

Two comedy legends for the price of one: Josiane Balasko and Gérard Depardieu star as the ordinary-looking temp and the BMW salesman (with a beautiful wife) who falls for her. Offbeat and determined – sometimes a little too determined – to undermine the clichés of the standard romcom.

Le mari de la coiffeuse (The Hairdresser's Husband)

dir Patrice Leconte, 1990, Fr, 80m

Sexy, offbeat and Gallic to the core. A sensual and surprisingly intense tale of love, longing, haircutting and Arabian dancing, courtesy of the fabulous Jean Rochefort. Celebrated composer Michael Nyman provides the score.

Les visiteurs (The Visitors)

dir Jean-Marie Poiré, 1993, Fr, 107m

The splendid Jean Reno and Christian Clavier play an 11th century French nobleman and his squire inadvertently transported through time to the 20th century. Said nobleman must seek out his modern day descendants to work out a route home, whilst also dealing with the trappings of modern day life and all that such technology has to offer.

Le bonheur est dans le pré (Happiness Is In The Field)

dir Étienne Chatiliez, 1995, Fr, 106m

Former footballer Eric Cantona (and his brother Joel) lifted the profile of this film but they are not its star turns. A simple plot device – miserable businessman (Michel Serrault) swaps lives with a dead namesake – sparks off a graceful, winding but charming film that induces smiles if not belly laughs.

Gazon maudit (French Twist)

dir Josiane Balasko, 1995, Fr, 107m

Adulterous husband Laurent (Alain Chabat) receives his comeuppance in the form of lesbian Marijo (played by Balasko herself) who moves in on his wife Loli (Victoria Abril). A classic French farce played only for laughs.

On connaît la chanson (Same Old Song) dir Alain Resnais, 1997, Fr, 120m

Hard to believer that the director of this fluffy, lip-synched musical homage to Dennis Potter was the *éminence grise* behind 1961's avant-garde monolith *Last Year In Marienbad*. They couldn't be more different – this is a very charming, very French, and very light comedy. If only the songs had been given more time to breathe.

Ma femme est une actrice

dir Yvan Attal, 2001, Fr, 91m

Actor-director Yvan Attal directs wife Charlotte Gainsbourg and himself in a nicely paced comedy of jealousy and the male ego under threat. It's not only the autobiographical element but also the splendid soundtrack composed by American jazz pianist Brad Mehldau that remind you of Woody Allen at his freshest.

Le placard (The Closet)

dir Francis Veber, 2001, Fr, 85m

French comedy regular Daniel Auteuil stars as an accountant who saves his job by pretending to be gay. That the role-reversals the film depends on don't entirely convince doesn't spoil the fun, including the pleasure of seeing Gérard Depardieu playing a homophobe who receives his comeuppance.

Les triplettes de Belleville (Belleville Rendezvous)

dir Sylvain Chomet, 2002, Fr, 81m

Grotesque, offbeat and with an eerie soundtrack, this animated marvel relates a surreal tale of a Tour de France cyclist captured by a mafia godfather and his square-shaped heavies. His grandmother and dog come to the rescue. In a world, and a class, of its own.

Germany

The German influence on international cinema has been strong, largely through the impact of the many directors who left the country after the rise of the Nazis and made second careers in Hollywood. Among the most notable figures were two great comedy luminaries, Ernst Lubitsch and Billy Wilder. However, much of Germany's home-grown comedy has failed to translate. Among Lubitsch's early movies were such oddities as *Der Stolz der Firma* (1914), a slapstick film set in the Jewish-clothing manufacturing sector, and an early female cross-dressing film, *Ich möchte kein Mann sin* (1920).

Among the many German comedy stars beloved at home but unknown abroad is the genial everyman **Heinz Ruhmann**, a legend in his own country with films such as the school drama *Die Feuerzangenbowle* (1944) in which a middle-aged man goes back to school. But the most success-ful modern director in international terms has been **Doris Dörrie**, who scored a big success with *Männer* (*Men*) in 1985. This quirky "New Man" comedy was the first in a string of comedy films including *Bin ich schön?* (*Am I Beautiful?*, 1998), and *Enlightenment Guaranteed* (2000), an interesting companion piece to Sofia Coppola's *Lost In Translation,* in which two brothers go to Japan to find themselves in a Zen monastery.

German cinema began finally to laugh at its own past in the 1990s. *Schtonk!* (1992) focused on the real-life events behind the faked Hitler diaries, while the unification of Germany created a new mini-genre: the unification comedy. The most extreme example was the gory *Das deutsche Kettensagenmassaker* (*The German Chainsaw Massacre*, 1990), where Germans fleeing from the East are slaughtered, packaged up and eaten in a tinned food scam. The most celebrated was *Good Bye, Lenin!* (2003), in which a loving son works hard to re-create communist East Berlin for his bedridden mother.

Though Dörrie has had her offers, Germany's biggest exports are big-budget action direc-tors such as **Wolfgang Petersen** and **Roland**

Broad humour in the Hitler Diaries-themed *Schtonk!*

253

Emmerich. The revitalization of the German film industry since unification has led to an increase in the number of talented filmmakers choosing to remain in their own country, and to a new found love of the comedy movie. In 2001, *Der Schuh des Manitu* (*Manitou's Shoes*) – a spoof German western – written, directed and starring **Michael Herbig**, became the country's highest earning home-language movie. Unfortunately, this, like many other German comedies, it is not widely available. *Shoes* can be found in a dubbed version, but most German comedies fare even worse, without even subtitles on the home-market-only DVDs.

Männer (Men)
dir Doris Dörrie, 1985, W. Ger, 99m

Fast, farcical but wearing very well for its years, *Men* runs through most of the repertoire of male-female misunderstandings in the cause of humour. A gorilla suit has a central role in which a philandering husband receives some of his own medicine in return. He fights back by moving in with her lover.

Schtonk!
dir Helmut Dietl, 1992, Ger, 111m

The Hitler diary controversies are the springboard for a slick and amusing media-frenzy romp. It's not subtle nor has it aged well, but a continental comedy with a lot of energy and a willingness to offend has something going for it.

Good Bye, Lenin!
dir Wolfgang Becker, 2003, Ger, 121m

In which Alex (Daniel Brühl) conceals the sudden collapse of East Germany from his ill, staunchly Communist mother. Veering more towards drama than comedy (despite a couple of standout moments) the tone is part satire, part elegy and wholly bittersweet.

Enlightenment Guaranteed (Erleuchtung garantiert)
dir Dorris Dörrie, 2000, Ger, 109m

Two brothers discover themselves in Japan courtesy of an urban nightmare in Tokyo and Zen monastery ritual. Uwe Ochsenknecht from Dörrie's *Men* is a welcome familiar face in a film that would make a splendid double-bill with Sofia Coppola's *Lost In Translation*.

India

Comedy has been an integral part of Bombay cinema since its inception. By the second half of the nineteenth century, it was as important in the Parsi-Urdu theatre as melodrama and the comedy of manners was for the colonial stage, and this tradition continued onto the silent screen. The advent of the talkies saw comedians Bhagwan, Johnny Walker and Jagdeep (among others) achieve star status by playing bit parts, a tradition continued nowadays by characters such as Johnny Lever.

Post-Independence saw the emergence of pure comedy cinema, with the production of a number of immensely successful romantic and screwball films. In the 1950s and 1960s, such stars as **Dev Anand** and **Shammi Kapoor** proved hugely popular playing trickster heroes with melodramatic character traits. But the playback singer **Kishore Kumar** was *the* comic star of the period with smash hits such as *Padosan* (1968). In addition, since the 1970s, the piquant flavours of Bombay *masala* movies – with their varied mixture of music, romance and dance (plus borrowings from western genres) – have owed a lot not just to melodrama, violence and sex, but also to comedy, which is often played out with great verve in song and dance sequences. This is exemplified in the classic *masala* action picture *Sholay* (1975), which begins with comedy and maintains a comic tenor throughout while also turning towards blinding violence and tragedy. In **Ram Gopal Varma**'s gangster films, too, *Satya* (1998) and *Company* (2002), the comic attains deadly apocalyptic overtones.

In recent times, most actors, including **Amitabh Bachchan**, **Sridevi** and **Shahrukh Khan**, have a substantial filmography of comedy *masala* roles in addition to more straightforward romantic or action parts. Both aspects justify their reputations as superstars. Over the last decade and a half, however, **Govinda** has emerged as *the* comic superstar – and has recently been elected to parliament – starring in some of the most edgy and subversive comedies ever to have come out of Bombay, notably *Coolie No.1*. The 2000s have also seen an increased emphasis on comedy which is in line with Hollywood fratpack movies of recent times, in which young men behave less than perfectly in their quest for a good time,

before (usually) succumbing to more traditional Indian values.

Padosan
dir Jyoti Swaroop, 1968, India, 157m

Kishore Kumar plays a dilettante babu who coaches Sunil Dutt in the ways of love to woo his padosan (neighbour), Saira Banu. The film reaches sublime heights of comic genius in the song "Mere samne wali khidki mein" ("At the window across the street") with Dutt miming to Kishore's "live" playback singing to serenade Banu.

Amar Akbar Anthony
dir Manmohan Desai, 1977, India, 184m

Amitabh Bachchan established his superstardom through his comic turn in this near perfect *masala* film based on Bollywood's favourite "brothers separated at birth" formula. The ironic dialogue is memorable, as are the songs. Bachchan's surreal comic piece to the song "My name is Anthony Gonsalves" is a high point, displaying Bombay cinema at its playful best.

Coolie No.1
dir David Dhawan, 1995, India, 134m

This film established Govinda as the master of bawdy subversive comedy, borrowing heavily from lower caste and Muslim *bazaar* comic repertoires. He plays an indigent coolie who stumbles into marriage with a rich man's daughter with surreal consequences. Karishma Kapoor's raunchiness matches Govinda's intentions to upend class and caste snobbery through sheer provocative humour.

Italy

Italy's comedy movie traditions run deep, not only through its important heritage of comedy theatre and clowning but also via a head start in the silent period when comic movie stars like Cretinetti (see p.6) were nurtured by burgeoning Italian film studios. There have been several waves of domestic success since those early days, but international recognition has been less forthcoming.

A prize case in point is the Neapolitan comedian **Totò**, whose real name, Antonio de Curtis Gagliardi Griffo Focas Comneno di Bisanzio, was so long as to seem a joke in itself. Totò was not so much an actor or clown as a frenzied, over-assertive, hungry and vulgar persona, one which could adapt to all manner of characters from the man in the street to legendary statesman Machiavelli or avant-garde playwright Luigi Pirandello. His heyday was in the postwar period, during which he was directed by a host of different directors in vehicles with titles such as *Totò cerca casa* (*Totò Goes Househunting*, 1949) or the intriguingly titled *Totò Tarzan* (1950). Few outside Italy have had the chance to see any of the 97 films he made between 1937 and 1967, but he did make an appearance in two of Italy's most notable successes: *L'ora di Napoli* (*The Gold Of Naples*, 1954) and the influential heist comedy *Soliti ignoti i* (*Big Deal On Madonna Street*, 1958).

Vittorio de Sica was an actor and successful romantic comedy director before becoming a cinema legend with his world famous landmark of neorealism *Ladri di biciclette* (*Bicycle Thieves*, 1948). Indeed he was a familiar – even iconic – presence in Italy's "white telephone" films of the 1930s, light comedies of class manners played out in Art Deco settings. He blended comedy with fantasy for 1951's *Miracolo a Milano* (*Miracle Of Milan*), before returning to romantic comedy, most notably with 1963's *Ieri, oggi, domani* (*Yesterday, Today And Tomorrow*). This multi-story tale of male–female relationships iconized the on-screen pairing of sultry **Sophia Loren** and **Marcello Mastroianni**, who had already patented his amused, knowing persona in successful films like *Divorzio all'italiana* (*Divorce Italian Style*, 1961). De Sica's *Matrimonio all'italiano* (*Marriage Italian Style*, 1964) once again paired Loren and Mastroianni; the suave actor continued in a humorous vein with such movies as *Oggi, domani, dopodomani* (*Today, Tomorrow, the Day after Tomorrow*, 1965), which was later released as the improbably named *Kiss The Other Sheik*.

A year later he collaborated with **Neil Simon**, Britt Ekland and **Peter Sellers** who took the leading role of a master criminal in *Caccia alla volpa* (*After the Fox*, 1966). The film neatly spoofed the neorealist idea that everyone was a potential movie star.

The incomparably glamorous pairing of Mastroianni and Loren was a highlight of *commedia all'italiania* (comedy Italian style). In these films upper-class conventions were mocked and the triumph of the commonplace was celebrated. Such comedies were in turn superseded by a cosier style of bourgeois comedy that proved less enduringly appealing overseas.

The 1970s offered an absurdist example of comic Italian cinema with Mastroianni once again taking the lead in the Italian/French restaging of General Custer's last stand, *Touche pas à la femme blanche* (*Don't Touch The White Woman*, 1973). He also appeared in director **Marco Ferreri**'s dark brand of the absurd, perfectly encapsulated in

La grande bouffe (1973) in which four men (one played by Mastroianni) gorge themselves in nihilistic abandon. **Federico Fellini's** *Amarcord* (1973) also kept the fantastic note alive with an imaginative and nostalgic portrait of his home town Rimini in the Fascist years. Confidently vulgar and one of the famous auteur's most accessible films, *Amarcord* (like most of Fellini's work) was too individual a film to inspire a trend in the comedy genre.

With a television boom in the mid-1970s cinema admissions plunged in Italy, and filmmakers were forced to rely on the numerous TV channels for funding. Consequently, a reportage-style visual aesthetic emerged, with an emphasis on dialogue and close-ups. This perfectly suited the emerging talents of comedian directors like Roberto Benigni (*Il piccolo diavolo/The Little Devil*, 1988), Maurizio Nichetti (*Ladri di sapontte/The Icicle Thief*, 1989) and Nanni Moretti (*Caro diario/Dear Diary*, 1993) who were considered part of a loose group of "new comics" (*i nuovi comici*) known for "dialect comedy" who emerged in the early 1980s. **Giancarlo Giannini** also reached an international audience with his lead role in **Nanni Loy's** dark 1984 hit, *Mi manda Picone* (*Where's Picone?*).

Maurizio Nichetti found success domestically with his satire on advertising, *Ho fatto splash* (*It Made A Splash!*, 1980), but it was *The Icicle Thief*,

The incomparably glamorous pairing of Mastroianni and Loren

which lampooned Italian neorealism and the modern media in general, that became a worldwide hit. More of an isolated humorist than a traditional movie comedian, **Nanni Moretti** has also drawn plaudits for his whimsical anti-naturalistic vein of humour. His episodic *Dear Diary* offered a uniquely personal brand of film humour. But of the three, it was **Roberto Benigni** who had the most impact, His mistaken identity romp *Johnny Stecchino* (1991) broke Italian box office records, but he was best known abroad for his cultish collaborations with US director **Jim Jarmusch**, *Down by Law* (1986) and *Night on Earth* (1991). That was until he won best foreign film and best actor for *La vita à bella* (*Life Is Beautiful*, 1997), the holocaust comedy drama that he scripted, directed and starred in. After an acting turn in the French comic-book derived *Astérix et Obélix contre César* (1999) the not always reliable Benigni came unstuck with his take on *Pinocchio* (2002), but he still retains the distinction of being one of only two people who have directed themselves to a best actor Oscar win, for *Life is Beautiful*. (Laurence Olivier in *Hamlet* (1948) was the other.)

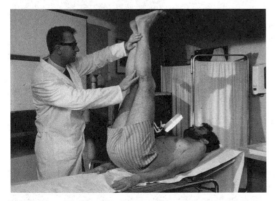

Nanni Moretti upends standard comedy practice in *Dear Diary*

Gentler humour hasn't disappeared in Italy either. **Gabriele Salvatores** detailed at least part of the Italian World War II experience, chronicling a group of Italian soldiers seconded to a Greek Island in 1991's delightful *Mediterraneo*. In recent years there has also been a trend towards sex and relationship comedies, of which **Gabriele Muccino**'s humorous look at pregnancy and parenthood, *L'ultimo baccio* (*The Last Kiss*, 2001) has been one of the most notable. It is surely only a question of time before comedy Italian-style makes it big again.

 ### I soliti ignoti (Big Deal On Madonna Street/Persons Unknown)
dir Mario Monicelli, 1958, Italy, 105m, b/w

Scripted by the brilliant duo of Age and Scarpelli, this crime caper is the antidote to French gangster classic *Rififi*. Womanizing boxer Vittorio Gassman and baby-minding Marcello Mastroianni excel, although they're upstaged by iconic clown Totò as the gang's safe-cracking mentor. Endlessly imitated.

Divorzio all'italiana (Divorce Italian Style)
dir Pietro Germi, 1961, Italy, 104m

With an Oscar for its screenplay and nominations for both its star and director, this noirish, neorealist farce rips into Catholicism and Sicilian codes of honour, as Marcello Mastroianni plans a crime of passion to end his intolerable marriage to shrewish Daniela Rocca.

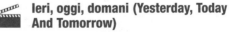 ### Ieri, oggi, domani (Yesterday, Today And Tomorrow)
dir Vittorio de Sica, 1963, Italy, 119m

Modish, Oscar-winning comedy of sexual manners, in which Sophia Loren plays a trio of modern women – black-marketeering Adelina, avoiding arrest by getting pregnant; spoilt Anna, ending her marriage because of a crashed car; and hooker Mara, sidelining a regular to save a troubled soul. Marcello Mastroianni exudes bemused charm as the saps suckered by Sophia's wiles.

Matrimonio all'italiano (Marriage Italian Style)

dir Vittorio de Sica, 1964, It, 102m

This smartly scripted adaptation of Eduardo de Filippo's play, *Filumena Marturano*, typifies the sassy Italian sex comedy of the early 1960s. Sophia Loren fully deserved her Oscar nomination, giving a sultry performance as a mistress who endures years of exploitation by wealthy lover Marcello Mastroianni before luring him into matrimony.

Il mio nome è nessuno (My Name Is Nobody)

dir Tonino Valerii, 1973, W Ger/Fr/It, 130m

Produced by Sergio Leone and scored by Ennio Morricone, this slapstick spaghetti spoof openly mocks generic convention, while also trading on the contrasting acting styles of Terence Hill's over-eager bounty hunter and Henry Fonda's world-weary gunfighter. Think Keystone meets Peckinpah.

Mi manda Picone (Where's Picone?)

dir Nanni Loy, 1984, It, 122m

The Mafia and Neapolitan bureaucracy are the principal targets of this pitch-black satire, in which red tape expert Giancarlo Giannini descends into the underworld after being hired by Lina Sastri to find her late husband's corpse. The assault on Italian corruption is made all the more savage by Loy's unflinching use of authentic locations.

Ladri di saponette (Icicle Thief)

dir Maurizio Nichetti, 1989, It, 85m

A glorious lampoon of the way movies are screened and watched on TV. A homage both to neorealist masterpieces like *Bicycle Thieves* and to cartoonish audiovisual trickery, the sequences in which an earnest, monochrome social drama becomes entangled with a tacky, full-colour soap commercial are frantically funny and technically inspired.

Johnny Stecchino

dir Roberto Benigni, 1991, It, 100m

Alternately manic and melancholic, this is a riotous reworking of the old lookalike ploy, with moll Nicoletta Braschi duping lovesick schoolbus driver Benigni into doubling for her hated mobster husband. Cross Jerry Lewis with Norman Wisdom, have him speak Italian, and you've got the idea.

 ## Mediterraneo

dir Gabriele Salvatores, 1991, It, 92m

The winner of the Academy Award for Best Foreign Film, this has all the sweetness of *Cinema Paradiso*, while also anticipating the contentious nostalgia of *Life Is Beautiful*. The relationships forged between a stranded unit of Italian soldiers and the residents of an Aegean island whose menfolk have been arrested by the Nazis are highly idealized. But Salvatores uncovers the humanity in the caricatures and clichés and uses warm wit to show that life went on, even in the midst of war.

 ## Il mostro (The Monster)

dir Roberto Benigni, 1994, It/Fr, 112m

Benigni is accused of being Roman serial killer "the Mozart of Vice" in this Sellersesque black comedy of errors that delights as much in its bad taste as in Benigni's pursuit by three incompetent cops. The set-pieces (centring on two parties, a supermarket and Benigni's apartment) provide the most laughs.

Caro diario (Dear Diary)

dir Nanni Moretti, 1993, It/Fr, 100m

Moretti won the Director's Prize at Cannes for this picaresque disquisition on Roman architecture, disposable culture, irresponsible film criticism and the state of the Italian health service. The Vespa tour of the capital and the resumé of recent happenings in a soap opera shouted across a volcanic Aeolian island are priceless.

 ## L'ultimo baccio (The Last Kiss)

dir Gabriele Muccino, 2001, It, 115m

Casting a fresh eye back towards the 1960s sex comedy, this polished ensemble piece explores the impact that Giovanna Mezzogiorno's pregnancy announcement has on her thirty-something boyfriend (Stefano Accorsi), his laddish mates and her mid-life crisis-stricken mother (Stefania Sandrelli).

Russia/USSR

It would be a mistake to think of Soviet cinema purely in terms of granite-faced, iron-willed heroes and heroines of labour forever frozen in a revolutionary montage. The 1920s in particular marked a high point in Russian humour (much of it absurdist and rather dark) with various Chaplin imitators and several clever satires.

One of the best silent comedies is *The Extraordinary Adventures Of Mr West In The Land Of The Bolsheviks* (1924), which takes equal delight in mocking both the pretensions of new socialism and American capitalism. Mention should also be made of **Vsevold Pudovkin** and **Nikolai Shipavsky**'s *Chess Fever* (1925) in which a young woman tries to wean her fiancé off an addiction to chess. Another early figure was **Yakov Protazanov** who was successful with *The Tailor From Torzhok* (1926) which features great Russian comic actor **Igor Ilyinsky** playing a man whose life is changed when he wins the State lottery. Ilyinsky was also to reappear in *The Festival Of St Jorgen* (1930) where his criminal character dresses up as a nun (this one never seems to fail), causing all sorts of comic capers and confusions.

Comedies of various kinds remained popular throughout the Communist years with musical comedy, as in Hollywood, proving very popular. **Georgi Alexandrov**'s were the best known, including *Volga Volga* (1934) – said to be Stalin's favourite film – in which happy peasants and petty bureaucrats feature in equal measure. **Ivan Preyev**'s "collective farm comedies", including *The Swineherdess And The Shepherd* (1941), made in a period of unparalleled agricultural tragedy in the Soviet Union, are even less likely to see a revival of interest.

The two giants of Russian comedy cinema are **Eldar Ryazanov** and **Leonid Gaidai**. Ryazanov, who has been making films since 1953, has had a string of successes with a variety of comedy dramas – though in recent years, as the tone of his films has become more serious, his critical reception has become more muted – among them *The Irony Of Fate* (*Ironiya sudby, ili S lyogkim parom!*, 1975), a romantic movie that has become a Russian New Year's TV viewing tradition. Of the films of **Leonid Gaidai** – who has been directing since 1956 – the most famous are the smuggling caper *Diamond Arm* (*Brilliantovaya ruka*, 1968) and *Kidnapping Caucasian Style* (*Kavkazskaya plennitsa, ili Novye priklyucheniya Shurika*, 1966). The latter, a comic romp set in the Caucasus (with plenty of broad stereotypical locals), reached more than 70 million viewers. Central to the plot are three stooge-like villains – played by Yevgeny Morgunov, Georgii Vitsin and former clown **Yuri Nikulin** – along with the character Shurik (**Aleksandr Demianenko**), a typical innocent and catalyst of chaos. Demianenko, who looks something like an early Jerry Lewis crossed with Mike Myers, featured in a string of Shurik films, including Gaidai's exuberant time-machine comedy *Ivan Vassilievich – Back To The Future* (*Ivan Vasilevich menyaet professiyu*, 1973), which was based on a short story by cult Russian author **Mikhail Bulgakov**.

Yuri Mamin's *Window To Paris* (*Okno v parizh*, 1993), a curious film that seems remarkably prescient of American indie hit *Being John Malkovich* (1999), has been one recent international export, but crossovers into Hollywood have been minimal. There has been

Ivan the Terrible attempts to impose his authority

Russian stand-up **Yakov Smirnoff**, who made a name for himself Stateside in movies such as *Moscow On The Hudson* (1984), *The Money Pit* (1986) and the Richard Pryor vehicle *Brewster's Millions* (1985) – but then again, perhaps we shouldn't go there... In general, Russian cinema comedy has pursued furrows of its own, such as **Aleksandr Rogozhkin**'s drinking-buddy movies *Peculiarities Of The National Hunt* (*Osobennosti natsionalnoy okhoty*, 1995) and *Peculiarities Of The National Fishing* (*Osobennosti natsionalnoy rybalki*, 1998), or become more derivative, with titles like *My Big Fat Armenian Wedding* (2004), and the exciting new things in Russian cinema have been taking place in other genres.

The Extraordinary Adventures Of Mr West In The Land Of The Bolsheviks (Neobychainiye priklucheniya mistera Vesta v strane bolshevikov)
dir Lev Kuleshov, 1924, USSR, 94m, bw

Nimble satire conducted with typical 1920s Soviet cinematic flair. One of the most entertaining propaganda movies of all time and for silent cinema fans compares favourably with the Hollywood films of the period.

The Irony Of Fate Or Enjoy Your Bath (Ironiya sudby, ili S lyogkim parom!)
dir Eldar Ryazanov, 1975, USSR, 185m

A Moscow man gets drunk in a sauna bath with friends and ends up in Leningrad, in an identical flat to his own, with a female stranger while his girlfriend waits in Moscow. The premise may sound unlikely, but a Russian audience used to the homogeneity of Soviet housing loved it. Starting slowly, it becomes a subtle, superbly acted romcom, combining elements of screwball, farce and arthouse drama. A true classic.

Ivan Vassilievich – Back To The Future (Ivan Vasilevich menyaet professiyu)
dir Leonid Gaidai, 1973, USSR, 93m

Characters from 1970s Moscow and Ivan the Terrible's medieval Russia (including the Tsar himself) exchange places, thanks to a time machine mix-up. Frenetic, fresh and funny, especially if you have seen Eisenstein's *Ivan* films.

Window To Paris (Okno v parizh)
dir Yuri Mamin, 1993, Rus/Fr, 88m

A quirky and original treat for those with a taste for the adventurous. This Russian-French co-production travels from the crumbling streets of St Petersburg to affluent Paris via a magical window in the attic of disillusioned aesthetics teacher, Nikolai Nikolaevich (Sergei Dontsov, who later starred in 2002's arthouse smash *Russian Ark/ Russkiy kovcheg*).

Scandinavia

Denmark, Finland, Iceland and Sweden

The popular view of Scandinavian countries does not tend to include humour as a major characteristic (think Kierkegaard, Ibsen and Ingmar Bergman), but in reality these northern climes have produced their fair share of comedy movies, just a few of which have penetrated international markets.

Apart from a brief "golden age" in the early twentieth century, **Danish cinema** hasn't had the highest of profiles until recently. On the other hand it has given the world one of the longest-running comedy series ever. *The Olsen Gang* (*Olsenbanden*, 1968–81) was unique in that it was successfully adapted for a parallel version in Norway (1969–84). While the Danish critics loved the series, Norwegian critics queued up to dish out a panning. A total of thirteen films were made in both countries (using different casts), with each film centring around a basic, unvarying premise. Released from jail, Egon Olsen is received outside by dimwitted sidekicks Kjeld and Benny, whereupon he is brought back to the kitchen of Yvonne/Valborg and unveils a new plan for a master scam. Though hugely popular in Denmark and Norway, the films have yet to receive much attention in the English-speaking world.

The same is not however true of **Dogme 95**, the brainchild of Danish filmmakers **Lars von Trier** and **Thomas Vinterberg**, which gave the world a new bible for back-to-basics filmmaking. Von Trier is a very amusing character (particularly off-screen) but his own films, such as *Breaking The Waves* (1996) and *Dancer In The Dark* (2000), take harrowing and melodramatic situations and then playfully intensify the pathos and drama. Probably the only one that verges towards real humour is the cult classic *The Kingdom* (*Riget*, 1994), a not-so-simple hospital horror soap parody that was made for TV but is frequently screened in repertory or festivals. The series of episodes introduced by von Trier himself as a kind of latter-day Alfred Hitchcock have a lot to amuse and intrigue in equal measure. *The Kingdom II* (*Riget II*) followed in 1997. There have been other Dogme films that have played for laughs, including *Mifune* (*Mifune sidste sang*, 1999) in which Rud (who has a mental age of eight) derails city sophisticate Kresten's life. This was followed by **Lone Scherfig**'s *Italian For Beginners* (*Italiensk for Begyndere*, 2000), in which a diverse group of Danes face up to the task of learning Italian as an escape from rather bleak daily lives, she also made Scottish suicide film *Wilbur Wants To Kill Himself* (*Wilbur begar selvmord*, 2002).

Finnish comedy, which has mostly stayed at home, has also proved to be the source for one of the biggest and most inventive names in independent world cinema. The prolific **Aki Kaurismäki**, along with his brother **Mika**, have been responsible for making roughly a fifth of their country's film industry output since the late 1980s. Aki's films have travelled well and his droll, stylish movies have captivated indie audiences the world over. Particularly successful have been 1989's *Leningrad Cowboys Go America*, a road movie/rock musical following a real Finnish band as they travel across the US, as well as 1990's darker *I Hired A Contract Killer*, set in a typically melancholic London. However, the tone lightened with the global success *The Man Without*

Dry humour and distinctive cinematography in *Leningrad Cowboys Go America*

A Past (*Mies Vailla Menneisyyttä*, 2002). He has also paid homage to silent cinema in *Juha* (1999) filmed entirely in black and white.

Sweden has periodically appeared on the global comedy radar. **Ingmar Bergman**'s romantic *Smiles Of A Summer Night* (1955) is perhaps the best of the arthouse legend's lighter films and makes the connection with Woody Allen (see Icons) a lot clearer for those who have only seen Bergman's austere parables such as *The Seventh*

Seal (1957). *Smiles* was set in the early twentieth century, and a later international success *My Life As A Dog* (1985) was also set in the past, this time Sweden of the 1950s. This charming portrayal of childhood foibles was not untypical of internationally recognized European films of the period – drama with comic touches taking centre stage rather than out-and-out comedy. Sweden's current leading director, **Lukas Moodysson**, like his illustrious predecessor Bergman, has also shown an occasional comic aptitude in his film *Together* (2000). This time the period under consideration was 1970s Sweden, in the form of members of a hippie commune.

Offbeat comedies, it seems, can appear from any part of the globe these days, and 2000's *101 Reykjavik* certainly fits into the new world cinema order: an Icelandic/Danish/Norwegian/French/German co-production, directed by Icelandic actor **Baltasar Kormákur**, and starring Spanish actress **Victoria Abril** in a brief break from the centre of the Spanish comedy scene.

Smiles Of A Summer Night (Sommarnattens Leende)
dir Ingmar Bergman, 1955, Swed, 110m, b/w

Bergman influenced both Stephen Sondheim (the stage show, *A Little Night Music*) and Woody Allen (*A Midsummer Night's Sex Comedy*), with this his first significant international success, a tale of couples coming together and falling apart in pursuit of love. Set during a summer weekend in 1900 at a country house party, it's a wonderfully evocative film that catches not only the mood but the heart of ardour as all those concerned search for romance; sometimes failing, sometimes succeeding.

My Life As A Dog (Mit Liv som Hund)
dir Lasse Hallström, 1985, Swed, 101m

As unusual as it is that a man named Lasse should make a film with "Dog" in the title, Hallström's film is a delightful mix of comedy and drama, focusing on a boy who is in turn focusing on a Russian dog sent into space, all of which he tries to follow from his native 1950s Sweden. He is however sent away from home and experiences numerous, admittedly episodic, events, that will inevitably come to shape his life. A film that may at first feel small scale, but that manages to touch on the breadth of life's experiences.

Leningrad Cowboys Go America
dir Aki Kaurismäki, 1989, Finland, 79m

A typically dry tale of a Finnish band trying to break the vast open spaces of America. It's knowing, but never

condescending, as the director charts the slow movements of his monosyllabic troupe across the plains of the US, en route to a gig in Mexico. The tone owes something to Jim Jarmusch, but the style is one Kaurismäki makes his own. The band hover between being real and manufactured – certainly after the success of the film, they got their world tour.

The Kingdom I (Riget I)
dir Lars von Trier, 1994, Den, 279 m

Utterly stunning, hilarious, unsettling and unpredictable. Stephen King remade this for American television, but the original is best, complete with von Trier's bizarre introductions and iconic opening sequence. Is it comedy? Absolutely, and much more besides.

Mifune (Mifune sidste sang)
dir Søren Kragh-Jaocobsen, 1999, Den, 101m

City slicker Kresten hasn't had the courage to tell his wife-to-be about his cerebrally challenged brother, Rud. After he dashes away from their wedding to take care of Rud following the death of their father, comedy ensues when prostitute Liva turns up to help with the housekeeping. Hilarious and beautifully acted – and the Dogme rough edges only make it more credible.

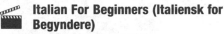 Italian For Beginners (Italiensk for Begyndere)
dir Lone Scherfig, 2000, Den, 112m

Adult education and Italian classes may seem like an unpromising premise for a comedy. But this one works very nicely, and the ordinary, well-balanced students make welcome companions before the school-trip denouement in romantic Venice.

101 Reykjavik
dir Baltasar Kormákur, 2000, Ice/Den/Nor/Fr /Ger, 88m

Almodóvar regular Victoria Abril as lesbian Lola moves in with unsympathetic diehard slacker Hlynur (who she gets pregnant by) and his mum, soon to be her true partner. A hot high concept is tempered by the verité chill of alcoholic ennui and Icelandic angst.

▐ The Man Without A Past (Mies Vailla Menneisyyttä)
dir Aki Kaurismäki , 2002, Fin, 97m

A middle-aged man beaten senseless loses his memory and finds a new life among homeless drifters and the Salvation Army. With Kaurismäki's typically laconic style, this arthouse comedy is surprisingly feel-good, benefiting from great cinematography and deceptively careful pacing.

▐ Together (Tillsammans)
dir Lukas Moodysson, 2000, Swe/Den/It, 107m

An abused wife and her two children join her hippie brother in a 1970s commune. Satirical (particularly about clothes and modish politics) and sweet by turns we get a kid's-eye view of a world where everyone is a little wiser by the close of the film.

Spain

When it comes to Spanish comedy all roads seem to lead to and from prolific director Pedro Almodóvar – or, to give him his full name, Pedro Almodóvar Caballero. The absence of a strong film industry in Spain in the repressed and repressive fascist regime of General Franco goes some way to explaining Almodóvar's huge success – this was a country ripe and ready to explore its new freedoms, commercial, sexual and social.

True there was some comedy before Almodóvar in the form of eclectic **Luis García Berlanga** who together with **Juan Antonio Bardem** directed *¡Bienvenido Mr Marshall!* (*Welcome Mr Marshall!*, 1952) a smart satire about the visit of Americans to a small Spanish town. In fact both directors went on to enjoy long and successful careers in Spain but it says something of the difficulties of the time that Bardem was arrested several times and once imprisoned, and neither could impact significantly on the international scene in the discouraging Francoist climate. Not even the "sexy Spanish" comedies of the late 1960s and early 1970s were quite what they sound. Whilst the rest of Europe was becoming increasingly permissive – this was the era of the soft-porn boom – there was little chance that these comedies of manners would wow the rest of the world in the way Almodóvar was shortly to do.

Condemned and celebrated for addressing a younger audience – the so-called *pasota* ("couldn't care less") generation – Almodóvar has been hugely influential on filmmakers throughout the world. Since the early days he has acted as his own producer and won cult arthouse audiences, while in the process also making big stars of stock company members **Carmen Maura**, Victoria Abril, **Antonio Banderas** and others. His early career, which included writing comic strips, parodic memoirs of a porn star (Patti Diphusa), and several Super 8 shorts, already demonstrated the traits that came to define his movies – sexually explicit, playful, gender- and genre-bending, and totally unique.

Almodóvar's films range from strong dramas to blistering comedies, often at the expense of a more conservative audience's sensibilities. Gay, transsexual and bisexual themes and strong character parts have been central to his oeuvre, though as the

Victoria Abril pushes the boundaries of Spanish comedy

years have passed the frenetic pacing, emotional excess and visual extravagance have thinned out a little. His breakthrough movie was *Pepi, Luci, Bom And The Other Girls* (*Pepi, Luci, Bom y otras chicas del monton*) in 1980, which documented the nascent Spanish punk scene, and shocked more than one casual viewer with its depiction of sex, drug, rape and more. It served Almodóvar well as a calling card, and by 1988 he was making huge international waves with *Women On The Verge Of A Nervous Breakdown* (*Mujeres al borde de un ataque de nervios*), helping to establish Antonio Banderas as a major international star along the way. In 1989 the decidedly kinky *Tie Me Up! Tie Me Down!* (*¡Atame!*) also found its way to the global screen, as did such other successes as *High Heels* (*Tacones lejanos*, 1991), *All About My Mother* (*Todo sobre mi madre*, 1999) and *Talk To Her* (*Hable con ella*, 2002). The latter two, especially, tip over the divide from comedy to drama, and are none the worse for that.

Almodóvar, however, is just one member of the **Escuela de Madrid** (Madrid School of comedy), which also includes directors **Juan José Bigas Luna** and Fernando Trueba. Luna,

in particular, caused a stir with two of his early films *Jamón, jamón* (1992) and *Golden Balls* (1993). Criticised for what was seen as an overdose of testosterone, Luna protested he was satirizing macho mores in his movies rather than applauding them. His follow up, *The Tit And The Moon* (1994), about a boy who pleads to the moon for a new breast of his own to suckle, was the last of his films to receive anything like mainstream distribution. **Fernando Trueba**, another prolific and central presence on the Spanish comedy scene, offered a gentler period take on male-female relations with *Belle Epoque* (1992); *The Girl Of Your Dreams* (*La Niña de tus ojos*, 1998), about a theatre troupe in Nazi Germany and starring **Penelope Cruz**, won fewer fans.

On home ground, comedy thrillers and action movies such as the locally successful series *Torrente* (1997) and *Torrente 2* (2001) have vied for home box office pole position with broad comedies like *Airbag* (1997), in which the main character loses his engagement ring on his stag night in the vagina of a prostitute – a particularly Latin mixture of traditional comedy and contemporary grossout that was a success in Spain but didn't attract international interest. Not so the films of cult Basque director (and former philosophy graduate) **Álex de la Iglesia**, the new wild man of Spanish cinema, who has a small but passionate following and a reputation for constant surprise. The sci-fi horror comedy *Mutant Action* (*Acción mutante*, 1993), for example, unveils a future world overlorded by good-looking people fighting a group of terrorists claiming rights for uglier folk. He also directed *Dying Of Laughter* (*Muertos de risa*, 1999), a satire on celebrity comedy double acts in which a duo end up viciously hating each other. But the pick of his films is probably the horror comedy *Day Of The Beast* (*El día de la bestia*, 1995), in which a Basque priest, certain that the Antichrist will be born in Madrid on Christmas Day, joins forces with a record store assistant with a yen for heavy metal to prevent the diabolic occurrence. Spanish comedy certainly has a strong flavour, at once black and colourful, and once the taste is acquired tends to become an addiction. We can expect Iglesia, Almodóvar and their colleagues to continue to push the boundaries for some time to come.

Pepi, Luci, Bom... (Pepi, Luci, Bom y otras chicas del monton)
dir Pedro Almodóvar, 1980, Spain, 80m

A riotous treatise on the status of women in post-Franco Spain or a chauvinist romp designed to offend bourgeois sensibility? Either way, there's plenty in Almodóvar's feature debut to shock and amuse, as Carmen Maura seeks revenge on a bullying cop by teaming his mousey wife with a lesbian punk rocker. Brash and provocative in the contemporary *pasota* ("couldn't care less") manner of the day.

What Have I Done to Deserve This? (¿Qué he hecho yo para merecer esto?!)
dir Pedro Almodóvar, 1984, Spain, 101m

Almodóvar is at his most Buñuelian in this Dadaist dissection of a dysfunctional family. Yet it's just as easy to spot traces of Billy Wilder, John Waters and Andy Warhol in both the nefarious activities indulged in by Carmen Maura's nearest and dearest and the desperate measures she resorts to in order to survive. Very much a woman on the verge.

The Law Of Desire (La lay del deseo)
dir Pedro Almodóvar, 1987, Spain, 100m

Who else could concoct an erotic comedy thriller centred on a gay love triangle involving a bartender, a government minister's son and a film director, who lives with his transsexual sister, whose lesbian ex-lover is played by a male transvestite? Revelling in the contrivance of his scenario, Antonio Banderas's enthusiastic participation in the sex scenes and Carmen Maura's scene-stealing brilliance, this is Almodóvar at the peak of his early powers.

Tie Me Up! Tie Me Down! (¡Atame!)
dir Pedro Almodóvar, 1989, Spain, 102m

Take extract of Buñuel, Sirk and Fassbinder and toss in some S&M and you have this quirky dissertation on love and lust, fantasy and reality, obsession and addiction, in which Antonio Banderas's recovered mental patient kidnaps ex-porn star Victoria Abril to persuade her to marry him. Some thought this too tame for Almodóvar. But it saw him tone down the camp kitsch in favour of the arthouse intensity for which he's now renowned.

Belle Epoque
dir Fernando Trueba, 1992, Spain, 110m

Engaging drama comedy in which a deserting soldier finds a very hospitable welcome in a female-dominated family. Each of the very different sisters attempts to seduce him in turn. Lush-looking, amorous humour in period costume. Penelope Cruz stars.

Jamón, jamón
dir José Bigas Luna, 1992, Spain, 94m

Spanish melodramatic playwright Federico Lorca meets Madrid school mayhem. All the cast sizzle away, particularly Javier Bardem and Penelope Cruz, but the humour is mostly black, and the luminously gritty Spanish outback locale seems more like someone's fantasy of Mexico. Sexy, if not exactly sidesplitting.

Huevos de oro (Golden Balls)
dir José Bigas Luna, 1993, Spain, 95m

Not since King Vidor's insane and proto-fascist drama *The Fountainhead* (1949) has architecture featured so heavily in a mainstream film. Bigas Luna's second feature is similarly insensitive, and the overdone machismo is almost painful to watch. Weird, but only darkly humorous.

El día de la bestia (Day Of The Beast)
dir Álex de la Iglesia, 1995, Spain, 104m

Iglesia's wildest, most irreverent outing, as it follows priest Alex Angulo on a macabre mission around Madrid to perform enough evil to summon Satan and prevent the birth of the Beast on Christmas Day 1995. A gleeful amalgam of Z grade exploitation, *The Exorcist*, *The Omen* and socko cartoons – that earned cult status home and abroad.

The Information: the wider picture

Laurel and Hardy entertain the troops
in British Guiana, 1942

The Information: the wider picture

You've seen the movies, bought the DVD, re-watched it countless times and learned the best gags off by heart – but now you want to know more, to go deeper into the laugh. But where to begin?

Film festivals and events

While there are relatively few festivals devoted to comedy movies alone, most of the world's major comedy festivals include films in their programme.

Similarly, most of the world's major film festivals include comedy in theirs. What follows is a brief rundown of the major funny fests around the globe – for a fuller listing, take a look at the British Council's searchable site **www.britfilms. com**.

Comedia, Montréal, Canada
www.hahaha.com/comedia

Part of Montréal's major ten-day Just For Laughs/ Juste pour rire festival, which was established in 1983 and is now one of the world's big three comedy events. The film festival, though a relatively small part of the overall event, is gaining speed, screening thirty or so international movies from student shorts to silent classics and mainstream premières. *July*

First Sundays Comedy Film Festival
New York, USA
www.firstsundays.com

Less a festival than a year-round event, with comedy shorts screened at a hip Lower East Side movie house on the first Sunday of every month. You might even get to see yourself on screen; each month an audience member is picked at random to star in one of the next month's movies.

Giggleshorts International Comedy Short Film Festival, Toronto, Canada
www.giggleshorts.com

The largest festival of international comedy shorts in the world, with screenings every two weeks at the National Film Board Centre in Toronto, and its own spin-off TV show on Canada's cable Movieola station.

International Comedy Film Festival of Peñiscola, Spain
www.festivaldepeniscola.com

Major festival, exclusively devoted to feature films, held in a lovely walled medieval city in Castellón province. *May/June*

Melbourne Comedy Short Film Festival, Melbourne, Australia
www.comedyfestival.com.au

Along with Edinburgh and Montréal, Melbourne hosts one of the world's big three comedy festivals. Mostly based around stand-up and cabaret, the month-long extravaganza also includes free screenings of international comedy shorts produced by young filmmakers. *March, April or May*.

Over the Fence Comedy Film Festival, Australia
www.overthefence.com.au

A touring movie festival that travels the length and breadth of Australia celebrating Australian humour. The emphasis is on emerging and independent filmmakers.

U.S. Comedy Arts Festival, Aspen, Colorado, USA
www.hbocomedyfestival.com

Sponsored by cable channel HBO, this high-profile four-day festival celebrates comedy in all its forms. Held at the height of the ski season in Aspen, and attracting as many industry bigwigs as fans, it's usually swarming with TV and movie execs as well as wannabe Woody Allens. The film section showcases independent features and shorts, and also rewards the best theatrically released comedy movies of the year. *February/March*

World of Comedy International Film Festival, Toronto, Canada
www.worldcomedyfilmfest.com

Everything to do with comedy movies: shorts, features, animation, mockumentaries, plus biopics and documentaries about comedy. Also a seminar series for aspiring comedy writers and directors. *February*

Books

In the reviews listed below, the US publisher follows the UK publisher. Unless otherwise stated, where only one publisher is listed, it is the same in both the US and the UK.

Biography and Autobiography

Woody Allen On Woody Allen

Woody Allen and Stig Bjorkman, 1995 (Faber and Faber/ Grove Press)

There are numerous books on the great Woody, ranging from standard biographies, through in-depth over-analyses, to day-by-day diary recordings of every single second of the shooting of *Radio Days* – but the most revealing is Allen in his own words. This volume is laid out in an occasionally wearing interview/dialogue style, but its scope is refreshingly broad, moving through his complete oeuvre and raising such subjects as his upbringing, his favourite movies and his filmmaking techniques. The new edition, published in 2004, benefits from 100 pages of new material. Also worth reading are the man's own collection of dryly humorous essays, three volumes – *Getting Even* (1971); *Without Feathers* (1975); and *Side Effects* (1980) – presented in 1992 as *The Complete Prose Of Woody Allen* (Crown Publications/Picador). For those wanting an outsider's view, one of the strongest is *Woody Allen: A Biography* by Eric Lax (Da Capo), which was written by a close friend. First published in 1991, it was updated in 2000 to cover all the events in the intervening period.

The Day The Laughter Stopped: The True Story Behind The Fatty Arbuckle Scandal

David Yallop, 1976 (Corgi/St Martin's Press)

A thorough look at the movie star whose career was ruined by an early, and ugly, Hollywood scandal – and whose scapegoating, which ushered in the Hays Code, effectively marked the end of a Tinseltown era.

Wired: The Fast Times And Short Life of John Belushi

Bob Woodward, 1985 (Faber/Pocket)

The writer who brought down Richard Nixon turns his hand to the cocaine-fuelled 1980s, focusing in on the iconic Belushi – too young, too much and far, far too stoned – as a metaphor for an era.

The Big Screen Comedies Of Mel Brooks

Robert Alan Crick, 2002 (McFarland and Co)

Each of Brooks's movies detailed and reviewed, complete with cast list, full credits and more. For those that have a hankering for contemporary Brooks (after a fashion, anyway) check out *The Producers: The Book, Lyrics And Story Behind The Biggest Hit In Broadway History – How We Did It* by Mel Brooks and Thomas Meehan, 2001 (Miramax). This delivers everything it says on the cover – an account of how Mel took his finest movie and rubbed Broadway's nose in it, plus costume designs, lyrics, photos and sketches galore.

Frank Capra: The Catastrophe Of Success
Joseph McBride, 1992 (Faber/St. Martin's Press)

A highly detailed and intelligent – if not particularly warmhearted – look at the life and filmic times of one of Hollywood's most influential directors. Revised edition published in 2000.

My Autobiography
Charles Chaplin and David Robinson, 1964 (Penguin Modern Classics/Plume)

Chaplin in his own words (augmented and abetted by Robinson), told with the benefit of hindsight though, thankfully, not always viewed through rose-tinted glasses. Robinson, a Chaplin expert, also authored the hefty *Chaplin: His Life And Art*, 1985 (Penguin/McGraw-Hill), a definitive account of the man's movies and his personal life.

Gérard Depardieu: A Biography
Marianne Gray, 1991 (Time Warner/St Martin's Press)

Somewhat out of date now, but as a readable and insightful account of the early life of M. Depardieu, it can't be bettered.

W.C. Fields By Himself: His Intended Autobiography
W.C. Fields and Ronald J. Fields, 1973 (Prentice Hall)

A collection of Fields's writings – sketches, anecdotes, scripts, letters – posthumously collected by his son. Great photos, too. For a biography, read *Man on the Flying Trapeze: Life and Times of W.C. Fields* (Faber/W W Norton) by Simon Louvish, 1997; the author, a serious fan and scholar, scuppers many of the myths surrounding Fields's early life as peddled by the man himself, and also

provides an affecting account of his later years.

Kate Remembered: Katharine Hepburn, A Personal Biography
A. Scott Berg, 2003 (Pocket/Putnam)

Written by a close friend, and offering an emotional, intimate portrait of the great actress. A good companion piece with Hepburn's own bestseller, *Me: Stories of My Life*, 1991 (Penguin/Random House).

Bob Hope: My Life In Jokes
Bob Hope and Linda Hope, 2003 (Hyperion)

As Hope neared his centenary he collected some of the best gags from his vast career to mark this momentous occasion, organizing them decade by decade to create a chronological account of his life and career. He died shortly before the work was published.

Buster Keaton: Tempest In A Flat Hat
Edward McPherson, 2004 (Faber/Haymarket)

Acclaimed, lively biography of the stone faced one, from his early vaudeville training to his career collapse and descent into alcoholism.

Mr Laurel And Mr Hardy: An Affectionate Biography
John McCabe, 1961 (Robson Books)

Although there are many books on the market concerning comedy cinema's finest double act, McCabe's tome benefits from the author having met and interviewed the duo towards the tail end of their career. Simon Louvish's *Stan and*

Ollie: The Roots of Comedy, 2001 (Faber/Thomas Dunne), a revealing account of their intertwined lives and mutual affection, is also worth a read.

King Of Comedy: The Life And Art Of Jerry Lewis
Shawn Levy, 1996 (St. Martin's Press)

Written without any help or assistance from Lewis, Levy's book gives credit where credit is due to the subject's lengthy career and noted charity work, but never shies away from exploring the despair behind the smile. Frank Krutnik's *Inventing Jerry Lewis*, 2000 (US: Smithsonian) takes a more academic approach, tracing the many faces of this complex and controversial performer.

The Harold Lloyd Encyclopedia
Annette M. D'Agostino Lloyd, 2003 (US: McFarland and Co)

Everything you ever wanted to know about Lloyd and his career, including an in-depth filmography of his vast back catalogue. The illustrations are great, too.

Pure Drivel 1999 (Phoenix/Hyperion
Shopgirl,2000 (Phoenix/Theia)
The Pleasure Of My Company 2003 (Phoenix/Hyperion).
Steve Martin

While there isn't yet a decent biography on this most serious of clowns, several examples of Martin's excellent writings are readily available. *Pure Drivel* is a wonderful collection of short comic essays and stories; the novella *Shopgirl* takes a different tack with a bittersweet tale of a young woman trapped by her job and her life, while *The Pleasure Of My Company* is the *pièce de résistance*, a brilliant comic novel about a man suffering from obsessive compulsive disorder, and just about everything else. Masterful.

The Marx Brothers Encyclopedia
Glenn Mitchell, 1996 (Reynolds and Hearn)

Mitchell's book leaves no stone unturned in its A–Z approach to all things Marxist. But for those wishing for the more personal touch, two autobiographies more than meet the mark: *Harpo Speaks,* by Harpo Marx and Rowland Barber, 1961 (Virgin/Limelight), in which finally we hear the voice of the silent one; and *Groucho and Me* by Groucho Marx (Virgin/ Da Capo), written in 1959, in which Groucho tells as much of his story as he wants to tell in his usual wise-

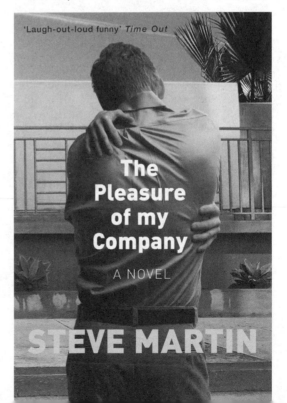

cracking style. In addition, Stefan Kanfer's entertaining *Groucho: The Life and Times of Julius Henry Marx*, 2000 (Penguin/Vintage) is particularly interesting for its account of Groucho's post-Brothers career.

Marilyn Monroe
Barbara Leaming, 1998 (Orion/Three Rivers)

Monroe has been the subject of so many salacious biographies – dealing with conspiracy theories, Presidential affairs and beyond – that Leaming's book comes across as refreshingly balanced, talking with numerous key players, including the generally reluctant Arthur Miller.

Cinderella Story: My Life In Golf
Bill Murray, 1999 (Bantam Doubleday Dell Publishing Group/Broadway)

A distinct oddity – part autobiography, but more a tale of one man's love of golf from his childhood days as a caddy through to his adult days on the pro-celebrity charity circuit. Oddly engaging, but it helps if you like the sport.

Pryor Convictions: And Other Life Sentences
Richard Pryor, 1995 (Mandarin/Pantheon)

Pryor's written prose is not as savage or insightful as his stand-up, but from his early whorehouse years to setting himself on fire and being wheelchair bound courtesy of MS, he sure has had a hell of a life.

The Pythons Autobiography
The Pythons, with Bob McCabe, 2003 (Orion)

The remaining Pythons (with family and surviving partner stepping in for Graham Chapman) tell their tale in more depth – and with more candour – than ever before. Plus, it's illustrated with more than 1000 photos, the majority of which are from their own archives and thus truly deserve the phrase "never before seen."

The Life And Death Of Peter Sellers
Roger Lewis, 1990 (Applause)

Lewis's controversial take on the difficult, troubled, but undeniably brilliant Sellers (made into a movie starring Geoffrey Rush) is offset by the altogether warmer *Remembering Peter Sellers* by Graham Stark, 1990 (UK: Robson Books), an affectionate, anecdote-heavy memoir by his longtime costar and cohort.

King Of Comedy: The Lively Arts
Mack Sennett and Cameron Shipp, 1954 (To Excel)

An edited selection of Sennett's own reminiscences on all things comic and cinematic.

Rewrites
Neil Simon, 1996 (Simon and Schuster)

An anecdotal autobiography, dealing with the period of his life from roughly age 30 to 46, and also taking time to talk about the creative nature of writing in general and comedy in particular.

A Wonderful Life: The Films And Career Of James Stewart
Tony Thomas, 1988 (Citadel Press)

A thorough and winning biography of

Hollywood's quintessential everyman.

Becoming Mae West
Emily Worth Leider, 1997 (Da Capo Press)

Proof that West was more than just cleavage and double entendre, this shows West the business woman, the writer and the woman trying to get ahead in a male-dominated industry. West's auto-biography, *Goodness Had Nothing to Do With It*, 1959 (Virago/Manor), tells her own story in her inimitable style.

Conversations With Wilder
Cameron Crowe and Billy Wilder, 1999 (Alfred A. Knopf)

Shortly before Wilder's death, writer-director Cameron Crowe spent some time with him recalling the old days, their respective attitudes towards film and comedy, and much more. A rare insight into the minds of two extremely talented men. It can easily be augmented with the deluxe boxed *Some Like It Hot* by Billy Wilder, Dan Auiler and Alison Castle, 2001 (Taschen) – Wilder and Diamond's screenplay, lavishly illustrated, containing scenes cut from the final classic film, and peppered with interviews with those involved.

General

American Film Comedy: From Abbott And Costello To Jerry Zucker
Scott and Barbara Siegel, 1994 (Prentice Hall/Macmillan)

Useful A–Z round up, thorough but not encyclo-pedic – and it halts in the early 1990s.

BFI Film And Modern Classics series
British Film Institute Publishing, London

The BFI have produced not far short of a hundred copiously illustrated short books on individual films in two series written by a wide variety of critics. There are several comedy titles including *Bringing Up Baby* (Peter Swaab, 2005), *Groundhog Day* (Ryan Gilby, 2004), *To Be Or Not To Be* (Peter Barnes, 2002), *Withnail and I* (Kevin Jackson, 2004). For a complete and up-to-date list go to www.bfi.org.uk/bookvid/books

The Carry On Companion
Robert Ross, 1996 (B.T. Batsford)

Each of the 31 *Carry Ons* lovingly detailed and analysed, with best scenes/lines/performances chosen from each. Revised in 2003.

Comedy Movie Posters
Bruce Hershenson and Richard Allen, 2000
(Partners Publishing Group/Bruce Hershenson)

A visual treat – a collection of key comedy movie posters from the thirties to the turn of the millennium.

The Comic Mind: Comedy And The Movies
Gerald Mast, 1979 (Chicago University Press)

Veteran overviewer Mast surveys comedy at the movies. Thoughtful but by no means a light read.

Ealing Studios Charles Barr, 1977
(Cameron and Hollis/University of California)

The story of the studios that brought us so many classics, complete with a follow-up look at the post-glory days of the famed studios, as well as a look at the life of founder Michael Balcon. The revised edition, 1999, looks at Ealing in the context of Thatcherite and post-Thatcherite Britain, with an improved filmography and biography.

Film Comedy
Geoff King, 2002 (Wallflower Press)

A detailed, analytical approach to the development of comedy on screen.

The Film Reader: Hollywood Comedians
ed. Frank Krutnik, 2002 (Routledge)

A collection of learned writings on and analyses of a host of comic screen legends, and the impact they have had, all the way from Buster Keaton to Chris Rock.

The Great Funnies: A History Of Film Comedy
David Robinson, 1969 (Studio Vista/E.P. Dutton)

You will do well to find this out-of-print book, which covers in brisk and readable style developments from the silents to Tati. But it's worth hunting out, particularly for its splendid black-and-white illustrations and in-depth coverage of silent comedians.

Romantic Comedy In Hollywood: From Lubitsch To Sturges
James Harvey, 1987 (Da Capo Press)

An in-depth look at the 1930s Hollywood movies that came to define screwball comedy.

Saturday Night: A Backstage History Of Saturday Night Live
Doug Hill and Jeff Weingrad, 1987 (Vintage Books/William Morrow)

Although outdated, this remains the definitive account of the beginnings and inner workings of *SNL* from the start through its glory days and into the troubled 1980s.

This Is Spinal Tap: The Official Companion
Karl French, 2000 (Bloomsbury)

Featuring a "pre-epilogue" by Michael McKean (aka David St. Hubbins), this volume contains not only the script but an A–Z of all things Tap and a look at the making of the world's finest – if you will – "mockumentary."

Quinlan's Illustrated Directory Of Film Comedy Stars
ed. David Quinlan, 1992 (B.T. Batsford/Chrysalis)

Quinlan's expert guide to around 300 screen comics, accompanied by full filmographies and potted biographies.

Writing the Comedy Film: Make 'Em Laugh
Stuart Voytilla, 2003 (Michael Wiese Productions)

Any attempt to analyse what makes the comedy movie tick might seem problematic, but at least the author has the good sense to run the range of examples, from Sturges to the Farrellys, the Marx Brothers to *American Pie*.

The Internet

General

As everyone knows the Web is a wonderful place for looking up everything from breaking news to shoe sizes of the rich and famous, but while it proves itself to be a haven for all things enshrined by the word "cult," the broad sweep of the comedy movie does not lend itself terribly well to such short-order categorization. While you can find countless designated sites for all manner of film genres, from horror to Taiwanese martial arts movies, the comedy movie per se is pretty ill-served. That's not to say that there aren't still a vast number of sites that allow you to delve and seek, look and learn. We've pinpointed a few of the best below. Happy hunting.

In addition to the sites reviewed below, every major **film magazine** and **trade paper** has its own website, so if you want to find out the current development status of *Dodgeball 2*, or to see if those rumours of an *Ishtar* trilogy are grounded in reality you could check out the likes of **www.empireonline.co.uk** or **www.variety.com** or **www.hollywoodreporter.com** or **www.ew.com/ew** (for *Entertainment Weekly*) or so on and so on – just pick your magazine and get typing. If you want to go a bit deeper, turn to the smart online film journal **www.sensesofcinema.com**. Devoted to the serious discussion of cinema, it's particularly good on directors, with regular interviews and analysis.

The Internet Movie Database
www.imdb.com

The mother of all movie reference sites, easy to use and navigate, with each of its 200,000 plus movie listings breaking down into separate sections on each cast/crew member, and such other details as awards, trivia, goofs, soundtrack listings, fan sites and so on. The comedy genre listings offer their own route through the IMDb's cornucopia of information, though at times the classifications put square pegs in round holes. For a subscription fee you can also access "IMDb pro," which gives you additional business-orientated information.

Ain't it Cool News
www2.aintitcool.com

For those who simply like to get their movie news in the form of gossip, speculation and numerous exclusives, this is an always entertaining, studio-busting must-see.

All Movie Guide
www.allmovie.com

Similar in style to IMDb, and sometimes more thorough, offering a wide range of fact-based material on a wide variety of movies.

Britmovie
www.britmovie.co.uk

Searchable database of British movies, directors and actors, with sections on genres (including comedy, and separately, *Carry On* movies) and movie studios, and a history of British film.

Cinema Sites
www.cinema-sites.com

A great place to find links for all those things that intrigue you, from festival listings through scripts to fan sites – it can even lead you to check out the splendidly titled Arbucklemania, for all things Fatty.

Funny.co.uk
www.funny.co.uk/news/cat_166-Film.html

All the latest news related to comedy movies, major new releases and stars.

Greatest Films
www.filmsite.org

You could get lost in this site for hours – based around a number of lists (from the American Film Institute, among other sources) of best movies, stars, scenes and quotes, it also features very long reviews and background history on all the classic Hollywood movies, detailed articles about film genres, a history of the movies and loads more.

Yahoo Movies and Film
dir.yahoo.com/Entertainment/Movies_and_Film/

Reliable site with a constantly updated rolling news format.

History

Bright Lights: Silent Film Comedians
www.brightlightsfilm.com/37/Silent1.htm

Lively analysis of Chaplin, Keaton, Lloyd and Langdon, also tracing the death of slapstick, from this excellent online film journal.

Britmovie: Carry On Sitcom
www.britmovie.co.uk/features/upton/sitcom00.html

Detailed article about that peculiarly 1970s British institution – the sitcom spin-off film.

Britmovie: Ealing Studios
www.britmovie.co.uk/studios/ealing/index.html

More good stuff from Britmovie, with a three-page history and full filmography of the great comedy studios.

Cinema Britain
members.aol.com/cinemabritain/

A detailed and well-written site devoted to the revitalization of the British film industry during the 1950s and 1960s, with a good account of comedy caper movies.

Entertainment Weekly – Gross-Out Movies
www.ew.com/ew/features/980731/gross/

There's lots of material on EW on the "retched genre" including a lively history with nods to *Animal House, Dumb and Dumber* and *There's Something About Mary*.

Greatest Films

www.filmsite.org

This indispensable site includes a decade-by-decade history of the Hollywood movie industry, with a detailed account of the comedy genre, including analyses of key movies and historic movie landmarks.

Rainbow Network – Celluloid Drag

www.rainbownetwork.com/Film

Register, go to the above address and then search for 'drag' and you will find an interesting account of drag's place in the comedy movie from Chaplin to *Mrs Doubtfire* with a follow-up piece also exploring the development of drag in the movies from the late 1960s onwards.

Saturday-Night-Live.com

www.saturday-night-live.com

The definitive *SNL* history, with a season-by-season breakdown (under "Miscellaneous Stuff"), cast and guest lists, and episode reviews (post-1997 only) written by site users.

Screen Online: Musical Comedy in the 1930s

www.screenonline.org.uk/film/id/592383

Overview of the musical comedy in post-war Britain, with features on Gracie Fields and George Formby.

Screwball Comedy

freespace.virgin.net/d.moore1/Donna2/Screwball_Comedy.htm

Enjoyable site covering everything you'd ever want to know about this peculiarly American genre, including features on screwball history, stars, all the best movie lines, and, of course, the movies themselves. It's also worth checking www.moderntimes.com/screwball/, a clearsighted and deft account with lots of images, a bibliography and good links.

Silent Era: The Silent Era Website

www.silentera.com

A comprehensive site for all things pre-talkies, for fans of Keaton, Chaplin, Lloyd and co to delight in.

The movies

If you're looking for a particular movie, your first stop should be to search the phenomenal **www.filmsite.org**, a list-lovers' paradise that features every conceivable 100 Best . . . list from numerous sources, with long, descriptive reviews (plus lots of dialogue), analyses and background history on all the classic Hollywood greats.

Also worth checking to see if your favourite movie is covered is **www.rottentomatoes.com**, which has a searchable database of more than 100,000 movie titles complete with scores of reviews from American papers, online magazines and cult publications.

Writing Comedy: David Zucker

www.robinkelly.btinternet.co.uk/zucker.htm

Zucker, of Z-A-Z comedy genius, gives a brisk rundown of comedy dos and don'ts, quoting scenes and gags from *Airplane!* in many of his examples.

Annie Hall

www.godamongdirectors.com/scripts/anniehall.shtml

The classic Allen script in full – stock your printer up with 120 sheets, then sit back and wait.

Bringing up Baby

www.dvdtalk.com/dvdsavant/s1548baby.html

A detailed, intelligent and accessible account of the classic screwball on this above-average DVD review site.

Dr Strangelove

www.indelibleinc.com/kubrick/films/strangelove/Internet

This classy site is packed with stills, audio files, articles and reviews, with interviews with writer Terry Southern and images and dialogue from the movie's alternative, rejected pie-fight ending.

The Ferris Bueller Page

www.idiotsavant.com/bueller

The place for Ferris fans to speculate on a sequel – email your ideas for a storyline and wait to hear back from Paramount. And check out www.80s.com/saveferris, which has some great, off-the-wall links.

The Gold Rush

www.dvdjournal.com/reviews/g/goldrush.shtml

Extremely full and enjoyable reviews, both of Chaplin's classic movie and of the MK2/Warner DVD (2003).

The Movie Sounds Page: Good Morning, Vietnam

www.moviesounds.com/vietnam.html

Hear those schizophrenic Williams ad libs in all their crazy glory on a range of downloadable sound files.

Groundhog Day: The Movie

www.transparencynow.com/groundhog.htm

An enjoyable and well-argued philosophical treatise on how *Groundhog Day* explores our "essential human desire to become whole".

A Hard Day's Night

www.popmatters.com/film/reviews/h/hard-days-night.shtml

Intelligent review of the groundbreaking Beatles movie, placing it in the context of its very specific 1960s moment.

It Happened One Night

www.sensesofcinema.com/contents/cteq/01/12/happened. html and www.moviediva.com/MD_root/reviewpages/ MDItHappenedOneNight.htm.

Two in-depth and accessible analyses of this early and influential screwball.

Kind Hearts And Coronets

www.screenonline.org.uk/film/id/441483/

Small but beautifully formed, complete with overview, video clips, contemporary reviews and production stills.

Local Hero

movie-reviews.colossus.net/movies/l/local_hero.html

No bells and whistles here, just an intelligent, considered and detailed review.

ACME Animal House

www.acmewebpages.com/animal/index.html

Nearly thirty years on and the original gross-out movie is alive and barfing – come here for news, links, interviews, photos, sound clips, cast information, shooting locations and all manner of Belushi trivia.

The Rushmore Academy

rushmore.shootangle.com/academy/films/rushmore

Laid out like a school prospectus, this site started as a shrine to *Rushmore* and has expanded to cover Wes Anderson's first film, *Bottle Rocket,* and his third, *The Royal Tenenbaums.* With articles, biographies and information about Anderson, Owen Wilson and others, plus links, photos and video clips.

Baz The Great – Strictly Ballroom

www.bazthegreat.co.uk

Lovingly compiled fan site with full details on *Strictly Ballroom,* the first of Baz Luhrmann's so-called Red Curtain Trilogy (followed by *Romeo and Juliet* and *Moulin Rouge!*) – and a movie that apparently Bill Clinton watched six times. Includes a transcript of the DVD commentary and interviews with people involved in the making of the movie.

Sullivan's Travels

www.moviediva.com/MD_root/reviewpages/ MDSullivansTravels.htm

An excellent analysis, complete with photos, personal accounts and background details.

This Is Spinal Tap

www.spinaltapfan.com

As daftly witty as the movie itself, this clever fan site more than evokes the sick and twisted spirit of the Tap with articles, an A to Z guide, and weird and wonderful world news.

To Be Or Not To Be
www.cinematicreflections.com/ToBeorNottoBe.html

A thoughtful review that claims this is not Ernst Lubitsch's most successful or most hilarious film, but instead a flawed masterpiece that bravely tackles pacifism with humanism and humour.

Les Vacances de M. Hulot
www.imagesjournal.com/issue10/reviews/tati/text.htm

DVD reviews of *M. Hulot's Holiday* and *Mon Oncle*, highlighting the director's themes and stylistic concerns.

Withnail and I WAV Gallery
home.c2i.net/ranash/withnail/firstpage.html

The best of quite a few sites offering quote-along audio and Realplayer clips, along with links to DVDs, books and other Withnailia.

Icons

Those seeking out their heroes and heroines on the Web are best off first doing a Google search, or by typing something along the lines of **www.stevemartin.com** and seeing where it leads. (In fact, when you do type in **www.stevemartin.com** it leads to an extremely well-designed, comprehensive and up-to-the-minute site with occasional personal messages from the man himself.) This tactic doesn't always work, however – those trying **johncleese.com** may be in for a bit of a shock – but it's a good starting point. To hunt down news stories about your favourite stars, check to see if they're listed on **www.topix.net**, which searches the Net for stories (sometimes

rather tenuous) about a range of people so you don't have to. Beyond that there are numerous fan-based directories: try **www.starseeker.com**, which has a good range of links to fan pages, or **www.fansites.com**, which has links to 2500 or more (for filmmakers as well as actors and actresses). For a monthly subscription fee you can even contact your favourites direct. And if you're after serious discussion and analysis of the work of the great comedy directors, check out **myweb.tiscali.co.uk/filmdirectors**, which has an alphabetical listing with links to journals and articles across the Net.

RadioLovers.com – Abbott and Costello
www.radiolovers.com/pages/abbottcostello.

Listen to twenty or so Abbott and Costello radio shows online, including their classic "Who's on First?" baseball routine.

Woody Allen
www.sensesofcinema.com/contents/directors/03/allen.html

After musing on the thesis "Is Allen a misanthrope?", follow the links to other offbeat, eclectic and illuminating Allen sites.

Arbucklemania
www.silent-movies.org/Arbucklemania

Impressive site dedicated to the "Prince of Whales". Along with the biography, bibliography and filmography, juicy extras include scholarly essays, trivia, movie clips and even a sound file of Roscoe – as the home page tells you, his "friends never called him Fatty" – saying "how do you do".

The Hand Of John Belushi

www.consciouschoice.com/1995-98/cc092/
palmbelushi0002.html

Chirologist John Pomeray takes a different angle on the legend that is Belushi, carefully analysing his sausage-shaped fingers, conic fingertips and longitudinal fate line.

Humorous Quotations Of Robert Benchley

www.workinghumor.com/quotes/robert_benchley.shtml

A raft of witticisms from this acerbic writer.

Mel Brooks Movie Site

www.ladyofthecake.com/mel/nfmain.htm

Devoted to seven of Brooks's movies – *The Producers, Blazing Saddles, Young Frankenstein, History of the World Part 1, Spaceballs, Robin Hood, Dracula* – with potted story, credits, quotes, sound files and images from each.

Frank Capra

myweb.tiscali.co.uk/filmdirectors/Cameron-Curtiz.htm

Links to online articles about the director and his legacy, taken from academic and film journals.

Screenonline: Carry On

www.screenonline.org.uk/film/id/467358

Intelligent and up-to-date articles about all the *CarryOn* films and their major stars. www.carryonline.com, the official website, is also good for trivia and regularly updated *Carry On* news.

Charlie Chaplin

www.clown-ministry.com/History/Charlie-Chaplin.html

There are plenty of Chaplin sites out there – this one gets our vote for contextualizing the Little Tramp in a history of clowning. Turn here for biographies of Charlie and his wives, reviews and quotes from his movies, a transcript of his barnstorming "Great Dictator" speech, some of his original song compositions, and loads more.

Coen Brothers

www.youknowforkids.co.uk

Everything you could possibly want to know about the Coens and their work, including, impressively, the scripts for each and every one of their movies.

Quotes from (and about) W.C. Fields

www.louisville.edu/~kprayb01/WCQuote.html#A8

There's no better way to get a handle on Fields's genius than by trawling through this abundance of aphorisms and flights of fancy. For a look at Fields's career as a virtuoso juggler, turn to www.juggling.org/fame/fields/index.html, which includes accounts from the "Great Man" himself of his early life.

The Ultimate Cary Grant Pages

www.carygrant.net

There's a wealth of stuff for Grant fans to look at out in cyberspace – get yourself started with this extraordinarily comprehensive site.

Katharine Hepburn at Reel Classics
www.reelclassics.com/Actresses/Katharine/katharine.htm

One of the more substantial Hepburn sites, with lots of links and a host of downloadable wallpaper stills from her best movies.

Bob Hope and American Variety
www.loc.gov/exhibits/bobhope/

Online version of the Library of Congress's splendid exhibition, held in 2000, focusing on Hope's beginnings and his legacy as a variety star. Lots of good vaudeville history, great visuals and detailed captions – top-notch culture in your own front room.

Chuck Jones – Academy of Achievement
www.achievement.org/autodoc/page/jon1pro-1

Celebrating the greatest thinkers and achievers of our age, Washington DC's Academy of Achievement spotlights Jones with a lengthy interview and lots of downloadable audio and video files. There's also an essay on Jones as auteur on **www.sensesofcinema.com/contents/directors/02/jones.html**.

Juha's Buster Keaton page
www.ida.liu.se/~juhta/buster/

A painstakingly compiled list of intriguing Buster links, directing you to everything from the Keaton museum in Kansas to the site of the "Blinking Buzzards", the British Buster Keaton Society.

Laurel and Hardy Memorabilia magazine
members.aol.com/oxford0614/

From the opening steel pan version of their theme tune to the advice on how to make a Laurel and Hardy diorama – not to mention the article on how they influenced 1960s boy band The Monkees – this gently nutty site more than lives up to the spirt of the great Mr Laurel and Mr Hardy.

The Straight Dope: Do the French really love Jerry Lewis?
www.straightdope.com/classics/a991001.html

No one knows quite what to make of Jerry Lewis nowadays, and the Web rages with debate about this genius clown/abhorrent oaf (delete as appropriate). To enter the fray, read this scathing account alongside **dir.salon.com/people/feature/2001/06/06/lewis/index.html**, a defence, penned by a wheelchair-bound critic, of Lewis's use of the word "cripple".

Steve Martin
www.stevemartin.com

Cartoonish and hip – if maybe just a bit too heavyhanded with the exclamation marks – Martin's official site is by far the best online source for the "wild and crazy guy."

Why a Duck – The Marx Brothers
www.whyaduck.com

Computer nerds and endlessly quotable one-liners are a match made in heaven, and so naturally there are lots of great Marx Brothers sites on the Net. This is one of the very best, splendidly entertaining, with everything from audio streaming and timed quizzes to Marx Brothers horoscopes.

Salon: Marilyn Monroe

dir.salon.com/topics/marilyn_monroe/index.html?ti=13

Among the glut of websites obsessed by Marilyn's image, this directory of smart articles taken from online cultural magazine *Salon* is a breath of fresh air.

Eddie Murphy Biography

www.tiscali.co.uk/entertainment/film/biographies/eddie_murphy_biog

Very detailed and considered five-page biography/filmography.

Shotgun Golf with Bill Murray

Sports.espn.go.com/sepn/page2

Is Murray the coolest actor on the planet? Without doubt, if starring in gonzo journalist Hunter S. Thompson's last article before his suicide – written for sports channel ESPN – is anything to go by.

Madcap Mabel

www.slapstick-comedy.com/Mabel/home.html

Attractive site with lots of photos, a breezy biography (which avoids any mention of Normand's alleged wild lifestyle), filmography, links and a good range of movie clips.

The Richard Pryor Show

www.tvclassics.com/pryor.htm

Fascinating account of a shortlived but seminal moment in Pryor's career – his low-rated, four-episode, transgressive TV series in 1977 – including an audio download.

Monty Python Sound

Filesbau2.uibk.ac.at/sg/python/Sounds.html

All the old favourites – the "Lumberjack Song", "Spam", "Always look on the bright side of life" – for you to download and sing along to at your leisure.

Sunset Gun: Adam Sandler – A Defense

sunsetgun.typepad.com/sunsetgun/2004/12/adam_sandlera_d.html

Glamorous and brainy, Kim Morgan loves movies and she *loves* Adam Sandler. She even goes so far as to compare him to Molière in this well-considered and thought-provoking piece.

Peter Sellers Appreciation Society

www.petersellersappreciationsociety.com

Delightfully old-fashioned looking, this online arm of the PSAS is devoted to preserving all things Peter. If you're moved to join the society on the spot, youll receive a quarterly magazine and lots of special offers and competitions.

The Jimmy Stewart Museum

www.jimmy.org

The online arm of Indiana's Jimmy Stewart museum – where "regular folks greet each other as pedestrian traffic flows lazily through the sidewalks of downtown" – is affectionate, folksy and in places just plain funny – check out the tongue-in-cheek virtual tour. A delightful tribute.

The Official Preston Sturges site

www.prestonsturges.com

Beautiful, stylish site devoted to the great director.

Frank Tashlin
www.sensesofcinema.com/contents/directors/03/tashlin.html

Accessible and thoughtprovoking piece, adapted from a PhD thesis, arguing against the tendency to see Tashlin simply as a director "whose cartoons somehow resemble features", and whose features are somehow "cartoony."

Jacques Tati
www.sensesofcinema.com/contents/directors/02/tati.html

Yet another fine article from this splendid movie journal, covering Tati and all his work with a fine-tooth comb.

Screen Online: Terry-Thomas
www.screenonline.org.uk/people/id/461962/

A brief biography, with detailed film analyses, video clips, stills and contemporaneous reviews of the toothy one's major movies.

Mae West: 1930 Interview
maewest.blogspot.com/2004/10/mae-west-1930-interview.html

Reading more like a list of trivia than an interview proper, this article, written in 1930, is full of fascinating snippets – that she could lift three men weighing 150lb each, say, or that she read only ancient history books.

24fps: Billy Wilder
www.24fpsmagazine.com/Archive/Wilder.html

Readable and detailed analysis of Wilder's work from a now-defunct movie ezine.

Robin Williams @ audible.com
www.audible.com/rw/site_link.html

For more than a year, Robin Williams hosted this award-winning Net-based chat show, featuring a series of half-hour programmes with the comedian talking/laughing with the likes of George Lucas, David Crosby, Eric Idle, Billy Crystal and others. All the shows are now available as audio books from the site.

Comedy around the world

African Comedy
www.allafricanmovies.com

Dip a toe into the Nigerian screen boom with 75 comedies listed on the website at the time of writing. The "number one etailer of African movies and entertainment" also covers productions from many other countries.

British Comedy
www.screenonline.org.uk/film

Educationally orientated site with snapshot accounts of the British comedy tradition. If you are in the UK and at a school, college or library you can download clips from 14 British comedies.

Comedy Directors
www.sensesofcinema.com/contents/directors

Commendable Australian website that takes its cinema seriously. The coverage of a good number of world cinema directors is very full and worth checking out with new names appearing all the time.

eBay
www.eBay.com

Many discount and bargain basement offers on individual films are to be found here, with surprisingly rare or surprisingly cheap finds to be had for the taking.

European Comedy
www.multilingualbooks.com/foreignvids

Seattle-based DVD and video dealer (not to mention books) with a wide range of international comedy titles and helpful orientation and notes. It is particularly strong on French comedy.

Hong Kong
www.hkmdb.com

Though IMDB has made great strides in improving its coverage of Asian cinemas the Hong Kong movie database goes into more depth and breadth and, just like in its western cousin, you can get lost for days.

Independent Viewing
www.greencine.com

Eclectic US rental site which now offers a streaming service (to PCs). There are a lot of comedies

here from all parts of the world and some excellent orientation primers on the likes of Hong Kong Horror comedies or British comedies amidst a range of excellent contextual material.

International Comedy
www.screenselect.co.uk

Excellent DVD rental service with wider range of international coverage than the norm. The navigation tools are not particularly great and the front end of the sight seems overly keen to push the usual Hollywood mainstream. But don't be discouraged. If you know what you are looking for this is a really good place to track down international comedy on DVD and rent at reasonable prices.

Russia on Screen
www.russiandvd.com

Etailer for Russian film and audio products most of which don't yet appear on Amazon.

World Cinema
www.moviemail-online.co.uk

A specialist UK DVD retailer run by big film enthusiasts, its website has lots of short articles. For an unusually broad range of international comedies, go to **1-World Festival Of Foreign Films** (www.1worldfilms.com/comedies).

Picture credits

The Publishers have made every effort to identify correctly the rights holders and/or production companies in respect of images featured in this book. If despite these efforts any attribution is incorrect the Publishers will correct this error once it has been brought to its attention on a subsequent reprint.

Cover Credits

Michael Palin in Monty Python's *Life Of Brian*; Python (Monty) Pictures Ltd

Illustrations

Corbis (245) (269): George Eastman House Collection (1) 9 Harry Langdon Corporation First National Pictures Inc (3) Edison Manufacturing Company (7) George Eastman House (9) Harry Langdon Corporation First National Pictures Inc: The Kobal Collection (8) Keystone Film Company (25) Kobal (55) TriStar Pictures Inc. Gracie Films Columbia (75) Warner Bros Crossbow Productions (87) Hawk Films Ltd Columbia Pictures 94 Channel Four Films/ PolyGram Filmed Entertainment/ Working Title Films Gramercy Pictures (95) Buster Keaton Productions Inc/United Artists (101) Charles Chaplin Productions/United Artists (111) Columbia Pictures Corporation (122) Python (Monty) Pictures Limited Handmade Films Ltd 142 M & A/ Australian Film Finance Corporation (AFFC)/ Beyond Films The Rank Organisation Film Productions Ltd. Miramax 164 Universal International Pictures (167) Keystone Film Company Triangle Film Corporation (202) Metro-Goldwyn-Mayer (212) Rastar Pictures Columbia Pictures (227) 20th Century Fox/ Twentieth Century-Fox Productions Ltd (257) Compagnia Cinematografica Champion/Les Films Concordia: Movie Store Collection (13) Columbia Pictures Corporation (16) Paramount Pictures (17) RKO (Radio) Pictures Inc/ Warners (21) Columbia Pictures Corporation (23) Metro-Goldwyn Mayer/ Loew's Inc (29) Columbia Pictures Corporation (33) Universal Pictures/Arwin Productions (38) Paramount Pictures Corporation (43) Paramount Pictures (46) Paramount Pictures (49) Too Askew Prod. Inc/View Askew Productions Miramax 51 Sofinergie Films/Miramax (57) Touchstone Pictures American Empirical Pictures/Mordecai Films /Buena Vista (64) Paramount Pictures (66) 20th Century Fox (68) Victoires Production/ Tapioca Films/ France (3) Cinéma (71) The Mirsch Corporation MGM (77) RKO Radio Productions/

Warners (81) Orion Pictures Corporation (88) Mediastream Vierte Film GmbH & Co. Vermarktungs KG/ Red Hour Films 20th Century Fox Film Corporation (102) Silver Screen Partners III/ Touchstone Pictures Buena Vista Pictures (109) Columbia Pictures Corporation (113) Ealing Studios Ltd Canal + (117) Jack Rollins & Charles H. Joffe Productions United Artists (119 20th Century Fox Film Corporation Aspen Productions Ingo Preminger Productions (124) Universal Pictures MCA (130) Crossbow Productions/Metro-Goldwyn-Mayer (MGM)/ Springtime Productions Embassy Pictures Corporation (132) Circle Films Inc. Twentieth Century Fox Film Corporation (137) Big Talk Productions/ Studio Canal/ Working Title Films United International Pictures Rogue Pictures (141) Ashton Productions/The Mirisch Corporation United Artists/MGM (146) 20th Century Fox (149) Romaine Film Corporation United Artists (158) Handmade Films Ltd. (161) Universal Pictures (169) Universal City Studios, Inc. (170) Cinema Guild Productions/ Rene Clair Productions United Artists (174) Movie Store (176) Motion Picture Corporation of America (MPCA) New Line Cinema (179) Charles Chaplin Productions/United Artists (181) Buena Vista Pictures/ Mike Zoss Productions/ Studio Canal/ Touchstone Pictures/ Universal Pictures/ Working Title Films (185) Metro-Goldwyn-Mayer (188) Paramount Pictures (195) Jerry Lewis Enterprises Paramount Pictures (197) Hal Roach Studios Inc/ Pathé Exchange Inc./The Harold Lloyd Trust (199) Aspen Film Society Warner Bros. (203) 20th Century Fox (207) Devoted Productions Warner Bros (216) Happy Madison Productions/ Jack Giarraputo Productions/ Revolution Studios Columbia Pictures (219) Jalem Productions Paramount Pictures (222) Universal Pictures Co Inc (229) Universal Pictures (231) The Mirsch Corportion MGM (233) Warner Bros Film Four/Mad Chance/Senator Film Produktion GmbH (240) CiBY 2000/Film Victoria/House and Moorhouse Films/Miramax Films (266) El Deseo S.A Miramax: Ronald Grant Archive (35) Paramount Pictures and Jurow-Shepherd Productions (73) New Line Cinema Capella International/ Juno Pix KC Medien AG/Moving Pictures (84) Gaumont/EFVE/ TF1 Films Productions/TPS Cinéma (92) Paramount Pictures Corporation (135) American Empirical Pictures Touchstone Pictures Buena Vista Pictures (144) Paramount Pictures Inc (154) Cady Films/Specta Films (172) Movie Store (177) Adder Productions/ Rank Organisation Film Productions Ltd.183 Paramount Pictures (193) Hal Roach Studios Inc./ MGM (205) Imagine Entertainment Universal Pictures (210) Fried/Woods Films TriStar Pictures (217) British Lion Film Corporation/ Charter Films Ltd Canal + (235) Esselte Video/Finnish Film Foundation/Finnkino Oy/Megamania/Svenska Filminstitutet/Villealfa Filmproduction Oy Orion Artificial Eye (246) Films Albatros Moviegraphs Inc (251) Da Ma Produzione/Les Productions Artistes Associés United Artists (253) Westdeutscher Rundfunk Bavaria Film international, Constantin Film, Artificial Eye (258) Ban Film/Le Sept Cinéma/Le Studio Canal+/Rai Uno Radiotelevisione/Sacher Film/ Fine Line Features/Artificial Eye (263) Esselte Video/Finnish Film Foundation/Finnkino Oy/Megamania/Svenska Filminstitutet/Villealfa Filmproduction Oy Orion Artificial Eye: (261) Mosfilm Image Entertainment Inc

Index

Page references to films discussed in the Canon chapter, people or things described in the Icons chapter, and specific feature boxes are indicated in **bold**.

S